BLIAINIRIS ÉIREANNACH AN DLÍ IDIRNÁISIÚNTA
IMLEABHAR 15, 2020

THE IRISH YEARBOOK OF INTERNATIONAL LAW
VOLUME 15, 2020

The *Irish Yearbook of International Law* supports research into Ireland's practice in international affairs and foreign policy, filling a gap in existing legal scholarship and assisting in the dissemination of Irish policy and practice on matters of international law. On an annual basis, the *Yearbook* presents peer-reviewed academic articles and book reviews on general issues of international law, as well as topics with significant interest for an Irish audience. Designated correspondents provide reports on international law developments in Ireland, Irish practice in international bodies, and the law of the European Union as relevant to developments in Ireland.

This volume of the *Yearbook* includes contributions on international humanitarian law, including intersections with international human rights law and the law of state responsibility, the concept of due diligence in international law, and the exercise of international criminal jurisdiction with specific reference to Irish law.

Bliainiris Éireannach an Dlí Idirnáisiúnta

Imleabhar 15, 2020

Curtha in Eagar ag
Bríd Ní Ghráinne, James Gallen and Richard Collins

The Irish Yearbook of International Law

Volume 15, 2020

Edited by
Bríd Ní Ghráinne, James Gallen and Richard Collins

•HART•
OXFORD · LONDON · NEW YORK · NEW DELHI · SYDNEY

HART PUBLISHING

Bloomsbury Publishing Plc

Kemp House, Chawley Park, Cumnor Hill, Oxford, OX2 9PH, UK

1385 Broadway, New York, NY 10018, USA

29 Earlsfort Terrace, Dublin 2, Ireland

HART PUBLISHING, the Hart/Stag logo, BLOOMSBURY and the Diana logo are
trademarks of Bloomsbury Publishing Plc

First published in Great Britain 2023

Copyright © The editors 2023

A catalogue record for this book is available from the British Library.

ISBN:	HB:	978-1-50996-629-5
	ePDF:	978-1-50996-631-8
	ePub:	978-1-50996-630-1

Typeset by Compuscript Ltd, Shannon

To find out more about our authors and books visit www.hartpublishing.co.uk.
Here you will find extracts, author information, details of forthcoming events
and the option to sign up for our newsletters.

Table of Contents

Contributors

Adedayo Akingbade, Lecturer in Law, Manchester Metropolitan University

Saeed Bagheri, Lecturer in International Law, School of Law, University of Reading

Michael A Becker, Assistant Professor, Trinity College Dublin

Pearce Clancy, Irish Research Council PhD Scholar and NUI EJ Phelan Fellow in International Law, Irish Centre for Human Rights, University of Galway

Richard Collins, Professor, School of Law, Queen's University Belfast

Rónán R Condon, Assistant Professor, School of Law and Government, Dublin City University

Rián Derrig, Postdoctoral Fellow, Sasakawa Global Ocean Institute, World Maritime University

James Gallen, Associate Professor, School of Law and Government, Dublin City University

Bríd Ní Ghráinne, Associate Professor, School of Law and Criminology, Maynooth University

Esther McGuinness, Senior Lecturer in Law and Head of the School of Law, Ulster University

Niall O'Shaughnessy, PhD Researcher, Department of Law, European University Institute

Harshit Rai, LLM Student, School of Law, University of Warwick

Eliza Walsh, Policy Advisor, Department of Foreign Affairs*

Paola Zichi, Postdoctoral Researcher, School of History, Queen Mary University of London

* The views expressed in this *Yearbook* article are those of the author and not of her employer.

Editorial

THIS VOLUME OF the *Irish Yearbook of International Law* is our first since commencing in post as joint Editors-in-Chief in the autumn of 2020. It was an unusual time to take over the editorship of the *Yearbook* and little did we know that almost two years later the world would still be struggling to emerge from the impact of a global pandemic. Undoubtedly, the editors themselves were not immune from the professional and personal pressures that the response to COVID-19 thrust upon many of us, as the delays in the publication of this volume attest. However, we are delighted to finally be able to publish volume 15 (2020) of the *Yearbook*.

Although much ground to a halt during the pandemic and the associated lockdowns and restrictions which followed, it was far from being a quiet year in international legal terms. As Michael Becker attests in his report, on top of dealing with issues related to pandemic emergency response and the fallout from Brexit, 2020 saw Ireland elected to a two-year term on the United Nations Security Council. In July, also, a particular highlight of the year was the appointment of Professor Siobhán Mullaly, Director of the Irish Centre for Human Rights at University of Galway and the founding editor of the *Irish Yearbook*, as UN Special Rapporteur on Trafficking in Persons, Especially Women and Children. As further detailed in Michael Becker's report, Professor Mullaly's appointment was actually one of three Irish appointments to Special Procedure Mandate Holders during 2020.

In June 2021, we were proud to host the first ever *Irish Yearbook of International Law* careers panel, aimed at law students in Ireland who are interested in careers in international law. We are immensely grateful to our panellists (Stephanie Barbour, James Gallen, Maeve O'Rourke and Eoin Murphy) for generously sharing their experiences of building a career in international law and for answering questions from over 80 aspiring international lawyers in attendance.

As we complete the editorial work for the *Yearbook* in early 2022, we have been deeply saddened by the loss of one of the leading lights of international law in Ireland, James Kingston, who has been legal adviser to the Department of Foreign Affairs since 2009. James not only had a brilliant legal mind, but was a fearless advocate for the international rule of law globally and a leading supporter of international law in Ireland, not least for the transformative role he had within and, more lately, as President of the Irish Branch of the International Law Association. He taught international law at Trinity College Dublin and was, in one way or another, usually supporting, contributing to or promoting many of the seminars, events and other initiatives in the international law calendar in Ireland. His loss has been felt very deeply across the international law community within Ireland, and the editors plan to dedicate volume 16 of the *Yearbook* to his memory.

James was also a mentor and friend to many of us international law scholars in Ireland. We are extremely grateful to both him and the Department of Foreign Affairs for their support of the *Yearbook*. We are also grateful to Hart Publishing for hosting and publishing the Yearbook, and for their support of the Irish Yearbook of International Law Best Paper Prize, which has been awarded to Saeed Bagheri for his article on the provision of military assistance to a state subjected to an armed attack in light of the contemporary law on state responsibility. Specifically, Bagheri addresses the question of whether and to what extent the assistance provided *in bello* to states involved in non-international armed conflicts (NIACs) comes within the scope of state responsibility, that is, whether it might amount to an internationally wrongful act as determined in the ILC Draft Articles on State Responsibility (ASR). Bagheri uses the example of Syria to highlight the scope and extent of state responsibility for assisting states in the course of a NIAC.

The current volume of the *Yearbook* includes two additional articles covering different aspects of international legal practice. This includes a contribution by Adedayo Akingbade, who looks at the contested and often confusing concept of due diligence in international law. Akingbade argues that the value of due diligence lies in its malleability and capacity to expand expectations of state conduct in the fulfilment of obligations. At the same time, however, he recognises the inherent limitations of the norm in driving conduct insofar as it relies on the decision-making of international courts and tribunals to concretise such expectations in the form of a binding legal norm applicable to particular circumstances and concrete situations.

In her contribution, which won the Irish Yearbook of International Law 'Best Student Paper Prize', Eliza Walsh addresses the *jus in bello* and discusses the fine line separating the existence of a NIAC and an internal disturbance. In this context, she claims, individuals are often left with lower levels of protection when it comes to fundamental human rights. In response, Walsh argues for the revival of the concept of 'fundamental standards of humanity' to provide a minimum level of protection in situations occupying the 'grey zone' between NIAC and internal disturbance.

In addition to the main articles, our book review section includes four contributions. Paola Zichi reviews Lori Allen's *A History of False Hope: Investigative Commissions in Palestine* (Stanford University Press, 2020), which in her words provides 'an interdisciplinary and challenging publication for students and academics in anthropology, history, and international law'. Niall O'Shaughnessy reviews Ntina Tzouvala's *Capitalism as Civilisation: A History of International Law* (Cambridge University Press, 2020), which, through its re-reading of the history of international law through the use of the gatekeeper concept of 'civilisation', has been warmly received by many in the discipline and recently received the American Society of International Law's 2020 Certificate of Merit for a pre-eminent contribution to creative scholarship. Pearce Clancy provides a review of James Upcher's *Neutrality in Contemporary International Law* (Oxford University Press, 2020), which is a particularly timely work in light of ongoing constitutional debates on this topic in Ireland in recent years. Finally, Harshit Rai has reviewed *Colonial Wrongs and Access to International Law* (Torkel Opsahl, 2020), a significant and weighty collection of essays edited by Morten Bergsmo, Wolfgang Kaleck and Kyaw Yin Hlaing, which, as Rai suggests, makes an important contribution to what is a 'complex and multidimensional theme'.

In addition to providing a book review in the volume, Pearce Clancy also joins as one of a number of new correspondents, taking over from Sandra Duffy in reporting on the topic of human rights in Ireland. Clancy's report begins with a brief introduction looking at the impact of the COVID-19 pandemic on human rights in Ireland, including some of the concerns raised by Irish Human Rights and Equality Commission in its report *Ireland's Emergency Powers During the COVID-19 Pandemic* (2020). In addition, and in line with previous years' reports, Clancy also sets out some of the major human rights cases brought before the superior courts in 2020, as well as challenges to Ireland before the European Court of Human Rights.

Complementing Clancy's report, Esther McGuinness provides an overview of human rights in Northern Ireland (NI). The COVID-19 pandemic features prominently in the first section of the report, including coverage of a range of human rights issues thrown up by NI measures and policy responses in light of the pandemic. Beyond this, McGuinness looks at two issues with particular relevance to the human rights situation in NI: the impact of Brexit and legacy issues arising from the Troubles. Finally, the report provides an overview of Northern Irish practice with regard to a number of key human rights: right to life; freedom from torture, inhuman and degrading treatment; freedom from slavery; right to liberty and security of person; right to a fair trial; right to private life; freedom of religion and belief, expression, association and the right to participate in public and political life; right to health; right to education; equality and non-discrimination; and, social rights.

Michael Becker also joins as a new correspondent, taking over from Dug Cubie in reporting on Ireland and International Law. Becker's report, like others', begins by noting the impact of the pandemic on Ireland and the array of international legal issues that it has thrown up. Among the issues and various aspects of Irish state practice extensively discussed, Becker focuses on the fallout from Brexit and in particular the negotiations with the UK throughout 2020, including on the implementation of the Northern Ireland Protocol, and broader trade and fisheries arrangements that led at the close of the year to the eventual conclusion of the Trade and Cooperation Agreement.[1] Becker also looks forward to the likely priorities and influence of Ireland in light of its successful election to the Security Council for a two-year term beginning in January 2021.

Another new addition to the *Yearbook*, Rián Derrig provides an overview of Irish practice related to the law of the sea. Of the issues covered in Derrig's report, he highlights policy and legislative initiatives in the areas of marine spatial planning and the protection of marine living resources through the designation of marine protected areas. Among the many other matters discussed, Derrig focuses on the implications for Ireland arising from the conclusion of the Trade and Cooperation Agreement between the UK and Ireland, noted above, in the context of a lengthy discussion on fisheries practice in the year. Another focus – arising also, at least in part, from post-Brexit fallout – is the reignited territorial and fisheries dispute between the UK and Ireland over Rockall.

---

[1] The UK-EU Trade and Cooperation Agreement 2020; effective 1 May 2021.

Finally, Rónán Condon returns as correspondent on the topic of Ireland and the EU. Like others, Condon begins his report addressing the impact of the COVID-19 pandemic and Brexit, which have particular implications in terms of the role of the EU in Ireland. However, the majority of Condon's report focuses on several high-profile cases that have arisen in areas such as environmental law, including *Friends of the Irish Environment v An Bord Pleanála*,[2] which not only touches on issues of substantive importance, but further sheds light on the complex constitutional dynamics thrown up by EU law obligations in the context of Ireland's relationship with international law. Furthermore, one of the most highly anticipated cases to arise in the year related to data protection law, in the form of the *Schrems II* case,[3] which resulted in the Court of Justice essentially rebuking the Commission's approach in this area and, as Condon suggests, highlights 'a clash of cultures of privacy across the Atlantic'.

Bríd Ní Ghráinne, James Gallen and Richard Collins
June 2022

---

[2] C-254/19, *Friends of the Irish Environment Ltd v An Bord Pleanála* (2020) ECLI:EU:C:2020:680.
[3] C-311/18, *Data Protection Commissioner v Facebook Ireland Ltd and Maximillian Schrems* (2020) ECLI:EU:C:2020:559.

Articles

Military Assistance and State Responsibility for 'in Bello' Violations during Non-international Armed Conflicts

SAEED BAGHERI*

MILITARY ASSISTANCE TO a state subjected to an armed attack and seeking the assistance of other states in self-defence is a well-accepted concept in international law. However, once the assisting state facilitates the preparation or commission of any acts violating the law of armed conflict (*jus in bello*), the question immediately arises of whether and to what extent the assistance provided to states involved in non-international armed conflicts (NIACs) comes within the scope of state responsibility for an internationally wrongful act (IWA). Having displaced the law of state responsibility as the lead regime on how to hold states responsible for their IWAs, this article aims to shed light on the rationale and prospects for effectively holding assisting states responsible for IWAs in NIACs. It seeks to answer the questions of when are assisting states responsible for *in bello* violations during NIACs, when are assisting states responsible for wrongful conduct attributable to them, when are they responsible for their aid and assistance, and whether and to what extent joint responsibility of the assisting state and the acting state would be the case. This is followed by an assessment of the alleged violations committed in the NIAC in Syria. The central argument builds on state responsibility under the ILC Draft Articles on State Responsibility, with a specific focus on the grounds for holding military allies responsible for *in bello* violations committed in conjunction with the acting state during NIACs.

I. INTRODUCTION

Seeking justice for international crimes is a topic that has seen many academics giving vent to their views from various aspects. Justice for international crimes remains a dominant theme of contemporary international law. One aspect that lacks scholarly

* Lecturer in International Law, University of Reading, Reading, UK, saeed.bagheri@reading.ac.uk. I extend my utmost thanks to Professor Michael N. Schmitt for his invaluable comments on an earlier draft of this article. I also would like to thank the anonymous peer-reviewers who read and gave insightful comments on earlier written versions of this paper. Finally, I would like to express my deepest thanks to the editors for their editorial comments. All thoughts and opinions expressed in this article are those of the author.

investigation is the study of international justice for violations of the law of armed conflict (*jus in bello*) committed in non-international armed conflicts.

Having relied on state responsibility for an internationally wrongful act (IWA), this article will use a case study from Syria to test a theory of state responsibility and responsibility of military partners (assisting states/third parties) for *in bello* violations during non-international armed conflicts (NIACs). The central argument to this analysis is based on the prohibition of indiscriminate attacks on civilians or civilian objects as subject to Article 13 of Additional Protocol (II) to the Geneva Conventions, which states that civilians 'shall not be the object of attack'. They shall enjoy the protection, unless and for such time as they take a direct part in hostilities. While there is a well-known and absolute prohibition on military intervention due to a mere request for assistance made by an opposition group in another state, military assistance is allowable at the request of the government of a state.[1] However, *in bello* violations by the assisting state have particular significance in terms of state responsibility for IWAs committed during the conflicts.

The experience of the NIAC in Syria since 2011 calls for a rethinking of the responsibility of assisting states under international law. The Syrian regime has fought against the opposition using a wide range of military means and has called on its regional and strategic allies, including Russia and Iran, for support. It has been reported that the Syrian regime has committed serious violations, including launching indiscriminate attacks on civilians and deliberately attacking protected objects.[2] Even if both the Iranian and Russian positions are accepted as assisting a state on request, it seems clear that they have breached their international legal obligations through wrongful aid and assistance to the Syrian regime in committing *in bello* violations.[3] This particularly relies on Common Article 1 of the Geneva Conventions,

---

[1] *Case Concerning Military and Paramilitary Activities in and against Nicaragua (Nicaragua v United States of America)* (*Nicaragua Case*), ICJ Judgment (27 June 1986) para 246. For discussion, see E De Wet, *Military Assistance on Request and the Use of Force* (Oxford, Oxford University Press, 2020); E de Wet, 'The (Im)permissibility of Military Assistance on Request During a Civil War' (2020) 7 *Journal on the Use of Force and International Law* 26; P Butchard, 'Territorial Integrity, Political Independence, and Consent: The Limitations of Military Assistance on Request under the Prohibition of Force' (2020) 7 *Journal on the Use of Force and International Law* 1.

[2] 'UN Commission of Inquiry on Syria: The Siege and Recapture of Eastern Ghouta Marked by War Crimes against Humanity' (UNHRC, 20 June 2018) www.ohchr.org/EN/HRBodies/HRC/Pages/NewsDetail.aspx?NewsID=23226&LangID=E; 'Attacks on Syrian Civilians and Aid Workers in Aleppo Were War Crimes' (OHCHR, 3 March 2017) www.ohchr.org/EN/NewsEvents/Pages/WarCrimesInAleppo.aspx.

[3] This is precisely because reports of the UN have explicitly stated on various occasions that all states have an obligation to refrain from giving assistance in violations of international law by involving in grave breaches of *jus in bello*. It has been reported that the Syrian government, with the help of Iran-backed militias and Russian aerial bombings, had reclaimed most of Syrian territory from the rebels in 2018. The campaign to retake Eastern Ghouta was based on continuous bombardment, which reportedly killed more than 170,000 of the 400,000 civilians that resided in the city within eight weeks. See M Sulce, *The War Report 2018: The Syrian Armed Conflict: Nearing the End?* (Geneva, Geneva Academy, 2019) 6; Human Rights Council (HRC), 'The Siege and Recapture of Eastern Ghouta, Conference', Room Paper of the Independent International Commission of Inquiry on the Syrian Arab Republic (18 June–6 July 2018), UN Doc A/HRC/38/CRP.3. See also HRC, 'Human Rights Council Holds Urgent Debate on the Situation in Syria's Eastern Ghouta', Commission Press Release (28 February 2012) www.ohchr.org/en/NewsEvents/Pages/DisplayNews.aspx?NewsID=22750&LangID=E; UN General Assembly (UNGA), 'Speakers Disagree over Suitable Level of Intervention for Stopping Atrocity Crimes, as General Assembly Concludes Debate on Responsibility to Protect', UN Doc GA/12038 (2 July 2018) www.un.org/press/en/2018/ga12038.doc.htm.

which creates obligations for all states to respect and ensure respect for *jus in bello* in all circumstances as a matter of customary international law.[4]

This article goes beyond the analysis of the extent to which the military allies' state officials or military commanders are individually responsible for violations committed in line with collective intentions of 'the acting state' and 'the assisting state'. Having tackled the Iranian and Russian military presence in Syria, the article determines how Iranian and Russian military aid or assistance to the Syrian regime constitutes a wrongful act where the Syrian regime and the assisting states violated their international obligations under *jus in bello*. Taking issue with the importance of state responsibility for IWAs, the article addresses state responsibility for *in bello* violations committed during NIACs. The key questions that will be answered in this article are: when is an act considered an IWA of the state; whether and to what extent are states responsible for wrongful conduct attributable to them; when are states responsible for their aid and assistance; and when is responsibility joint?

The article concludes that no state is allowed to ignore the provisions of the Geneva Conventions protecting civilians and civil objects during armed conflicts. Rather, they are committed to respecting and ensuring respect for *jus in bello* in all circumstances as a universal responsibility contained in Common Article 1 of the 1949 Geneva Conventions. This general obligation stems from the general principles of the law of armed conflict to which the Geneva Conventions merely give specific expression.

The purpose of this article is therefore to present lessons for the future that the Syrian case might bring to ongoing debates regarding seeking justice for assisting states and the impact of unlawful military assistance on *jus in bello*.

II. STATE RESPONSIBILITY FOR *IN BELLO* VIOLATIONS

A. Conceptual Framework

Under the contemporary international law of armed conflict, serious violations of the conventional and customary rules of *jus in bello* during international armed conflicts and NIACs have long been recognised as 'war crimes' under Article 8 of the Rome Statute, which contains a detailed provision outlining the requirements for responsibility.[5] It is worth reiterating here that *jus in bello* implicitly confers upon

---

[4] See MN Schmitt and S Watts, 'Common Article 1 and the Duty to "Ensure Respect"' (2020) 96 *International Law Studies* 702.

[5] The International Criminal Court (ICC) is the only permanent international court with jurisdiction to prosecute individuals for the international crimes of genocide, crimes against humanity, war crimes and the crime of aggression. The Rome Statute has listed war crimes and the elements of the crimes in Art 8. It has also phrased the grounds for individual criminal responsibility for all war crimes within the jurisdiction of the ICC in Art 25. See C de Than and E Shorts, *International Criminal Law and Human Rights* (London, Sweet & Maxwell, 2003) 121–23; PJ Stephens, 'Collective Criminality and Individual Responsibility: The Constraints of Interpretation' (2014) 37 *Fordham International Law Journal* 517.

parties to NIACs a functional international legal personality, and that violations of *jus in bello* by such parties entail their international legal responsibility.[6] Moreover, states, according to Article 146 of the Geneva Convention (IV), have an obligation to 'provide effective penal sanctions for persons committing or ordering to be committed' any grave *in bello* breaches to avoid impunity of perpetrators of such violations and to prevent them from finding a safe haven in third countries.

Regardless of the nature of the conflict, crimes committed during armed conflicts, as serious violation of the laws and customs of war, are among the gravest international crimes. They must be considered a matter of international concern, given that international crimes cannot be left to the state that would normally have jurisdiction over them.[7] When serious violations of *jus in bello* occur during armed conflicts, both state responsibility for IWAs and individual responsibility for war crimes are important. Although individual criminal responsibility has been discussed over the past three decades, particularly with the creation of the ICC, criminal responsibility of a state for an IWA has never been determined in international law. Rather, imposing sanctions against states for IWAs is an effective mechanism that has been foreseen by the Draft Articles on Responsibility of States for Internationally Wrongful Acts (ASR) adopted by the International Law Commission (ILC) in 2001.[8]

Before turning to *in bello* violations, it is necessary to identify what exactly constitutes an IWA of states. It is important to note here that the existence of a breach of a legal obligation and attribution are the constitutive elements of an IWA of a state. This largely relies on a permissive reading of Article 2 ASR, which states:

> There is an internationally wrongful act of a State when conduct consisting of an action or omission:
>
> (a)   is attributable to the State under international law; and
> (b)   constitutes a breach of an international obligation of the State.

These two constitutive elements have also been highlighted by the International Court of Justice (ICJ) on numerous occasions in key cases. The Court has explicitly identified the key requirements for the creation of international responsibility in the *Nicaragua Case* and the *Case Concerning United States Diplomatic and Consular Staff in Tehran*. According to the ICJ, it must be determined how far, legally, the acts in question may be regarded as imputable to the state, and whether the acts are compatible or incompatible with the obligations of the state in question under the treaties in force or under any other rules of the applicable international law.[9]

When one considers the requirements of attribution and breach of international legal obligations in force for that state at that time, *in bello* violations committed by states'

---

[6] See M Sassòli, 'State Responsibility for Violations of International Humanitarian Law' (2002) 8 *International Review of the Red Cross* 411.

[7] de Than and Shorts (n 5) 13.

[8] ILC, 'Draft Articles on Responsibility of States for Internationally Wrongful Acts' (Annex to the UNGA Resolution A/RES/56/83, 85th plenary meeting, 2001) (2001) 2 *Yearbook of the International Law Commission* 26.

[9] *Nicaragua Case* (n 1) para 226; *Case Concerning United States Diplomatic and Consular Staff in Tehran (United States of America v Iran)*, ICJ Judgment (24 May 1980) paras 56 and 90. See also Arts 12–13 ASR.

military forces quickly become apparent as IWAs of the states. Although it is widely accepted that *jus in bello* is increasingly implemented against and for the benefit of individuals, Sassòli has rightly argued that it is also part of the first layer of public international law in that it is implemented between states. Sassoli has also indicated that 'violations are attributed to states and measures to stop, repress and redress them must therefore be directed against the State responsible for the violations'.[10]

As previously discussed, attribution is another core element of IWAs, and needs to be identified along with the existence of a breach of an international legal obligation.[11] The breach of an international obligation of a state by the groups or individuals acting on behalf of the state would be considered an IWA of the state if there is evidence that the act committed is 'attributable' to the state in question. The legal attribution of conduct to states is so fundamental that laid down in Article 4 ASR, which states:

1. The conduct of any State organ shall be considered an act of that State under international law, whether the organ exercises legislative, executive, judicial or any other functions, whatever position it holds in the organization of the State, and whatever its character as an organ of the central Government or of a territorial unit of the State.
2. An organ includes any person or entity which has that status in accordance with the internal law of the State.

Another reading of Article 4 is that the act is considered an act of state if it is committed by its organs, so establishing a breach is an obvious next step within the meaning of Article 2 under which the state will incur responsibility.[12] On this understanding, respect for treaty (the 1949 Geneva Conventions and 1977 Additional Protocols) rules and the customary rules of *jus in bello* are considered the most distinctive international obligations of states, the direct violation of which by a state involved in an armed conflict or through assisting another state involved in an international conflict or NIAC may generate international responsibility of the state in the sense of Article 4.

Ultimately, a breach of an international legal obligation will in many cases be triggered because of the state's aid and assistance. This, therefore, begs the key question, when are states responsible for their aid and assistance? Article 16 ASR provides that:

A State which aids or assists another State in the commission of an internationally wrongful act by the latter is internationally responsible for doing so if:
(a) that State does so with knowledge of the circumstances of the internationally wrongful act; and
(b) the act would be internationally wrongful if committed by that State.

This is highlighted in the present research precisely to elucidate how an illegitimate joint contribution in violation of *jus in bello* would imply the legal responsibility of the state for an IWA. Accordingly, this article serves as a basis for discussion with respect to an IWA, which is composed of 'attribution' and 'breach', while attribution

---

[10] Sassòli (n 6) 402.
[11] See generally M Milanovic, 'Special Rules of Attribution of Conduct in International Law' (2020) 96 *International Law Studies* 295.
[12] See J Vidmar, 'Some Observations on Wrongfulness, Responsibility and Defences in International Law' (2016) 63 *Netherlands International Law Review* 351.

is determined by the secondary rules found in the law of state responsibility and breach lies in the primary rules – that is, *jus in bello*, which is the primary focus of this article.

While not taking issue with the importance of individual responsibility, the model of 'individual culpability'[13] for collective violence, including war crimes, adopted by international criminal law despite the collective nature of these crimes means that such crimes may not be perceived as evidence of overlap between individual criminal responsibility and state responsibility. As reaffirmed in the ICJ's *Advisory Opinion on the Legality of the Threat or Use of Nuclear Weapons*, the basic rules of *jus in bello* are 'intransgressible' in character and their violation is viewed as entailing an aggravated state responsibility. This principle is derived from the breaches committed by state organs, and the breach of specific obligations of states concerning the punishment of perpetrators as well.[14] When one considers state responsibility for IWAs, it becomes apparent that any wrongful act amounting to grave breaches of *jus in bello* entails both individual criminal responsibility and state responsibility for IWAs attributable to them, which are regulated both by customary international law and by treaties.[15] This is precisely subject to serious breaches of obligations under peremptory norms of general international law regulated by Article 40 ASR, which states:

1. This chapter applies to the international responsibility which is entailed by a serious breach by a State of an obligation arising under a peremptory norm of general international law.
2. A breach of such an obligation is serious if it involves a gross or systematic failure by the responsible State to fulfil the obligation.

According to the ILC Commentary on Article 40 ASR, a grave or serious breach is one which involves 'a gross or systematic failure by the responsible State to fulfil the obligation in question'. While it defines a 'systematic' violation as one which would have to be carried out in an organised and deliberate way, a 'gross' violation refers to the intensity of the violation or its effects.[16] Though it is difficult to identify which rules of *jus in bello* belong to peremptory norms of general international law, it would be enough to note that *jus in bello* obviously prohibits any form of agreement that adversely affects the situation of protected persons. As Sassòli has argued, it is

> difficult to find [a particular *in bello* rule] that does not directly or indirectly protect rights of protected persons in armed conflicts. In both international and non-international armed conflicts, those rules furthermore protect 'basic rights of the human person' which are classic examples for [peremptory norms].[17]

---

[13] Stephens (n 5) 513. For a detailed discussion, see M Drumbl, 'Collective Violence and Individual Punishment: The Criminality of Mass Atrocity' (2005) 99 *Northwestern University Law Review* 539.

[14] *Legality of the Threat or Use of Nuclear Weapons*, Advisory Opinion, ICJ Reports (1996) para 79; ILC, 'Commentary on Article 40 of Draft Articles on Responsibility of States for Internationally Wrongful Acts' (2001) 2 *Yearbook of International Law Commission* 113 para 5; BI Bonafè, *The Relationship Between State and Individual Responsibility for International Crimes* (Leiden, Martinus Nijhoff Publishers, 2009) 28.

[15] See Bonafè (n 14) 28; G Werle, 'Individual Criminal Responsibility in Article 25 ICC Statute' (2007) 5 *Journal of International Criminal Justice* 956.

[16] See ILC, 'Commentary on Article 40' (n 14) 113 paras 7–8.

[17] See Sassòli (n 6) 414.

Jus in bello is a set of peremptory norms from which no derogation is permitted. In particular, the basic rules of *jus in bello* are considered as peremptory norms of general international law under the ILC's Draft Conclusions (2019)[18] on identification of peremptory norms of general international law. While the ILC has not specified what rules of *jus in bello* ought to be considered as basic, it seems reasonably clear to all states that there is a particular set of *in bello* rules that are deemed as peremptory norms of general international law. It is broadly accepted, for instance, that the immunity of civilians from direct attack, the protection of *persons hors de combat* and those who do not take a direct part in hostilities, the prohibition of targeting persons who are no longer participating in hostilities, proportionality, military necessity and the prohibition of the use of weapons or methods of warfare that are likely to cause unnecessary losses are the basic rules of *jus in bello*.[19] Therefore, they are deemed as peremptory norms of general international law.

It is also widely accepted that the peremptory nature of the basic rules of *jus in bello* applies in all circumstances, regardless of the classification of the conflicts. That is to say, states should refrain from facilitating any *in bello* violations during both international armed conflicts and NIACs.

Ultimately, even the circumstances precluding the wrongfulness of an otherwise unlawful act, including 'consent, self-defence, countermeasures, force majeure, distress and necessity',[20] cannot preclude the wrongfulness of any act of a state which is not in conformity with an obligation arising under a peremptory norm of general international law.[21] Even the Geneva Conventions themselves stipulate that no state may absolve itself or another state of any responsibility incurred in respect of grave breaches.[22]

Under the general rules on attribution of IWAs, it is highlighted here that states are responsible for such violations committed in them by itself, by another state and by non-state actors. Furthermore, all states should invoke the international responsibility of the states which have committed such grave and serious violations during international armed conflicts and NIACs.

B. Attribution of Breaches to a State

Before turning to the responsibility of assisting states for *in bello* violations arising from military assistance during NIACs, this section briefly sets out the general rule on holding states responsible for IWAs. This general rule describes the principle of

---

[18] ILC, 'Peremptory Norms of General International Law (Jus Cogens)', adopted by the Drafting Committee on First Reading (Seventy-First Session, 29 April–7 June and 8 July–9 August 2019), UN Doc A/CN.4/L.936 (29 May 2019).

[19] More importantly, state practice establishes these rules as norms of customary international law applicable in both international armed conflicts and NIACs. See in general JM Henckaerts and L Doswald-Beck, *Customary International Humanitarian Law – Volume I: Rules* (Cambridge, Cambridge University Press, 2005). See also *Nicaragua Case* (n 1) para 218.

[20] Arts 20–25 ASR.

[21] Art 26 ASR.

[22] See Sassòli (n 6) 414.

'attribution' for the purposes of state responsibility in international law. Article 2 ASR states: 'There is an IWA of a state when conduct consisting of an action or omission: (a) is attributable to the state under international law.' However, it must be shown that IWAs have been perpetrated by state organs or by a person or entity empowered to exercise elements of the governmental authority on behalf of the state in question. Given the broad scope of the definition of 'state organ', the ASR has also made it clear which governmental organs come within this category. Article 4 ASR states:

1.   The conduct of any State organ shall be considered an act of that State under international law, whether the organ exercises legislative, executive, judicial or any other functions, whatever position it holds in the organization of the State, and whatever its character as an organ of the central Government or of a territorial unit of the State.
2.   An organ includes any person or entity which has that status in accordance with the internal law of the State.

It is also well known that the reference to a 'state organ' covers all the individual and collective entities which make up the organisation of the state and act on its behalf. It includes an organ of any territorial governmental entity within the state on the same basis as the central governmental organs of that state. It is, ultimately, through the principle of 'attribution' that states should be held responsible for all IWAs committed by any organ of a state regardless of classification, exercising functions and level in the hierarchy. This rule is of a customary character.[23]

It should also be noted, in any event, that any state organ, whether legislative, executive or judicial, or any other person who exercises authority on behalf of that state comes within the 'attributable' perimeters for state responsibility. As the ICJ has confirmed in the case of *United States Diplomatic and Consular Staff in Tehran*, there should be sufficient evidence to prove that an operation was officially authorised by the government of the perpetrator.[24] There can be no doubt that states' militaries are considered state organs and acting under state authority. This precisely relies on the ultra vires conduct of state organs reflected in Article 7 ASR, which

makes it clear that the conduct of a state organ or an entity empowered to exercise elements of the governmental authority, acting in its official capacity, is attributable to the state even if the organ or entity acted in excess of authority or contrary to instructions.[25]

This is particularly the case where the state provides significant military assistance at the official request of another state. What happens in such cases is that the conduct of a state soldier who murders a civilian will still be attributable to the soldier's state even if such conduct was committed against the express orders of the soldier's superior.[26]

---

[23] ILC, 'Commentary on Article 40' (n 14) 40 paras 1–6. For a detailed analysis, see G Zyberi, 'Responsibility of States and Individuals for Mass Atrocity Crimes' in A Nollkaemper and I Plakokefalos (eds), *The Practice of Shared Responsibility in International Law* (Cambridge, Cambridge University Press, 2017) 236–62.

[24] *Case Concerning United States Diplomatic and Consular Staff in Tehran* (n 9) para 58. For a discussion, see de Than and Shorts (n 5) 17–18.

[25] ILC, 'Commentary on Article 7 of Draft Articles on Responsibility of States for Internationally Wrongful Acts' (2001) 45 para 1.

[26] Milanovic (n 11) 380.

Therefore, all states remain responsible for IWAs attributable to them that violate international law, in particular *jus in bello* rules and international human rights law.

III. RESPONSIBILITY FOR THE BREACHES ARISING FROM MILITARY ASSISTANCE

There are reasons to consider military aid unlawful within the context of the current legal regime. State responsibility comes into question when the perpetrator and co-perpetrator act pursuant to a common plan to commit a certain act as an illegitimate joint contribution in violation of *in bello* rules. This will set out the well-established rules of state responsibility for wrongful assistance and complicity in the wrongful conduct of a third state, rather than directly attributing that conduct to the assisting state.[27] The NIAC in Syria is a credible case, which underscores the grave *in bello* violations and IWAs committed by the Syrian regime with support of its partners.

A. Legitimate Scope of Military Assistance

Military assistance at the request of the states involved in an armed conflict is one of the most highly disputed and controversial subjects of international law. It is also one of the most significant limits on state sovereignty and territorial integrity. It can be defined as when a state seeks assistance from other states to defend its borders from outside attacks, internal disturbances and isolated guerrilla or terrorist activities. However, military assistance in this vein has been accepted by the international community of states when consent has been granted by a state to 'reinforce its authority'.[28] As reaffirmed by United Nations Security Council (UNSC) Resolution 387 (1976), it is the 'inherent and lawful right of every State, in the exercise of its sovereignty, to request assistance from any other State or group of States'.[29] In this respect, the jurisprudence of the ICJ is more illustrative. According to the ICJ, and contrary to the principle of non-intervention (as per customary international law) due to a mere request for assistance made by an opposition group in another state, military assistance is permissible at the request of the government of a state. This is evidence that stems from the wording of the ICJ in the *Nicaragua Case*:

> Indeed, it is difficult to see what would remain of the principle of non-intervention in international law if intervention, which is already allowable at the request of the government of a State, were also to be allowed at the request of the opposition.[30]

[27] ibid 355–62.
[28] GH Fox, 'Intervention by Invitation' in M Weller (ed), *Oxford Handbook of the Use of Force in International Law* (Oxford, Oxford University Press, 2015) 821; TC Heller and AD Sofaer, 'Sovereignty: The Practitioner's Prospective' in D Krasner (ed), *Problematic Sovereignty: Contested Rules and Political Possibilities* (New York, Colombia University Press, 2001) 24–25.
[29] UNSC Resolution 387, UN Doc S/RES/387 (31 March 1976).
[30] *Nicaragua Case* (n 1) para 246.

Nevertheless, as Brownlie has argued, a problem arises when the legal status of the government that is alleged to have given consent is in doubt.[31] Further, doctrine and state practice limit the requests of the established and internationally recognised government of a state for assistance (which is often made in the form of detachments of armed forces or the supply of military equipment)[32] in particular circumstances. Given the unpredictable impact of military assistance, the legitimacy of any assistance by request depends on the requirement of the de facto character of the inviting government and its effective control over its territory.[33]

There is no precise definition of effective control or what constitutes it. The most widely accepted view is that effective control, as the test for a government's capacity to represent the state, has largely been measured by the degree to which the government has a certain level of unconditional control and commands the obedience of the people within the state. In addition, all population groups and institutions within the jurisdiction of the state recognise and accept the incumbent government's superiority and its right to represent the state as a whole. This suggests that the government does not become a de facto government unless it establishes itself in such a way that all within its influence recognise its control, and that there is no opposing force assuming to be a government in its place.[34] Ultimately, the acting state will be able to request military assistance if its government is de facto and has effective control over its territory.[35]

It is also perhaps worth making explicit that military assistance by request is still controversial in terms of validity, legality and enforceability if the acting state is engaged in a NIAC. In principle, third-party states must legally refrain from interfering, assisting or participating in NIACs in which the control of a state is divided between warring factions; military assistance will be controversial even if it is by the request of the acting state's established government.[36] As an exception, however, there is a well-accepted view indicating that military assistance by request in an internal armed conflict[37] is considered justified if there is a war against a violent, armed

---

[31] I Brownlie, *International Law and the Use of Force by States* (Oxford, Oxford University Press, 1963) 317.

[32] R Jennings and A Watts (eds), *Oppenheim's International Law – Volume 1: Peace* (London & New York, Longman, 1996) 435.

[33] Broadly speaking, the authority which has come to power and exercises full control over the country would have to be regarded as the legitimate government of the state and is therefore entitled to give consent to military assistance that may be regarded as valid under international law. See G Hafner, 'Present Problems of the Use of Force in International Law' (2009) 73 *Annuaire de l'Institut de Droit International* 321.

[34] See Arbitration Between Great Britain and Costa Rica – Opinion and Award of William H Taft, Reports of International Arbitral Awards (Recueil Des Sentences Arbitrales) – Aguilar-Amory and Royal Bank of Canada Claims (Great Britain v Costa Rica) (Washington, DC, 18 October 1923) 382. See also SD Murphy, 'Democratic Legitimacy and the Recognition of States and Governments' (1999) 48 *International and Comparative Law Quarterly* 566; D Wippman, 'Military Intervention, Regional Organizations, and Host-State Consent' (1996) 7 *Duke Journal of Comparative and International Law* 212; E de Wet, 'From Free Town to Cairo via Kiev: The Unpredictable Road of Democratic Legitimacy in Governmental Recognition' (2014) 108 *American Journal of International Law Unbound* 203.

[35] Arbitration Between Great Britain and Costa Rica (n 34) 381–82.

[36] R Jennings and A Watts (n 32) 438. See also C Nowak, 'The Changing Law of Non-intervention in Civil Wars – Assessing the Production of Legality in State Practice after 2011' (2018) 5 *Journal on the Use of Force and International Law* 40; E Lumsden, 'An Uneasy Peace: Multilateral Military Intervention in Civil Wars' (2003) 35 *New York University Journal of International Law and Politics* 795.

[37] G Nolte, 'Intervention by Invitation', *Max Planck Encyclopaedia of International Law* (2010) para 1, https://opil.ouplaw.com/view/10.1093/law:epil/9780199231690/law-9780199231690-e1702?print=pdf.

non-state actor or terrorist group committing atrocities against the state forces and civilians.[38] Under these circumstances, military assistance is acceptable only by the request of a state that is being subjected to an armed attack and is seeking the assistance of other states in self-defence.[39] In other words, a state may provide military assistance only once the victim state has requested it to fight terrorism and violent armed non-state actors. As discussed earlier, such assistance with the consent of the acting state is allowed as a circumstance precluding the wrongfulness of an otherwise unlawful act, unless the assistance amounts to a serious violation of peremptory norms of general international law.

It is well established that military assistance to armed non-state actors or rebel groups is prohibited. Moreover, any form of direct or indirect intervention in NIACs is prohibited that is

> in violation of the [UN Charter], of the principles of non-intervention, of equal rights and self-determination of peoples and generally accepted standards of human rights and in particular when its object is to support an established government against its own population.[40]

Notwithstanding this, the ICJ has confirmed the general rule that military assistance is already allowable at the request of the government.[41]

As subject to the law of state responsibility, consent is one of the circumstances precluding the wrongfulness of an otherwise unlawful act enumerated in Article 20 ASR. However, as discussed earlier, there are no circumstances under Article 26 ASR in which consent or any other circumstance precluding wrongfulness can be used as a basis for committing human rights violations, such as assassinations, torture or any form of inhumane treatment, or attacking civilians and civilian objects within the acting state's territory.

In its commentary on Article 16 ASR, the ILC states that state responsibility for aid or assistance in the commission of an IWA 'can arise when a State voluntarily assists or aids another State in carrying out conduct which violates the international obligations of the latter, for example, by knowingly providing an essential facility or financing the activity in question'.[42] However, it should be emphasised that aid or assistance by the assisting state should not be confused with responsibility of the acting state. In such a case, the assisting state will only be responsible to the extent that its conduct has caused harm or has contributed to the IWA; it is not responsible for the actions of the acting state[43] (this will be discussed in the last section).

Aside from the above, any type of operation by the assisting state must comply with the relevant provisions of international human rights law and *jus in bello*,

---

[38] The operations under 'such interventions may involve actual fighting by the foreign troops but [these operations] may also be limited to power projection or to other forms of active military support'. ibid para 1.

[39] *Nicaragua Case* (n 1) para 176.

[40] MG Hafner (2011) 'Present Problems of the Use of Force in International Law: A Report of Sub-Group C on Military Assistance on Request' (Institut De Droit International, 2011) Art 3(1), www.idi-iil.org/app/uploads/2017/06/2011_rhodes_10_C_en.pdf.

[41] *Nicaragua Case* (n 1) para 246.

[42] ILC, 'Commentary on Article 16 of Draft Articles on Responsibility of States for Internationally Wrongful Acts' (2001) 66–67.

[43] ibid. See also B Graefrath, 'Complicity in the Law of International Responsibility' (1996) 29 *Belgian Review of International Law* 380.

as well as any conditions imposed by the acting state. This is where the acting state seeks assistance to defend its borders from external attacks, internal disturbances and isolated guerrilla or terrorist activities. Although the consent of the acting state justifies the use of military force by the assisting state in its territory, there exists a general rule of international law according to which all states are subject to the applicable law, including *jus in bello*, during military operations, even within a foreign territory in support of the acting state.

To highlight the limitations on military assistance by request with actual examples, the legality and impact of the Russian and Iranian military assistance to the Syrian regime involved in a NIAC are considered in the last section.

B. Responsibility of Assisting States for Indiscriminate Attacks in Violation of *Jus in Bello*

The state responsibility in both international armed conflicts and NIACs begins with violation of the general principles of *jus in bello*, including military necessity, distinction between combatants and non-combatants, and proportionality in attacks, which concerns how much force is morally appropriate.

For the purpose of this article, indiscriminate attacks against civilians and civilian objects during NIACs, particularly armed attacks by the state involved in a NIAC and its invited military allies, come to the fore as the subject of the principle of distinction intended to protect civilian persons and objects. Under Article 13 of Protocol II to the 1949 Geneva Conventions, all civilian populations affected by NIACs shall enjoy general protection against the dangers arising from military operations and shall not be the object of attack, unless they take direct part in hostilities. Though a number of states have not ratified Protocols I and II, the general obligation to uphold the principle of distinction is valid as a rule of customary international law applicable in both international armed conflicts and NIACs.[44]

No doubt there are legal obligations and responsibilities for *in bello* violations, but it is worth being explicit here that the *jus in bello* rights and obligations are the same for fighters of each party in an international armed conflict or NIAC. Common Article 3 to the Geneva Conventions and Additional Protocol (II) is offset by the fact that only the provisions of Common Article 3 are applicable to both signatory and non-signatory parties.[45] As Pictet has argued,

> the mere fact of the legality of a government involved in an internal conflict suffices to bind that Government as a Contracting Party to the Convention ... If an insurgent party applies Article 3, so much the better for the victims of the conflict. No one will complain. If it does

[44] Henckaerts and Doswald-Beck (n 19) 3.

[45] As the ICJ pointed out in the *Nicaragua Case*, Art 3, which is common to all four Geneva Conventions of 12 August 1949, is declaratory of customary international law. According to the Court, 'Article 3 defines certain rules to be applied in the armed conflicts of a non-international character. There is no doubt that, in the event of international armed conflicts, these rules also constitute a minimum yardstick, in addition to the more elaborate rules which are also to apply to international conflicts; and they are rules which, in the Court's opinion, reflect what the Court in 1949 called "elementary considerations of humanity".' See *Nicaragua Case* (n 1) para 218.

not apply it, it will prove that those who regard its actions as mere acts of anarchy or brigandage are right.[46]

In view of this, care has been taken to state that the fighters in a NIAC, including government forces and organised armed groups, would, of course, be responsible for *in bello* violations.[47] Under the principle of distinction, indiscriminate attacks directed against civilian objects by the military forces of a state involved in a NIAC and its military allies would also be considered a serious violation of Common Article 3 to the Geneva Conventions, which protects persons taking no active part in the hostilities. Such attacks would also be considered 'wilful killing' of persons who are recognised as *hors de combat*. According to Rule 47 of the International Committee of the Red Cross (ICRC)'s Customary International Humanitarian Law Study, 'a person *hors de combat* is: (a) anyone who is in the power of an adverse party; (b) anyone who is defenceless because of unconsciousness, shipwreck, wounds or sickness; or (c) anyone who clearly expresses an intention to surrender'.[48] The prohibition on targeting persons *hors de combat* is a norm of customary international humanitarian law which prohibits 'violence to life and person, in particular murder of all kinds', against persons placed *hors de combat*.[49]

Whilst states involved in NIACs may not be willing to admit to the existence of armed conflict and the application of Common Article 3 as a matter of law, its provisions are frequently applied in practice.[50] Indiscriminate attacks against protected persons in NIACs thus constitute a grave breach of *jus in bello* and the acting state cannot consent to such breaches.[51]

This is regardless of whether the government forces and their military allies use force in self-defence against one or more organised groups. When states use force in self-defence with the assistance of military allies invited to the conflict, they must be held responsible for the measures taken that are incompatible with the UN Charter. In terms of state responsibility for IWAs, Article 21 ASR clearly indicates that 'the wrongfulness of an act of a state is precluded if the act constitutes a lawful measure of self-defence taken in conformity with the UN Charter'.

IV. EMPIRICAL TEST: LESSONS FROM SYRIA

To exemplify the arguments discussed in this article concerning responsibility of military allies for *in bello* violations committed on behalf of the acting state, this

---

[46] J Pictet, *Commentary on the Geneva Conventions of 12 August 1949 – Volume III* (Geneva, ICRC, 1960) 37–38.

[47] According to the ICRC's Customary International Humanitarian Law Study, a state is responsible for *in bello* violations attributable to it. State practice establishes this rule as a norm of customary international law applicable to violations committed in both international armed conflicts and NIACs. See Henckaerts and Doswald-Beck (n 19) Rule 149, 164–65.

[48] ibid 164–65.

[49] ibid 164.

[50] UK Ministry of Defence, *The Manual of the Law of Armed Conflict* (Oxford, Oxford University Press, 2004) 387; Pictet (n 46) 37–38.

[51] Sassòli (n 6) 414.

section briefly delves into the justifications made by Iran and Russia for active assistance to the Syrian government during the NIAC in Syria and their responsibility for the violations committed at the request of the Syrian regime.

A. Rationales for the Aid and Assistance Provided to the Syrian Regime

The International, Impartial and Independent Mechanism created by the UN General Assembly in 2016 has collected, analysed and preserved evidence of all violations committed by all sides in Syria. Apart from the Syrian regime, the responsibility of its military allies, including Iran and Russia, which were invited by the Syrian regime to support Syria's so-called counter-terrorism operations, is an issue under international criminal justice.

The Syrian regime's strategic allies, including Iran and Russia, have played a substantial role in supporting the Syrian government to keep control of the capital with the seat of government, much of the western part of the country and almost all the coastal region. Both Iran and Russia have close ties to Syrian President Bashar al-Assad's regime. Along with financial support, military advice and training, Iran has reportedly deployed thousands of members of the Iranian Revolutionary Guard in support of the Syrian regime to fight Islamic State[52] and opposition groups since 2011. Likewise, Russia has played an active role in support of Assad's regime, having deployed approximately 4000 personnel to Syria since November 2015. It has also been reported that the Russian forces have included ground forces, naval units, combat aircraft and helicopters, which have been used in airstrikes against Islamic State and other opposition groups since their arrival in the country in late August 2015.[53] It is well known that their primary and common objective has been aiding the Syrian government to retake control of the strategic territory it had lost to Islamic State and opposition groups.

Even if one accepts that the conflict in Syria is complex due to the multiple external interventions with different justifications, responsibility for *in bello* violations

---

[52] Islamic State, also known as IS, Islamic State of Iraq and the Levant (ISIL), Islamic State of Iraq and Syria (ISIS), or the Arabic acronym Daesh/Da'ish, is one of the most powerful Islamic jihadist groups that has ever existed. The group, which arose shortly after US forces left Iraq, consolidated its power by occupying major parts of Iraqi and Syrian territory over a very short period and declaring an Islamic Caliphate, and its acts of violence and terrorism focused the international community's attention on the Middle East. The emergence of Islamic State took the international community by surprise, particularly after the group declared a worldwide caliphate. Pro-democracy protests against President Bashar al-Assad in Syria, which initially began peacefully in March 2011, led to the killings of several protestors and plunged the country into chaos. This allowed Islamic State to take advantage of the situation and to expand its influence, while Syrian society remained repressive on the eve of the 2011 uprisings. See S Jayaraman, 'International Terrorism and Statelessness: Revoking the Citizenship of ISIL Foreign Fighters' (2016) 17 *Chicago Journal of International Law* 178; H Wimmen, *Syria's Path from Civic Uprising to Civil War* (Washington, DC, Carnegie Endowment for International Peace, 2016) 4; P Sluglett, 'Deadly Implications: The Rise of Sectarianism in Syria' in M Beck, D Jung and P Seeberg (eds), *The Levant in Turmoil: Syria, Palestine, and the Transformation of Middle Eastern Politics* (New York, Palgrave Macmillan, 2016) 39–55.

[53] TD Gill, 'Classifying the Conflict in Syria' (2016) 92 *International Law Studies* 355; M Hakimi, 'Defensive Force against Non-State Actors: The State of Play' (2015) 91 *International Law Studies* 1.

is unproblematic with regard to targeting civilians because the absolute *jus in bello* prohibition on civilian targeting applies either way.[54] It is, of course, worth noting here that Russia and Iran, as assisting states invited by the Syrian government, have also played a vital role in fighting Islamic State on the Syrian government's side. It is also well known that other states, including the USA, Turkey and Gulf Arab states, have intervened in Syria without the consent of the Syrian government to fight against Islamic State and backed opposition groups.[55] Though IWAs of other intervening states are subject to state responsibility under the ASR, this is technically beyond the scope of this article. This article does not discuss thoroughly all the aspects of the war and the responsibility of all states involved in the conflict. As far as possible, the aim of this article is to highlight and examine the responsibility of the states invited by the government of the acting state involved in a NIAC.

The consent and request of the Syrian government are the major justifications and legal basis for military assistance by third-party states to the Syrian regime in defending its integrity and independence. Clearly, military assistance at the request of the acting state is a circumstance precluding wrongfulness and therefore is not at odds with the principle of territorial sovereignty, which provides that integrity and political independence of states are inviolable.[56] In a sense, sovereign equality is based on the states' commitment to respecting the personality, territorial integrity and political independence of other states. In that sense, military assistance by request indicates the consent of the legitimate government of a victim state (which is confronted by armed attacks) given to another state to use armed force against its enemies.

As discussed earlier, the permissibility of military assistance by request in NIACs such as the one in Syria is still a subject of controversy among the international community.[57] However, there is evidence of state practice (in which the acting state's consent is a justification for intervention in internal conflicts)[58] that is mostly based on the permissibility of military assistance by request of the acting state. The stronger view based on practice indicates the permissibility of the use of force in Syria due to the fact that Bashar al-Assad's regime, as the internationally recognised legitimate government

---

[54] See JA Green and C Waters, 'Military Targeting in the Context of Self-Defence Actions' (2015) 84 *Nordic Journal of International Law* 6.

[55] See K Bannelier-Christakis, 'Military Interventions against ISIL in Iraq, Syria and Libya, and the Legal Basis of Consent' (2016) 29 *Leiden Journal of International Law* 745. See also 'Syria War: A Brief Guide to Who's Fighting Whom' (*BBC News*, 7 April 2017) www.bbc.co.uk/news/world-middle-east-39528673.

[56] Declaration on Principles of International Law Concerning Friendly Relations and Co-operation Among States in Accordance with the Charter of the United Nations, UNGA, Resolution 2625, UN Doc A/RES/25/2625 (24 October 1970).

[57] Legal justification for unlawful intervention in civil wars is found in the 1975 Resolution of the Institute of International Law on the Principle of Non-intervention in Civil Wars, in which civil wars are defined as internal or NIACs between the government of a state and insurgent movements, whose aim is to overthrow the government or the political, economic or social order of the state, or to achieve secession or self-government for any part of the state; or a NIAC between two or more groups contending for control of the state in the absence of an established government. See Justitia et Pace Institut de Droit International, 'The Principle of Non-intervention in Civil Wars' (Session of Wiesbaden, 14 August 1975) Art 1, www.idi-iil.org/app/uploads/2017/06/1975_wies_03_en.pdf.

[58] 'The Legal Framework for the United States' Use of Military Force Since 9/11', speech delivered by Stephen W Preston at the Annual Meeting of the American Society of International Law, Washington, DC (10 April 2015) www.defense.gov/Newsroom/Speeches/Speech/Article/606662/.

of Syria, which has not been replaced by another political entity as a result of the ongoing war, has given consent. In other words, the consent and request of Bashar al-Assad as the official head of the Syrian government, who was elected in accordance with the Syrian Constitution, constitute justification for third-party intervention in Syria. This was also the Iranian authorities' justification for assisting a large pro-government militia known as the National Defence Forces. According to the Iranian authorities, Iranian forces are present in Syria in response to the Syrian government's request to support Bashar al-Assad's regime, and they will leave Syria if the Syrian government declares that their presence in Syrian territory is no longer necessary.[59]

It appears that both Iran and Russia have been worried about the durability and survival of the Syrian regime because it is threatened not only by Islamic State, but also by various domestic rebel groups, including the Syrian National Coalition, the Interim Government, the Turkish-backed Free Syrian Army, the Syrian Salvation Government, Hayat Tahrir al-Sham and the National Coordination Committee for Democratic Change, who are all opposing the Syrian government for very different reasons.[60] This could be observed more specifically where the Iranian forces fought against rebel groups in the defence of Bashar al-Assad's regime. At this stage, the legitimacy of the military assistance remains problematic since it has led to serious violations of *jus in bello*. It has been reported, for example, that the Syrian regime committed serious crimes amounting to war crimes in launching indiscriminate attacks on civilians.[61]

Thanks to Russian and Iranian support, Assad's regime has taken back control of much of western Syria. However, despite the Iranian and Russian positions being widely accepted as action in assistance at the request of the acting state, they still seem to be in violation of the international law of armed conflict. It has been explicitly identified in UN reports and decisions of international tribunals on many occasions that all states have an obligation to refrain from giving assistance in violation of *jus in bello* (negative obligations) through participation in war crimes and crimes against humanity during international armed conflicts and NIACs.[62]

The UN General Assembly (UNGA) Resolution on the human rights situation in Syria has condemned the continued widespread and systematic gross violations of human rights and fundamental freedoms by the Syrian authorities, such as the use of heavy weapons and force against civilians, massacres, arbitrary executions, extrajudicial killings, the killing and persecution of protestors, human rights defenders and journalists, arbitrary detention, enforced disappearances, interference with access

---

[59] Gill (n 53) 355–56; 'IRGC Official Hits Back at US's Pompeo over Anti-Iran Remarks' (*Tasnim News*, 25 May 2018) www.tasnimnews.com/en/news/2018/05/25/1734519/irgc-official-hits-back-at-us-s-pompeo-over-anti-iran-remarks; 'Iran Says to Maintain Military Presence in Syria Despite US Pressure' (*Reuters*, 28 August 2018) www.reuters.com/article/us-mideast-crisis-syria-iran/iran-says-to-maintain-military-presence-in-syria-despite-u-s-pressure-idUSKCN1LD1JQ.

[60] For general information, see B Haddad and E Wind, 'The Fragmented State of the Syrian Opposition' in M Kamrava (ed), *Beyond the Arab Spring: The Evolving Ruling Bargain in the Middle East* (Oxford, Oxford University Press, 2014) 397–436; D Byman, 'Six Bad Options for Syria' (2016) 38(4) *The Washington Quarterly* 171.

[61] 'Attacks on Syrian Civilians and Aid Workers in Aleppo Were War Crimes' (OHCHR, 3 March 2017) www.ohchr.org/EN/NewsEvents/Pages/WarCrimesInAleppo.aspx; 'UN Commission of Inquiry on Syria: The Siege and Recapture of Eastern Ghouta Marked by War Crimes against Humanity' (UNHRC, 20 June 2018) www.ohchr.org/EN/HRBodies/HRC/Pages/NewsDetail.aspx?NewsID=23226&LangID=E. See also n 2 above.

[62] See de Than and Shorts (n 5) 121–23; Stephens (n 5) 517.

to medical treatment, torture, sexual violence and ill-treatment, including against children, as well as any human rights abuses by armed opposition groups.[63] The Resolution has also emphasised the need to conduct an international, transparent, independent and prompt investigation into abuses and violations of international law, with a view to holding to account those responsible for violations and abuses, which may include crimes against humanity and war crimes.[64]

It should be kept in mind that all states have an obligation to respect the fundamental rules of *jus in bello* and the implementation of the obligations contained in Common Article 1 of the 1949 Geneva Conventions.[65] Ever since the adoption of the UN Charter in conjunction with international law regulating the use of force and *jus in bello*, it has commonly been accepted that under no circumstances, even in support of the acting state, can any state involved in any form of armed conflict be excused of human rights violations such as assassination, torture or other kinds of inhumane treatment, or attacking civilians and civilian targets within the acting state's territory. Using this logic, continuing to assist the Syrian regime when there is significant evidence that the government is committing serious crimes inside its borders entails the involved states' international responsibility for supporting and closing their eyes to the violations of *jus in bello* through excessive, indiscriminate and disproportionate force against opposition groups in the course of the war on terrorism.

Russia's military assistance to Syria serves as another example of military assistance at the request of the Syrian government. The presence of the Russian military in Syrian territory became a common sight during the war with Islamic State. Regarding the legality of the use of force in foreign territory, the Russian military operations in Syria do not require much commentary since the operations were undertaken at the request of the Syrian government. According to the Russian authorities, 'on 30 September 2015, following a request of the Syrian leadership, the President of Russia asked for and received the consent of the Federation Council to use the armed forces of the Russian Federation in the Syrian Arab Republic'.[66] In that sense, Russia's military assistance to Syria is similar to the US-led coalition's assistance to Iraq, whereas the states participating in the airstrikes against Islamic State, in legally justifying their actions, largely relied on a general assertion that military action in a state's territory with the consent of its government is legal. The US authorities stated that:

> we believe that any actions we would take, to include airstrikes, would be consistent with international law, as we have a request from the Government of Iraq. So, we [have] essentially been asked and invited to take these actions by the Government of Iraq, and that provides the international legal basis.[67]

---

[63] UNGA, 'Situation of Human Rights in the Syrian Arab Republic', Resolution A/HRC/21/L.32 (24 September 2012) para 4.

[64] ibid para 10.

[65] See in general U Palwankar, 'Measures Available to States for Fulfilling Their Obligation to Ensure Respect for International Humanitarian Law' (1994) 298 *International Review of the Red Cross* 9.

[66] Letter dated 1 September 2015 from the Permanent Representative of the Russian Federation to the United Nations addressed to the Secretary-General (S/2015/678), UN Doc S/2014/695 (30 September 2015) 4, 30. See also M Bodner, 'Russia Begins Airstrikes in Syria' (*Moscow Times*, 30 September 2015) www.themoscowtimes.com/2015/09/30/russia-begins-air-strikes-in-syria-a49973.

[67] The White House Office of the Press Secretary, 'Background Briefing by Senior Administration Officials on Iraq' (8 August 2014) https://obamawhitehouse.archives.gov/the-press-office/2014/08/08/background-briefing-senior-administration-officials-iraq.

For the same reason, Russia joined in the pre-existing NIAC between Syria and Islamic State and therefore became a party to the conflict alongside the Syrian government. However, the problem that arises in this case is that Russia's operations also deliberately targeted other groups that opposed the Syrian regime.[68] It has been reported that the majority of its operations have targeted areas under the control of rebel groups and civilians where none of Islamic State's fighters were located. In other words, Russia's military operations at the request of the Syrian government had little impact on Islamic State and more impact on civilians and the opposition groups, particularly those who backed the Western powers.[69] Yet, the majority of states apathetically tolerated the unlawful operations carried out under the guise of military assistance justified by consent.

B. International Responsibility of Assisting States for *in Bello* Violations

Over and above these precedents, regardless of what the assisting states assert as the legal basis for supporting Iraq or Syria – military assistance at the request of effective or ineffective governments – the humanitarian impact of such actions must be considered the primary concern of the international community. The aim of this is to answer the questions of when the assistant states are responsible for their aid and assistance and when responsibility for them is joint.

It is universally recognised that no international or regional treaty or convention accepts the targeting of civilians in fighting armed non-state actors or any violent groups. Having dealt with the humanitarian consequences of the US, Russian and Iranian interventions in both Iraq and Syria, it appears clear that the military operations undertaken at the request of the partially effective governments of Iraq and Syria exceeded their primary objective of defending the acting state's borders from external attacks, internal disturbances and isolated guerrilla or terrorist activities.[70] Even taking the requests of the Iraqi and Syrian governments into consideration, the major question remains whether the main objective of the military assistance was to aid the acting state to protect its people from terrorist actions and to minimise civilian casualties, given the increased number of civilian casualties and the targeting of civilian property and natural resources in the wake of extraterritorial use of force within the territory of the acting states. Particularly in Syria, this has led to additional challenges regarding serious violations of *jus in bello*.

---

[68] V Koutroulis, 'The Fight Against the Islamic State and Jus in Bello' (2016) 29 *Leiden Journal of International Law* 836; J Borger, 'Russia Committed War Crimes in Syria, Finds UN Report' (*The Guardian*, 2 March 2020) www.theguardian.com/world/2020/mar/02/russia-committed-war-crimes-in-syria-finds-un-report.

[69] See M Czuperski et al (eds), *Distract, Deceive, Destroy: Putin at War in Syria* (Washington, DC, Atlantic Council, 2016) 11–12, 20; Borger (n 68).

[70] Although more than two states engaged in the war with Islamic State, this did not internationalise the NIAC between Iraq and Islamic State. Instead, the military operations of third states are integrated into the pre-existing NIAC and are regulated by *jus in bello* since no state has argued the inapplicability of this law to the initial phase of external military operations. For more discussion, see Koutroulis (n 68) 832.

While the use of force may be justified under military necessity and military assistance by request, it can also make the assisting states responsible for any violations of *jus in bello* due to the disproportionality of the attacks with regard to their foreseeable impacts on civilians. It is worth noting that state responsibility for IWAs extends to all states assisting in the *in bello* violations. The elements of assistance amounting to state responsibility are clearly defined and formalised by Article 16 ASR, which has generally been well received by the international community of states. To reiterate the elements of state responsibility for IWAs under Article 16, military assistance involves state responsibility if the assisting state has 'knowledge of the circumstances of the wrongfulness of the act', and 'the acts committed by the assisting State in support of the acting State would be internationally wrongful'.

In the interests of clarity regarding wrongfulness of the acts committed by the assisting state, it should be noted here that the prohibition on targeting civilians and civilian objects is a well-known, absolute and peremptory obligation under *jus in bello*.[71] There can be no doubt, therefore, that the alleged violations of *jus in bello* committed in Syria amount to IWAs as they constitute serious violations of peremptory norms of general international law.

One might consider the issue of 'knowledge of the circumstances of the IWA' critical to the responsibility of the assisting state. However, there can be no doubt that an assisting state is under an obligation to engage in prior investigations before committing assistance to the acting state that is allegedly responsible for serious violations of *jus in bello*.[72] In this article, Iran and Russia would be in the same situation as they have assisted and unlawfully supported the Syrian regime despite the wide range of allegations and the reports published by the UN concerning the Syrian regime's responsibility for indiscriminate attacks against civilians.[73] Official statements made by the Iranian and Russian authorities concerning the invitation by the Syrian government to assist Assad's regime in fighting opposition within the Syrian territory make such an assertion plausible.[74] What began in Syria in 2011 has been a NIAC between anti-government rebel groups and the Syrian government backed by Russia and Iran. Iran reportedly provided combat troops to support the Syrian army since 2012,[75] and Russia has been a direct participant in the conflict since 2015.[76] They fought on the Syrian regime's side and played an important

---

[71] See Green and Waters (n 54) 7–8. For a detailed assessment, see E De Wet, 'Complicity in Violations of Human Rights and Humanitarian Law by Incumbent Governments Through Direct Military Assistance on Request' (2018) 67 *International & Comparative Law Quarterly* 301.

[72] HP Aust, *Complicity and the Law of State Responsibility* (Cambridge, Cambridge University Press, 2011) 336.

[73] See n 2 above.

[74] ibid.

[75] SK Dehghan, 'Syrian Army Being Aided by Iranian Forces' (*The Guardian*, 28 May 2012) www.theguardian.com/world/2012/may/28/syria-army-iran-forces; Global Conflict Tracker, 'Civil War in Syria' (last updated 11 March 2022) www.cfr.org/global-conflict-tracker/conflict/civil-war-syria; S Dadouch, 'After Backing Assad, Iran and Russia Compete for Influence and Spoils of War' (*Washington Post*, 20 May 2021) www.washingtonpost.com/world/middle_east/syria-war-russia-iran-influence/2021/05/19/7d26851e-a9d1-11eb-bca5-048b2759a489_story.html.

[76] M Yacoubian, 'What Is Russia's Endgame in Syria?' (United States Institute of Peace, 16 February 2021) www.usip.org/publications/2021/02/what-russias-endgame-syria; Global Conflict Tracker (n 75).

role in its campaign against the rebels. With Russian aerial support and the Iranian Revolutionary Guard's troop deployments, the Syrian government steadily regained control of territory from opposition forces in Aleppo in 2016.[77] However, it has been well evidenced and reported that abuses of the Syrian forces, including the use of disproportionate force, indiscriminate attacks against civilians, the systematic destruction of civilian property, enforced disappearances, torture, sexual violence and deaths in custody, amount to crimes against humanity. The Russian- and Iranian-backed atrocities, shelling of civilians and widespread violations of human rights and international law committed in Syria have taken hundreds of thousands of Syrian lives.[78] Despite all the evidence above and promises by the UN to take action, the ongoing deployment and presence of Iranian troops and Russian aerial operations in support of the Syrian regime[79] may be enough to conclude that Russia and Iran have supported the Syrian regime with knowledge of the circumstances of the IWAs.

ILC has ultimately made it clear that 'State practice supports assigning international responsibility to a State which deliberately participates in the internationally wrongful conduct of another through the provision of aid or assistance, in circumstances where the obligation breached is equally opposable to the assisting State'.[80] However, it is worth noting here that the assisting state would only be responsible for its own act in deliberately assisting another state to breach an international obligation by which they are both bound; it is therefore not responsible, as such, for the act of the acting state within the meaning of Article 16 ASR.[81] But this is not the only possible reading of the ASR. The international law of state responsibility further specifies joint responsibility of a state in connection with the act of another state. This is particularly the case where the assistance is a necessary element in the IWA and in the absence of which it could not have occurred: here, the injury suffered can be concurrently attributed to the assisting and the acting state.[82] As previously discussed, keeping control of the large part of the country, including the capital, the western part of the country and almost all of the coastal region, would

See further S Adams, *Failure to Protect: Syria and the UN Security Council* (New York, Global Centre for the Responsibility to Protect, 2015).

[77] See Global Conflict Tracker (n 75).

[78] European Parliament, 'Syria: Syria: Assad Regime, Russia and Iran are Responsible for Heinous Crimes', Press Release (15 March 2018) www.europarl.europa.eu/news/en/press-room/20180309IPR99435/syria-assad-regime-russia-and-iran-are-responsible-for-heinous-crimes. See also 'Syria: UN Commission Chair Warns the General Assembly that War against the Syrian People Continues Unabated (UNHRC, 25 October 2021) www.ohchr.org/EN/HRBodies/HRC/Pages/NewsDetail.aspx?NewsID=27703&LangID=E; '76th Session of the United Nations General Assembly Third Committee, Statement by Mr Paulo Sérgio Pinheiro – Chair of the Independent International Commission of Inquiry on the Syrian Arab Republic' (UNHRC, 25 October 2021) www.ohchr.org/EN/HRBodies/HRC/Pages/NewsDetail.aspx?NewsID=27701&LangID=E. See also nn 2 and 50 above.

[79] See 'Disappearance and Detention to Suppress Dissent a Hallmark of a Decade of Conflict in Syria – UN Report' (UNHRC, 1 March 2021) www.ohchr.org/EN/HRBodies/HRC/Pages/NewsDetail.aspx?NewsID=26811&LangID=E; 'UN Commission of Inquiry on Syria: Unprecedented Levels of Displacement and Dire Conditions for Civilians in the Syrian Arab Republic' (UNHRC, 20 March 2020) www.ohchr.org/EN/HRBodies/HRC/Pages/NewsDetail.aspx?NewsID=25638&LangID=E.

[80] See ILC, 'Commentary on Article 16' (n 42) 66 para 7.

[81] ibid para 10.

[82] ibid.

not have been achieved without substantial support from Iran and Russia. It has, however, been documented and reported that the Russian and Iranian joint military campaign based on continuous bombardment in the commission with Syrian forces killed thousands of civilians.[83] This would be considered a form of state responsibility for complicity in the wrongful conduct of a third state with knowledge of the circumstances of IWA, as well as with a view to facilitating the commission of that act.[84] This brings clarity to the concept of joint responsibility of both the assisting state and the wrong-doing acting state for *in bello* violations. This last point is evident from the first paragraph of Article 47 ASR on 'plurality of responsible States', which states:

1.   Where several States are responsible for the same internationally wrongful act, the responsibility of each State may be invoked in relation to that act.

This is a general principle dealing with situations where two or more states might combine in carrying out together an IWA through breaching the same obligation in circumstances where they may be regarded as acting jointly in respect of the entire operation.[85] Crucially, the joint responsibility of the two or more states will depend on the circumstances and on the international obligations of each of the states carrying out IWAs through breaching the same legal obligations.[86] On this understanding, the default position is, therefore, that IWAs and *in bello* violations by the Syrian regime and violations of the same rules by Iran and Russia through assisting the Syrian regime in doing so would and should bring their joint responsibility to the extent that they have breached the same legal obligations and the law applicable to the NIAC in Syria. This would, of course, fall within the realm of the general attribution standards of state responsibility of co-perpetrators for IWAs, dealt with in Chapter II (Articles 4–11) of the ASR. And this makes sense. There is, therefore, incontrovertible evidence for engaging the responsibility of the assisting state for *in bello* violations during military assistance. At this point, the perpetrator states making reparations for *in bello* violations and international sanctions being imposed on the states' authorities depending on their international responsibility are the most convenient responses in the context of the current legal regime.

Above all, valuing 'necessity' above 'proportionality' and the protection of civilian objects would be considered a significant obstacle to apportioning responsibility for *in bello* violations. It should be kept in mind that necessity is a customary rule of *jus in bello* limiting the military actions of armed forces. Necessity only permits measures that are necessary to accomplish a legitimate military objective and are not otherwise prohibited by *jus in bello*, while the only legitimate military objective is to weaken the military capacity of the enemy while taking into consideration that civilians and civilian objects must be protected against attacks if they are not

---

[83]   See n 3 above.

[84]   Milanovic (n 11) 362. See also ILC, 'Commentary on Article 16' (n 42) 66 para 3. More generally, see M Milanovic, 'Intelligence Sharing in Multinational Military Operations and Complicity under International Law' (2021) 96 *International Law Studies* 1274; Aust (n 72) 192–268.

[85]   ILC, 'Commentary on Article 47 of Draft Articles on Responsibility of States for Internationally Wrongful Acts' (2001) 124 para 2.

[86]   ibid 125 para 6.

proportionate to the expected military advantage. Necessity is inadmissible if the purpose for which the measure was taken was itself contrary to *jus in bello*.

As pointed out by the International Criminal Tribunal for the Former Yugoslavia (ICTY):

> The protection of civilians in times of armed conflict, whether international or internal, is the bedrock of modern humanitarian law … Indeed, it is now a universally recognised principle recently stated by the [ICJ] that deliberate attacks on civilians or civilian objects are absolutely prohibited by international humanitarian law.[87]

Therefore, no limitations or amnesty may be applied to bar the prosecution of such violations, even if the perpetrators are not party to the treaties that established the mentioned violations, given that customary international law and the customary rules of the international treaties bind even non-party states. This is the primary objective of the use of universal jurisdiction as a legal measure, as it ensures that the worst human rights crimes, war crimes and crimes against humanity will not remain unpunished. However, this is not the focus of this article as it is mainly dealing with the extent to which states should be held responsible for war crimes.

V. CONCLUDING REMARKS

In light of the foregoing considerations, it would be convenient to merely conclude that the *in bello* violations committed by the acting state involved in a NIAC with contribution from its military partners would be subject to state responsibility. Put differently, military assistance does not find support in international law if the assistance is incompatible with an international obligation of the assisting state. It has been argued in this article that the assisting state is only responsible for its own act in deliberately assisting another state to the extent that its conduct has caused or contributed to the IWA of the acting state involved in a NIAC. It has also been argued that the assisting and acting states would be jointly responsible if the assistance were a necessary element in the IWA in the absence of which it could not have occurred.

This article has sought to elucidate that even if one accepts that military assistance at the request of a state involved in a NIAC is compatible with the law on the use of force, the consent of the acting state never precludes the wrongfulness of military operations in violation of peremptory norms of international law, including the law governing the conduct of hostilities.

In effect, all the steps identified above would be used for the core objective of international law, which aims to prohibit and restrict *in bello* violations and any other forms of IWAs to deter states from breaching international legal obligations in similar circumstances. State responsibility for *in bello* violations committed directly or in support of a state involved in NIACs contributes to the main purpose

---

[87] International Tribunal for the Prosecution of Persons Responsible for Serious Violations of International Humanitarian Law Committed in the Territory of the Former Yugoslavia since 1991, *Prosecutor v Zoran Kupreskic et al* (Trial Judgement), IT-95-16-T, ICTY (14 January 2000) para 521.

of international criminal justice, which is to assert that there is no impunity for international crimes. Overall, holding both assisting and acting states responsible for their IWAs and conduct amounting to serious violations of peremptory norms of international law in the sense of Article 40 ASR would have a deterrent role in preventing future violations.[88]

While the focus of article is on state responsibility for wrongful aid and assistance in NIACs, it has been argued that the peremptory nature of the basic rules of *jus in bello* applies in all circumstances, regardless of the classification of the armed conflicts. Therefore, states have obligations to refrain from facilitating any *in bello* violations during both international armed conflicts and NIACs.

---

[88] See International Tribunal for the Prosecution of Persons Responsible for Serious Violations of International Humanitarian Law Committed in the Territory of the Former Yugoslavia since 1991, *Prosecutor v Zoran Kuprerskic et al* (Trial Chamber), Case No IT-95-16-T (Judgement of 14 January 2000) paras 848–49; UNSC Resolution 827, UN Doc S/RES/827 (25 May 1993).

Due Diligence in International Law: Cause for Optimism?

ADEDAYO AKINGBADE

Abstract

Due diligence is not a new concept in international law. It has been used to address state conduct in significant transboundary harm, the law of the sea, protection of aliens and violence in the private sphere in human rights law, especially in the context of violence against women. However, the role of due diligence in international law has been questioned – particularly whether it makes primary obligations weaker and whether its usage adds a clear value. This article examines what the role of due diligence is, its potential and whether there is a reason to be optimistic about the concept in international law. It argues that the potential value of the concept lies in its malleability and capacity to expand what is required of the state in fulfilling its obligations, yet limitation persists because due diligence relies on international courts and tribunals to crystallise what it entails into a hard legal standard.

I. INTRODUCTION

DUE DILIGENCE HAS been termed a familiar stranger.[1] Nonetheless, it has been applied in different areas of international law – for example, in the prevention of transboundary harm, the law of the sea and violence against women. Therefore, it is imperative to address what its role and potential contribution are to international law; particularly if there is a reason to be optimistic about due diligence in the assessment of state conduct.

This article begins by discussing why due diligence emerged and its subsequent role in the law of state responsibility. Due diligence's entry is tied to the arising need to attribute responsibility for the sovereign's action or omissions concerning the harm committed by private persons in the age of absolutism. Therefore, the initial impact and relevance of due diligence can be found in the responsibility for harm done to aliens and the state's failure to fulfil its obligations of neutrality. Hence, due

---

[1] A Peters et al, 'Due Diligence in the International Legal Order – Dissecting the Leitmotif of Current Accountability Debates' in H Krieger et al (eds), *Due Diligence in the International Legal Order* (Oxford, Oxford University Press, 2020) 1.

diligence has been in play concerning the state's duty to use its apparatus to prevent harm and the state's duty to prevent, investigate, pursue and prosecute perpetrators.

Beyond the context of the protection of aliens, the article shows that due diligence has expanded and developed in international environmental law, the law of the sea, human rights and violence against women. In this expansion, due diligence has also been used as a standard of conduct that states must meet when fulfilling their obligations. There is also consensus that as 'a qualifier of behaviour',[2] due diligence is a tool for promoting better state response or conduct. As such, this contribution understands due diligence as an element of primary obligation. Furthermore, this article contends in the final section that due diligence's continuous relevance is in its potential to scrutinise state conduct in changing circumstances where existing standards are no longer sufficient. However, such relevance may be limited where there are gaps in state accountability in some thematic areas and those gaps are not filled because there is no crystallised hard legal standard of due diligence developed by international courts/tribunals in such areas.

II. EARLY IMPACT OF DUE DILIGENCE

Due diligence comes from the Latin word *diligentia*, which can be translated as care or circumspection.[3] It stems from domestic legal traditions linking back to Roman civil law.[4] However, both common and civil law systems recognise the duties of diligent conduct.[5] Under the traditions of both systems, a person can be liable for accidental harm caused to others if the injury is occasioned by the person's failure to meet the standard required of a *diligens paterfamilias* – that is, the standard required of a prudent head of a household.[6] Burdick explains that these Roman law underpinnings indicate a connection between culpability and due diligence.[7] Accordingly,

> [c]ulpa [fault] and diligentia are … inseparably associated, since culpa is the lack of due diligence, and the degree of diligentia or care required in any given case regulates inversely the degree of culpa or negligence that will subject one to liability in case of loss.[8]

The above implies that, in its domestic origins, due diligence was instrumental in attributing the responsibility of an actor concerning harm caused by them. This due diligence functionality of establishing responsibility influenced the writings of Grotius on state responsibility.[9] Elements of due diligence in Roman traditions

---

[2] ibid 2.

[3] ibid.

[4] P Dupuy, 'Due Diligence in the International Law of Liability' in Organisation for Economic Co-operation and Development, *Legal Aspects of Transfrontier Pollution* (Paris, OECD, 1977) 369.

[5] M Monnheimer, *Due Diligence Obligations in International Human Rights Law* (Cambridge, Cambridge University Press, 2021) 78.

[6] ibid; see also R Zimmerman, *The Law of Obligations: Roman Foundations of the Civil Tradition* (Oxford, Oxford University Press, 1996) 1009; RW Lee, *An Introduction to Roman-Dutch law*, 4th edn (Oxford, Clarendon Press, 1946) 324.

[7] WL Burdick, *The Principles of Roman Law and Their Relation to Modern Law* (Clark, NJ, Lawbook Exchange, 2004) 415.

[8] ibid.

[9] See SM Blanco, *Full Protection and Security in International Investment Law* (London, Springer Nature, 2019) 386.

were then invoked to address questions surrounding states' responsibility for private actions in the protection of aliens in international law.[10] These are the issues bordering on when states bear responsibility for the actions of individuals. Indeed, as Blanco notes, due diligence was introduced between the pre-modern idea that the nation is responsible for the acts of its members and doctrines, acknowledging no responsibility for private injuries to aliens.[11]

Thus, in addressing the uncertainties between states and harm caused by their private citizens, Grotius laid the foundations for the concept of responsibility due to lack of due diligence.[12] It was discussed in regard to a state ruler's accountability for his subjects in the age of absolutism, where the sovereign wields all governmental power.[13] So Grotius posited that the sovereign could become complicit in the crimes of private individuals through the principles of *patientia* and *receptus*.[14] Under *patientia*, a community or its ruler is responsible for a crime committed by the subject where they had knowledge of the crime but failed to prevent it.[15] This same duty extends to situations where the sovereign's subjects commit a crime against foreign sovereigns or subjects. Similarly, a ruler under *receptus* is responsible for not extraditing or prosecuting offenders who are using the ruler's realm as a refuge from justice.[16] There is a duty on the sovereign 'to punish the offenders as guilty, in case they could be found, or surrender them'.[17] He also explained that 'a man who is privy to a Fault and does not hinder it, when in a Capacity and under an Obligation of so doing, may properly be said to be the Author of it'.[18] In essence, Grotius underpinned that the sovereign is under a duty to take appropriate steps in response to the injurious acts of private individuals. In the knowledge of harm or risk of harm, an absence of action implies that the sovereign incurs responsibility.

Wolff echoed the Grotian concept of responsibility and due diligence. However, unlike Grotius, he differentiated the state from its ruler.[19] This differentiation might have been influenced by the fact that the age of absolutism was wearing off, and all governmental authority no longer resides with the sovereign. Wolff explained that the state is under a duty not to allow any of its subjects to harm foreign nationals or foreign states.[20] Where an injury occurs, the ruler is required to compel the offender to repair the loss suffered; and if it is a criminal act, the offender is punished.[21] Though the nation and ruler are different entities, Wolff noted that an act is imputed

---

[10] See JA Hessbruegge, 'The Historical Development of the Doctrines of Attribution and Due Diligence in International Law' (2003) 36 *New York University Journal of International Law and Policy* 266.

[11] Blanco (n 9) 376.

[12] See Hessbruegge (n 10) 283; see also J Kulesza, *Due Diligence in International Law* (Leiden, Brill Nijhoff, 2016) 1–3.

[13] Kulesza (n 12) 3.

[14] H Grotius, *On the Law of War and Peace* (S Neff trans, Cambridge, Cambridge University Press, 2012) 292.

[15] ibid.

[16] ibid.

[17] ibid 284.

[18] H Grotius, *The Rights of War and Peace Book II*, J Barbeyrac edn (Indianapolis, Liberty Fund, 2005) 1056.

[19] C Wolff, 'Jus gentium methodo scientifica pertractactum' (1749) in J Brown Scott (ed), *Classics of International Law* (J Drake trans, Oxford, Clarendon Press, 1934) 536.

[20] Hessbruegge (n 10) 288.

[21] ibid.

to the ruler and, by implication, the nation where the ruler approves private individuals' harmful acts.

Drawing from Wolff, Vattel explained that a nation would be guilty of its citizens' crime if its conduct allows its citizens to plunder and maltreat foreigners – especially where there is a failure to organise the manners and maxims of government appropriately.[22] Vattel's arguments show that states are under an obligation to protect foreigners within their territory from any potential harm. The state must ensure that actions within its territory do not become harmful to other states. Vattel also noted that if one state counterfeits another state's currency it harms the latter, and this counterfeiting incurs responsibility.[23] He reiterated the Grotian principle that requires the state to effect reparation of damage caused by a subject and punish the offender or carry out the offender's extradition. Where there is a refusal to punish or extradite, the relevant state will incur responsibility as an accomplice in the harm.[24]

The influence of Wolff and Vattel concerning due diligence and state responsibility for harmful conduct towards foreign states is apparent in the 1872 *Alabama Claims Arbitration*.[25] Great Britain (GB) had allowed the construction and escape of vessels planned to be used by the Confederacy against the USA. The arbitral tribunal examined GB's obligation of neutrality in the US civil war. GB argued that due diligence should be exercised per their affairs and efforts prescribed by national laws instead of international law.[26] The tribunal rejected GB's definition as narrow. Instead, it adopted the more demanding definition from the USA. The tribunal explained that due diligence is informed or determined by international law, and it requires efforts that are in exact proportion to the risks or threats that parties may be exposed to from a failure to fulfil the obligations of neutrality. GB incurred responsibility here as the measures used in pursuit of the escaped vessels 'were so imperfect as to lead to no result'.[27] As such, the tribunal clarified that due diligence requires a show of vigilance and adopting necessary means to prevent harm to another state.[28] Therefore, the state is responsible for the actions of individuals if it did not exercise due diligence in performing its duties.[29]

Hall noted that to avoid responsibility, the state must demonstrate that its failure to prevent the commission of harmful acts or an omission to do certain acts has been within the reasonable limits of error.[30] That is, the state must show that the injurious acts could not have been prevented by appropriate acts under the circumstances.[31] As was said in *Alabama*, the government's amount of care and its response must be

---

[22] E de Vattel, *The Law of Nations*, 6th edn by J Chitty T. & J. W. Johnson & Co., Law Booksellers 1883) 163.

[23] ibid 47.

[24] ibid 162–63.

[25] Award rendered on 14 September 1872, Reports of International Arbitral Awards 2012, vol XXIX, 125–34.

[26] ibid.

[27] ibid 130.

[28] ibid 129–32.

[29] Kulesza (n 12) 21.

[30] WE Hall, *A Treatise on International Law*, 3rd edn (first published 1884, Oxford, Clarendon Press, 1890) 213–17.

[31] ibid.

proportional to the state of affairs existing at the time.[32] Furthermore, since administrative officials and naval and military commanders are under the state's control, injurious actions done by them are actions of the state until the state renounces such actions.[33] Where these officials harm a foreign state or its nationals, the state must punish the officials and provide necessary reparations.[34] By implication, the state's conduct must not condone or encourage public officials' injurious actions toward a foreign state or its nationals.

In connection with the above, the influence of Hall is visible in the Mixed Claims Commission Italy–Venezuela constituted under the Protocols of 13 February and 7 May 1903, specifically in *Sambiaggio*.[35] Hall explained that when a government cannot control the harmful acts of private persons within its territory because of insurrection, it cannot be responsible for injuries suffered by aliens.[36] Where the state has lost much control in the case of internal insurrection, it will be difficult for it to take appropriate steps to protect aliens and their interests. In *Sambiaggio*, the tribunal examined Venezuela's protection obligations concerning Sambiaggio and other Italians resident in Venezuela.[37] Referencing Hall, the tribunal explained that it could not hold Venezuela responsible for the harm inflicted by private actors since the state has lost control of its territory.[38] Here, due to the insurrectional war, the state could not exercise due diligence in the use of its apparatus to prevent harm. However, the Amador Report[39] suggests that the state's responsibility may change if it is manifestly negligent in adopting measures to prevent or suppress an insurrection. The state will be responsible for injuries caused to an alien by measures taken by its armed forces or other authorities if they harm private persons.[40] Here, it means the state may still be responsible even in the face of internal insurrection.

Nonetheless, as Pisillo-Mazzeschi,[41] Baldwin[42] and Barnidge[43] argue, the broader implication is that due diligence has been in play concerning the state's duty to use its apparatus for preventing private harm, particularly in the protection of aliens. It is also in play in the state's duty to prevent, investigate, pursue and apprehend perpetrators.[44] This role of due diligence became apparent in the litigations between the USA and Mexico. For example, in *Janes*,[45] a claim was made by the USA for the

---

[32] ibid 216.

[33] ibid 213–14.

[34] ibid.

[35] *(Italy v Venezuela)* (1903) 10 RIAA 499, Reports of International Arbitral Awards 2006, vol X, 499–525.

[36] Hall (n 30) 219.

[37] *Sambiaggio* (n 35) 500–01.

[38] ibid 515–21; see also *Santa Clara Estates Case (Supplementary Claim)*, (1903) UNRIAA IX 2006, 455, where similar conclusions were reached.

[39] F v Garcia Amador, 'International Responsibility, Second Report' (15 February 1957) Document A/CN.4/106, 120.

[40] ibid.

[41] R Pisillo-Mazzeschi, 'The Due Diligence Rule and the Nature of the International Responsibility of States' (1992) 35 *German Yearbook of International Law* 9.

[42] SE Baldwin, 'Protection of Aliens by the United States' (1914) 13 *Michigan Law Review* 17.

[43] RP Barnidge, Jr, *Non-State Actors and Terrorism: Applying the Law of State Responsibility and the Due Diligence Principle* (The Hague, TMC Asser Press, 2007).

[44] ibid; Pisillo-Mazzeschi (n 41) 29.

[45] *Janes (USA) v United Mexican States* (1925) UNRIAA IV 2006, 82–98.

murder of Everett Janes, an American citizen working in Mexico.[46] The Mexican authorities delayed action and even failed to take appropriate steps to apprehend the perpetrator. The Claims Commission held that there was an evident lack of diligence on the part of the Mexican authorities to apprehend and punish the perpetrator.[47] Like *Alabama*, the Commission explained that the failure to take timely and efficient action towards the perpetrator's apprehension indicates a lack of due diligence and, as such, Mexico will be responsible for the harm.[48] The responsibility of states for not exercising due diligence in the prevention of harm caused by their private citizens to aliens was subsequently confirmed in similar cases.[49] This role of due diligence in attributing responsibility has also been acknowledged in ILC Special Rapporteur Garcia Amador's second report on international responsibility.[50] The report reiterated the articulations above, noting that a state is responsible for an injury to a foreigner from its failure to exercise due diligence to prevent the injury.[51]

Therefore, due diligence emerged and had its initial impact on states' responsibility for private actors, particularly in the prevention of harm against aliens.[52] As an offshoot of this initial impact, there has been an emergence of due diligence requiring states to endeavour to reach the result set out in an obligation.[53] Also, it has expanded to other areas of international law – not just in the sense of state responsibility for harm committed by individuals, but also in the case of responsibility for harm committed by the state.[54] However, due diligence in its expansion has also developed as a tool for prescribing the standard of conduct required to discharge international state obligations. As we will see below, due diligence is a useful and flexible tool in, for instance, the prevention of transboundary environmental harm or protection of women from domestic violence.

III. LESSONS FROM ENVIRONMENTAL LAW AND THE LAW OF THE SEA

Due diligence has significantly developed in the area of transboundary environmental harm and the law of the sea.[55] Particularly, the concept has been instrumental in the obligation to prevent significant transboundary harm. In the 1949 *Corfu Channel* case,[56] the International Court of Justice (ICJ) explained that a state has

---

[46] ibid 83.

[47] ibid 82–86.

[48] ibid 90; in *William E Chapman (USA) v United Mexican States* (1930) UNRIAA IV 2006, 632, the arbitral commission confirmed Mexico's responsibility for lack of diligence in the pursuit and apprehension of culprits.

[49] See *Thomas H Youmans (USA) v United Mexican States* (1926) UNRIAA IV 2006, 110–17; *Neer (USA) v United Mexican States* (1926) UNRIAA IV 2006, 60–66; *Chase (USA) v United Mexican States* (1928) UNRIAA IV 2006, 337.

[50] Garcia Amador (n 39) 106, 122–23.

[51] ibid.

[52] T Koivurova, 'Due Diligence', *Max Planck Encyclopaedia of Public International Law* (2013) 1, 9.

[53] ibid.

[54] In international environmental law, a state can become responsible for not exercising due diligence in the prevention of transboundary harm to other states.

[55] Kulesza (n 12) 11.

[56] *Corfu Channel Case (UK v Albania)* (Merits) [1949] ICJ Rep 4.

an obligation not to knowingly allow its territory to be used for acts contrary to the rights of other states. This enunciation is a general obligation that has been given a broader interpretation in the context of significant transboundary harm and the setting of minimum standards in international environmental law. Hence, *Corfu Channel* constitutes a precedent in favour of due diligence in environmental law, and there is a subsequent manifestation of this precedent.[57] The International Law Commission's Draft Articles on Prevention of Transboundary Harm from Hazardous Activities with Commentaries (ILC Prevention Articles)[58] provides that there is a duty on the state of origin to take all appropriate measures to prevent significant transboundary harm or to minimise its risk to other states.[59] In addition, the Commentaries explain that this is an obligation of prevention requiring the exercise of due diligence from states.[60] In terms of what this requirement means, the Commentaries explicated that it is the state's conduct concerning its obligation that is relevant under due diligence.[61]

Thus, due diligence requires the state to exert its best possible efforts to minimise the risk of transboundary harm.[62] Certainly, this effort will depend on the circumstances of the potential harm, and the state is to keep itself updated on the technological changes and scientific developments in the area.[63] In *Pulp Mills on the River Uruguay*,[64] Argentina instituted proceedings against Uruguay in respect of their construction of two pulp mills on the River Uruguay with reference to its transboundary effects on the quality of the waters of the River Uruguay.[65] *Pulp Mills* is significant because it covers the themes highlighted by the ILC in the Prevention Articles – due diligence, environmental impact assessment (EIA), notification, consultation and cooperation.[66] Also, until *Pulp Mills*, no international court had held that there is a specific duty on states to carry out an EIA in cases of significant transboundary risk.[67] The ICJ further affirmed that fulfilling the obligation to prevent environmental harm requires the exercise of due diligence. That is, it 'entails not only the adoption of appropriate rules and measures but also a certain level of vigilance'.[68] This vigilance implies that where a party is planning works that may affect the river and indeed occasion transboundary harm, as in this case, it must undertake an EIA on the potential effects of the works in the light of perceived risks.[69]

---

[57] Pisillo-Mazzeschi (n 41) 39.

[58] Text adopted by the International Law Commission at its fifty-third session in 2001 and submitted to the General Assembly as a part of the Commission's report covering the work of that session (A/56/10).

[59] ibid Art 3, 154.

[60] ibid Commentary 7.

[61] ibid; Kulesza (n 12) 11.

[62] Text adopted by the International Law Commission (n 58) Commentary 10.

[63] ibid Commentary 11.

[64] *Argentina v Uruguay*, Judgment, ICJ Reports 2010, 14.

[65] ibid para 1, p 25.

[66] A Boyle, 'Pulp Mills Case: A Commentary', 1 www.biicl.org/files/5167_pulp_mills_case.pdf.

[67] ibid 2; see also CR Payne, 'Pulp Mills on the River Uruguay: The International Court of Justice Recognizes Environmental Impact Assessment as a Duty under International Law' (2010) 14(9) *American Society of International Law Insights*.

[68] *Pulp Mills* (n 64) para 197, p 79.

[69] ibid para 205, p 83.

The other implication from *Pulp Mills* is that being vigilant and, consequently, undertaking an EIA is evidence of the exercise of due diligence on the part of the state.[70] Boyle similarly argued that an EIA is a necessary element of due diligence in preventing and controlling transboundary harm.[71] Therefore, the state's duty to be vigilant, which has roots in *Alabama*,[72] and the duty to undertake an EIA represent the specific type of conduct expected of a state regarding its obligations in transboundary harm. For example, these include requirements to notify, inform, consult, cooperate, conduct risk assessments, monitor, warn, publicly explain or take reasonable precautions.[73] These action points represent due practical steps the state should take to prevent transboundary harm before commencing environmental works. Pisillo-Mazzeschi[74] and Fitzmaurice[75] pointed out that what is required of the state is to make every effort to reach the specified result in an obligation. In this case, the result is the prevention of transboundary harm, and the relevant state must make every effort to undertake an EIA at the start of an environmental project.[76]

In the 2015 *Border Area and Road* case,[77] the ICJ provided links between due diligence, EIA and the duty to consult and negotiate. In the case, Costa Rica alleged that Nicaragua invaded and occupied its territory, conducting dredging works in the San Juan River in violation of its obligations.[78] Affirming its position in *Pulp Mills* concerning due diligence, the ICJ explained that

> if the environmental impact assessment confirms that there is a risk of significant transboundary harm, a State planning an activity that carries such a risk is required, in order to fulfil its obligation to exercise due diligence in preventing significant transboundary harm, to notify, and consult with, the potentially affected State in good faith, where that is necessary to determine the appropriate measures to prevent or mitigate that risk.[79]

Thus, due diligence triggers the need to carry out an EIA and to notify and consult the potentially affected state where the EIA confirms there is a risk of significant harm.[80] Hence, the above quote from the court's judgment offers sequential steps that start with an EIA. That is, an EIA, then a risk of transboundary harm confirmed, then notification and consultation. These steps represent a set standard that is indicative of the exercise of due diligence in preventing significant transboundary harm.[81]

---

[70] ibid.
[71] A Boyle, 'Developments in International Law of EIA and their Relation to the Espoo Convention' (2012) 20 *Review of European Community & International Environmental Law* 227.
[72] *Alabama Claims Arbitration* (n 25).
[73] Peters et al (n 1) 12.
[74] Pisillo-Mazzeschi (n 41) 41.
[75] M Fitzmaurice, 'Legitimacy of International Environmental Law. The Sovereign States overwhelmed by Obligations: Responsibility to React to Problems beyond National Jurisdiction?' (2017) 77 *Heidelberg Journal of International Law* 339.
[76] See R Yotova, 'The Principles of Due Diligence and Prevention in International Environmental Law' (2016) 75 *CLJ* 445.
[77] *Certain Activities Carried Out by Nicaragua in the Border Area (Costa Rica v Nicaragua) and Construction of a Road in Costa Rica along the San Juan River (Nicaragua v Costa Rica)*, Judgment, ICJ Reports 2015, 665.
[78] ibid para 1.
[79] ibid para 104, p 45.
[80] *Pulp Mills* (n 64) para 104.
[81] See, eg Payne arguing that carrying out EIA is now a requirement for the State under international law. C Payne, 'Environmental Impact Assessment as a Duty under International Law: The International Court of Justice Judgment on Pulp Mills on the River Uruguay' (2010) 1 *European Journal of Risk Regulation* 317.

They also inform state conduct[82] – as attention is on state behaviour – precisely what they should do or what they are actively doing to fulfil their prevention obligations in environmental law. As such, for states to meet their obligations, they will have to establish various domestic and transboundary procedures to prevent significant transboundary damage.[83]

However, the ICJ in the *Border Area and Road* case was unclear about the method and criteria that should be used to assess the degree of risk of transboundary harm that would be sufficient to trigger a state's obligation to carry out an EIA.[84] This has practical implications for the exercise of due diligence in the context of transboundary harm. If there is no threshold of risk that triggers the duty to conduct an EIA, then there is a lack of clarity in determining whether a state has exercised due diligence in preventing transboundary harm. There should be a threshold for assessing the risk, and that threshold should not be decided by the states involved, but rather by international law. Perhaps, as Desierto argues, the ICJ should have drawn on the Prevention Articles, which tie in the concept of significant risk of transboundary harm to the 'physical consequences' of activities, taking into consideration current 'developments in scientific knowledge' in the assessment of risks.[85] Activity may involve a risk of significant transboundary harm even though those responsible for carrying out the activity underestimated the risk or were even unaware of it.[86] As such, the risks should be assessed objectively, based on an appreciation of the possible harms resulting from an activity that a properly informed observer ought to have.[87] While objective assessments might be a way out of ascertaining what threshold of risk triggers the need for an EIA, there is a likelihood that the states involved in the activity may disagree. The disagreement may be because objective assessments might still need some level of specificity of requirements or pointers that can guide states on when an EIA should be carried out. Consequently, this might be a signal that due diligence needs to be further fleshed out by, for example, international courts/tribunals to fill gaps and strengthen the continuous crystallisation of a legal standard in transboundary harm.

The role of international tribunals in crystallising what due diligence entails is also apparent in the law of the sea. For example, the International Tribunal for the Law of the Sea (ITLOS) in the *Seabed Mining Advisory Opinion*[88] had the opportunity to interpret the obligation to ensure compliance and liability for damage provided

---

[82] N McDonald, 'The Role of Due Diligence in International Law' (2019) 68 *International and Comparative Law Quarterly* 1044.

[83] ILA Study Group on Due Diligence in International Law, First Report (7 March 2014) 28.

[84] See *Border Area and Road* case (n 77) paras 104–05; see also D Desierto, 'Evidence but Not Empiricism? Environmental Impact Assessments at the International Court of Justice in Certain Activities Carried Out by Nicaragua in the Border Area (Costa Rica v Nicaragua) and Construction of a Road in Costa Rica Along the San Juan River (Nicaragua v Costa Rica)' (*EJIL: Talk!*, 26 February 2016) www.ejiltalk.org/evidence-but-not-empiricism-environmental-impact-assessments-at-the-international-court-of-justice-in-certain-activities-carried-out-by-nicaragua-in-the-border-area-costa-rica-v-nicaragua-and-con.

[85] Prevention Articles (n 58) paras 15 and 16.

[86] ibid.

[87] ibid para 14.

[88] Responsibilities and Obligations of States Sponsoring Persons and Entities with Respect to Activities in the Area, 1 February 2011, ITLOS Reports 2011, 10.

in Article 139 of the United Nations Convention on the Law of the Sea. Referring to the ILC Commentary in the Prevention Articles[89] and the ICJ's findings in *Pulp Mills*, ITLOS explained that the obligation to ensure requires the exercise of due diligence, which is not an obligation to achieve a result in every case.[90] As such, it is an obligation to deploy adequate means, exercise the best possible efforts, do the utmost and use a certain level of vigilance to obtain the result.[91]

The obligation to exercise due diligence adds another layer in the sense that state conduct should be attentive to the reality of the issue at stake, as we have seen in *Alabama*. Also, the standard of conduct required from the state may change or evolve as measures considered sufficiently diligent at a particular time may become less diligent in the light of new knowledge or riskier circumstances.[92] For environmental law, the general level of knowledge or information will continuously shift because of new insights and information.[93] Hence, the sequence of action required from the state will evolve or shift so that it is relative or proportional to the existing issues. However, factors that may change the level of conduct required from the state do not include its capacity to implement and enforce environmental measures. That is, ITLOS does not consider the development level of a state to be a factor in whether it has exercised due diligence in its conduct.[94] The basis of this is to adopt and push for the highest standards in environmental protection – which means the required action from the state is not only to avoid potential responsibility, but to do the utmost in protecting a common heritage of humanity.[95] Indeed, ITLOS itself warned that differentiated lower standards might result in the emergence of the equivalent of states 'of convenience' – where legal spaces are created for some developed states to perform at a lower standard in respect of their environmental obligations.[96] Also, the uniform application of the highest standards of protection of the marine environment will be jeopardised.[97]

Similarly, a further application of the standard requirements of due diligence from the *Seabed Advisory Opinion* can be seen in *The Sub-regional Fisheries Commission (SRFC) Advisory Opinion* submitted to ITLOS.[98] Here, ITLOS was requested to provide an advisory opinion on the flag state's obligations in cases where illegal, unreported and unregulated (IUU) fishing activities are conducted within the exclusive

---

[89] See Prevention Articles (n 58) Art 3.

[90] ibid para 110. It is not one that 'dictates the prefect achievement of result'.

[91] ibid.

[92] ibid para 117.

[93] D French, 'From the Depths: Rich Pickings of Principles of Sustainable Development and General International Law on the Ocean Floor – The Seabed Disputes Chamber's 2011 Advisory Opinion' (2011) 26 *International Journal of Marine & Coastal Law* 525.

[94] *Seabed Mining Advisory Opinion* (n 88) paras 158–59.

[95] T Poisel, 'Deep Seabed Mining: Implications of Seabed Disputes Chamber's Advisory Opinion' (2012) 19 *Australian International Law Journal* 226; see also French (n 93) 559.

[96] See *Seabed Mining Advisory Opinion* (n 88) 159; D Freestone, 'Advisory Opinion of the Seabed Disputes Chamber of International Tribunal for the Law of the Sea on "Responsibilities and Obligations of States Sponsoring Persons and Entities with Respect to Activities in the Area"' (2011) 105 *American Journal of International Law* 755.

[97] ibid.

[98] ITLOS Case No 21, Request for Advisory Opinion submitted by the Sub-Regional Fisheries Commission, Advisory Opinion, 2 April 2015, ITLOS Reports 2015, 4.

economic zones of third party states.[99] Reiterating *Pulp Mills*, ITLOS clarified that the obligations of the flag states concerning IUU fishing require due diligence in their discharge.[100] It further explained that these obligations do not involve the achievement of compliance in IUU fishing by vessels flying the state flag in every situation.[101] Instead, what is required is for the flag state to take all necessary measures and actions to ensure compliance and to prevent IUU fishing by fishing vessels flying its flag.[102] These requirements to take all necessary measures will enable authorities to fight illegal fishing more efficiently.[103]

The flag state of a fishing boat, therefore, has an obligation of conduct.[104] Due diligence obligations can well be categorised as obligations of conduct – those primary obligations that require states to endeavour to reach the result set out in the obligation.[105] Obligations of conduct focus on the behaviour of states. So, due diligence can be used as a legal standard of conduct – in the sense of acting with due diligence – but only by reference to a pre-existing rule of international law. If a state has acted with the required diligence under a particular rule, it can be said that the state has not violated the rule.[106] For example, for a state party to fall below the due diligence standard, it must engage in conduct at variance with its control obligations in IUU fishing.[107] Importantly, ITLOS elucidated the specific conduct required of the state to satisfy the standard of due diligence in IUU fishing. For example, a flag state should adopt sanctions of sufficient gravity to deter and disincentivise violations and deprive offenders of IUU fishing benefits.[108] This elucidation indicates that, as far as the IUU obligations require due diligence, a particular standard of care is expected of the flag state.[109] An identical conclusion was also reached in the *South China Sea Arbitration*[110] – where it was explained that since China had not taken any steps to enforce rules against fishers engaged in poaching endangered species in the sea, it was not exercising any form of due diligence.[111] Thus, from the context of IUU fishing and even poaching of endangered species, we can identify that due diligence performs an important task because it applies to new

---

[99] ibid para 85.

[100] See also ibid paras 125–32.

[101] ibid para 129.

[102] ibid.

[103] V Ventura, 'Tackling Illegal, Unregulated and Unreported Fishing: The ITLOS Advisory Opinion on Flag State Responsibility for IUU Fishing and the Principle of Due Diligence' (2015) 12 *Brazilian Journal of International Law* 50.

[104] D Freestone, 'International Tribunal for the Law of the Sea, Case 21' (2016) 1 *Asia Pacific Journal of Ocean Law & Policy* 131.

[105] Koivurova (n 52) 2.

[106] McDonald (n 82) 1044.

[107] G Handl, 'Flag State Responsibility for Illegal, Unreported and Unregulated Fishing in Foreign EEZs' (2014) 44 *Environmental Policy & Law* 163.

[108] SRFC Advisory Opinion (n 98) paras 138–39.

[109] ER van der Marel, 'ITLOS Issues Its Advisory Opinion on IUU Fishing' (*The NCLOS Blog*, 21 April 2015) https://site.uit.no/nclos/2015/04/21/itlos-issues-its-advisory-opinion-on-iuu-fishing/.

[110] *South China Sea Arbitration, The Republic of the Philippines and The People's Republic of China*, PCA Case No 2013-19, Permanent Court of Arbitration, 12 July 2016.

[111] ibid para 1203. For further analysis of this case, see B Oxman, 'The South China Sea Arbitration Award' (2017) 24 *University of Miami International & Comparative Law Review* 235.

situations where no specific or limited regulation exists.[112] Also, the international court or tribunal faced with a question of due diligence has the flexibility to assess its specific content and, consequently, what conduct is required of the state in a particular context.[113] However, while the exercise of due diligence by states will contribute to a reduction in illegal, unreported and unregulated fishing, the current due diligence requirements alone will not directly revive already heavily depleted fisheries.[114] For example, more needs to be done to combat artisanal fishing that over-extracts marine resources by fishing beyond the maximum sustainable yield for a region.[115] So, through the articulations of ITLOS, the current standards of due diligence may also be redefined and updated to deal with the gap left by unsustainable artisanal fishing practices.[116]

IV. VIOLENCE AGAINST WOMEN: DUE DILIGENCE AND THE PUBLIC/PRIVATE DIVIDE

The application of due diligence to determine whether states are meeting their international human rights law obligations was first introduced by the Inter-American Court of Human Rights in the *Velasquez Rodriguez* case.[117] In this case, Velasquez, a university student in Honduras, was violently detained without a warrant and tortured by members of the Honduran armed forces. In the judgment, the court explained that an illegal private act that violates human rights could lead to the state's responsibility for harm where there is a lack of due diligence to prevent the violation or in responding to it.[118] This decision is reminiscent of the application of due diligence in the context of private harm against aliens described earlier.[119] Thus, what is again clear in *Velasquez* is that if the state's apparatus acts in a manner that allows for violations to go unpunished and reasonable efforts are not taken to restore the victim's full enjoyment of rights, the state has failed to act with due diligence.[120] As Shelton and Gould pointed out, a state's diligence is not legally deficient because of the act that causes harm. Instead, it is because of what was lacking in the authorities' conduct.[121] Indeed, the language in *Velasquez* provided the foundation for the subsequent application of due diligence in violence against women (VAW).

---

[112] Koivurova (n 52) para 44.

[113] See V Schatz, 'Fishing for Interpretation: The ITLOS Advisory Opinion on Flag State Responsibility for Illegal Fishing in the EEZ' (2016) 47 *Ocean Development & International Law* 337.

[114] A Telesetsky, 'The Global North, the Global South, and the Challenges of Ensuring Due Diligence for Sustainable Fishing Governance' (2017) 26 *Transnational Law & Contemporary Problems* 436.

[115] ibid.

[116] See, eg H Tuerk, 'The Contribution of the International Tribunal for the Law of the Sea to International Law' (2007) 26 *Penn State International Law Review* 289.

[117] *Case of Velásquez-Rodríguez v Honduras*, Judgment of 29 July 1988, Inter-AmCtHR (Ser C) No 4 (1988).

[118] ibid para 172.

[119] See nn 42–52 above.

[120] *Velasquez* (n 117) para 176.

[121] D Shelton and A Gould, 'Positive and Negative Obligations' in D Shelton (ed), *The Oxford Handbook of International Human Rights Law* (Oxford, Oxford University Press, 2013) 562.

Consequently, states could be held responsible for failing to effectively prevent and address VAW – particularly at the hands of persons in the private sphere.[122] Although in *Velasquez* the decision still concerned victims' violations in the public sphere and through the state machinery, the introduction and appropriation of due diligence in VAW put visible acts of violence against women within the private sphere.[123] The introduction of due diligence in VAW necessitated a redefinition in the standard of conduct required of states towards more protection for women, especially in the case of intimate partner violence.[124] The use of due diligence to respond to the problem of the public/private divide indicates that there is potential for it to be used as a tool to address state behaviour that has previously ignored human rights abuses in the private sphere.

With General Recommendation No 19, the UN Committee on the Elimination of Discrimination Against Women adopted due diligence as a tool to assess a state's obligations in VAW.[125] Similarly, Article 4 of the Declaration on the Elimination of Violence against Women (DEVAW)[126] requires the state to exercise due diligence to prevent, investigate and punish acts of VAW, whether those acts are perpetrated by the state or by private persons.[127] Furthermore, Article 7(b) of the Inter-American Convention on the Prevention, Punishment, and Eradication of Violence against Women (Convention of Belém do Pará)[128] has similar provisions requiring the state to apply due diligence concerning their obligations in combating VAW.[129] In addition, the Coomaraswamy Report on VAW[130] made some articulations about the application of due diligence. According to the report, the test is whether a state takes its duties seriously. This seriousness or inaction will be evaluated through the actions of state agencies and private actors on a case-by-case basis.[131] Referencing General Recommendation No 19, DEVAW and *Velasquez*, the report showed that inaction in fulfilling state duties has implications – that is, if a state does not respond to the attendant crimes in VAW, it is as guilty as the perpetrators.[132]

Furthermore, noting gaps in the enforcement of protective obligations, the Ertürk Report on VAW[133] moved further by using due diligence to redraw the protection

---

[122] P García-Del Moral and MA Dersnah, 'A Feminist Challenge to the Gendered Politics of the Public/Private Divide: On Due Diligence, Domestic Violence, and Citizenship' (2014) 18 *Citizenship Studies* 661.

[123] ibid 665.

[124] See, eg LD Obreja, 'Human Rights Law and Intimate Partner Violence: Towards an Intersectional Development of Due Diligence Obligations' (2019) 37 *Nordic Journal of Human Rights* 63.

[125] UN Committee on the Elimination of Discrimination Against Women (CEDAW), CEDAW General Recommendation No 19: Violence against Women, 11th Session, 1992, para 9.

[126] UN General Assembly, Declaration on the Elimination of Violence against Women, A/RES/48/104, 20 December 1993.

[127] ibid.

[128] Organization of American States (OAS), Inter-American Convention on the Prevention, Punishment and Eradication of Violence against Women 1994 (Convention of Belem do Para).

[129] ibid.

[130] Report of the Special Rapporteur on violence against women, its causes and consequences, Ms Radhika Coomaraswamy, submitted in accordance with Commission on Human Rights Resolution 1995/85 (5 February 1996) E/CN.4/1996/53.

[131] ibid.

[132] ibid para 120.

[133] Y Ertürk, Special Rapporteur on violence against women, its causes and consequences, 'The Due Diligence Standard as a Tool for the Elimination of Violence against Women' (20 January 2006) UN Doc E/CN.4/2006/61.

levels of conduct for states' enforcement. According to the report, the response of due diligence to VAW should be at different levels of intervention, namely, individual women, the community level, the state and the transnational level.[134] The report uses due diligence to holistically capture these different levels of causes and consequences of VAW. At the level of individual women, state efforts must target women's empowerment. This target action would involve education, skills training and access to productive resources to improve women's self-awareness and self-reliance.[135] State efforts should also be geared towards victims of VAW, and those at risk of VAW should have access to support systems that suit their needs.[136] At the community and family level, human rights discourses should be complemented with an approach based on 'cultural negotiation'.[137] Cultural negotiation means discouraging culture-based norms that give validity to gender-based violence in private spheres.[138] Overall, the report seeks to expand the application of due diligence to push new minimum levels of conduct in addressing VAW at all levels of manifestation – including the public and private spheres.

Indeed, the CEDAW Committee has taken advantage of due diligence's capability to respond to state conduct in the private sphere. In *AT v Hungary*,[139] the victim had been subjected to severe domestic violence and serious threats by her partner.[140] She argued that the Hungarian authorities had failed to provide adequate protection for her and her two children.[141] Hungary had no legal mechanism for obtaining protection or restraining orders, and the criminal proceedings against her husband had been dragging on for years while he remained free.[142] The CEDAW Committee determined that Hungary had indeed failed in its protection obligations.[143] It explained that the state's failure to act in this case represents the general landscape in Hungary, and there is an entrenched traditional stereotype regarding the role of women.[144] In their decision, they recommended that Hungary act with due diligence by expeditiously introducing a specialised law prohibiting domestic violence against women, which would also provide for protection and exclusion orders.[145] Thus, due diligence was used as a tool by the CEDAW Committee to delineate that states like Hungary adopt specialised mechanisms that address harm in the private sphere within the context of VAW.[146]

---

[134] ibid.
[135] ibid paras 78–81.
[136] ibid.
[137] ibid paras 85–88.
[138] ibid paras 85.
[139] Communication No 2/2003, UN Doc CEDAW/C/32/D/2/2003 (26 January 2005).
[140] ibid para 2.1.
[141] ibid.
[142] ibid paras 3.1–3.2.
[143] ibid paras 9.2–9.3.
[144] ibid para 9.4.
[145] ibid para 11(e).
[146] See also *Goekce v Austria*, Communication No 2/2003, Views of the Committee on the Elimination of Discrimination against Women; *Yildirim v Austria*, Communication No 6/2005; *Kell v Canada*, Communication No 19/2008; *VK v Bulgaria*, Communication No 20/2008; *Isatou Jallow v Bulgaria*, Communication No 32/2011.

Furthermore, the corresponding application of due diligence in the Inter-American system has also provided a means to re-envision human rights law to better respond to violations with gender-specific causes and consequences.[147] The victim alleged that the Brazilian government condoned the violence perpetrated by her husband against her. Brazil also failed to punish her husband, and he had remained free.[148] The Commission found that the violence perpetrated by the husband was part of a pattern of negligence and lack of effective action by the state in prosecuting perpetrators. It noted that such discriminatory judicial ineffectiveness fosters a climate that encourages domestic violence – since the public sees that the state will not take effective action to punish violence.[149] Citing the Convention of Belém do Pará, the Commission described Brazil's conduct and climate of impunity as a systemic failure on the part of a state to meet the due diligence standard to ensure that women are protected from violence and gender-based discrimination.[150] Thus, due diligence provides a juridical bridge from the traditional state-centric and public sphere-focused human rights law to the role the state may have in the relationship between individuals.[151]

Similarly, in *Jessica Lenahan Gonzales et al v United States*,[152] the claimants argued that the USA violated their rights by failing to exercise due diligence to protect Jessica Lenahan and her daughters from harm perpetrated by her ex-husband even though Ms Lenahan held a restraining order against him.[153] They alleged that the police failed to adequately respond to Jessica Lenahan's repeated calls that her husband had taken their minor daughters in violation of the restraining order.[154] The Inter-American Commission observed that due diligence is used to interpret the content of state obligations towards the problem of violence against women.[155] Due diligence provides a way of understanding what a state's human rights obligations mean in practice when it comes to violence perpetrated against women, including domestic violence.[156] Citing *Maria da Penha Maia Fernandes*,[157] the Commission explained that the state has to act with the due diligence necessary to investigate and sanction human rights violations in domestic violence cases.[158] Restraining orders are critically part of the due diligence conduct of states in cases of domestic violence. They are often the only remedy available to women victims (and children) to protect them from imminent intimate partner harm. They are only useful, however, if they are diligently enforced.[159] The Commission concluded that the USA failed to

---

[147] *Maria da Penha Maia Fernandes v Brazil*, Case 12.05 1, Inter-AmCtHR, Report No 54/0 1, OEA/Ser.L/V/II.111, doc 20, rev 16 (2000).
[148] ibid paras 1–20.
[149] ibid para 56.
[150] ibid. See also para 20.
[151] Abi-Mershed (n 147) 128.
[152] Inter-American Commission on Human Rights, Merits, Report No 80/11, Case 12.626.
[153] See ibid paras 1–58.
[154] ibid.
[155] ibid para 123.
[156] ibid para 125.
[157] *Maria da Penha Maia Fernandes* (n 148).
[158] *Jessica Lenahan* (n 153) para 131.
[159] ibid para 163.

act with due diligence to protect Jessica Lenahan and her daughters from domestic violence.[160]

Thus, notably from the above, the public–private dichotomy obscures the violence experienced in private life.[161] Due diligence challenges this public–private divide by articulating the relationship between state responsibility and violations by private residents. Those focusing on addressing gender violence have shown interest in developing due diligence in this area for this reason.[162] Applying due diligence to VAW has helped to bring violations of rights in the private sphere under scrutiny.[163] Hence, the potential of due diligence lies in the renewed interpretation or expansion of existing levels of conduct and full implementation of obligations of prevention, protection and compensation – so that it responds more effectively to the specificities of violence against women at all levels.[164]

The European Court of Human Rights in *Opuz v Turkey*[165] amplified the need for states to exercise due diligence by using it to pierce the private sphere in the context of VAW, especially where the situation poses a danger to the potential victim. In the case, the court examined whether Turkey displayed due diligence or acted in preventing the killing of the applicant's mother.[166] Turkey argued that criminal proceedings were commenced against the perpetrator but were discontinued after the applicant withdrew their complaint.[167] The Turkish authorities also claimed that further interference by them would amount to a breach of privacy rights.[168] Interestingly, the court rejected this argument, stating that the authorities should have considered the circumstances of the situation. For instance, the ex-husband had regularly issued death threats against the applicant and her mother.[169] In such indicative instances, due diligence requires authorities to take further measures that would have a real prospect of altering a negative outcome or mitigating the harm suffered.[170] In the court's opinion, branding the issue as a 'private matter' or 'family matter' is incompatible with the discharge of the state's positive obligations.[171] Also, such uninformed branding cannot remove the applicant and her mother from danger. The court noted that there was no uniform practice amongst the contracting states in terms of continuing with proceedings when the complainant in a domestic violence case withdraws the complaint.

---

[160] ibid para 199. For similar cases, see *Claudia Ivette Gonzalez and Others (Mexico)*, Inter-AmCtHR, Report No 54/01, Case 12.051, paras 160–255; *Case of González et al ('Cotton Field') v Mexico*, Preliminary Objection, Merits, Reparations and Costs, Judgment of 16 November 2009, Inter-AmCtHR (Ser C) No 205.

[161] DJ Liebowtiz and J Goldscheid, 'Due Diligence and Gender Violence: Parsing Its Power and Its Perils' (2015) 48 *Cornell International Law Journal* 306.

[162] ibid 307.

[163] Y Ertürk, 'The Due Diligence Standard: What Does It Entail for Women's Rights?' in Benninger-Budel (n 147) 33.

[164] ibid.

[165] ECtHR Application no 33401/02, 9 June 2009.

[166] ibid para 137.

[167] ibid paras 140–45.

[168] ibid.

[169] ibid.

[170] ibid para 136.

[171] ibid para 144.

Nonetheless, there is an acknowledgement of the duty on the part of the authorities to strike a balance in enforcing the victim's privacy rights.[172] Thus, given the circumstances of the situation, Turkish authorities should have exercised due diligence by pursuing criminal proceedings against the ex-husband as a matter of public interest.[173] More importantly, the court elaborated on the nature of state obligations concerning violence in the family, particularly acknowledging the problems created by the invisibility of the crime and highlighting the seriousness with which states must respond.[174] Furthermore, like the *Lenahan* decision and the *Maria da Penha Maia Fernandes* case, this articulation in *Opuz* contributes to building the due diligence content, particularly extending what is the minimum a state is required to do in the context of the private sphere in VAW.[175]

However, due diligence, in the context of VAW, is not a silver bullet. While it has helped to deconstruct the public/private divide, VAW persists.[176] As much as attention has been brought to the public/private divide, more needs to be done for due diligence to be more impactful in addressing VAW in practice. This includes continuous activism, grassroots efforts and advocacy, all of which historically used due diligence to challenge the public/private divide. Advocacy groups could use documents like the United Nations Development Fund for Women (UNIFEM) Ten Point National Accountability Checklist on ending VAW.[177] It was written for policy-makers, parliamentarians and advocates seeking to promote due diligence in the establishment and to track state action and policies in response to VAW.[178] A more recent example is the Due Diligence Project's (DDP) Due Diligence Framework.[179] The DDP is a research-based advocacy group that aims to enhance understanding of a state's due diligence obligations to prevent, protect, prosecute, punish and provide redress for VAW. Also, it aims to develop a due diligence framework with a set of guidelines for compliance.[180] Its work could be taken up at the UN Special Rapporteur level, where more attention could be drawn to expanding due diligence to address gaps in accountability.

---

[172] ibid para 138.

[173] ibid para 145.

[174] M Burton, 'The Human Rights of Victims of Domestic Violence: Opuz v Turkey' (2010) 22 *Child & Family Law Quarterly* 131.

[175] See C Bettinger-Lopez, 'Introduction: Jessica Lenahan (Gonzales) v United States of America: Implementation, Litigation, and Mobilization Strategies' (2012) 21 *Journal of Gender Social Policy and Law* 228.

[176] See, eg UN Women, 'Facts and Figures: Ending Violence against Women' (*UN Women*, March 2021) www.unwomen.org/en/what-we-do/ending-violence-against-women/facts-and-figures#notes.

[177] See UN Women, 'Ending Violence against Women and Girls: UNIFEM Strategy and Information Kit' (*UN Women*, 2010) www.unwomen.org/en/digital-library/publications/2010/1/ending-violence-against-women-and-girls-unifem-strategy-and-information-kit.

[178] J Sarkin, 'A Methodology to Ensure that States Adequately Apply Due Diligence Standards and Processes to Significantly Impact Levels of Violence Against Women Around the World' (2018) 40 *Human Rights Quarterly* 17.

[179] ZA Aziz and J Moussa, 'Due Diligence Framework: State Accountability Framework for Eliminating Violence against Women' (Due Diligence Project, 2016) http://duediligenceproject.org/resources/.

[180] ibid 5.

V. IMPLICATIONS OF USING DUE DILIGENCE AS A TOOL FOR EXPANDING THE SCOPE OF OBLIGATIONS

Over the years, due diligence's conceptualisation, functionality and contemporary relevance have increased in international law. Due diligence provides a way of understanding what state obligations mean in application, for example, when it comes to responding to the problem of violence against women.[181] Sarkin has called due diligence an oversight tool,[182] and Ertürk explained that it is a framework for action in respect of obligations.[183] Mullally has also argued that due diligence can be potentially expanded to the context of asylum adjudications – where its introduction would require much greater scrutiny of states' legislative and policy frameworks on domestic violence asylum claims.[184] The reasonableness of relocation alternatives would also be open to greater questioning to assess whether state obligations are being fulfilled.[185] Also, Davitti argued that due diligence is a tool capable of reconceptualising protection standards in investment discourses where the interests of all actors, especially the most vulnerable, can be better reflected and protected.[186] It would seem that Mullally and Davitti see the re-envisioning potential in due diligence.

Due diligence's contemporary relevance is in its potential to redefine the existing standard of conduct required of states in the fulfilment of their obligations. It is receptive to changes so that new levels of conduct are set or shaped in the light of evolving circumstances. Therefore, due diligence should be seen as a rallying point for the required action that states must carry out.[187] It has the potential to lay out what new conduct the states should be exhibiting, particularly in the face of a change in circumstances. It can also function as a yardstick against which states' efforts towards their obligations may be measured.[188] So, instead of providing answers to questions of breach of obligations, due diligence tends to inquire whether states have taken reasonable and appropriate efforts to avoid or mitigate injury to other states.[189]

However, what happens when acting with due diligence no longer signifies only acting reasonably, but transforms into meeting more stringent and concrete legal standards? The crystallisation of due diligence into concrete legal standards is already at play in international law. This is because of the use of due diligence as a

---

[181] RM Celorio, 'The Rights of Women in the Inter-American System of Human Rights: Current Opportunities and Challenges in Standard-Setting' (2011) 65 *University of Miami Law Review* 854.

[182] Sarkin (n 179).

[183] Ertürk (n 164) 27, 37.

[184] S Mullally, 'Domestic Violence Asylum Claims and Recent Developments in International Human Rights Law: A Progress Narrative?' (2011) 60 *International and Comparative Law Quarterly* 483.

[185] ibid.

[186] D Davitti, 'On the Meanings of International Investment Law and International Human Rights Law: The Alternative Narrative of Due Diligence' (2012) 12 *Human Rights Law Review* 443.

[187] Sarkin (n 179) 4.

[188] See J Bourke-Martignoni, 'The History and Development of the Due Diligence Standard in International Law and Its Role in the Protection of Women against Violence' in Benninger-Budel (n 147) 47.

[189] International Law Association (ILA) Study Group on Due Diligence in International Law, Second Report (July 2016) 3.

tool by international courts and tribunals (as shown above). For example, regarding obligations to prevent significant transboundary harm, acting with due diligence now legally requires an EIA and the duty to notify and consult the relevant states. Similarly in the context of VAW, the introduction of due diligence through women's advocacy within the echelons of the UN has redefined the standards so that states become attentive to abuses in the private sphere.[190] International courts like the Inter-American Court of Human Rights have contributed to the crystallisation of due diligence into a legal standard in VAW. The consequence is that the international legal order has a more attentive or relevant legal standard within a thematic area. Importantly, the involvement of state parties in international litigation (as shown in the previous sections) before the courts increases the strictness of the applicable standard 'into a more demanding system of legal accountability. An example of this is the obligation to undertake environmental impact assessment (EIA) which has now been considered by the ICJ on several occasions and progressively strengthened.'[191] This article sees due diligence as a standard which may form part of secondary rules, and it can also form part of primary rules. For example, Article 7(b) of the Convention of Belém do Pará provides that states 'apply due diligence to prevent, investigate and impose penalties for violence against women'.[192] Also, as shown above, due diligence can be used to determine whether the state in question is internationally responsible for its omissions concerning a non-state actor's conduct that is contrary to international law.[193]

The transformation of due diligence from what is reasonable to concrete legal standards in the thematic areas discussed above also shows some limitation regarding the concept and cause for pessimism. Due diligence alone cannot respond to gaps in the implementation of state obligations unless its contents and what it entails are crystallised or concretised into a legal requirement by international courts and tribunals or treaty provisions – otherwise, it does not become a hard legal standard.

However, this is not to say that there is no reason to be optimistic about due diligence – given its reliance on courts and tribunals to be crystallised. Indeed, the concept is not static. The contents of due diligence themselves are not fixed, even if they have been crystallised into a hard legal requirement. Also, the Commentaries to the 2001 Articles on Responsibility of States for Internationally Wrongful Acts (ARSIWA) describe due diligence as a standard of primary obligation that varies from one context to another for reasons which essentially relate to surrounding circumstances, the object and purpose of the treaty provision or other rule giving rise to the primary obligation.[194] This classification of due diligence is not surprising as international practice and most international legal scholarship acknowledge that due diligence is an element of primary rules and not a general principle of responsibility.[195]

---

[190] See García-Del Moral and Dersnah (n 122).
[191] ILA (n 190).
[192] Convention of Belem do Para (n 128).
[193] See also R Mackenzie-Gray Scott, 'Due Diligence as a Secondary Rule of General International Law' (2021) 34 *Leiden Journal of International Law* 359.
[194] Art 2, Commentary.
[195] A Ollino, *Due Diligence Obligations in International Law* (Cambridge University Press 2022) 62.

However, in the Commentaries to ARSIWA, due diligence is mentioned as a way of measuring the breach of an obligation by states. Due diligence has the capability to form part of the primary rules. It can also operate as part of the secondary rules.[196]

As such, the flexibility of the concept and the standard of reasonableness it entails can be used as a basis for advocacy – even at a soft law status – regarding what is required of a state concerning its obligations in international law, in the sense that what the relevant state is doing is unreasonable – even if the current hard legal standard allows it. It can be used by non-governmental organisations (NGOs) and civil society organisations as a basis to pressure states and push the boundaries of an extant standard to be more attentive to current circumstances.[197] One method of doing this is that NGOs can submit amicus curiae briefs that articulate due diligence and what it entails before international courts, regional human rights courts and, for example, the UN Human Rights Committee. Due diligence can also be used in reports of UN Special Rapporteurs to challenge and point out gaps in current standards.

There is scepticism about using due diligence. One could argue, like Hathaway and Foster, that since due diligence is concerned with state responsibility, it is conceptually unfit or will be at odds with a regime designed to protect individuals from harm.[198] This argument is limited because it conceptualises due diligence only within the paradigm of state responsibility. Indeed, conceptualising due diligence this way is understandable given the concept's origins. However, limited conceptualisation will lead to conclusions only associated with state responsibility. It blinds the potential of due diligence to prescribe standards of conduct to be met by states to fulfil their obligations.

Kamminga argued that since due diligence conduct is one of means and not results, it presents a potentially dangerous weakness.[199] He explained that, as an obligation of conduct, due diligence could be used as a defensive standard – where the state could defend their position that even though the result was not achieved, it still acted with due diligence.[200] He then pointed out that there is a risk due diligence undermines positive obligations existing within treaties.[201]

However, due diligence does not undermine positive obligations. The relationship between due diligence and positive obligations makes due diligence in international law a positive development. The concept seeks to push states to carry out their positive obligations as it is used to describe prudent steps to be taken by states to avoid a range of bad outcomes in the discharge of their positive obligations.[202] Positive obligations require the state to carry out certain acts and the standard of due diligence allows a wide margin of flexibility as to the substance of conduct required to carry out those acts.

---

[196] See, eg Scott (n 194).

[197] See, eg Ertürk, 'Special Rapporteur on Violence against Women' (n 133).

[198] J Hathaway and M Foster, *The Law of Refugee Status*, 2nd edn (Cambridge, Cambridge University Press 2014) 314.

[199] MT Kamminga, 'Due Diligence Mania: The Misguided Introduction of an Extraneous Concept into Human Rights Discourse' (2011) Maastricht Faculty of Law Working Paper No 2011/07 1.

[200] ibid 5.

[201] ibid 6.

[202] McDonald (n 82) 1049.

For example, in environmental law, due diligence indicates conduct or behaviour a state must follow to effectively protect other states from transboundary harm through legislative and administrative action.[203] It is thus demanding in the sense that states go beyond legislation by adopting useful measures to meet their positive obligations in international environmental law.[204] These measures should not be mere formalities preordained to be ineffective.[205] Due diligence does not subtract from positive obligations. Instead, it gives additional value to the interpretation of positive obligations. It is an oversight mechanism that assists in scrutinising the will and processes used in fulfilling positive obligations.[206] It allows deficiencies in state conduct to be detected and corrected.[207] It provides a platform for determining what it means to fulfil an obligation and analysing the duty-bearer's actions or omissions.[208]

Due diligence does not only describe steps to be taken to fulfil a positive obligation; it has the potential to redefine standards of conduct in the face of changing circumstances, albeit reliant on international courts/tribunals to make it a hard legal standard. This potential could be useful in demanding a more significant response from the states as things evolve or new problematic trends come to light. As we saw in *Alabama*, Great Britain wanted a narrow interpretation of due diligence.[209] The tribunal rejected this argument and gave a broader and more demanding standard that must match or be in exact proportion to the risks to which either of the belligerents may be exposed from a failure to fulfil the obligations of neutrality on their part.[210] The standard is not static – as the conduct required of the state would correspond with the new circumstances of a fluid situation. For example, as in *Alabama*, the circumstances changed after the ships escaped from British territory. The tribunal noted that the subsequent measures taken to pursue the escaped ships were so inadequate in the situation that they could not lead to any result.[211] The Treaty of Washington (1871), on which the *Alabama* litigation is based, indicated how states are required to use due diligence at every stage: firstly, to prevent the fitting and equipping of any vessel intended to carry on war against another state; and secondly, to use to prevent the departure of any vessel intended for war.[212] So, depending on whether the vessels are in a construction stage or finished stage, where prevention of departure is then required, or the escape stage, where another specific action is needed, the type of conduct required changes.

---

[203] See P Birnie et al, *International Law and the Environment*, 3rd edn (Oxford, Oxford University Press, 2009).

[204] A Byrnes, 'Article 2' in MA Freeman et al (eds.), *The UN Convention on the Elimination of All Forms of Discrimination Against Women: A Commentary* (Oxford, Oxford University Press, 2012) 69.

[205] *Velasquez* (n 117) para 177.

[206] See, eg *Pulp Mills* (n 64) para 197.

[207] Sarkin (n 179) 17.

[208] The Special Rapporteur on violence against women, its causes and consequences, 'Summary Paper: The Due Diligence Standard for Violence against Women', www2.ohchr.org/english/issues/women/rapporteur/docs/SummaryPaperDueDiligence.doc.

[209] *Alabama Claims Arbitration* (n 25).

[210] ibid.

[211] ibid.

[212] ibid; see also T Bingham, 'The Alabama Claims Arbitration' (2005) 54 *International & Comparative Law Quarterly* 16.

Similarly, in international environmental law, we see some of the potential of due diligence to change expectations of required conduct in light of circumstances. In transboundary harm, the required degree of care is also proportional to the degree of hazardousness of the activity involved. The degree of harm itself should be foreseeable, and the state must know or should have known that the activity has the risk of causing significant transboundary harm.[213] Furthermore, depending on the activity, carrying out an EIA before an environmental activity is not mandatory. However, if the activity carries some potential risk of transboundary harm by default, the conduct required will change.[214] The ILC Draft Articles explained that activities involving a risk of causing significant transboundary harm usually have some general identifiable characteristics.[215] So, where the activity bears some of these identifiable potential risks, the standard will then require an EIA from the state and, subsequently, the duty to notify and consult with the state that may be potentially affected will follow.[216] It is entirely plausible that the process is sequential in the sense that notification and consultation follow the outcome of an EIA process.[217] Therefore, depending on the preliminary nature of the environmental activity, the standard of conduct required of the state may include carrying out an EIA and/or notification and consultation. In *Seabed Mining Advisory Opinion*, it was explained that due diligence might change over time as measures considered sufficiently diligent at a specific moment may change in light of new scientific or technological knowledge.[218] For instance, prospecting for minerals is generally less risky than the exploitation of minerals. Thus, the standard of due diligence in prospecting minerals would be less onerous, and in the case of the exploitation of minerals, the standard might shift towards requiring more demanding conduct from the relevant state.[219]

VI. CONCLUSION: OPTIMISM?

Due diligence emerged as an element within state responsibility culminating in its early relevance in the context of alien protection. The application of due diligence then expanded and developed in other areas like significant transboundary harm in environmental law, the law of the sea and violence against women. In these

---

[213] PSRao, Special Rapporteur, 'International Liability for Injurious Consequences Arising out of Acts not Prohibited by International Law (Prevention of Transboundary Damage from Hazardous Activities)' (5 May 1999) A/CN.4/501.

[214] See *Pulp Mills* (n 64); *Border Area* (n 77); *ILC Prevention Articles* (n 58).

[215] For these characteristics, see Commentary 9, Art 7, *ILC Prevention Articles* (n 58).

[216] See n 194 above; Kulesza (n 12).

[217] J Brunnée, 'Reflection Procedure and Substance in International Environmental Law Confused at a Higher Level?' https://esil-sedi.eu/post_name-123/.

[218] *Seabed Mining Advisory Opinion* (n 88) para 117; see also *ILC Prevention Articles* (n 58) Commentary to Art 3. Similar to *Alabama*, the Commentary said that the standard of due diligence against which the conduct of the state should be examined is that which is generally considered to be appropriate and proportional to the degree of risk of transboundary harm. For example, activities which may be considered ultrahazardous require a much higher standard of care and a much higher degree of vigour on the part of the state.

[219] T Poisel, 'Deep Seabed Mining: Implications of Seabed Disputes Chamber's Advisory Opinion' (2012) 19 *Australian International Law Journal*. 29.

applications, due diligence reinforces a standard of conduct that states must meet or display in the fulfilment of their positive obligations. Notably, we see in the VAW context that the due diligence standard has been reinterpreted to pierce the private sphere and increase state responses at all levels where VAW could thrive or manifest. It has also been argued that the application of due diligence can be expanded to issues like domestic violence claims in asylum adjudication in order to provide adequate protection standards to, for example, women seeking asylum from a culture of violence in the origin state.

There is a reason for optimism as due diligence's flexibility provides a tool for advocacy and the possibility of redefining existing standards of conduct when they are no longer attentive to extant problems. The value and, indeed, the continued relevancy of due diligence lies in the potential that it can be extended or stretched to meet new and evolving situations or contexts. It provides a platform to design what is due in state conduct. It can also be used to analyse extant requirements to increase state accountability and redraw required responses in a changing situation. This potential in due diligence can change what is required of states so that such requirements can match changes in circumstances and set new minimum conduct, respectively. Global issues are innately dynamic as new challenges arise, and formerly existing requirements may be insufficient. So, due diligence can present a malleable standard to set new or additional requirements for states in the face of growing challenges. Thus, due diligence adds more to the advocacy arsenal. Notwithstanding the potential that due diligence holds, for due diligence to redefine an existing standard of conduct required to fulfil an obligation, it has to be crystallised by international courts or tribunals. Such reliance means it may take some time for a redefined due diligence standard in soft law and probably at the advocacy level to transform into a concrete legal standard.

In addition, there could be concerns about the consistency of standards where there is a constant evolution of due diligence requirements to meet new circumstances or close gaps through judicial recognition. For example, where due diligence forms part of the provisions of a treaty (as in the Convention of Belém do Pará), it is possible that what due diligence entails in the prevention of violence against women later changes to close new gaps. In this case, the implication is that state parties have signed up to a treaty where the standards of their obligations are now different, probably stricter than what it was at the point of ratification. States might be wary of changing standards and could argue that there is a level of uncertainty about what exercising due diligence constitutes or what is expected of them. There was an indication of this in the *Alabama Claims Arbitration* – where the USA and GB gave different interpretations of the definition and requirements of due diligence as provided for in Article (vi) of the Treaty of Washington (1871). So, there is always the possibility that the malleability of due diligence and its evolution through judicial recognition may place uncertain standards on state parties. Consequently, the concept of due diligence occupies the border across optimism, advocacy, possibility of increasing the attentiveness of legal standards to new circumstances and wishful legal thinking for solutions to new problems in international law.

The Fine Line between Non-international Armed Conflicts and Internal Disturbances and a Call for the Revival of the Concept of 'Fundamental Standards of Humanity'

ELIZA WALSH

Abstract

The imprecise definitions for non-international armed conflicts (NIACs) and internal disturbances have resulted in numerous scenarios where the line distinguishing an armed conflict from an internal disturbance is extremely blurred. This means the protection afforded to victims is often hampered for a number of reasons, such as the inadequacy of domestic law or derogations from human rights treaties. In evaluating this 'grey zone' between NIACs and internal disturbances, this paper proposes a new angle for the definition of internal disturbances and the revival of the concept of 'fundamental standards of humanity' for those situations lying on the spectrum somewhere between a NIAC and an internal disturbance.

I. INTRODUCTION

IT HAS BEEN recognised that there are currently 26 states with ongoing non-international armed conflicts (NIACs) in the world today, which is a stark contrast to only five instances of international armed conflicts (IACs) that presently exist in the international community.[1] Furthermore, in 2018 alone, there was an 11 per cent increase in political violence and a 24.5 per cent increase in riots and protests from the previous year.[2] All of this is to say that the modern structure of hostilities has drastically changed from what it was when international humanitarian law (IHL) was first conceptualised, when the market for conflict was saturated with IACs, and NIACs rarely existed or at least were not formally recognised.[3] This paper focuses on this contemporary reality of hostilities and the difficulty with

---

[1] Geneva Academy, 'RULAC – Conflicts' (*RULAC*, 2021) www.rulac.org/browse/conflicts.
[2] ACLED, 'ACLED 2018: The Year in Review' (11 January 2019) https://acleddata.com/2019/01/11/acled-2018-the-year-in-review/.
[3] D Turns, 'The Law of Armed Conflict (International Humanitarian Law)' in M Evans (ed), *International Law*, 5th edn (Oxford, Oxford University Press, 2018) 843–46.

classifying situations caught on the spectrum between NIACs and internal disturbances, to which IHL does not apply, and discusses potential improvements in this
area.

Conflating the idea of armed conflict with something not officially classified as an
armed conflict but improperly referred to as a 'war', such as the so-called Mexican
'War on Drugs' or the US declaration of the 'War on Terror', can have serious implications for the protection individuals are afforded in such times.[4] The term 'war' is
used frequently in society as a form of rhetoric in response to a grave situation to
assure the public that the state or authority labelling it as 'war' is treating such a
calamity with the utmost concern and condemnation.[5] However, simply labelling a
situation as a 'war' does not mean it is a war in the legal sense subject to *jus in bello*,
but instead could be more clearly qualified as opposition against crisis.[6]

The fine line dividing internal disturbances and NIACs has been referred to as a
'grey zone' or 'shadow area', given the identification of which side of the line a situation lies, whether on the NIAC side or the internal disturbance side, is not a simple
determination.[7] The difficulty with this fine line comes down to definitional matters,
given the understanding of NIACs is still quite vague as they are imprecisely defined
as a conflict 'not of an international character'.[8] Unfortunately, this uncertainty is
also found with internal disturbances, given they are scarcely elaborated upon. As a
result, this has caused a severe gap in the understanding of what constitutes a NIAC
and an internal disturbance, meaning the protection afforded to victims caught in
these situations is often hampered for a number of reasons, such as the inadequacy
of domestic laws or derogations from human rights treaties, despite violations of the
most basic human rights norms that occur in such situations.[9]

This paper will ask the question what can be done in this area to develop greater
clarity, and the answer proposed in response will be that a new definition for internal
disturbances is required that places the emphasis on when an internal disturbance
comes to an end rather than meeting the criteria necessary for the establishment of a
NIAC. Shifting the focus, in instances where the situation could arguably be classified as either a NIAC or an internal disturbance, would create a concrete end to an
internal disturbance and allow for the situation to switch into the realms of IHL. In
addition, this paper will call for the revival of the notion of 'fundamental standards
of humanity', which sets a core body of rules promoting the principle of humanity
applicable at all times, including in the grey zone situations falling in the borderlines
between NIACs and internal disturbances.

---

[4] H Duffy, *The 'War on Terror' and the Framework of International Law*, 2nd edn (Cambridge, Cambridge University Press, 2015) 347.

[5] 'Text: President Bush Addresses the Nation' *Washington Post* (20 September 2001) www.washingtonpost.com/wp-srv/nation/specials/attacked/transcripts/bushaddress_092001.html.

[6] SP Marks, 'Branding the War on Terrorism: Is There New Paradigm of International Law' (2006) 14 *Michigan State University Journal of International Law* 71, 72.

[7] A Eide, A Rosas and T Meron, 'Combating Lawlessness in Gray Zone Conflicts through Minimum Humanitarian Standards' (1995) 89 *American Journal of International Law* 215; JD Vigny and C Thompson, 'Fundamental Standards of Humanity: What Future?' (2002) 20 *Netherlands Quarterly of Human Rights* 185.

[8] Art 3 Common to 1949 Geneva Conventions.

[9] Vigny and Thompson (n 7) 185–86.

In section II, the requirements that need to be satisfied for both internal disturbances and NIACs will be outlined, with due regard being paid to the difficulty in deciphering the difference between the two, while also using the Mexican 'War on Drugs' as an example to illustrate these ambiguities. The section will also discuss the effects of this fine line and propose a new angle for a definition of internal disturbances. Section II will then analyse the concept of 'fundamental standards of humanity' and call for its restoration.

II. DECIPHERING THE DIFFERENCE BETWEEN NON-INTERNATIONAL ARMED CONFLICTS AND INTERNAL DISTURBANCES

A. Non-international Armed Conflicts

i. *Classification of Non-international Armed Conflicts*

The classification of conflicts under IHL 'occupies a pivotal, conceptual, and practical place in the international legal system. It reflects the contents, limits, and separation of fundamental international legal categories, such as war and peace, and international personality.'[10] It was only in the mid-twentieth century, with the enactment of Common Article 3 of the Geneva Conventions, that the concept of a NIAC was recognised as being regulated by international law.[11] Therefore, the introduction of Common Article 3 was a watershed moment in the development of IHL, as it recognised non-state actors (NSAs) as parties to a conflict with their own share of obligations for the first time. However, the drafters of the Geneva Conventions were careful to emphasise that it 'shall not affect the legal status of the Parties to the conflict'.[12]

One of the key differentiating factors between IACs and NIACs is the level of intensity necessary. For IACs, given the prohibition on the use of force between states contained within the UN Charter, it is assumed that where there is such a use of force, it will trigger the rules applicable for IACs.[13] However, it is not such a simple determination when it comes to NIACs, as states are permitted to use force against NSAs within their own territory for the purposes of law enforcement, meaning the threshold for the classification of a NIAC is higher than for an IAC.[14] It has come to be understood that in order for a situation to be classified as a NIAC, the hostilities must be sufficiently intense and the parties must be organised. This can be traced to the definition of armed conflict in the 1995 *Tadić* decision by the International Criminal Tribunal for the former Yugoslavia (ICTY) Appeals Chamber, which stated, 'An armed conflict exists whenever there is a resort to armed

---

[10] I Kalpouzos, 'International Law and the Classification of Conflicts' (2013) 26 *Leiden Journal of International Law* 767, 767.

[11] Turns (n 3) 846.

[12] N Melzer, *International Humanitarian Law, A Comprehensive Introduction* (Geneva, International Committee of the Red Cross, 2016) 53.

[13] Art 2(4) UN Charter.

[14] Melzer (n 12) 54.

force between States or protracted armed violence between governmental authorities and organised armed groups or between such groups within a State'.[15] The rationale behind these criteria was to eliminate those instances of hostilities falling below the threshold of NIACs to which IHL does not apply. As was stated in the ICTY Trial Chamber in *Delalic* 'in order to distinguish from cases of civil unrest or terrorist activities, the emphasis is on the protracted extent of the armed violence and the extent of organisation of the parties involved'.[16] This was further emphasised in the ICTY Appeals Chamber in *Kordic and Cerkez*, where it was noted 'the requirement of protracted fighting is significant in excluding mere cases of civil unrest or single acts of terrorism'.[17] A minimum degree of organisation is necessary to carry out any military operation and therefore it is the case that the parties in a NIAC must be organised. It is assumed state forces are sufficiently organised, so this question of organisation primarily relates to NSAs. The *Tadić* definition does not explicitly mention what an 'organised armed group' consists of; however, a number of factors have been developed with the progression of case law. The ICTY Trial Chamber in *Prosecutor v Milošević* found 'a sufficient body of evidence pointing to the KLA [Kosovo Liberation Army] being an organized military force, with an official joint command structure, headquarters, designated zones of operation, and the ability to procure, transport, and distribute arms'.[18] Furthermore, the *Haradinaj* case laid down a number of factors such as

> the existence of a command structure and disciplinary rules and mechanisms within the group; the existence of a headquarters; the fact that the group controls a certain territory; the ability of the group to gain access to weapons, other military equipment, recruits and military training; its ability to plan, coordinate and carry out military operations, including troop movements and logistics; its ability to define a unified military strategy and use military tactics; and its ability to speak with one voice and negotiate and conclude agreements such as cease-fire or peace accords.[19]

In the same *Milošević* decision, the intensity was analysed with regard to the length or protracted character of the hostilities, the seriousness of the violence, the spread of hostilities over the territory, the types of weapons used and the increase in government forces being deployed.[20] The *Haradinaj* case set out a number of factors to be considered when determining the intensity of a situation, none of which are intended to be an essential criterion in and of itself, which include

> the number, duration and intensity of individual confrontations; the type of weapons and other military equipment used; the number and calibre of munitions fired; the number of persons and type of forces partaking in the fighting; the number of casualties; the extent of material destruction; and the number of civilians fleeing combat zones. The involvement of the UN Security Council may also be a reflection of the intensity of a conflict.[21]

---

[15] *Tadić*, ICTY Appeals Chamber, 2 October 1995, para 70.
[16] *Delalic et al*, ICTY Trial Chamber, 16 November 1998, para 184, in A Cullen, *The Concept of Non-international Armed Conflict in International Humanitarian Law* (Cambridge, Cambridge University Press, 2010) 122.
[17] *Kordic and Cerkez*, ICTY Appeals Chamber, 17 December 2004, para 341.
[18] *Milošević*, ICTY Trial Chamber, 12 December 2007, para 23.
[19] *Haradinaj et al*, ICTY Trial Chamber, 3 April 2008, para 60.
[20] *Milošević* (n 18) para 28.
[21] *Haradinaj et al* (n 19) para 49.

Imperatively, when it comes to analysing what is meant by intensity, a great deal hinges on the interpretation of the word 'protracted'.[22] However, there seems to be some disagreement as to how protracted should be understood, with some regarding protracted as meaning the intensity of the conflict, whereas others argue protracted and intensity are two distinct criteria and should not be conflated with one another.[23] If a layman with no knowledge of IHL were to try and understand the term 'protracted', they would undoubtedly believe there was a durational or temporal element to it, given a typical English dictionary definition refers to it as 'lasting for a long time or made to last longer than necessary'.[24] However, the layman's understanding and the IHL understanding are two separate and diverse notions.[25] Dinstein is firmly of the view that the two are separate criteria and are not to be assimilated with one another. He acknowledges the fact that the Trial Chamber in *Haradinaj* recognised protracted 'as referring more to the intensity of the armed violence than to its duration'.[26] However, he rebuts this argument by evidencing the *Gombo* Pre-trial Chamber decision in the International Criminal Court (ICC), which separated intensity and protracted.[27] Dinstein's argument is that a NIAC does not simply come about in an instant, but rather, it is preceded by a series of isolated and sporadic internal disturbances which culminate in the outbreak of a NIAC. In other words, there needs to be a 'germination' phase, and only when it is no longer isolated or sporadic can a NIAC exist.[28]

On the other side of the argument, it is suggested that protracted should be looked at holistically in the context of the entire period of hostilities and should not require the hostilities to be continuous or sustained.[29] This understanding encompasses the idea that in order for the rules relating to NIACs to apply, the hostilities 'must be high enough to exclude isolated or sporadic acts of violence, but low enough to include situations of internal conflict where hostilities are not necessarily carried out on a continuous basis'.[30] Indeed, for greater clarification of the term 'protracted', one can look to the *La Tablada* decision of the Inter-American Commission on Human Rights, which concerned an attack on an Argentine military base that lasted just 30 hours in total.[31] The Commission was tasked with deciding whether the hostilities were simply an internal disturbance or whether they constituted a NIAC, and ultimately found that IHL was indeed applicable, noting that where the material conditions for the characterisation of an armed conflict have been met, an armed conflict may exist despite the brevity of the hostilities.[32]

---

[22] Cullen (n 16) 341.

[23] Y Dinstein, *Non-international Armed Conflicts in International Law* (Cambridge, Cambridge University Press, 2014) 32–34.

[24] C McIntosh, 'Protracted', *Cambridge Advanced Learner's Dictionary*, 4th edn (Cambridge, Cambridge University Press, 2013).

[25] M Hrnjaz and J Simentić Popović, 'Protracted Armed Violence as a Criterion for the Existence of Non-international Armed Conflict: International Humanitarian Law, International Criminal Law and Beyond.' (2020) 25 *Journal of Conflict & Security Law* 473, 477.

[26] *Haradinaj et al* (n 19) para 49; Dinstein (n 23) 35.

[27] *Gombo*, ICC Pre-trial Chamber, 15 June 2009, paras 231 and 235; Dinstein (n 23) 35.

[28] Dinstein (n 23) 32.

[29] Cullen (n 16) 128.

[30] ibid.

[31] Case 11.137 (*La Tablada*), Report No 55/97 of the Inter-American Commission on Human Rights, 18 November 1997.

[32] ibid paras 152–56.

An important point to note for the purposes of this paper is that the term 'protracted' was intended to be used to distinguish NIACs from acts of 'banditry, unorganized and shortlived insurrections, or terrorist activities', meaning 'protracted' is an element which distinguishes a NIAC from an internal disturbance.[33] The 1997 *Tadić* ICTY Trial Chamber decision elaborated on the words put forward by the Appeals Chamber in the 1995 case and stated:

> The test applied by the Appeals Chamber to the existence of an armed conflict for the purposes of the rules contained in Common Article 3 focuses on two aspects of a conflict; the intensity of the conflict and the organization of the parties to the conflict.[34]

Therefore, despite the Appeals Chamber recognising 'protracted' as referring to the duration, the Trial Chamber interpreted it as referring to intensity.[35] The Trial Chamber in *Haradinaj* also found 'The criterion of protracted armed violence has therefore been interpreted in practice, including by the *Tadić* Trial Chamber itself, as referring more to the intensity of the armed violence than to its duration'.[36] Declaring that duration and intensity are two separate criteria goes to the principle of legality, as it would be unjust for a person who may have committed a crime in the initial stages of a conflict to be held liable in international criminal law, as they may not have understood, nor may it have been officially considered, that there was an armed conflict ongoing at that time.[37]

The view of the majority presently appears to be that 'protracted' should be interpreted to mean intensity, and duration is not a necessary requirement; indeed, the International Committee of the Red Cross (ICRC) has noted that Common Article 3 should be applied as widely as possible when human lives are at stake.[38] It is important to fully grasp how a NIAC comes about in order to differentiate it from an internal disturbance. While there is undoubtedly more information at hand to define what constitutes a NIAC as opposed to an internal disturbance, there still remains a great level of uncertainty in this area, as manifested not only in the opposing views on the term 'protracted', but also in the vagueness of the definition 'not of an international character'. Presumably the drafters of Common Article 3 deliberately left this ambiguity to ensure greater support from states not wishing to relinquish a further fraction of their sovereignty, but nevertheless it is problematic for the purposes of separating NIACs from internal disturbances.

ii. Case Example: Can the Mexican 'War on Drugs' Be Classified as a Non-international Armed Conflict?

In order to fully grasp the complexity of the situation under discussion in this paper, where the lines between NIACs and internal disturbances are so blurred that

---

[33] *Tadić*, ICTY Trial Chamber, 7 May 1997, para 562 in DA Lewis, 'The Notion of "Protracted Armed Conflict" in the Rome Statute and the Termination of Armed Conflicts under International Law: An Analysis of Select Issues' [2020] *International Review of the Red Cross* 1098.

[34] *Tadić*, ICTY Trial Chamber, 7 May 1997, para 562 in Hrnjaz and Simentić Popović (n 25) 477.

[35] Hrnjaz and Simentić Popović (n 25) 477.

[36] ibid.

[37] Lewis (n 33) 1100.

[38] J Caplin, 'Politics in Conflict: Why the Intersects of States Inescapability Infuse International Humanitarian Law, The Case of Mexico's Drug War' (2016) 8 *Elon Law Review* 107.

determining the classification is next to impossible, an example case study will be analysed. The Mexican 'War on Drugs' is a prominent example that has garnered support on both sides of the fence, ie those who consider it a NIAC and those to whom it is an internal disturbance.

Drug cartels have been present in Mexico for much of the twentieth and twenty-first centuries. The dynamics of the cartels have changed and evolved since the beginning of the 'War on Drugs', with various cartels emerging, disintegration and splitting into different factions, which has left today just two dominant cartels, Cartel de Sinaloa (CDS) and Cartel Jalisco Nueva Generación (CJNG), alongside numerous weaker and smaller cartels.[39]

For years, it was the policy of Mexican presidential administrations to deal with these drug-trafficking organisations (DTOs) 'through an opaque strategy of accommodation, payoffs, assigned trafficking routes, and periodic takedowns of uncooperative capos [bosses]'.[40] However, following his election in 2006, President Calderón chose to declare a 'war' on Mexico's increasingly powerful criminal groups, placing the emphasis on his militarised security strategy. However, this strategy had disastrous effects for the safety of civilians, with a 260 per cent increase in homicides from 2007 to 2010.[41] In 2012, the newly elected President Enrique Peña Nieto engaged in much of the same activities as that of Calderón, creating a national gendarmerie described as a 'paramilitary police force', consisting of primarily military personnel.[42] The current President, Andrés Manuel López Obrador, ran on the promise of bringing an end to the 'War on Drugs'. He repeatedly promoted that 'we will fight them with intelligence and not force. We will not declare war.'[43] However, this policy has been met with some earnest criticism, one critic stating that 'his anti-crime strategy barely changes anything, it's not different from that of previous governments, and even accentuates the use of the armed forces for public security'.[44] The law enforcement styles of all three administrations produced the opposite of what they were hoping to achieve, namely increased homicide rates and grave human rights violations.

The combination of these militarised law enforcement policies and the fierce nature of the DTOs has produced disastrous human rights catastrophes, leaving Mexico with a notorious and credible reputation for violence, causing society to

---

[39] Comisión Mexicana de Defensa y Promoción de los Derechos Humanos (CMDPHD), ITESO; Universidad Jesuita de Guadalajara and Grotius Centre for International Legal Studies (Universiteit Leiden), 'La Situación de La Violencia Relacionada Con Las Drogas En México Del 2006 al 2017: ¿es Un Conflicto Armado No Internacional?' (2019) Leiden IHL Clinic Report Series No 28, www.cmdpdh.org/publicaciones-pdf/cmdpdh-la-situacion-de-la-violencia-con-las-drogas-2006-a-2017.pdf; Geneva Academy, 'RULAC – Mexico' (*RULAC*, 3 April 2020) www.rulac.org/browse/countries/mexico#collapse1accord.

[40] A Nill Sánchez, 'Mexico's Drug "War": Drawing a Line Between Rhetoric and Reality' (2013) 38 *Yale Journal of International Law* 467.

[41] ICRC, 'Mexico, The "War on Drugs"', https://casebook.icrc.org/case-study/mexico-war-drugs.

[42] Nill Sánchez (n 40) 472.

[43] C Kahn, 'As Mexico's Dominant Cartel Gains Power, The President Vows "Hugs, Not Bullets"' (*NPR*, 23 July 2020) www.npr.org/2020/07/23/893561899/as-mexicos-dominant-cartel-gains-power-the-president-vows-hugs-not-bullets?t=1622454752728.

[44] C Quackenbush, '"There Is Officially No More War." Mexico's President Declares an End to the Drug War Amid Skepticism' *TIME Magazine* (31 January 2019) https://time.com/5517391/mexico-president-ends-drug-war/.

refer to it as a 'war', which as a result has opened calls to recognise the situation as a NIAC.

Proponents of the notion that the 'War on Drugs' constitutes a NIAC argue that the intensity of the situation as well as the complex organisation of the cartels satisfies the necessary criteria for the establishment of a NIAC.[45] By way of analogising the 'War on Drugs' with the intensity and organisation criteria laid down in *Haradinaj*, we can see that there are numerous indicators that these conditions have been satisfied. Traditionally, the command structures of the DTOs were based upon a hierarchy, often related through family, such as with the CDS.[46] This hierarchal structure is reflected in the fact that security forces routinely target high-level members of cartels, in an attempt to bring down the whole DTO.[47] In present times, it is far more common for organisations to structure themselves as a more horizontal, multifaceted organisation.[48] For example, the CJNG has been described as 'much more an ecosystem than it is a vertically integrated organization'.[49] This modern approach is frequently advanced as an argument that DTOs do not have a sufficient command structure to be considered organised.[50] However, as a counter to that argument, if cartels can continue to function and control their members using this approach, then a traditional structure may not be necessary; however, where this horizontal approach results in the cartel becoming so disjointed that there is no longer any coherent command structure, the organisation criterion would no longer be satisfied.[51]

Undoubtedly the strongest argument in opposition to the contention that the DTOs are sufficiently organised is the fact that they are in a constant state of flux. Mexican DTOs have continuously evolved, splintered and disintegrated since the commencement of the 'War on Drugs': whereas at one point there were as many as nine cartels on the go, now the cartels with the greatest relative strength are CDS and CJNG.[52]

In terms of territorial control, although there is undoubtedly a struggle between the various cartels for control of territory, this should not be mistaken for an insurgent struggle over control of territory; rather, the struggle is for control of the trafficking routes.[53] It is true that a lot of the DTOs have control over an area in terms of bribery, and extortion of local enterprises and law enforcement, but that is not to

---

[45] *Tadić* (n 15) para 70.

[46] 'Revealed: How Mexico's Sinaloa Cartel Has Created a Global Network to Rule the Fentanyl Trade' *The Guardian* (8 December 2020) www.theguardian.com/world/2020/dec/08/mexico-cartel-project-synthetic-opioid-fentanyl-drugs.

[47] MT Wotherspoon, 'Mexico's Drug War, International Jurisprudence, and the Role of Non-international Armed Conflict' (2012) 3 *International Humanitarian Legal Studies* 291, 306.

[48] ibid.

[49] 'Mexico's Jalisco New Generation Cartel Blazes a Bloody Trail in Rise to Power' *Washington Post* (10 July 2020) www.washingtonpost.com/world/the_americas/mexico-jalisco-new-generation-cartel-omar-garcia-harfuch/2020/07/10/0666b600-c14d-11ea-b4f6-cb39cd8940fb_story.html.

[50] Nill Sánchez (n 40) 485 and 486.

[51] Caplin (n 38) 115.

[52] CMDPHD et al (n 39); JS Beittel, 'Mexico: Organized Crime and Drug Trafficking Organizations' (Congressional Research Service 2020) 9 and 10, https://fas.org/sgp/crs/row/R41576.pdf.

[53] Nill Sánchez (n 52) 491.

say that the state is totally defunct in these regions.[54] Indeed, many armed groups do not view the complete absence of governance as an asset; rather, they prefer a functioning state which they can manipulate to allow them to continue with their illegal activities undisturbed.[55]

The extent of violence that the cartels have caused throughout the 'War on Drugs' is a strong indication of the weapons and equipment that DTOs have in their arsenal. DTOs come prepared with rifles, pistols, grenades and armoured vehicles.[56] Listed among the weapons used by the cartels are AK-47 rifles, N-PAP M70 rifles, PAP M92 PV pistols, AR-15 rifles, high-calibre guns, grenades and high-power rocket launchers, as well as armoured vehicles.[57]

It is also evident that this weaponry is backed by more than a sufficient amount of manpower to carry out the functions of the cartel.[58] The numbers of cartel members have been matched by the number of police and armed forces that are present to combat them. Indeed, it was estimated at one point that there were 100,000 'foot soldiers' making up the cartels across Mexico – a number that may underestimate the reality, given the discrete nature of DTOs – opposed by 130,000 Mexican militarised law enforcement personnel.[59] That said, due to the high homicide rates and number of arrests amongst the cartels, it is imperative for the cartels to be able to continually recruit new members in order to carry out their operations. There are a number of techniques that have been employed by cartels over the years to gain new members, such as social media and specifically designated recruitment groups. A technique employed by most of the cartels, and arguably the most persuasive, is the promise of safety from the cartel for themselves and their families.[60]

Furthermore, while the cartels have engaged in military-style operations, the attacks that the cartels perpetrate for the most part are brief ambush-style and 'shoot and run' encounters, rather than full military-style operations, which is another potential counter-argument to it being considered a NIAC.[61] However, that is not to say that the cartels are incapable of planning and coordinating logistics and movements.[62] For example, the CDS can point to its operations to help its leader

---

[54] Beittel (n 52) 2.

[55] JM Hazen, 'Understanding Gangs as Armed Groups' (2010) 92 *International Review of the Red Cross* 380.

[56] 'Mexican Standoff: At Least 39 Dead in Mass Shootout with Drug Cartel' (RT, 23 May 2015) www.rt.com/news/261417-mexico-shootout-drug-cartel/.

[57] ibid; C Woody, 'Gunmen Shot down a Helicopter in One of Mexico's Most Lawless Regions' (*Business Insider*, 7 September 2016) www.businessinsider.com/knights-templar-shoot-down-helicopter-tierra-caliente-mexico-2016-9?international=true&r=US&IR=T; E de Cherisey, 'Mexico's CJNG Drug Cartel Adopts Military Posture' (*Janes*, 25 August 2020) www.janes.com/defence-news/news-detail/mexicos-cjng-drug-cartel-adopts-military-posture.

[58] Caplin (n 38) 121.

[59] ibid.

[60] CMDPHD et al (n 39) paras 62, 91 and 120.

[61] M Cawley, 'Ambush of Mexico Soldiers Reminder of Jalisco Cartel's Power' (*Insight Crime*, 14 May 2014) https://insightcrime.org/news/brief/ambush-of-mexico-soldiers-reminder-of-jalisco-cartels-power/; 'Police Officers Die in Mexico Roadside Ambush' (*Al Jazeera*, 8 April 2015) www.aljazeera.com/news/2015/4/8/police-officers-die-in-mexico-roadside-ambush.

[62] Wotherspoon (n 47) 299.

'El Chapo' escape from prison, not once but twice, as evidence of their ability to coordinate and carry out complicated operations.[63]

Crucial to the functioning of cartels, and another factor contributing to their organisation, is their ability to conclude and negotiate agreements. Over time, the cartels began to realise that creating bonds and allegiances would assist them in succeeding with their goals, by giving them greater manpower and control over a wider area.[64]

With the onslaught of violence has come material destruction. Cartels have set cars aflame to block roads, torched businesses which refused to pay protection money to the cartel and destroyed items of the state such as military helicopters.[65] Towns have been wholly deserted as a result of the violence, exemplifying that the violence is not just destructive of civilian lives, but also renders areas uninhabited due to the mass exodus of persons.[66] As a result of the incessant violence, Mexico is suffering a severe migration problem both internally and externally. There are numerous conflicting sources of the number of people who have been displaced as a result of the violence; however, the general consensus is that the numbers range in the hundreds of thousands.[67]

The intensity element provides the most robust argument in favour of the 'War on Drugs' being considered a NIAC, given the ample evidence of violence between the cartels and the sheer gravity of the violence, which has resulted in immeasurable catastrophes. Homicide rates grew by 22 per cent in 2016 and by 23 per cent in 2017. In 2018, homicides exceeded 33,000, with a rate of 27 per 100,000; 2019 was the deadliest in Mexico's recent history, with 35,588 homicides; and in 2020, despite the pandemic, the violence continued near record highs.[68] The only stumbling block to the argument that the 'War' is a NIAC is the brevity and spontaneity of the attacks when compared to other recognised NIACs. For example, in the *Haradinaj* case at the ICTY, an armed conflict was recognised between the Kosovo Liberation Army and Serbian forces as there were daily clashes consisting of 'regular confrontations between the two forces involving prolonged fire for a period of days'.[69]

Drug cartels are similar to insurgent groups in many respects, but diverge in other critical areas. Unlike insurgent groups, DTOs do not wish to overthrow the government, and in fact in many circumstances seek to keep the government in power so

---

[63] Beittel (n 52).

[64] Wotherspoon (n 47) 308.

[65] T Wilkinson, 'Mexico Launches Military Push to Restore Order in Michoacan State' *LA Times* (21 May 2013) www.latimes.com/world/la-xpm-2013-may-21-la-fg-wn-mexico-military-push-20130521-story.html.

[66] J Kryt, 'Fighting Mexico's New Super Cartel' (*Daily Beast*, 12 July 2017) www.thedailybeast.com/fighting-mexicos-new-super-cartel; A Macias, 'Mexican Marines Rained Bullets on Villages during the Failed Operation to Capture Drug Kingpin "El Chapo" Guzmán' (*Business Insider*, 19 October 2015) www.businessinsider.com/afp-el-chapo-manhunt-leaves-bullet-riddled-homes-cars-2015-10?international=true&r=US&IR=T.

[67] 'Displacement Due to Criminal and Communal Violence' (Internal Displacement Monitoring Centre, 2011) 3–5 www.internal-displacement.org/sites/default/files/publications/documents/201111-am-mexico-overview-en.pdf; F Sandoval, 'The Displaced of Sinaloa' (*Insight Crime*, 25 September 2012) https://insightcrime.org/investigations/the-displaced/.

[68] Internal Displacement Monitoring Centre (n 67) 1; *Washington Post* (n 49).

[69] Nill Sánchez (n 40) 482.

that they can be extorted and ensure that their drug trafficking goes under the radar of the state. Taking into consideration all of the above information, there are plausible arguments to be made that the criteria for a NIAC have been met. However, it may not always be fitting to apply the lens of IHL to situations such as the Mexican 'War on Drugs'. The application of IHL to non-conflict settings requires cautious analysis at every step of the process, questioning whether the methodology and assumptions relating to IHL are suitable for those situations which are not armed conflicts.[70] Thus, even though there is an argument to be made that it is in fact a NIAC, one should not try to fit a square peg into a round hole. The common understanding of armed conflict, as enunciated in the Geneva Conventions, is no longer adequate for the analysis of these novel situations on the borderline between NIACs and internal disturbances, meaning that this habitual understanding of IHL would need thoughtful reconsideration if it is to take into account these modern types of hostilities.

B. Internal Disturbances

i. What is an Internal Disturbance?

The category of violence that falls below NIACs are the situations referred to in Article 1(2) of Additional Protocol II (APII) to the Geneva Conventions, those being 'internal disturbances and tensions, such as riots, isolated and sporadic acts of violence and other acts of a similar nature'. It has been noted in the 2016 Commentary on the Geneva Conventions by the ICRC that this is not solely applicable to APII NIACs, but also NIACs stemming from Common Article 3.[71] There is a distinct lack of clarity in this area as to what is meant by an internal disturbance and where the line between internal disturbances and NIACs should be drawn. The 1987 Commentary to APII outlines that

> there are internal disturbances, without being an armed conflict, when the State uses armed force to maintain order; there are internal tensions, without being internal disturbances, when force is used as a preventive measure to maintain respect for law and order.[72]

The clearest definition for what constitutes an internal disturbance was proposed by the ICRC to a group of government experts in 1971 as

> situations in which there is no non-international armed conflict as such, but there exists a confrontation within the country, which is characterized by a certain seriousness or duration and which involves acts of violence. These latter can assume various forms, all the way from the spontaneous generation of acts of revolt to the struggle between more or less

---

[70] Hazen (n 55) 378.
[71] ICRC, 'Commentary on the First Geneva Convention' (2016) para 431, https://ihl-databases.icrc.org/applic/ihl/ihl.nsf/Comment.xsp?action=openDocument&documentId=59F6CDFA490736C1C1257F7D004BA0EC; ICRC, 'Commentary of 1987 on Article 1 AP II' (1987) https://ihl-databases.icrc.org/applic/ihl/ihl.nsf/Comment.xsp?action=openDocument&documentId=15781C741BA1D4DCC12563CD00439E89.
[72] ibid.

organized groups and the authorities in power. In these situations, which do not necessarily degenerate into open struggle, the authorities in power call upon extensive police forces, or even armed forces, to restore internal order. The high number of victims has made necessary the application of a minimum of humanitarian rules.[73]

There are lots of elements that can be taken from this definition which shed light on the classification of internal disturbances. The placement of the words 'as such' is quite significant, suggesting an understanding that the situation is almost adjacent to a NIAC but lies just below that threshold. This is another indicator of the difficulty identifying the difference between NIACs and internal disturbances, given it is not clear just how far below the threshold of a NIAC an internal disturbance must lie before it crosses the boundary line into the application of *jus in bello*.

The 'seriousness or duration' words allude to the protracted element contained within the understanding of NIACs, and although it is not a NIAC, there is still a need for it to be characterised by some degree of seriousness or for it to be for an extended period of time. In respect of NIACs, it now seems settled, albeit with some disagreement, that 'protracted' should be interpreted to mean the intensity of the situation and that duration is not a defining element. This is comparable to the ICRC definition for internal disturbances, given the duration aspect is not required for internal disturbances either, provided the seriousness element has been met. If duration is not necessarily required for either internal disturbances or NIACs, although it is possible for an internal disturbance to exist purely if it is characterised by duration, then the common denominator is the intensity. An internal disturbance characterised by duration but not seriousness has a low probability of transforming into a NIAC, given duration is not considered a defining element for the commencement of a NIAC. However, an internal disturbance characterised by seriousness, and not necessarily duration, has a strong possibility of moving into the sphere of the applicability of IHL if the violence moves from serious to intense. As noted earlier, this 'protracted' or intensity element is therefore a key factor in distinguishing a NIAC from an internal disturbance.

The next phrase worth noting is 'from the spontaneous generation of acts of revolt to the struggle between more or less organized groups and the authorities in power'.[74] This wording suggests that the level of violence for internal disturbances exists on a spectrum, with 'spontaneous' and sporadic incidents being at one end and at the other end, with a greater degree of violence, the 'struggle' between the groups and the authorities. The latter end of the spectrum suggests the situation is relatively severe, though not to the extent that it would satisfy the intensity criteria necessary for a NIAC, again illustrating the struggle of differentiating a NIAC from an internal disturbance, given the ambiguity as to where the line between 'struggle' and intensity lies. It is also worth noting here that the definition relates to groups against the authorities in power, though the Commentary makes it clear that internal disturbances also come under the Common Article 3 NIACs, thereby not eliminating the possibility of no state involvement.[75]

---

[73] ICRC, 'Commentary of 1987 on Article 1 AP II' para 4475.
[74] ICRC, 'Commentary of 1987 on Article 1 AP II' (n 71).
[75] ibid.

This ICRC definition notes that there must be extensive use of police and potentially the use of the armed forces, which seems to complicate the already existing contentious relationship between NIACs and internal disturbances. It has been stated in the ICRC Commentary on Common Article 3 that in NIACs 'the legal Government is obliged to have recourse to the regular military forces against insurgents', emphasising that in order for a NIAC to exist the domestic law enforcement system must be incapable of handling the situation and so the armed forces are required.[76] However, if this ICRC definition for internal disturbances is stating that armed forces may be utilised in such circumstances without it being transformed into a NIAC, then this wholeheartedly goes against what is laid out in the Commentary for NIACs and only serves to further complicate this area.

The distinction between internal disturbances and NIACs is both a legal and political question as states have continuously tried to reject the application of IHL within their territory due to their unwillingness to grant NSAs a sense of legitimacy and leave open the possibility to prosecute the armed groups for their acts.[77] As a result, the lack of an authoritative and cogent definition of what constitutes an internal disturbance has left a cavernous gap in the application of IHL, rendering already arduous determinations of the applicability of IHL even more burdensome. The implications of such an obscurity in practice means that there may well be internal disturbances that could affably fulfil the criteria for a NIAC, but nevertheless remain in the zone of hostilities where IHL is not applicable, due to the inconclusiveness of a definition of an internal disturbance that further buttresses a state's unwillingness to classify it as an armed conflict.

ii. Case Example: Is the Mexican 'War on Drugs' an Internal Disturbance?

In order to exemplify the difficulty of classification when a situation could arguably constitute a NIAC or an internal disturbance, one needs to have regard to the opposing arguments to the contention that it is a NIAC and examine the propositions that declare it is simply an internal disturbance. Regard will be had to the ICRC definition noted earlier, as this appears to be the most comprehensive definition available of what constitutes an internal disturbance. To reiterate, the elements to be considered in this context are: (i) the confrontations in the country must be characterised by seriousness or duration, and must include acts of violence; (ii) the form of the violence must be on the spectrum from a spontaneous act of revolt to a struggle between the parties; (iii) the parties must be more or less organised groups; and (iv) there must be an extensive use of police and/or armed forces.[78]

Firstly, with regard to the necessity of the confrontations being 'characterised by seriousness or duration', as discussed above, the intensity of the situation provides the strongest argument to classify the situation as a NIAC. Therefore, this can be

---

[76] ICRC, 'Commentary on Article 3 Common to the 1949 Geneva Conventions' (2016) https://ihl-databases.icrc.org/ihl/full/GCI-commentaryArt3; D Stephens, 'Military Involvement in Law Enforcement' (2010) 92 *International Review of the Red Cross* 456.

[77] Melzer (n 12) 88, 162.

[78] ICRC, 'Commentary of 1987 on Article 1 AP II' (n 71).

said to be characterised by seriousness, given that it is of a lesser degree than the intensity element necessary to classify it as a NIAC. Looking at the duration aspect, despite the length of the 'War on Drugs' as a whole, it would be incorrect to say that the violence has been continuous and habitual for that length of time, given that many cartels have dissolved and changed since it commenced, as well as the sporadic, brief and inconsistent nature of their 'shoot and run' operations.[79] However, as it only has to be characterised by seriousness *or* duration, the sporadic nature of the acts would not be an issue as the seriousness requirement would have been met. That said, it would be more appropriate to classify the violence somewhere on the internal disturbance spectrum between the sporadic nature of 'spontaneous generations of acts of revolt' and the 'struggle', which would seem to indicate a greater force that is just falling short of the intensity required for a NIAC.

Although the cartels have exemplified many of the factors of organisation, the ever-changing character and splintering of the cartels is an argument that has been put forward to show their disorganised character.[80] Based on the analysis of organisation necessary for a NIAC, which for the most part was satisfied, it could be inferred that these DTOs would be considered 'more or less' organised for the purposes of the internal disturbances definition.

With respect to the use of police and armed forces, the security strategy employed by each Mexican administration since the 'War on Drugs' commenced has been to militarise the law enforcement operations, with thousands of police and armed forces personnel being deployed across Mexico.[81] However, as noted above, the armed forces element has been a key factor in distorting the lines between NIACs and internal disturbances, due to the fact that the ICRC definition for internal disturbances says that military involvement is possible for internal disturbances but the ICRC Commentary to Common Article 3 says that use of the military is an indicator of it being a NIAC. Therefore, it may be best to reconsider the use of armed forces in the classification of a situation if they may be utilised in internal disturbances without converting the situation to a NIAC, while, on the other hand, they have been noted as a defining element of the existence of a NIAC.

Following the definition from the ICRC noted above, there is a very strong argument that the situation in Mexico is an internal disturbance, especially when we consider the intensity aspect that is required, and the 'more or less' organised nature of the parties. However, there is presently no exceptional clarity as to where to draw the line between the end of an internal disturbance and the beginning of a NIAC, thereby making it very difficult to definitely label the situation as a NIAC or an internal disturbance, which may result in drastic repercussions for victims in such situations if the law is not adequately protecting them.

Victim rights groups across Mexico have consistently campaigned for greater human rights protections for victims in their society.[82] Such human rights organisations note

---

[79] Wotherspoon (n 47) 299.
[80] Caplin (n 38) 111.
[81] ICRC, 'Mexico, The "War on Drugs"' (n 41).
[82] L Villagran, 'The Victims' Movement in Mexico' (Wilson Center Mexico Institute, University of San Diego, August 2013) www.wilsoncenter.org/sites/default/files/media/documents/publication/victims_mexico_villagran.pdf.

how the Mexican government has a responsibility to protect its citizens, but it is unfortunately often the case that the government plays alternative roles, of both protector and aggressor.[83] They argue that it is the system itself that is creating the victims and if change is to come about what is needed is a full-scale reform.[84] Indeed, it is clear that the system currently in place in Mexico is not protecting the victims in society. This, coupled with the state's persistent unwillingness to reform, makes it clear that there is a need for evolvement in the area of the law relating to NIACs and internal disturbances to account for the current deficiencies and to strengthen the protections afforded to victims.

C. The Fine Line between NIACs and Internal Disturbances

i. The Suitability of IHL as a Framework to Regulate Situations Caught on the Fine Line between NIACs and Internal Disturbances

The difficulty with delineating the boundary line between NIACs and internal disturbances comes down to definitional matters. The lack of an authoritative definition for internal disturbances and the vagueness of the term 'not of an international character' for NIACs results in a disparity in the theory of the classification of each situation. In the situations falling between the two, it is not the case that neither classification legal framework applies; in practice, it is more often the case that the situation exists on a spectrum occupying both classifications at different times or oscillating between them. On the side of the line where IHL does not apply, fundamental rights may be curtailed as a result of inadequate domestic laws or by the declaration of a state of emergency allowing the state to derogate from certain human rights provisions. In these instances, victims are stranded in a metaphorical purgatory where the law does not adequately protect them.

A potential advantage of a situation falling within the realms of IHL is that the individuals participating in hostilities have the potential to be held liable for a war crime. In internal disturbances, individuals are subject to domestic criminal law; however, internal disturbances may occur in states with a corrupt government, resulting in few or no convictions as the state shields individuals from prosecution for actions which under international criminal law would constitute a war crime.[85] Providing the opportunity for an individual to be held liable for war crimes offers the guarantee that there will be no impunity for the actions of individuals in hostilities. This is extremely valuable for victims who have been at the hand of such atrocious crimes, by recognising the brutality that they endured, which often is the best remedy that can be offered.[86] With individuals being vulnerable to prosecution for war crimes, state forces will be forced to go out of their way to verify that their actions are compliant with IHL, because in the context of NIACs state

---

[83] ibid 8.
[84] ibid 18.
[85] Caplin (n 38) 147.
[86] ibid 153.

forces are permitted to kill fighters so long as they are taking part in hostilities.[87] Therefore, amplified adherence to the principles of proportionality and distinction in IHL would potentially result in a reduction in the loss of civilian lives if individuals were conscious of the fact that their actions could entail international criminal punishment.

However, that is not to say that acknowledging a situation as a NIAC will solve all of the problems. There is an unspoken assumption that because something is officially regulated by IHL it automatically makes it more humane than any other form of hostilities; however, this is not always the case.[88] Firstly, given the fundamental nature of NIACs, NSAs are persistently intertwined with, overlapping and penetrating into society, thereby making it an arduous endeavour to determine whether a person is a civilian or an integral component in the armed group's framework. As a result of the permissibility of the use of lethal force in armed conflicts, albeit under strict circumstances, state forces may view this as a free pass to kill individuals with the justification of military necessity.[89] In order for IHL to be effective, it relies on a state not being perforated with corruption, as a corrupt state could abuse the principles of IHL for its own advantage. Therefore, in instances of internal disturbances, a shift from international human rights law (IHRL) and domestic law to IHL may result in the direct opposite of what was hoped to be achieved, namely civilian casualties.[90]

Despite internal disturbances technically qualifying as 'peacetime' disturbances, the amount of violence that is perpetrated in such instances can be truly staggering, and in certain instances higher than in some armed conflict situations.[91] The most common pattern of abuse in internal violence is undoubtedly the arbitrary deprivation of life, particularly of civilians, by both NSAs and the state's armed forces.[92] In addition to the execution of civilians, torture and cruel, inhumane and degrading treatment are frequently employed on civilians and persons who form part of the opposition as a means of gathering information.[93] Linked to this is the arbitrary detention that is imposed on individuals in times of internal disturbances, where the persons are detained for extended periods of time without the guarantee of due process rights. In addition to all of this, women and children are particularly vulnerable in times of internal violence, not only in terms of being the target of an attack, but also in the impact on their health, education, development and well-being.[94] These heinous crimes call for the enactment and strengthening of the law in order to provide a degree of protection to individuals in such situations.

---

[87] ibid 135 and 136.

[88] C af Jochnick and R Normand, 'The Legitimation of Violence: A Critical History of the Laws of War' (1994) 35 *Harvard International Law Journal* 49, 50.

[89] Caplin (n 38) 50.

[90] ibid 136.

[91] M Harroff-Tavel, 'Violence and Humanitarian Action in Urban Areas: New Challenges, New Approaches' (2010) 92 *International Review of the Red Cross* 336.

[92] Minimum humanitarian standards: analytical report of the Secretary-General submitted pursuant to Commission on Human Rights Resolution 1997/21, UN Doc E/CN.4/1998/87 (5 January 1998) 8 and 9.

[93] ibid.

[94] ibid.

IHRL applies in all instances of the use of force in peacetime; therefore, it may not be appropriate to apply IHL if this would mean that civilians could in certain circumstances be lawfully attacked.[95] As will be discussed below, a more appropriate solution may be to stipulate a set of rules that would incorporate elements of both IHL and IHRL and would be applicable in all circumstances, including internal disturbances. Regardless of the approach taken, the incoherent definitions of both NIACs and internal disturbances call for reform, as the current stance of IHL fails to take into account the modern realities of hostilities where a situation cannot fit neatly into a NIAC or an internal disturbance, but instead lies somewhere on the spectrum between the two.

ii. A New Definition for Internal Disturbances

In order to overcome the problem with the fine line between NIACs and internal disturbances, greater clarity is needed on the exact parameters of when an internal disturbance ends and when a NIAC begins. The description of internal disturbances in APII is intentionally vague, and when coupled with the equally ambiguous definition of a 'conflict not of an international character' it is clear that there is ample scope for situations to fall in the grey zone between the two. A possible solution to this issue would be to shift the focus to when an internal disturbance ends rather than focusing on meeting the criteria for when a NIAC begins. At first glance, one could argue that determining the end of an internal disturbance and the beginning of a NIAC is the same thing. However, there is indeed a difference and this difference is why there remains cases which overlap both categories.

Where there are credible arguments to be made that the criteria for a NIAC and an internal disturbance are both satisfied, arguably an internal disturbance could persist indefinitely. However, if a definition were to say that beyond a certain specified point an internal disturbance is converted into a NIAC, it would help to alleviate the distorted situation where hostilities can fall on either side of the line. Of course, it is acknowledged that an internal disturbance may just naturally come to an end without ever evolving into a NIAC; however, the purpose of using this new angle for a definition would be to account for those situations that are characterised by such an intensity that they affably could be a NIAC but are still considered an internal disturbance. To best explain this concept, we can look back to the example of the Mexican 'War on Drugs'. The situation in Mexico has been ongoing for years and objectively one could argue that the criteria of intensity and organisation have been met, so why is it still considered an internal disturbance? In instances such as Mexico, if there was a definition which enunciated that beyond a certain specified point the internal disturbance would automatically be converted to a NIAC, rather than solely focusing on whether the factors necessary for the existence of a NIAC have been met, this would help to alleviate the ambiguity of the so-called grey zone on the spectrum between the two classifications.

---

[95] Harroff-Tavel (n 91) 348.

For recognition of a NIAC, a great deal hinges on the actual recognition from the state itself of it being an armed conflict. One can compare this to another concept in international law, namely, state recognition. With the declaratory theory for the recognition of a state, the criteria laid down in the Montevideo Convention on the Rights and Duties of States need to be satisfied, and it is only then that an entity can be recognised by the international community as a state.[96] However, there are circumstances where it is possible for an entity to meet the criteria of the Montevideo Convention but nevertheless not constitute a state, due to lack of formal recognition.[97] Similarly, a situation may meet the criteria for a NIAC but nevertheless not be classified as an armed conflict due to lack of authoritative recognition from the state or international bodies such as the UN Security Council. Therefore, given the state is a central actor in recognising the existence of an armed conflict, if the state was aware that certain actions would definitively bring an end to an internal disturbance and convert it to a NIAC, it could refrain from intensifying the hostilities by not carrying out those actions, and this would potentially lower the extent of violence.

It would undoubtedly be difficult to identify what would bring an end to an internal disturbance, and more importantly to get the parties to agree to such a definition, given the inevitable hesitancy of states to relinquish any further fraction of their sovereignty to the international community. However, the stagnation in the development of the law in this area is evidence that different avenues need to be explored, and this is a potential option that could be worth investigating. This novel form of hostilities, where the situation falls imprecisely somewhere on the line between a NIAC and an internal disturbance, signals the necessity for an evolvement in IHL. Indeed, IHL has often developed in response to past catastrophes. Therefore, IHL needs thoughtful reconsideration to update its rules in order to regulate and account for this modern-day type of fighting.[98]

III. REVIVAL OF THE CONCEPT OF 'FUNDAMENTAL STANDARDS OF HUMANITY'

It is, of course, important to generate some precision in this area for the purposes of legal clarity; however, the most pressing impetus for coherency in this area must be the protection of victims. In this legal state of limbo that exists between NIACs and internal disturbances, the protection that victims are afforded can be radically curtailed for a number of reasons, such as corruption of governments or derogations from human rights norms. Over the years, a concept known as 'minimum humanitarian standards' which later evolved into 'fundamental standards of humanity' was developed to try and rectify this issue for the benefit of individuals caught in the entanglement between NIACs and internal disturbances. The general idea behind the notion of fundamental standards of humanity is that there should be a degree

[96] J Crawford, *Brownlie's Principles of Public International Law*, 9th edn (Oxford, Oxford University Press, 2019) 135.
[97] J Vidmar, 'The Concept of the State and Its Right of Existence' (2015) 4 *Cambridge Journal of International and Comparative Law* 549.
[98] A Henriksen, *International Law*, 2nd edn (Oxford, Oxford University Press, 2019) 280.

of humanitarian protection afforded to all persons at all times, including internal disturbances.[99] If IHRL instruments were always universally applied and respected, it is possible that there would not be a need for a declaration such as the fundamental standards of humanity. However, what this concept seeks to achieve is to raise situations where IHRL and IHL protections are curtailed up to the same level of protection afforded where these instruments are complied with. The fundamental standards of humanity are not stating that the existing human rights norms are ineffective, but rather saying that their applicability is not always adequate, and by creating a non-derogable instrument that encapsulates the effectiveness of the core existing human rights norms, as well as potential new norms focused towards modern hostilities, it would further enhance the protection already in place.

A. History and Development of Fundamental Standards of Humanity

Talk around minimum humanitarian standards arose in the midst of the 1977 Diplomatic Conference that resulted in the two Additional Protocols to the Geneva Conventions. A few years after the adoption of the Additional Protocols, Theodore Meron, a prominent spearhead in the development of minimum humanitarian standards, wrote about the 'inadequate reach of humanitarian and human rights law and the need for a new instrument' when it came to the problems surrounding protections afforded to individuals in internal disturbances.[100] He commended the progress achieved by the 1977 Protocols, but noted that the 'exceedingly high level' of applicability of the Protocols meant that the 'prospects for the formal application of the Protocol … [were] poor'.[101] There remained a lacuna in the law in circumstances where the state refused to acknowledge the existence of an armed conflict or had derogated from a large number of human rights instruments, or where the tensions did not reach the threshold of armed conflict.[102]

In the aftermath of the Conference, suggestions were put forward to create

> a short, simple and modest instrument to state an irreducible and non-derogable core of human rights that must be applied at a minimum in situations of internal strife and violence (even of low intensity) that are akin to armed conflicts, even though the government concerned contests the armed character of the conflict.[103]

Meron suggested that such a declaration, 'which would not require formal accession or ratification by states', would prevent a 'twilight zone' where there is a dispute in the applicable law.[104] The discussion was geared towards four primary areas where it was thought that there was not adequate protection: (i) the non-ratification

---

[99] T Meron, 'On the Inadequate Reach of Humanitarian and Human Rights Law and the Need for a New Instrument' (1983) 77 *American Journal of International Law* 589, 604.

[100] ibid.

[101] Meron (n 99) 599, cited in E Crawford, 'Road to Nowhere? The Future for a Declaration on Fundamental Standards of Humanity' (2012) 3 *International Humanitarian Legal Studies* 43, 51.

[102] Meron (n 99) 603 in Crawford (n 101) 51.

[103] A Schüller, 'Fundamental Standards of Humanity – Still a Useful Attempt of an Expired Concept?' (2010) 14 *International Journal of Human Rights* 744, 747; Meron (n 99) 604.

[104] Meron (n 99) 603; Crawford (n 101) 51.

of the relevant instruments of international law; (ii) the possibility of derogating from human rights guaranteed by relevant international treaties; (iii) the threshold of applicability of international humanitarian law; and (iv) the problem of NSAs.[105]

Following on from this, the International Law Association produced the Paris Declaration, which set out a number of minimum human rights standards applicable in cases of states of emergency, which provided valuable guidance for the future development of a framework on minimum humanitarian standards.[106] The ICRC then created a Code of Conduct laying out the non-derogable 'hard core' of human rights which apply in all situations. Gasser, the publisher of this Code of Conduct, argued that Common Article 3 forms part of customary law and therefore applies not only in every armed conflict, but also in internal disturbances and tensions.[107] It was not intended for this Code to provide legitimacy to those at which it is aimed, but merely to pronounce the principles that must be respected at all times, hoping that by taking this approach it would garner greater support from those states that were reluctant to afford such legitimacy to NSAs.[108] In contrast to Gasser's concept, which reiterated and concreted already existing norms, Meron proposed that not only should the already existing norms be included, but so too should those abuses that are not effectively addressed by these existing norms.[109]

As the discussion in this area increased, in December 1990 a meeting was held in Turku, Finland, where a group of experts concluded a declaration of minimum humanitarian standards, also known as the Turku Declaration, laying down standards applicable in all circumstances, including internal disturbances and tensions.[110] The Declaration contains 18 articles, four of which are based on general principles, six are based on principles of IHL and seven are based on principles drawn from IHL and IHRL.[111] In 1994, the Turku Declaration was transmitted to the Commission on Human Rights in the hope of its adoption.[112] However, the Commission decided not to deal with the Declaration but instead call for the initiation of the negotiation of a new instrument.[113] Subsequently, a meeting of international experts, including states from the Nordic Group, the ICRC and South Africa, met in Cape Town to discuss this issue, with the results being presented to the Commission on Human Rights, whereupon the Commission requested the Secretary General of the UN to produce a report on these fundamental standards of humanity.[114] The meeting in Cape Town did not produce any significant results due to the members being unable to decide on the necessity for a formal legal document or the scope of such a document.[115]

---

[105] Vigny and Thompson (n 7) 186 and 187.

[106] RB Lillich, 'The Paris Minimum Standards of Human Rights Norms in a State of Emergency' (1985) 79 *American Journal of International Law* 1072; Schüller (n 103) 747.

[107] HP Gasser, 'A Measure of Humanity in Internal Disturbances and Tensions: Proposal for a Code of Conduct' (1988) 262 *International Review of the Red Cross* 38; Schüller (n 103) 747.

[108] Gasser (n 107) 50.

[109] T Meron, 'Draft Model Declaration on Internal Strife' (1988) 262 *International Review of the Red Cross* 59; Schüller (n 103) 749.

[110] Schüller (n 103) 747.

[111] UN Doc E/CN.4/Sub.2/1991/55 (2 December 1990).

[112] Vigny and Thompson (n 7) 188 and 189.

[113] ibid; Resolution 1995/29, Minimum humanitarian standards.

[114] ibid; UN Doc E/CN.4/1997/77Add.1; Resolution 1997/21 (n 92).

[115] Crawford (n 101) 55.

In 2000, a further meeting of international experts was held in Stockholm, with the results being presented to the Commission later that year, which the Commission took note of in Resolution 2000/69.[116] This pattern of meetings and drafting reports was repeated in the UN for many years, with a current total of 27 UN documents being produced since 1991.[117]

The main hinderance in the development of the law in this area, as with many issues in international law, relates to the sovereignty of states. States wish to benefit from the ambiguity of the law in this area and ensure that the international community does not have the right to get involved in matters within their domestic jurisdiction, in addition to their unwillingness to grant any sense of legitimacy to NSAs when they may be involved. The lack of state interest in the development of this area essentially means that 'the adoption of a document that outlines these fundamental standards is no more imminent than when the issue first moved to the United Nations'.[118]

B. Why are Fundamental Standards of Humanity Necessary?

Fundamental standards of humanity are necessary for a number of reasons. With regard to human rights law, there are three key areas that necessitate an instrument on fundamental standards of humanity. First is the ability to derogate from human rights norms in times of public emergency. States are much more in favour of declaring states of emergency than classifying a situation as an armed conflict, as not only does this mean that IHL does not apply, but it also leaves scope for states to derogate from certain fundamental human rights norms that are ordinarily guaranteed in peaceful circumstances.[119] For example, with the situation in Mexico, President Enrique Peña Nieto's administration enforced serious measures under the 'El Pacto por México', which were not explicitly related to the 'War on Drugs'. Despite protests from the population to these changes, the government continued to assert that the enhanced and militarised law enforcement measures introduced by these laws were necessary for the security of the Mexican people. The implementation of restrictions in times of states of emergency does not necessarily mean that this is an illegitimate restriction on fundamental rights; however, it is in the instances where

[116] Vigny and Thompson (n 7) 190.
[117] Crawford (n 101) 45; UN Doc E/CN.4/Sub.2/DEC/1991/107 (24 October 1991); UN Doc E/CN.4/Sub.2/RES/1994/26 (28 October 1994); UN Doc E/CN.4/RES/1995/29 (1995); UN Doc E/CN.4/RES/1996/26 (1996); UN Doc E/CN.4/1996/80/Add.1 (4 January 1996); UN Doc E/CN.4/1996/80/Add.2 (28 February 1996); UN Doc E/CN.4/1996/80/Add.3 (11 March 1996); UN Doc E/CN.4/1997/77 (24 December 1996); UN Doc E/CN.4/RES/1997/21 (1997); UN Doc E/CN.4/1997/77/Add.2 (20 February 1997); UN Doc E/CN.4/RES/1998/29 (1998); UN Doc E/CN.4/1998/87 (5 January 1998); UN Doc E/CN.4/1998/87/Add.1 (12 January 1998); UN Doc E/CN.4/1999/92 (18 December 1998); UN Doc E/CN.4/RES/1999/65 (1999); UN Doc E/CN.4/2000/94 (27 December 1999); UN Doc E/CN.4/RES/2000/69 (2000); UN Doc E/CN.4/2001/91 (12 January 2001); UN Doc E/CN.4/DEC/2001/112 (25 April 2001); UN Doc E/CN.4/2002/103 (20 December 2001); UN Doc E/CN.4/DEC/2002/112 (25 April 2002); UN Doc E/CN.4/2004/90 (25 February 2004); E/CN.4/DEC/2004/118 (21 April 2004); UN Doc E/CN.4/2006/87 (3 March 2006); UN Doc A/HRC/8/14 (3 June 2008).
[118] Crawford (n 101) 45.
[119] Schüller (n 103) 749.

there is an abuse of the provisions allowing for derogations that there is cause for concern.[120] Any derogation must be strictly required by the exigencies of a situation that threatens the life of the nation and cannot contradict any other non-derogable international requirements.[121] Ultimately it is the state itself that will decide whether the life of the nation is threatened or not, indicating quite a circular system whereby the state declares there is an emergency and can restrict human rights without outside interference verifying the legitimacy of that declaration.

Secondly, in situations of internal violence NSAs are one of the main participants; however, given they are not states, they cannot ratify IHRL instruments and therefore these groups are arguably not legally bound by IHRL and will not be subject to the same international legal responsibility as a state would be for human rights abuses.[122] In situations of armed conflict, NSAs are bound to respect the laws of IHL and can be prosecuted where they have violated it, but in those instances that fall below the threshold of an armed conflict there are not the same international legal implications for NSAs as a collective group as there are for a state. Therefore, it is the responsibility of the state to regulate such individuals, although in instances where the state and NSAs corruptly work together, it can result in NSAs effectively operating above the law.[123]

Finally, there are some areas of IHRL which lack specificity to clearly pronounce what is required or prohibited in times of internal violence, in contrast with IHL, which clearly stipulates what are considered violations of IHL. For example, the right to life is laid out in a number of IHRL instruments; however it has been noted that there is no specific guidance of when an arbitrary deprivation of life has occurred under IHRL.[124] Indeed, there are some human rights instruments which provide greater guidance for domestic policing, such as the UN Basic Principles on the Use of Force and Firearms by Law Enforcement Officials.[125] Therefore, an instrument of a similar nature to these Basic Principles, that explicitly and comprehensively outlines key human rights provisions that are to be applied in domestic law enforcement systems, would be very beneficial for the promotion of human rights in internal disturbances.[126]

With respect to IHL, as outlined above, there are three key issues which necessitate an instrument outlining fundamental standards of humanity. First, determining when IHL actually becomes applicable is a key weak spot; second, the protection guaranteed in Common Article 3 and APII is minimal when compared to the rules for IACs; and third, the ambiguous wording of a conflict 'not of an international character' has left plenty of scope for states to contest the applicability of IHL within their territory. As a result, this means that there are instances of internal violence

---

[120] UN Doc E/CN.4/1998/87 (n 92) 14.
[121] Art 4 ICCPR.
[122] UN Doc E/CN.4/1998/87 (n 92) 15.
[123] ibid.
[124] ibid 17.
[125] UN Basic Principles on the Use of Force and Firearms by Law Enforcement Officials – Adopted by the Eighth United Nations Congress on the Prevention of Crime and the Treatment of Offenders, Havana, Cuba, 27 August–7 September 1990.
[126] ibid 18.

where the parameters of acceptable action of armed forces and NSAs is not clearly regulated.

There have been questions as to whether in fact there is a need for a declaration on the fundamental standards of humanity if it would merely restate already existing norms developed through treaties, customs and cases. In fact, numerous reports on this topic by the UN Secretary General have noted that 'there [is] no apparent need to develop new standards'.[127] One could argue that the fundamental standards of humanity do not change anything and are already being applied in domestic law or IHRL. However, the purpose of the fundamental standards of humanity is not to undermine the frameworks already in place but to bring the situations where such frameworks are not being adequately applied, for reasons such as derogations from human rights treaties and others outlined above, up to the same standard as what is already accounted for in domestic law and IHRL.

Criticism has not only come from states but, worryingly, also from human rights and humanitarian law advocates arguing that despite the fact that they both intend to protect human beings, IHL and IHRL have different philosophical underpinnings and it would not be appropriate to try and encompass the two areas of law under one instrument.[128] It is true that there is a great overlap between a number of IHRL and IHL provisions, but more significantly there is a great divergence, especially in the areas of right to life and detention. Indeed, there has been great discussion and disagreement on the interplay and intersections of IHL and IHRL in recent times (which are beyond the scope of this paper) on issues such as *lex specialis* and which framework is applicable in different scenarios, which is something that would have to be kept in mind when developing these standards. In response to such a criticism, it would appear that the optimal solution would not be to try and conflate IHL and IHRL with one another, but rather to focus on what the two have in common, with an adequate balance between the two to ensure the finest protection. Increasingly over time, the common denominator between the two areas has been the principle of humanity, and this is the ground that should be built upon.[129]

Furthermore, concerns have been raised over the lack of enforcement measures that would accompany such a declaration, especially if it does not establish any new laws but merely reformulates the existing ones.[130] In response, one could argue that it is indeed an issue that there is no enforcement measure; however, the harsh reality is that this is the case for all aspects of international law, barring any potential deterrence from international criminal prosecution. However, the absence of an enforcement mechanism does not mean that these rules would inevitably be disrespected. The persistent narrative around IHL is that it is never respected and is continuously violated; in reality, however, this is not always the case.[131] In addition, many of the obligations under IHL and IHRL are negative rather than positive obligations,

---

[127] Crawford (n 101) 58.

[128] AL Svensson-McCarthy, 'Minimum Humanitarian Standards – From Cape Town Towards the Future' (1994) 53 Rev, International Commission of Jurists 5; Crawford (n 101) 59.

[129] Meron (n 99) 594.

[130] Crawford (n 101) 59.

[131] ICRC, 'IHL in Action: Respect for the Law on the Battlefield' https://ihl-in-action.icrc.org/.

meaning that states would not need to take concrete action to comply with the law but must merely refrain from certain actions.

In fact, there is a great need for an instrument such as the Turku Declaration to bring together both IHL and IHRL.[132] The Geneva Conventions are almost universally ratified, but the same cannot be said for the Additional Protocols and IHRL. An instrument that brings together the core principles of IHRL and IHL in one document, encompassing all of those measures that states have not ratified or derogated from but which would be applicable at all times, including in times of internal disturbances, would be advantageous for those victims caught in the crossfire in situations such as Mexico, discussed above. Furthermore, by their very nature, NSAs are unable to sign human rights or IHL treaties; therefore, it would be extremely valuable if such a declaration left open the possibility for NSAs to pledge their commitment to the declaration, especially in instances of internal disturbances.[133] These grey zone situations are becoming increasingly prevalent in recent times, with the surge in NIACs and internal disturbances. There is thus a dire need for developments in the law to match the pace of the ever-evolving nature of hostilities in these contemporary times.

C. Future of Fundamental Standards of Humanity

Unfortunately, despite the necessity for such an instrument, the discussion of this topic and its place on the agenda of states has petered off in the last 20 years. The last dedicated UN document on this issue was in 2008 and concluded merely that 'the Human Rights Council may wish to keep itself informed of relevant developments'.[134] While the academics' contribution to the development of the law in this area, with the adoption of Turku Declaration, is both important and commendable, the success of a fundamental standards of humanity instrument is unfortunately not dependent on legal scholars; rather, the success is dependent on the willingness of states and NSAs to be bound by, or at least to sign their commitment to, such an instrument.[135] In fact, one could argue that the Turku Declaration is an instrument with no practical influence for those who should be at the centre of attention when progressing the law in this area, namely the victims. Despite the dormant nature of the topic of fundamental standards of humanity, this conception has not expired; rather, it remains a pressing issue that should be at the forefront of states' minds when looking to develop the law, especially given the complicated and unfolding nature of hostilities that presently exist.[136]

The adoption of a legally binding document is unlikely, given the inevitable hesitancy of states to relinquish any (more) of their sovereignty, especially those who

---

[132] Crawford (n 101) 71 and 72.
[133] ibid 64.
[134] Fundamental standards of humanity: report of the Secretary-General, UN Doc A/HRC/8/14 (3 June 2008) 15.
[135] Schüller (n 103) 765.
[136] Vigny and Thompson (n 7) 191.

have not even ratified Additional Protocol II. Therefore, the most likely option would be the creation of a fully elaborated declaration to which states, NSAs and any other interested parties can come together and negotiate, discuss and declare their commitment. While the involvement of parties other than states is not the norm when it comes to negotiating multilateral agreements, that is not to say that it is completely unrealistic. Indeed, the conference establishing the 1977 Additional Protocols allowed the participation of national liberation movements, and the Ottawa Conference, which produced the 1997 Convention on the Prohibition of the Use, Stockpiling, Production and Transfer of Anti-Personnel Mines and on their Destruction, allowed for 'irregular participation'.[137] Therefore, for an instrument such as the fundamental standards of humanity, parties who have an interest in the development of this area should and could be given the opportunity to have their voice heard.

In order to revive this issue, a new approach is certainly needed, as the previous pattern of drafting UN reports has not proved to be fruitful. In the years following the Cape Town Workshop, 'the prototype instrument has progressed through two UN committees, has been dropped from annual consideration by the UN to biennial revision, and has undergone a name change'.[138] Yet, the UN appears to be no closer to an agreed upon and accepted instrument than it was in 1990 in Turku. With the UN seemingly having reached an impasse in the development of this area, alternative options need to be looked at to revitalise the conversation around fundamental standards of humanity.[139] One option that has been advanced is to produce an instrument which would serve as an educational tool and be widely disseminated amongst states, NSAs, international organisations and other interested actors in this field, to ensure greater respect for these rules.[140] While this would be beneficial to raising awareness of these principles and explaining how they operate, in reality an educational tool is far from an adequate solution for what is needed in this area. An educational tool, which parties would not have committed themselves to, will be of little interest to those victims on the ground who continue to be the subject of mass violence. Another possibility that has been put forward is to follow the method of the San Remo Manual on the Law of Armed Conflict at Sea, which was a non-binding document adopted outside of a UN-based mechanism.[141] The Manual swiftly progressed from a theoretical conception to final adoption in a period of seven years, which is a stark contrast to the 30 years of slow progress of the fundamental standards of humanity.[142] To move this issue along, it is possible that by placing responsibility for it into the hands of an organisation other than the UN, could be the push that this topic needs. Organisations such as Geneva Call, who are familiar with the law in this area as well as the process of getting NSAs to sign deeds of commitment,

---

[137] ibid 69 and 70.
[138] Crawford (n 101) 56.
[139] ibid.
[140] Vigny and Thompson (n 7) 186.
[141] L Doswald-Beck, 'The San Remo Manual on International Law Applicable to Armed Conflicts at Sea' (1995) 89 *American Journal of International Law* 192.
[142] ibid 68 and 69.

may provide a more productive option. This would mean that the process would not be strictly limited to those who are state parties at the UN, but would allow for non-state armed groups to sign up to these commitments, as well as those who have not been granted admission to the UN system, or any other interested parties.[143]

The approach taken with the Turku Declaration is that of restating rather than expanding the applicable IHL and IHRL standards, which undoubtedly was intended to restore some faith for those states who may have been reluctant to agree to such a declaration as a result of their hesitance in granting legitimacy to NSAs.[144] However, the potential drawback of adopting such an approach for a future instrument would be that without any change to the existing declaration, there would be no change in states' desire to adopt new measures. The current framework has repeatedly bounced back and forth within the UN system and thus it appears that a change rather than continuing with the existing document is what is needed here. A proposal for a new declaration needs to be revaluated from the perspective of the reality of modern hostilities and with the intention of getting parties to agree to it without jeopardising the purpose for which it was intended. Redrafting the declaration, with the help of not only states but also international organisations, NSAs and organisations like Geneva Call, may provide for a more well-rounded and holistic approach that takes each of the potential parties' interests into account. Inviting all parties with an interest in internal disturbances may make them more inclined to cooperate with an instrument which they helped to enact. While the work of the academics at Turku, Cape Town and elsewhere is praiseworthy and has undoubtedly assisted in moving this area forward, it is imperative that not only academics but those who are directly involved in internal disturbances have their say on what they believe a declaration on fundamental standards of humanity should look like for such an instrument to be even remotely successful.

Although criticism has been levelled at the effectiveness of IHL and IHRL, and whether in fact an additional instrument is merely another 'piece of paper', the central focus around the implementation of such measures must always be the victims and those individuals who are most vulnerable in situations of internal disturbances. Therefore, if an additional instrument can provide even a minute degree of extra protection for these individuals, it is surely better than none at all.[145]

IV. CONCLUSION

Throughout history, the central focus of IHL was continuously placed upon IACs – with good reason, given their prominence as the predominant form of conflict. In recent years, however, hostilities have shifted principally to NIACs and internal disturbances, which, as a result, have been accompanied by numerous situations falling into the grey zone on the spectrum between NIACs and internal disturbances. Unfortunately, as IHL has developed over the years, internal disturbances have

---

[143] Crawford (n 101) 69 and 70.
[144] ibid 69.
[145] ibid 71.

seemed to slip below the radar, with the sole focus being placed on meeting the criteria to be considered an armed conflict rather than emphasising and showcasing those instances where the criteria for the existence of a NIAC have not been met. However, in order to determine when IHL applies, it is also necessary to consider those circumstances where the laws of war are not applicable, for the purposes of the process of elimination. The lack of discussion and uncertainty in this area has meant there are an increasing number of situations where the line between NIACs and internal disturbances is indistinct.

The central question of this paper related to the grey zone that exists in the overlap between NIACs and internal disturbances, and what can be done to enhance the protections for victims in such situations, where fundamental guarantees are drastically curtailed for a number of reasons, including the inapplicability of IHL, derogations from human rights norms or the actions of NSAs. To answer this question, in section II, the conflict classification of IHL was discussed by noting the criteria necessary for NIACs, as well as the definition, or lack thereof, for internal disturbances. The Mexican 'War on Drugs' was put forward as an example to illustrate the difficulty caused by this lack of a definition and the problems with determining what side of the line hostilities lie, especially in situations where there are plausible assertions to be made for both a NIAC and an internal disturbance. It was argued that in order to overcome this shortfall a clear and comprehensive definition of what constitutes an internal disturbance is necessary. A potential angle for a new definition of internal disturbances was advanced which aspires to curtail the difficulties in determining what side of the line a situation lies. This new angle for a definition would place the emphasis not only on whether a situation meets the criteria for the commencement of a NIAC, but also at what point an internal disturbance comes to an end. By shifting the focus to when an internal disturbance ends, it takes into consideration these borderline cases, with a greater reflection not only on whether a set of criteria which determine the establishment of a NIAC have been met, but also the cut-off point of when an internal disturbance crosses the boundary into IHL. Finally, a call was made to revive the concept of fundamental standards of humanity in order to alleviate some of the effects on victims left stranded on the border between internal disturbances and NIACs, where there is a lack of protection to manage human rights abuses.

The golden thread that links the issues of fundamental standards of humanity and the difficulties with demarcating the lines between NIACs and internal disturbances all comes down to the sovereignty of states. Indeed, with the majority of areas in international law where there is controversy for one reason or another, it usually all comes back to state sovereignty. Until states are willing to relinquish a fraction of this sovereignty for the benefit of victims caught in the grey zone, progression and development in this area will be unsuccessful. Therefore, in order to advance *jus in bello* and force it to maintain pace with these modern constructions of hostilities, what is required is greater cooperation between states, lawmakers, non-governmental organisations, international organisations, the academic community and any other interested parties, and a willingness to negotiate a new framework for this area of law.

The final words shall be left to the esteemed Hersch Lauterpacht, who noted the fundamental underpinnings of IHL, which ultimately go to heart of how the law relating to internal disturbances should be developed, when he stated that 'Rules of warfare are not primarily rules governing the technicalities and artifices of a game. They have evolved or have been expressly enacted for the protection of actual or potential victims of war.'[146] Therefore, at the forefront of the development of the law in this area must persistently be the protection of victims on the fine line between NIACs and internal disturbances.

[146] H Lauterpacht, 'The Problem of the Revision of the Law of War' (1952) 29 *British Yearbook of International Law* 360, 364.

Correspondent Reports

Human Rights in Ireland 2020

PEARCE CLANCY*

THE NOVEL CORONAVIRUS (COVID-19) pandemic dominated both news cycles and modes of living around the world in 2020, with Ireland being no exception. The virus became the most significant global public health crisis since the influenza pandemic of 1918 and necessitated sudden and severe action from governments in order to contain its spread. In Ireland, these powers emanated from several legislative provisions, beginning with the Health (Preservation and Protection and other Emergency Measures in the Public Interest) Act 2020 (Health Preservation Act) in March 2020.[1] Ireland did not declare a state of emergency in order to cope with the pandemic, as Article 28 of the Irish Constitution does not allow for such measures outside the context of 'war or armed rebellion'. Rather, the provisions came into force via several pieces of primary legislation, and 67 (as of November 2020) elements of delegated legislation enacted by the Minister for Health.

A report commissioned by the Irish Human Rights and Equality Commission and authored by the COVID-19 Observatory at Trinity College, Dublin detailed the impact of the COVID-19 emergency measures on human rights in Ireland throughout 2020.[2] Amongst the lockdown measures introduced were restrictions on international travel, mandatory wearing of face masks, and restrictions on the numbers and locations of gatherings. This precipitated concern in areas such as freedom of assembly, freedom of movement, freedom of religion and the right to liberty. Rule of law concerns arose with regard to the issuance of regulations; differentiation of the legal status of laws, regulations and public health advisories; and the clarity and timing of government announcements of new regulations.[3] While a number of cases were brought to the superior courts on such issues, they largely remained undecided as of 31 December 2020.

The report also examined the disproportionate impact of the lockdown measures on vulnerable groups. Essential workers with home caring responsibilities were heavily impacted by measures including the closure of schools, with extra childcare burdens being imposed particularly on mothers.[4] School closures also impacted the ability of some children to access education, particularly in rural areas, where

---

* Many thanks to Dr Sandra Duffy for providing invaluable assistance and support during the drafting of this report, and for sharing helpful materials at the outset.
[1] Irish Human Rights and Equality Commission, *Ireland's Emergency Powers During the Covid-19 Pandemic* (2020) 22.
[2] ibid.
[3] ibid 64.
[4] ibid 77.

internet infrastructure is weakest.[5] Travellers and persons living in Direct Provision were harshly impacted by both the pandemic itself and the lockdown measures.

I. HUMAN RIGHTS IN THE SUPERIOR COURTS

A. *Friends of the Irish Environment v Government of Ireland*

On 31 July 2020, the Supreme Court rendered its decision in the 'leapfrog appeal' from the High Court of *Friends of the Irish Environment v Government of Ireland* (*FIE v Government*),[6] a landmark case which attracted considerable national[7] and global attention.[8] The issue before the Supreme Court concerned 'whether the Government of Ireland … has acted unlawfully and in breach of rights in the manner in which it has adopted a statutory plan for tackling climate change'.[9]

In the High Court in 2019, the applicants, Friends of the Irish Environment (FIE), contended that the government's National Mitigation Plan (the Plan) failed to meet the standards of the Constitution and European Convention on Human Rights (the Convention), and that the Plan was ultra vires the relevant legislation. The purpose of the Plan, adopted under the Climate Action and Low Carbon Development Act 2015, was to facilitate the transition to a low carbon, climate resilient and environmentally sustainable economy by the end of 2050.[10] FIE objected that the Plan committed to an increase in carbon emissions, as opposed to a decrease, in the immediate future. Thus, FIE argued that even if the target of zero net emissions was to be achieved by 2050 pursuing this strategy, such an approach would nonetheless contribute to a greater global volume in emissions by the same year.[11]

Thus, FIE alleged that the Plan failed to vindicate both constitutional and Convention rights. Namely, FIE relied on the constitutional rights to life, bodily autonomy[12] and a third, unenumerated right to an environment consistent with

---

[5] ibid 80.
[6] [2020] IESC 49.
[7] See, inter alia, R Kennedy, M O'Rourke and C Roddy-Mullineaux, 'When Is a Plan Not a Plan? The Supreme Court Decision in "Climate Case Ireland"' (2020) 27(2) *Irish Planning & Environmental Law Journal* 60; Á Ryall, 'Climate Case Ireland: Implications of the Supreme Court Judgement' (2020) 27(3) *Irish Planning & Environmental Law Journal* 106; see also O Kelleher, 'The Supreme Court of Ireland's Decision in Friends of the Irish Environment v Government of Ireland ("Climate Case Ireland")' (*EJIL:Talk!*, 9 September 2020) www.ejiltalk.org/the-supreme-court-of-irelands-decision-in-friends-of-the-irish-environment-v-government-of-ireland-climate-case-ireland/.
[8] See, eg P Alston, V Adelmant and M Blainey, 'Litigating Climate Change in Ireland' (2020) New York University School of Law Public Policy and Legal Theory Paper Series Working Paper No 20-19; see also, following the Supreme Court's decision, V Adelmant, P Alston and M Blainey, 'Courts, Climate Action and Human Rights: Lessons from the *Friends of the Irish Environment v Ireland* Case' (2021) https:// papers.ssrn.com/sol3/papers.cfm?abstract_id=3855759.
[9] [2020] IESC 49, para 1.1.
[10] ibid para 4.1.
[11] ibid para 4.3.
[12] ibid para 5.3.

human dignity.[13] FIE further advanced arguments on the Convention right to life under Article 2, and the right to respect for private and family life under Article 8,[14] which the state is required to respect pursuant to the European Convention on Human Rights Act 2003. In addition, FIE argued that the Plan was ultra vires – in other words, that it failed to meet the standards set out in the Act.[15]

The applicants' claims were ultimately unsuccessful in the High Court, wherein MacGrath J refused all reliefs sought by FIE.[16] In reaching this determination, the trial judge concluded that FIE had failed to establish a breach of Articles 2 and 8,[17] that the underlying contestation regarded matters of policy and was thus outside the legitimate remit of the judiciary,[18] and finally that the contents of the Plan were within the margin of appreciation enjoyed by the government and was thus intra vires.[19] Nonetheless, it is of note that the learned judge accepted 'for the purposes of this case' that there is an unenumerated right to an environment consistent with human dignity, albeit that such a right was not breached by the Plan.[20]

In the Supreme Court, Clarke CJ prioritised the vires issues, before turning to the issues of standing and the alleged unenumerated – or derived – right to a healthy environment. The Court interrogated the correct interpretation of the Act, specifically section 4, which stipulates that the overriding requirement of a national mitigation plan is that it must, in accordance with section 4(2)(a), 'specify the manner in which it is proposed to achieve the national transition objective', ie the transition by 2050 to a 'low carbon, climate resilient and environmentally sustainable economy'.[21]

The government contended that the Act was a matter of policy and was therefore not justiciable.[22] However, the Court held that

> where the legislation requires that a plan formulated under its provisions does certain things, then the law requires that a plan complies with those obligations and the question of whether a plan actually does comply with the statute in such regard is a matter of law rather than a matter of policy.[23]

Having decided this, the Court then explored whether the level of specificity displayed in the Plan met that which was mandated by the Act. It concluded that there was 'a clear present statutory obligation on the Government, in formulating a plan, to at least give some realistic level of detail'[24] of how the Plan was to meet its

---

[13] ibid para 5.4.
[14] ibid para 5.8.
[15] ibid paras 5.44–5.45.
[16] [2019] IEHC 747.
[17] ibid para 5.17.
[18] ibid paras 5.23–5.24.
[19] ibid paras 5.49–5.50.
[20] [2019] IEHC 747, para 133; see also the judgment of Barrett J in *Friends of the Irish Environment v Fingal County Council* [2017] IEHC 695, para 264.
[21] [2020] IESC 49, para 6.17.
[22] ibid para 6.23.
[23] ibid para 6.27.
[24] ibid para 6.45.

objectives, and that the Plan fell 'a long way short of the sort of specificity which the statute requires'.[25] Clarke CJ stated that he did not

> consider that the reasonable and interested observer would know, in any sufficient detail, how it really is intended, under current government policy, to achieve the [National Transitional Objective] by 2050 on the basis of the information contained in the Plan.[26]

Importantly, in its analysis on whether quashing the Plan in such a way would constitute a 'collateral attack' on the legitimacy on the 2015 Act itself, the Chief Justice affirmed that the Court's decision 'does not carry with it any suggestion that there is any problem concerning the consistency of the 2015 Act with the Constitution'.[27]

Having determined that the Plan should be quashed on specificity grounds, and having dispensed with the vires issues, the Court then proceeded to consider 'the question of the standing of FIE to mount rights-based claims both in respect of certain rights guaranteed by the Constitution and also under the 2003 Act'.[28] The question arose as to whether FIE could be said to have standing to question the Plan under the rights to bodily integrity and life in the Constitution and Articles 2 and 8 of the Convention, despite not being itself, as an incorporated legal entity, prejudiced by the alleged breach of said rights. Despite being personal rights, which are accorded to individuals, FIE pointed out that in some cases, entities other than natural persons have been given standing to challenge on the basis of such rights.[29]

However, the Court disagreed and accepted the government's argument that Irish constitutional law does not accept an *actio popularis*.[30] The question which therefore arose was whether FIE had standing based on an exception to the general rule.[31] The Court observed that 'no real attempt has been made to explain why FIE has launched these proceedings and why individual plaintiffs have not commenced the proceedings, or sought to be joined',[32] and that the extension of the standing rules necessary to hold in favour of FIE would therefore be improper. Clarke CJ accordingly held that FIE had no standing to argue constitutional or Convention rights-based claims.[33]

Finally, despite having quashed the Plan and, moreover, concluded that FIE's rights-based argumentation could not be accepted by the Court on *locus standi* grounds, Clarke CJ nonetheless considered it necessary, in light of the decisions of Barrett and MacGrath JJ in the High Court,[34] to 'make at least some [obiter] observations' on the question of the alleged constitutional right to a healthy environment.[35] At the outset, Clarke CJ expressed his disapproval of the term 'unenumerated rights', preferring instead to refer to such rights as 'derived rights'.

---

[25] ibid para 6.46.
[26] ibid para 6.46.
[27] ibid para 6.31.
[28] ibid para 7.1.
[29] ibid paras 7.2–7.3.
[30] ibid para 7.4.
[31] ibid paras 7.5 and 7.7.
[32] ibid para 7.18.
[33] ibid paras 7.22 and 7.24.
[34] In [2017] IEHC 695 and [2019] IEHC 747, respectively.
[35] [2020] IESC 49, para 7.25.

The learned judge suggested that this terminology more accurately 'conveys that there must be some root of title in the text or structure of the Constitution from which the right in question can be derived'.[36]

In his obiter dicta on the substance of the alleged right, Clarke CJ exhibited considerable scepticism, questioning what the parameters of such a right may be and whether, in a practical sense, it could be said to advance constitutional protections beyond already identified rights.[37] Ultimately, Clarke CJ concluded in the negative, with the learned judge observing 'the asserted right to a healthy environment to be an either unnecessary addition (if it does not go beyond the right to life and the right to bodily integrity) or to be impermissibly vague (if it does)'.[38] Clarke CJ thus denied that a right to a healthy environment – or, formulated another way, a right to an environment consistent with human dignity – could be derived from the Constitution.[39]

B. *Damache v Minister for Justice, Equality and Law Reform*

On 14 October 2020, the Supreme Court handed down the judgment of Dunne J in *Damache v MJELR*,[40] concerning the power of the Minister for Justice, Equality and Law Reform (the Minister) to revoke the citizenship of naturalised Irish citizens and the procedure by which such a decision may be challenged. The relevant provision – section 19 of the Irish Nationality and Citizenship Act 1956 – provides for the revocation of a certification of naturalisation when the Minister is satisfied, inter alia: '(1) … (b) that the person to whom it was granted has, by any overt act, shown himself to have failed in his duty of fidelity to the nation and loyalty to the State'.

Section 19 continues:

(2) Before revocation of a certificate of naturalisation the Minister shall give such notice as may be prescribed to the person to whom the certificate was granted of his intention to revoke the certification, stating the grounds therefor and the right of that person to apply to the Minister for an inquiry as to the reasons for the revocation.

(3) On application being made in the prescribed manner for an inquiry under subsection (2) the Minister shall refer the case to a Committee of Inquiry appointed by the Minister consisting of a chairman having judicial experience and such other persons as the Minister may think fit, and the Committee shall report their findings to the Minister.

The facts of *Damache* are complex. The appellant, Ali Charaf Damache, was born in Algeria and came to Ireland seeking asylum in July 2000. After failing in his

---

[36] ibid para 8.6; note also the similarity in terminology in Alston et al, 'Litigating Climate Change in Ireland' (n 8).

[37] [2020] IESC 49, para 8.10.

[38] ibid para 8.14.

[39] ibid para 9.5.

[40] [2020] IESC 63.

asylum application in 2002, the appellant married an Irish citizen by birth and was subsequently naturalised in 2008. He received his Certificate of Naturalisation in the same year, along with a letter which alerted him to section 19.[41] Following the publication in 2007 of insensitive cartoons depicting the Prophet Muhammad in a Swedish newspaper, the appellant was the subject of a criminal investigation concerning, amongst other activities, the making of threatening telephone calls.[42] In 2010, a search warrant was executed pursuant to the Offences against the State Act 1939, and the appellant was arrested. The appellant successfully brought judicial review proceedings in the Supreme Court to prohibit his trial on the basis that evidence seized on foot of this search warrant was unconstitutionally obtained.[43]

While the appellant was being investigated in Ireland, US authorities in Philadelphia issued a warrant for his arrest in November 2010. The warrant alleged that Damache was involved in a conspiracy to create a 'terrorist cell' in Europe and was implicated in the attempted theft of US identity documents used by a co-conspirator in Pakistan. US authorities requested his extradition in January 2013, and an arrest warrant was issued in Ireland in February of the same year.[44] Two further important events took place in February 2013: (i) the appellant pleaded guilty to 'sending a message of a menacing character by telephone' before Waterford Circuit Court; and (ii) the appellant was arrested and brought to the High Court for extradition proceedings. The applicant unsuccessfully sought various forms of relief in connection to the latter proceedings.[45]

Nonetheless, the appellant mounted judicial review proceedings challenging the state's decision not to prosecute him on the matters contained in the extradition request, while also seeking a declaration that the relevant provisions of the Extradition Act 1965 were unconstitutional. His proceedings seeking leave brought the appellant twice in 2014 to the High Court[46] and once briefly to the Supreme Court.[47] Substantive judicial review and extradition proceedings, meanwhile, saw the appellant being granted relief,[48] albeit only temporarily, as the High Court's decision was reversed in part by the Court of Appeal.[49] In any event, by the time the Court of Appeal rendered its ultimate decision, the appellant had been arrested by Spanish authorities in Barcelona on foot of an extradition request from the USA. Damache was extradited to the USA in July 2017 and pleaded guilty in July 2018 before a federal court in Philadelphia to materially assisting an 'Islamist terrorist conspiracy' while resident in Ireland in or about 2010. He was sentenced to 15 years' imprisonment in October 2018, with credit for time served in Ireland and Spain.[50]

---

[41] ibid para 2.
[42] [2019] IEHC 444, para 8.
[43] ibid paras 10–11; see also *Damache v DPP* [2011] IEHC 197; *Damache v DPP* [2012] IESC 11.
[44] [2019] IEHC 444, para 12.
[45] ibid para 14.
[46] *Damache v DPP* [2014] IEHC 114; *Damache v DPP* [2014] IEHC 139.
[47] See [2019] IEHC 444, para 15.
[48] *Attorney General v Damache* [2015] IEHC 339.
[49] *Attorney General v Damache* [2018] IECA 130.
[50] [2019] IEHC 444, para 16.

Following his guilty plea, in October 2018, the appellant received a notice pursuant to section 19(2) of the 1956 Act informing him that the Minister intended to revoke his citizenship due to a failure to uphold his fidelity to the nation and the state. He was invited to indicate whether he wished for a committee to be formed, as provided for under section 19(3); however, the appellant never provided a response to the Minister.[51] Instead, the appellant filed judicial review proceedings seeking *certiorari* of the notice of intention to revoke his citizenship and an order of prohibition restraining the revocation, alleging that section 19(3) is inconsistent with the Constitution, the Convention and EU law.[52]

In the High Court, in dismissing the appellant's claims, Humphreys J ruled:

> The legislature has provided for the procedure of an independent committee of inquiry chaired by a judicial figure to report prior to any decision on the revocation of the applicant's nationality. That process should be allowed to continue and indeed to conclude. Accordingly, the proceedings are dismissed …[53]

The appellant sought leave to appeal Humphreys J's decision, which was granted by the Supreme Court as a 'leapfrog appeal', owing to the Minister's concession that the constitutionality of section 19 being conclusively and authoritatively settled was in the interests of justice.[54]

The appellant requested the Supreme Court to declare section 19 to be unconstitutional on the basis that the decision to revoke citizenship was of such gravity that it must be made by an independent body, and that such decisions were only capable of being made by the courts. The committee envisaged by section 19(3), the appellant submitted, was insufficient, and amounted to an unconstitutional usurpation by the executive of the judicial authority to administer justice.[55] The Irish Human Rights and Equality Commission, acting as amicus curiae, rejected the claim that the revocation of citizenship amounted to the administration of justice, and is traditionally considered to be within the powers of the executive, as opposed to the courts.[56] The Minister shared the view that a section 19 decision could not be interpreted as the administration of justice, further noting that the executive's power to revoke the citizenship of naturalised citizens follows from its competence to grant citizenship to such persons in the first place, and that these powers are clearly communicated to successful applicants upon receiving a Certificate of Naturalisation.[57]

Dunne J agreed that

> it has never been part of the function of a court to make a decision in relation to the naturalisation of any individual. It can be seen therefore that from an historical point of view it has long been the function of the executive to decide on issues of naturalisation and it has never been the role of the courts to make such decisions.[58]

---

[51] ibid paras 17–18.
[52] [2020] IESC 63, para 11.
[53] [2019] IEHC 444, para 68.
[54] [2020] IESC 63, paras 7–8.
[55] ibid para 37.
[56] ibid para 53.
[57] ibid paras 56–62.
[58] ibid para 67.

Thus, the claim that the revocation of a naturalised citizen's citizenship may be considered to be within the administration of justice was rejected.[59] Similarly, Dunne J disagreed with the notion that the fact that revocation would necessarily impact upon the appellant's rights – such as the right to remain in the state – renders it a decision only possible to be reached by the courts. The Court stressed that while his loss of citizenship may render the appellant liable to be deported from the state in the future, this would not be automatic, and thus should be seen as 'the making of an entirely separate decision and order'.[60]

Having rejected the appellant's arguments concerning the administration of justice, the Court then heard argumentation regarding whether section 19 afforded the requisite fair procedures to those having their citizenship revoked. Consistent with section 19(3), as noted above, should an individual who has been notified of an intention to revoke under section 19 wish to contest the same, a committee of inquiry shall be formed. Both the individual and the Minister present their submissions to the committee, which then provides a final recommendation to the Minister, albeit one that is non-binding.[61] The composition of such committees are decided by the Minister, although two members must come from the legal profession – with one of these to have 'judicial experience', tasked with acting as chair – and one to be a former member of Dáil Éireann.[62]

The appellant averred that this process was void of any effective independent decision-maker,[63] and was tainted by pre-judgement on the part of the Minister.[64] The Irish Human Rights and Equality Commission largely agreed, arguing that, due to the gravity inherent to revoking citizenship, robust procedural safeguards ought to exist, including, crucially, an independent and impartial arbiter.[65]

Dunne J disagreed with the appellant and amicus curiae. According to the learned judge, the fact that the members of the committee of inquiry were to be appointed by the Minister does not suggest that their independence is in any way compromised. In this, Dunne J put considerable stock in the fact that the chair was to be occupied by 'a person having judicial experience'.[66] However, the Court nonetheless took issue that it was the Minister that was to make the final decision on whether or not to proceed with the revocation.[67] Dunne J declared section 19 to be unconstitutional, concluding that

> the process provided for in s. 19 does not provide the procedural safeguards required to meet the high standards of natural justice applicable to a person facing such severe consequences as are at issue in these proceedings by reason of the absence of an impartial and independent decision maker.[68]

---

[59] ibid paras 67, 69 and 73.
[60] ibid para 70.
[61] ibid para 74.
[62] ibid paras 75–76.
[63] ibid para 77.
[64] ibid para 82.
[65] ibid paras 92 and 94.
[66] ibid para 124.
[67] ibid para 128.
[68] ibid paras 129 and 134.

C. Family Reunification and the International Protection Act 2015

In 2020, the Supreme Court heard a considerable number of cases concerning the International Protection Act 2015 (the 2015 Act) and the question of family reunification, or cases which otherwise address relating issues. The majority of these decisions were rendered in joined cases, and a notable number were 'leapfrog appeals' directly from the High Court.

i. MAM (Somalia) v Minister for Justice, Equality and Law Reform

On 19 June 2020, MacMenamin J delivered the decision of the Supreme Court in the combined cases of *MAM (Somalia) v MJELR* and *KN, EN, SM and YM v MJELR*.[69] The issue before the Court concerned whether MAM and KN, being refugees residing in Ireland who had subsequently acquired Irish citizenship, could avail themselves of family reunification. The primary contemporary legislation governing this process is the 2015 Act, which was introduced to replace the Refugee Act 1996 (the 1996 Act) and related instruments.

Section 18(1) of the 1996 Act had provided that a

> refugee in relation to whom a declaration [recognising their refugee status] is in force may apply to the Minister for permission to be granted to a member of his or her family to enter and to reside in the State.[70]

Eligible family members included spouses, parents of refugees of less than 18 years of age and children aged under 18 years.[71] The 2015 Act, meanwhile, under section 56(9), allowed for a 'sponsor' to 'make an application to the Minister for permission to be given to a member of the family of the sponsor to enter and reside in the State'. Eligible family members included spouses, civil partners, parents of refugees of less than 18 years of age and children of refugees aged under 18 years.[72] Importantly, the 2015 Act includes a clause, section 47(9), not found in the 1996 Act which invalidates any 'refugee declaration or a subsidiary protection declaration given, or deemed to have been given, under this Act … where the person to whom it has been given becomes an Irish citizen'.[73]

The first named appellants in both cases came to Ireland fleeing their native homes and were granted section 17 declarations by the Minister recognising their status as refugees.[74] Both women subsequently became Irish citizens, albeit prior to the introduction of the 2015 Act – ie while the 1996 Act was still in force.[75] Nonetheless, following the enactment of the 2015 Act, both submitted applications for family

---

[69] [2020] IESC 32.
[70] ibid para 5.
[71] Refugee Act 1996, s 18(3)(b).
[72] International Protection Act 2015, s 56(9)(a)–(d).
[73] International Protection Act 2015, s 47(9).
[74] [2020] IESC 32, paras 9 and 15.
[75] ibid paras 10 and 15.

reunification.[76] These applications were refused, with the Minister citing as justification section 47(9), arguing that as MAM and KN were now Irish citizens, they may no longer avail themselves of section 56(9) of the 2015 Act.[77]

MAM and KN brought judicial review proceedings, heard in tandem, to the High Court, arguing that their applications should be processed under section 18(1) of the 1996 Act, not the 2015 Act, and thus the exclusionary proviso of section 47(9) ought not apply.[78] Humphreys J, speaking for the High Court, in considering the meaning of 'refugee' in the 1996 Act (someone outside their 'country of nationality'),[79] nonetheless concluded that the effect of that instrument was equivalent to that of the 2015 Act, including section 47(9).[80] This is because, in the opinion of Humphreys J, based on an ordinary reading of the text of the 1996 Act, 'one no longer is a refugee if one becomes a citizen' of the state.[81] On appeal to the Court of Appeal, Baker J largely upheld the decision of Humphreys J,[82] although he broke with the High Court in holding that section 47(9) may not be retroactively applied to individuals issued with declarations pursuant to the 1996 Act.[83] More substantively, however, Baker J upheld Humphrey J's ruling that naturalised Irish citizens may not be concurrently classified as refugees.[84]

In the Supreme Court, tasked with resolving the question as to whether an individual may retain their refugee status under the 1996 Act after becoming a citizen, MacMenamin J undertook a detailed analysis of the full breadth of the Act. In particular, the learned judge put considerable emphasis on the section 2 definition of a refugee as including

> a person who, owing to a well founded fear of being persecuted … is outside the country of his or her nationality and is unable or, owing to such fear, is unwilling to avail himself or herself of the protection of that country.[85]

MacMenamin J noted that the Minister's case essentially hung on the contention that MAM and KN had assumed Ireland as their new 'country of nationality' and could thus no longer be considered to qualify as a refugee, being in situ in Ireland.[86] However, this was given a short thrift by the learned judge:

> For the purposes of s. 2, that appellant's '*country of nationality*' was not Ireland, but Somalia. The '*well founded fear*' which she had of persecution was from persecution in Somalia, not Ireland. There is nothing in the section to suggest that, by becoming a citizen, and by some metamorphosis, the appellant's '*country of nationality*' had altered to being Ireland. Her '*country of nationality*' was and remained Somalia.[87]

---

[76] ibid paras 10 and 16.
[77] ibid paras 13 and 20.
[78] [2018] IEHC 113; note that IK is not a party to the current appeal; for a helpful summary of the High Court decision, see S Duffy, 'Human Rights in Ireland 2018' (2020) 13 *Irish Yearbook of International Law* 119, 126–29.
[79] Refugee Act 1996, s 2(1).
[80] [2018] IEHC 113, paras 24–25.
[81] ibid para 24.
[82] [2020] IESC 32, para 27; [2019] IECA 116.
[83] [2019] IECA 116, paras 142–44.
[84] ibid paras 105 and 146.
[85] Refugee Act 1996, s 2.
[86] [2020] IESC 32, para 58.
[87] ibid para 62 (emphasis in original).

The learned judge continued by identifying that the Minister's interpretation of the Act resulted in absurdity – in essence, as refugees fleeing persecution in their country of origin, and thus fearing persecution by the relevant state, if it were to be accepted that their country of origin were now Ireland, this would mean that they *ipso facto* fear persecution by the Irish state. However, far from fearing persecution by the state, they wished to bring their families under its protection.[88] Similarly, MacMenamin J noted that throughout the Act, where the drafters sought to refer to Ireland it was denoted as 'the State', whereas section 2 concerns itself with the 'country of nationality', necessarily excluding Ireland.[89] It was accordingly held that an individual may at once be a refugee for the purposes of the 1996 Act and an Irish citizen; however, the learned judge took care to stress that this says nothing as to the function of the 2015 Act.[90]

The Court thus duly reversed the Court of Appeal's decision.[91] Finally, it is interesting to note that in the course of his judgment, MacMenamin J rejected the claim that the legislative intention of the 1996 Act was to incorporate the 1951 Refugee Convention into Irish law. The judge was of the opinion that there are no statutory words in the Act that would lend themselves to inferring such an intent.[92]

ii. X v Minister for Justice, Equality and Law Reform

The decision of Dunne J in *X v MJELR*[93] was handed down on 9 June 2020 following a 'leapfrog appeal' from the High Court, wherein the case was presided over by Barrett J.[94] The issue before the Court was whether 'child', as it appears in section 56(9) of the 2015 Act, ought to be taken to refer only to biological and adopted children or construed more broadly. As noted above, section 56 allows for family reunification requests to be submitted by a 'sponsor' with a view to securing permission for a 'member of the family' to enter and reside in the state. Section 56(9)(d) defines 'member of the family' to include 'a child of the sponsor who … is under the age of 18 years and is not married'. Thus, the question was whether a section 56 application in respect of a minor which is not the biological or adopted child of the sponsor, but for whom they serve a parental function, may succeed.[95]

X, the respondent, is a Cameroonian national and enjoys subsidiary protection in the state.[96] X has two children, living with his mother in Cameroon, and sought to bring them to Ireland. The mother of the children, who does not appear to be his wife, allegedly abandoned the children and left for the UK to pursue an education and live with another man, with whom she has two further children. In addition, X informed his solicitors that while he lived in Cameroon, he suspected that the mother

---

[88] ibid para 68.
[89] ibid para 74.
[90] ibid para 105.
[91] ibid para 106.
[92] ibid para 82.
[93] [2020] IESC 30.
[94] [2019] IEHC 284.
[95] [2020] IESC 30, para 2.
[96] ibid para 5.

of his children may have been unfaithful and could not be certain as to whether he is the biological father of his children. He never sought to verify the biological parentage of the children, as he said that he could not face the reality of discovering that he was not their biological father.[97] Despite this, X has been appointed as the sole legal guardian of the children by the Western Appeal Court in Cameroon.[98] After an initial series of unsuccessful attempts at seeking family reunification under the European Union (Subsidiary Protection) Regulations 2013,[99] now repealed and no longer in force, a final application was made in 2017 pursuant to the 2015 Act.[100] This final application was rejected by the Minister on the grounds that X refused to undergo a DNA test, and so had 'failed to fully establish the familial link between himself and the two minor children'.[101]

In High Court judicial review proceedings, Barrett J held that 'child' in this context should be interpreted broadly. It was noted in particular that 'There is a wide diversity of familial structures and the relationship is not confined (presumably deliberately not confused) by the 2015 Act to a biological father'.[102] Similarly, the Court recognised that 'Instances can arise where a man might for good reason prefer not to know that children whom he has treated as his children are not his biological children' and that the 2015 Act did not require X to consent to DNA testing, and his refusal to do so could not be considered to be a failure to 'cooperate fully in the investigation' of his application, as mandated by section 56(3).[103]

On appeal to the Supreme Court, the Minister's central submission was that Barrett J erred in law in interpreting the meaning of 'child' in section 56(9) of the 2015 Act.[104] It was argued that the omission of a definition of the term in the 2015 Act was a clear legislative choice, indicating that the Oireachtas intended to narrow the meaning of 'child' relative to the 1996 Act.[105] X, in responding, insisted that the Court accept and follow Barrett J's broader approach.[106] It was argued, inter alia, that the text of the Act does not indicate that the Oireachtas intended its operability to be limited to biological and adoptive children, but that 'child' in section 56 should encompass a ward or a child in respect of whom the sponsor is *in loco parentis*.[107] This was asserted to be necessary to avoid situations whereby separate treatment would be afforded to biological and non-biological children in the same household, as well as children of same-sex couples who are the biological child of only one, or neither, of the parents.[108] Acting as amicus curiae,

---

[97] ibid para 7.
[98] ibid para 9.
[99] ibid paras 5, 7 and 12–15.
[100] ibid para 16; note also at para 19 that although the basis for the final application appeared to be confused at the outset, in the High Court both parties agreed that the relevant statutory instrument was the 2015 Act.
[101] ibid paras 16–17.
[102] [2019] IEHC 284, para 1.
[103] ibid para 4.
[104] [2020] IESC 30, para 37.
[105] ibid para 51.
[106] ibid para 59.
[107] ibid para 62.
[108] ibid para 67.

the UN High Commissioner for Refugees urged the Court to adopt a broad interpretation to the question of family life.[109] The amicus stressed that 'child' ought to be 'construed so as to be capable of embracing non-biological children who form a genuine family unit with the qualified person, even where they have not been legally adopted'.[110]

Dunne J commenced by interrogating the legislative history, and thus the legislative intent, behind the 2015 Act. In particular, the learned judge noted that the provisions of the 2015 Act are 'clearly more restrictive than its legislative predecessors'.[111] Dunne J thus quickly came to the conclusion that 'child of the sponsor' in section 59(6)(d) can only be read as referring to the sponsor's biological or adopted child. The learned judge stated:

> I find it very hard to understand how the phrase 'child of the sponsor' can be read as including a relationship of father/child where that relationship is not a biological/adoptive relationship. I accept that that there is now a wide diversity of family structures as noted by the trial judge but I cannot agree with his conclusion that the relationship of father/child is not confined to a biological father in the context of this legislation.[112]

Interestingly, in addressing the concerns raised by X regarding situations where such a narrow interpretation may be problematic, Dunne J remained steadfast in her position:

> I accept that this may give rise to certain anomalies and one of the areas mentioned in the course of submissions was the situation in relation to surrogate children or indeed the children of a partner or spouse of the sponsor who were not the biological children of the sponsor. That there may be anomalous situations is undoubtedly the case but unfortunate though that may be, the fact that there may be anomalous situations created by the legislation does not in my view affect the interpretation of the statute.[113]

The Court then moved to consider whether the Minister erred in requiring X to undergo DNA testing. Dunne J held there is 'no basis for challenging the decision of the Minister based on the refusal of DNA testing by Mr. X'.[114] The learned judge noted that the Minister is duty-bound to investigate the relationship between the sponsor and the person or persons who are the subject of a family reunification application, and that the sponsor is obliged to fully cooperate in said investigation.[115] Similarly, it was stressed that X himself had called the parentage of the children into question[116] and that, it having been established that section 56 requires the 'child of the sponsor' to be biological or adoptive children, a court decision recognising X as a de facto parent would not suffice.[117] Accordingly, the Court allowed the Minister's appeal.[118]

---

[109] ibid para 100.
[110] ibid para 102.
[111] ibid para 106.
[112] ibid para 107.
[113] ibid para 107.
[114] ibid para 116.
[115] ibid para 109.
[116] ibid para 112.
[117] ibid para 111.
[118] ibid para 124.

iii. Gorry v Minister for Justice, Equality and Law Reform

McKechnie J, speaking for the Supreme Court, issued his judgment on 23 September 2020 on the joined cases of *Gorry v MJELR* and *ABM and BA v MJELR* following an appeal from the Court of Appeal.[119] The question faced by the Court concerned whether a non-national spouse of an Irish citizen has a right *ipso facto* to remain and reside in the state with their spouse. It is of interest that in the case at hand both of the non-national spouses at issue had been the subject of deportation orders by the Minister. Before proceeding, it may also be useful to stress that, while Mr and Ms Gorry separated following the initial judgment of the High Court in their case, creating what McKenchie J referred to as 'an element of mootness', the Supreme Court nonetheless proceeded 'given the importance of the issues raised'.[120]

The background to the *Gorry* case is as follows. Ms Gorry is a Nigerian citizen, whereas Mr Gorry is an Irish citizen.[121] Ms Gorry was notified in September 2005 of a deportation order which was made against her, and she was ordered to present to the Garda National Immigration Bureau on 29 September. She failed to do so and instead remained in the state, evading deportation.[122] The Gorrys met in 2006, and were married in Nigeria in September 2009, following advice received from the Immigration Office. In December 2009, Ms Gorry applied for a visa and for her deportation order to be revoked in light of her marriage to Mr Gorry. This application was refused in February 2010.[123] In March 2010, after returning to the state from a visit to Nigeria, Mr Gorry suffered a heart attack, and was advised that he should not fly or return to Nigeria again.[124] A second request for revocation was made in November 2010, citing Mr Gorry's health issues. However, this application was again rejected by the Minister in July 2012.[125]

This decision, which is the subject of the challenge, recognised that the right to family life under Article 8 of the Convention applies to the Gorrys. However, it noted nonetheless that the removal or exclusion of a family member from the state may not infringe Article 8 provided that there are no 'insurmountable obstacles' to the family living together in the country of origin of the excluded member. The Minister concluded no such obstacles existed preventing Mr Gorry from living in Nigeria.[126] Following this, the Minister then considered whether family rights under Article 41 of the Constitution were engaged. Having accepted that they were, the Minister asserted that

> there appears to be no authority which supports the proposition that an Irish citizen or a person entitled to reside in the State may have a right under Article 41 of the Constitution to reside with his or her spouse in this jurisdiction.[127]

[119] [2020] IESC 55.
[120] ibid para 35.
[121] ibid para 18.
[122] ibid para 19.
[123] ibid para 20.
[124] ibid para 21.
[125] ibid para 22.
[126] ibid para 23.
[127] Quoted in ibid para 25.

Regardless, Ms Gorry returned to Ireland in September 2012 without the permission of the Minister,[128] and the Gorrys successfully sought leave to seek an order of *certiorari* quashing the Minister's decision.[129] Having regard to Mr Gorry's health problems, Mac Eochaidh J of the High Court quashed the Minister's decision in January 2014.[130] Crucially, the learned judge also expressed his view that the marriage of a national and non-national may engage a prima facie right of residence in the state.[131] Mac Eochaidh J did, however, stress that such a right is not absolute, may be defeated by a legitimate countervailing policy objective and may not be engaged in all circumstances – citing, by way of example for this last point, 'The couple who marry on a whim in a drive-in church in Las Vegas having met earlier in the evening'.[132]

It is now useful, at this stage, to outline the facts of *ABM*. ABM and his wife, BA, are both Nigerian nationals.[133] ABM arrived in the state in September 2006,[134] whereas BA had arrived in 2000.[135] Having been unsuccessful in seeking asylum, BA was granted permission to remain in the state in June 2007. She subsequently became an Irish citizen in August 2013.[136] Meanwhile, in June 2008, ABM was notified that a deportation order had been made and he was ordered to present himself to the Garda National Immigration Bureau, but failed to do so and remained in the state, evading deportation.[137] ABM applied to have the deportation order revoked in January 2014, and subsequently underwent a civil marriage ceremony with BA in February 2015.[138] The Minister was notified in July 2015 that BA had fallen pregnant.[139]

A formal decision was made by the Minister on 20 July 2015 that ABM was to be deported, and he was once again ordered to present to the Garda National Immigration Bureau.[140] The Minister based his decision on the fact that Article 41 rights are not absolute and may be restricted, and contested that 'an Irish citizen, or a person entitled to reside in the State, may have a right, under Article 41 of the Constitution, to reside with his or her spouse in this jurisdiction'.[141]

ABM and BA were granted leave to bring judicial review proceedings and sought an injunction to restrain ABM's deportation pending the outcome. This application was refused by Stewart J on 4 August 2015, ABM was deported on 22 September 2015 and BA gave birth in December 2015.[142] Humphreys J issued the judgment of the

---

[128] ibid para 27.
[129] ibid para 28.
[130] ibid paras 29–30.
[131] [2014] IEHC 29, para 42; quoted in [2020] IESC 55, para 31.
[132] [2014] IEHC 29, paras 42 and 44.
[133] [2020] IESC 55, para 37.
[134] ibid para 39.
[135] ibid para 38.
[136] ibid para 42.
[137] ibid para 43.
[138] ibid paras 44–45.
[139] ibid para 46.
[140] ibid para 46.
[141] ibid para 49.
[142] ibid para 50.

High Court on 29 July 2016, refusing to quash the Minister's decision,[143] rejecting Mac Eochaidh J's suggestion in *Gorry* that there is a prima facie right to live with one's spouse and expressing the opinion that it needs 'slight rephrasing'.[144] Rather, according to Humphreys J:

> A married couple, one of whom is a citizen, should receive *prima facie* acknowledgement and consideration of their status under Article 41 of the Constitution, but that does not mean either that a deportation decision has to be phrased in any particular way (still less to use terms such as '*prima facie*'), or that such acknowledgment amounts to a right or even a *prima facie* right in any particular case or precludes the deportation of any particular applicant.[145]

Thus, in the opinion of the learned judge, it is ultimately for the Minister to balance the relevant competing interests. In his opinion, this had been done with due regard to Article 41 and was not done in a manner which could be described as unlawful or disproportionate.[146] ABM and BA were accordingly denied their requested relief.

On 27 October 2017, the Court of Appeal issued its judgment on the joint appeal of *Gorry*,[147] the related case of *Ford v Minister for Justice, Equality and Law Reform*[148] and *ABM*.[149] The judgment was delivered by Finlay Geoghegan J. The learned judge made the point that the Minister ought to begin the required analysis by considering the rights of applicants under the Constitution, following which rights under the European Convention should be interrogated.[150] Nonetheless, Finlay Geoghegan J found that the Minister had, in effect, assumed that the content of both was identical, and thus erred in law by failing to properly weigh the applicants' rights against state interests.[151]

Crucially, although the learned judge agreed that the decision of a family under Article 41 to live within the state should be respected, she rejected the claim that such a decision gives rise to any such prima facie right.[152] Despite disagreeing with the trial judge on issues of substance, the judge nonetheless upheld the order of *certiorari* in *Gorry* on the basis that the Minister had erred in law.[153] Hogan J also issued a concurring opinion, putting emphasis on the distinction in content between Article 41 of the Constitution and Article 8 of the Convention, and the failure of the Minister to properly account for this.

In the Supreme Court, McKechnie J agreed with Finlay Geoghegan and Hogan JJ that the Minister had erred in conflating Article 41 and Article 8.[154] The learned

---

143 [2016] IEHC 489.
144 [2016] IEHC 489, para 35.
145 ibid para 35.
146 ibid para 57.
147 [2017] IECA 282.
148 [2015] IEHC 720; [2017] IECA 281.
149 [2017] IECA 280.
150 [2017] IECA 282, para 56.
151 ibid paras 57, 88, 91 and 96.
152 ibid para 76.
153 ibid paras 106–07.
154 [2020] IESC 55, para 127.

judge quite forcefully rejected the Minister's assertions that the Court disregard the difference in language between the two – Article 41 requires the state to 'protect' family rights, whereas Article 8 merely requires it to 'respect' them – and held that 'the relative strength of the protections under the Constitution and the Convention is therefore relevant to the Minister's decision'.[155] The Court instructed the Minister that the 'proper approach' is to begin by taking note of the constitutional interests of the applicants under Article 41, and to then weigh Article 41 and Article 8 against the relevant state interests.[156] On the basis that the Minister failed to do this, and expressing agreement with the decision of the Court of Appeal, the Supreme Court upheld the order of *certiorari* in *Gorry* and *ABM*, dismissed the Minister's appeals and recommended that the matter not be remitted to the Minister.[157]

On a related matter, McKechnie J spent considerable time on the supposed unenumerated – or derived – right of spouses to cohabitate, prompting a concurring judgment from O'Donnell J (as he then was) disagreeing on this point. In the opinion of McKechnie J:

> For my own part, I would consider that it must surely be the case that, as regards two married Irish citizens, a right of cohabitation can be regarded as one of the rights of the marital family protected by Article 41 of the Constitution. I could not regard the right of the married citizen couple to live together as anything other than fundamental to Article 41's protection of the family 'in its *constitution* and *authority*'. The right to live together flows from the protection of the family in its 'constitution' – I agree that such term must be understood, in this context, to refer to the composition, or structure, of the family … I would therefore express the view, though *obiter*, that Irish citizens married to one another have a right of cohabitation which is firmly anchored in the text of Article 41 of the Constitution, in addition to Article 40.3.[158]

That said, the learned judge nonetheless agreed with Finlay Geoghegan J that it is incorrect to describe this as a prima facie right, even though he does not view it to be absolute.[159]

In his lengthy concurring opinion, O'Donnell J expressed concern that the majority's allusion to a right of cohabitation would 'encourage litigation on consequent delay and obstruction of the decision-making process'.[160] McKechnie J's approach, O'Donnell J suggests, 'provides little guidance as to the weight to be afforded to the respective considerations' in the balancing of individual and state interests, an issue exacerbated by the supposed existence of a right to cohabitation.[161] On the substantive question of the existence of a right to cohabit, the learned judge was unconvinced that Article 41 contained 'some unspecified super-rights to be discerned by future generations of judges and limited by equally unspecified considerations

---

[155] ibid para 137.
[156] ibid paras 191–95.
[157] ibid paras 226–27.
[158] ibid para 169.
[159] ibid para 177.
[160] [2020] IESC 55, concurring opinion of O'Donnell J para 12.
[161] ibid para 16.

including the common good and ensuring the integrity of the social welfare system', viewing it as

> an inevitable risk that in good times the interests of the State in the common good will be undervalued and in bad times, when it is perhaps most important to maintain and protect rights which may be temporarily unpopular, those rights may be overborne.[162]

Nonetheless, O'Donnell J recognised that the issue was essentially obiter, as the case fell on the specific manner in which the Minister undertook his analysis. Even so, he contested the existence of a right to cohabit:

> I do not consider, therefore, that I am required to approach this case through the prism of a constitutionally protected right to cohabit, still less one said to be protected by Article 41.1. The judgment of McKechnie J would appear to be the first time this court would hold that there is a general right to cohabitation protected by Article 41 with all that such entails. For the reasons set out above, I do not agree. Cohabitation by a married couple, and indeed by any couple in a committed and enduring relationship is, however, something the State is required to have regard to in its decision making and to respect.[163]

McKechnie J's response, included in the main judgment, hinged on a defence of identifying a right to cohabit derived from Article 41, and the tradition the location of derived rights – 'formerly "unenumerated rights"'[164] in the Irish Constitution – citing the recent example of *FIE v Government of Ireland*.[165]

iv. A v Minister for Justice, Equality and Law Reform

On 8 December 2020, the Supreme Court handed down its decision in the 'leapfrog appeal' of the joined cases of *A v MJELR*, *S v MJELR* and *I v MJELR*, authored by Dunne J.[166] *A* and *S* concern the question as to whether the distinction between pre- and post-flight marriages in section 56(9)(a) of the 2015 Act is repugnant to the Constitution and Convention. Put more simply, at issue in *A* and *S* was whether limiting the 2015 Act's family reunification mechanisms with regard to spouses to marriages entered into *before* the sponsor received international protection constituted unlawful discrimination.[167] *I*, meanwhile, concerned the time limit imposed in section 56(8) for reunification applications, and whether such a time limit was contrary to the Constitution and Convention.[168] Under this provision, applications must be made within 12 months of international protection being granted to the person acting as sponsor.

The facts are relatively straightforward. A is an Afghan national who, owing to the ongoing situation in Afghanistan, fled and was granted asylum in Ireland in 2015. Following this, A married his wife in April 2017 in Pakistan and, following

---

162 ibid para 15.
163 ibid para 62.
164 [2020] IESC 55, para 223.
165 ibid para 223.
166 [2020] IESC 70.
167 ibid para 4.
168 ibid para 5.

the advice of his solicitor, submitted an application for family reunification later that month. This application was refused in October 2017 on the basis that their marriage 'was not subsisting at the time [A] applied for international protection', as required by section 56(9)(a) of the 2015 Act.[169]

A and S, facing effectively the same situation, sought orders of *certiorari* in respect of the Minister's decision, and, before Barrett J, argued that section 56(9)(a)'s limitation to pre-flight spouses constituted an infringement of the Article 41 rights of the family and unlawful discrimination relative to the treatment of pre-flight families seeking family reunification, thus failing to 'guard with special care the institution of Marriage', as required by Article 41.3.1° of the Constitution.[170] Despite the Minister's arguments that the provision was intended only to reunite pre-flight couples, that opening the eligibility up to post-flight marriages would allegedly risk abuse by human traffickers and those entering into 'marriages of convenience',[171] and that the pre-flight restriction was supposedly required 'to comply with the State's international obligations',[172] the learned judge agreed with the applicants and deemed the portion of section 56(9)(a) at issue to be unconstitutional.

Turning to the Convention, Barrett J was confronted by the judgment of Humphreys J in *RC (Afghanistan) v MJELR*,[173] a case decided in the same year, wherein the High Court considered section 56(9)(a) to be in conformity with the Constitution and Convention. Barrett J, however, declined to follow the decision of Humphreys J. The Court argued that because the learned judge in *RC* did not appreciate the persuasiveness of the European Court of Human Rights precedent in *Hode and Abdi v the United Kingdom*,[174] it ought not to follow *RC*.[175] Accordingly, following an in-depth analysis of the findings in *Hode*, Barrett J, concluded that section 56(9)(a) infringed Article 14 of the Convention, read together with Article 8.[176] A and S were granted orders of *certiorari* quashing the Minister's decisions, and succeeded in having section 56(9)(a) declared unconstitutional, with the affirmation that had the Court not ruled as such regarding the constitutionality of the provision, it would have issued a declaration of incompatibility pursuant to the European Convention of Human Rights Act 2003.[177]

I concerned a Nigerian national, abandoned by her mother in 2011 at the age of 10 and granted refugee status in September 2014 pursuant to the 1996 Act. I recommended contact with her mother and younger sister in 2018, and in July of

---

[169] [2019] IEHC 547, para 1.
[170] ibid paras 6–7.
[171] The notion of 'marriages of convenience' was considered in detail by the Supreme Court in 2020 in *MKFS (Pakistan) and AF and NFJ (an infant suing by and through his mother and next friend AF) v MJELR* [2020] IESC 48 (per McKechnie J).
[172] [2019] IEHC 547, para 8.
[173] [2019] IEHC 65.
[174] [2013] 56 EHRR 27; Humphreys J believed that '*Hode* however was decided on certain factors which do not apply here': see [2019] IEHC 65, para 23.
[175] [2019] IEHC 547, para 11.
[176] ibid para 21.
[177] ibid paras 22 and 25.

the same year an application for family reunification was made on her behalf. This application was rejected in September 2018, when I was 17 years of age, on the basis that it was not submitted within 12 months of the granting of refugee status, as required by section 56(8). Hence, I filed for judicial review of the Minister's decision, and was granted leave to appear before Humphreys J in the High Court.[178]

Humphreys J held that I had failed to establish the evidential basis for the claim that the section 56(8) time limit was inconsistent with the Constitution, the Convention or EU law, and further held that the applicant had alternative remedies available to her. Regarding the Convention, it was similarly concluded that the applicant's claim that the time limit was disproportionate for the purposes of Article 8 had not been sufficiently proven.[179]

The questions put to the Supreme Court on the appeal of these cases was thus, following the judgment in *A*, whether the High Court was correct in finding section 56(9)(a) to be unconstitutional and, following the judgment in *I*, whether the High Court was correct in finding section 56(8) to be constitutional.[180] At the outset, however, Dunne J first addressed the decision of Barrett J in *A* to depart from the precedent set by Humphreys J in *RC*. Citing concerns of judicial comity, Dunne J lamented that:

> The problem is that whilst one knows that there is a difference of approach and that the trial judge in the instant cases clearly is of the view that the earlier decisions were wrong, it is impossible to ascertain precisely why that is so. A mere reference to the line of case law to be found in *Worldport/Kadri* is not a sufficient explanation of the reasons for departing from judgments which had been delivered on the same or similar issues just months previously.[181]

Thus, the learned judge voiced concern that Barrett J's decision 'appears to have had the effect of overturning the decision made just a short period before in *R.C.*, creating uncertainty as to the status of the provision affected'.[182] Charleton J issued a separate concurring opinion on this specific issue. Noting that 'there is an obvious draw towards not confronting the reasoning of another judge for fear of drifting into the expression of apparent disrespect',[183] Charleton J stressed that 'a system of first-instance and appellate opinions will undermine itself if law becomes a shifting sand which never crystallises into a legal principle that is generally applicable to all cases over which a judicial decision declares itself to govern'.[184]

More substantially on the question of the constitutionality of section 56(9)(a), Dunne J considered each of the Minister's justifications of the distinction between pre- and post-flight marriages in turn. Regarding the supposed international

---

[178] [2020] IESC 70, para 43.
[179] Quoted in ibid para 54.
[180] ibid para 56.
[181] ibid para 65.
[182] ibid.
[183] [2020] IESC 70, concurring opinion of Charleton J para 4.
[184] ibid para 6.

obligations of the state to do so, the Court expressed frustration that the Minister had not been more specific:

> I think it is unfortunate that the Minister has not explained with sufficient clarity how a requirement to comply with the State's international obligations could justify a difference in treatment between those who married pre-application and those who married post-application without reference to any specific international obligation, such as an EU Directive or any other measure, Treaty or Convention to which Ireland is a party which might create such a requirement ... I am not convinced that the Minister has established this by the evidence before the Court as a reason for a difference in treatment.[185]

Having dismissed this explanation, the learned judge questioned the contention that section 56(9)(a) allowed the Minister to undertake a more careful consideration of marriages entered into after the application for international protection. Dunne J expressed difficulty with this claim, commenting that it is 'hard to see' precisely how the relevant section allows for 'more careful consideration' in this respect. Accordingly, on the basis that the obligations of the Minister with regards immigration control 'are no greater and no less in the case of pre-application or post-application marriages', this justification was similarly dismissed.[186]

Considerably more time was dedicated to interrogating the Minister's argument that the intention of section 56(9)(a) was to permit 'a person who has been granted a declaration of refugee status or international protection the ability to reunite with the spouse from whom they have been involuntarily and forcibly separated'.[187] In this sense, post-flight marriages were asserted to be outside the intended scope of the provision. The Court thus posed the question of whether that distinction was justifiable. Dunne J expressed her agreement with Humphreys J in *RC* on this issue, approving the latter judge's acceptance of the Minister's argument that post-flight couples may be distinguished from their pre-flight counterparts in that 'Persons who marry after the making of an application for International Protection do not have their marriage involuntarily sundered by reason of the persecution or serious harm grounding their application for International Protection'.[188] Dunne J affirmed that post-flight marriages, and thus A and S, 'are not in the same position as a person whose relationships have been ruptured by the persecution which caused them to flee from their country or origin', and thus held section 56(9)(a) to be consistent with the Constitution.[189] This followed into the Court's analysis on the question of compatibility with the Convention.[190]

Accordingly, the Minister's appeal was allowed regarding the constitutionality and conformity with the Convention of section 56(9)(a). Regarding *I*, the Court rejected the applicant's assertion that she was not being held as equal before the law, as required by Article 40.1 of the Constitution, as 'the time limit imposed by

---

[185] [2020] IESC 70, para 95.
[186] ibid para 96.
[187] ibid para 97.
[188] [2019] IEHC 65, para 19; [2020] IESC 70, paras 97–99.
[189] [2020] IESC 70, para 99.
[190] ibid para 106.

s. 56(8) applies to all refugees, minors and adults alike'.[191] Further, Dunne J held that the 2015 Act is not the only means by which family reunification may be pursued, and that 'the State is entitled to have regard to the requirements of immigration control' in deciding and legislating for such measures.[192] The learned judge concluded that I was 'not subject to any difference in treatment by reference to any characteristic that is relevant to an issue in relation to equality such as sex, age, gender, religion or other relevant status', and thus found section 56(8) to be consistent with Article 40.1 of the Constitution.[193] This analysis was largely replicated regarding I's Convention rights.[194]

II. IRELAND BEFORE THE EUROPEAN COURT OF HUMAN RIGHTS

A. *LF v Ireland, KO'S v Ireland and WM v Ireland*

On 10 November 2020, the European Court of Human Rights ruled three cases, *LF v Ireland*,[195] *KO'S v Ireland*[196] and *WM v Ireland*,[197] to be inadmissible. These cases concerned the practice of performing symphysiotomies on women either in advance of or during labour in Ireland from the 1940s until 1980s, during which time a reported 1500 symphysiotomies were carried out. The Court, in *LF*, described the procedure as involving

> partially cutting through the fibres of the pubis symphysis (the joint uniting the pubic bones) so as to enlarge the capacity of the pelvis. The procedure allows the pubis symphysis to separate so as to facilitate natural childbirth where there is a mechanical problem.[198]

The practice was largely abandoned elsewhere in Europe by the mid-twentieth century as Caesarean sections became more common. In Ireland, however, the practice remained until the 1980s[199] due to the dominance of Catholic doctrine.[200] The prevalence of the procedure left a significant number of women, many of whom neither consented or knew the procedure had been carried out on them, with chronic physical, mental and sexual health issues.

Public awareness of the practice largely emerged in the 2000s, including calls for independent inquiries, the introduction of support systems by the Health Service Executive, televised documentaries and a public apology by the Catholic Medical Missionaries of Mary and the Institute of Obstetricians and Gynaecologists of the Royal College of Physicians in Ireland.[201] Moreover, two reports on the procedure

---

[191] ibid para 124.
[192] ibid.
[193] ibid para 125.
[194] ibid paras 132–33.
[195] Application no 62007/17.
[196] Application no 61836/17.
[197] Application no 61872/17.
[198] *LF v Ireland* (n 195) para 8.
[199] ibid para 12.
[200] ibid para 13.
[201] ibid paras 14–17.

and its effects were commissioned by the Department of Health and Minister for Health, authored by Professor Oonagh Walsh of University College Cork and Judge Yvonne Murphy, respectively.[202] An *ex gratia* scheme was introduced in July 2014 offering compensation to women who had undergone symphysiotomies or pubiotomies between 1940 and 1990. The scheme was administered by Judge Harding Clark, who also produced a report on its operation.[203]

In outlining the inadmissibility ruling in the present case, it is important also to note the complex and winding domestic litigation in *Kearney v McQuillan and North Eastern Health Board*.[204] Kearney, who had been subjected to a non-consensual symphysiotomy in 1969 immediately *after* her child was born, was refused relief by Dunne J in the High Court on the basis that there was a 'real and serious risk of an unfair trial', and that the delay between the procedure and the litigation was such that the proceedings were unduly prejudicial against the hospital. This was due to the fact that many of the personnel concerned, including the consultant gynaecologist, were either deceased or their whereabouts were otherwise unknown.[205] On appeal, to avoid her claim being struck out, the applicant reformulating to argue that 'the principal issue was that there had been no justification whatsoever for the performance of a symphysiotomy following delivery by caesarean section'.[206] The Supreme Court accepted this reformulation and affirmed that this removed the risk of prejudice.[207] Kearney was successful following her return to the High Court, which concluded that there was no reasonable justification for the symphysiotomy. Thus, expressing alarm that 'It is disturbing to consider how close this victim of grave medical malpractice came to being sacrificed on the altar of fair procedures', Ryan J granted the applicant €450,000 in damages.[208] In the Supreme Court, MacMenamin J reduced this figure to €325,000.[209]

The substantive reasoning of the three cases at hand is included in the decision of *LF*, and will be focused on here.[210] LF was admitted to Coombe Hospital in Dublin on 18 September 1963, by which point her baby was apparently overdue.[211] Owing to a narrow sub-pubic arch, it was concluded that the foetus's 'head could not be made to engage in the pelvis', and a symphysiotomy was performed.[212] The applicant's daughter was born 12 days after the symphysiotomy, by which point

---

[202] ibid paras 18–19 and 52–71.
[203] ibid paras 20 and 72–87.
[204] [2006] IEHC 186; [2010] IESC 20; [2012] IEHC 127; [2012] IESC 43.
[205] *LF v Ireland* (n 195) para 22.
[206] ibid para 23.
[207] ibid para 24.
[208] [2012] IEHC 127, paras 84–85.
[209] *LF v Ireland* (n 195) para 26.
[210] For crucial analyses of these cases, see, inter alia, M Enright, 'Symphysiotomies and an Overlooked Violation of Article 3 ECHR' (*Irish Centre for Human Rights Blog*, 21 December 2020) https://ichrgalway.wordpress.com/2020/12/21/symphysiotomies-and-an-overlooked-violation-of-article-3-echr/; C O'Mahony, 'The Irish Symphysiotomy Cases in the ECtHR: Focusing on Procedure to the Exclusion of Substance' (*Durham University Obstetric Violence Blog*, 20 April 2021) www.durham.ac.uk/research/institutes-and-centres/ethics-law-life-sciences/about-us/news/obstetric-violence-blog/the-irish-symphysiotomy-cases-in-the-ecthr/.
[211] *LF v Ireland* (n 195) para 4.
[212] ibid paras 5–6.

LF had not yet recovered from the procedure, and was thus 'physically unable to look after her daughter and had to rely on friends and relatives for assistance. As a consequence, the applicant claimed that she was unable to bond with her.'[213] Issues continued into the future, including back and hip pain, urinary incontinence and psychological problems. As she was not informed that a symphysiotomy was performed, this was attributed to 'normal complications of childbirth'.[214]

LF became aware that these issues may have been due to a symphysiotomy after a friend saw a televised documentary on the subject.[215] She sought relief in the High Court, but, to avoid her claim being struck out, agreed to limit her claim to there being no justification for the performance of the symphysiotomy, following the precedent in *Kearney*.[216] Despite agreeing to this limitation, the trial judge was not convinced, and in May 2015 the High Court held against the applicant.[217] The applicant similarly failed in the Court of Appeal, wherein the Court sought to distinguish her case from *Kearney*, noting that in the latter case the symphysiotomy was unjustifiable as the child had already been born, which was not the case for LF.[218] A further attempt to appeal to the Supreme Court was denied,[219] and LF did not apply to the *ex gratia* payment scheme, believing that 'there was no possibility of any acknowledgement of a breach of her rights; the quantity of the awards did not reflect the gravity of the harm inflicted on her; and the application window was unreasonably short'.[220]

In the European Court of Human Rights, LF claimed that, due to the Supreme Court decision in *Kearney*, she was precluded from making any complaint to the Irish courts, being effectively required to limit her claim to the lack of justification for her symphysiotomy, and that this breached Articles 3 and 8 of the Convention, read in conjunction with Article 13.[221] Similarly, it was argued that Article 3 was breached in its procedural aspect due to the state's failure to conduct an independent and thorough investigation into the practice of symphysiotomies.[222]

The Court proceeded on the basis that the applicant's reformulation of her claims in the Irish courts, and the fact that she did not apply under the *ex gratia* payment scheme, did not mean that she had failed to exhaust all domestic remedies.[223] Commenting on the manner in which the applicant was advised to reformulate her claim, the Court held that:

> On the basis of the material available, the position adopted by the Irish courts was one which had been reasonably open to them when faced with the difficult task of balancing the plaintiff's right of access to court in relation to a medical procedure performed several

---

[213] ibid para 9.
[214] ibid para 10.
[215] ibid para 27.
[216] ibid para 29.
[217] ibid para 33.
[218] ibid para 37.
[219] ibid para 40.
[220] ibid para 42.
[221] ibid para 91.
[222] ibid para 92.
[223] ibid paras 100 and 112.

decades previously against the defendant's right to a fair trial ... As such, by virtue of the fact of hearing the applicant's reformulated claim alone the Contracting State cannot be said to have exceeded the margin of appreciation afforded to it in ensuring that its positive obligation under Article 8 of the Convention was met.[224]

Emphasis was put on the fact that LF did not 'call into question the adequacy of the formulated and narrower basis on which she had decided to pursue her claim following the Supreme Court judgement in *Kearney*', putting forward the belief that, if LF objected to this, 'it was open to her, and indeed incumbent on her, to challenge this' at the time.[225]

The Court similarly expressed its reluctance to break with the findings of the domestic courts with regard to the legitimacy of the practice. It held that:

> In the applicant's case, as noted previously, the High Court found that the practice of prophylactic symphysiotomy in 1963 was not a practice without justification and that such a procedure without trial of labour was a reasonable although limited option. This assessment was endorsed by the Court of Appeal, which noted that the procedure was performed for a range of clinical reasons which at the time were approved by those at the very top of the obstetric profession in the respondent State ... it is not possible ... to refute the domestic courts' position in relation to the standards of practice and medicine in the respondent State at the relevant time and as regards the justification or therapeutic necessity for the procedure in the applicant's case.[226]

The state's views were similarly adopted with regard to the question of the alleged failure to undertake an independent and thorough inquiry. The Court found no reason to doubt the independence of the report authored by Professor Walsh,[227] and noted that the review overseen by Judge Yvonne Murphy led to the introduction of the *ex gratia* payment scheme.[228] Taking heed of the fact that Judge Harding Clark's report on the operation of said scheme was 'met with considerable ire by many women who had undergone the procedure and was criticised by the Commissioner for Human Rights [of the Council of Europe] for its "patronising tone"',[229] the Court nonetheless declined to query whether it was appropriate with regard to Ireland's obligations under the Convention.

The Court thus held that the complaint was inadmissible, offering the following as its conclusion:

> Nevertheless, in the present case, it would now be next to impossible for the domestic courts to conduct any meaningful – and, from the point of view of the defendant hospital, fair – inquiry into whether in her case the symphysiotomy had been performed with her full and informed consent. In these circumstances, where the actions complained of were not directly attributable to the State or to any of its agents, and were demonstrated not to have been carried out in bad faith or to have been unjustified by the relevant practice standards, the Court considers that in the particular circumstances of this case the civil proceedings,

---

[224] ibid para 114.
[225] ibid para 116.
[226] ibid para 118.
[227] ibid para 120.
[228] ibid paras 121–22.
[229] ibid para 124.

supplemented by the independent Walsh report, the *ex gratia* payment scheme, which enabled all the women who had undergone a symphysiotomy to obtain a not inconsequential award of compensation, and the provision of access, free of charge, to healthcare and individual pathways of care, sufficed to meet any obligation the State may have been under to provide redress.[230]

B. *Keaney v Ireland*

On 17 March 2020, the European Court of Human Rights rendered its decision in *Keaney v Ireland*,[231] wherein Vincent Keaney complained that the delay in his domestic civil proceedings – in excess of 11 years – constituted a breach of his Article 6.1 right to have his case heard within a 'reasonable time'.[232] It was further claimed that, as there was no remedy available to Keaney for this delay, the Article 13 right to an effective remedy had similarly been breached. This case follows a long string of cases before the Court concerning the long waiting times in the Irish superior courts.

The facts in *Keaney* are as follows. In 2003, Keaney sought to entirely separate his business and property interests from those of his former business partner.[233] Nonetheless, in February 2006, the applicant commenced legal proceedings claiming that he had suffered deceit, fraud, misrepresentation and undue influence on the part of 18 defendants throughout the period of 2000–03.[234] The issue was assigned to the Commercial List of the High Court, and the applicant was directed to submit a statement of claims.[235] As this statement, once submitted, was 'poorly particularised', the applicant submitted an amended version, without being granted leave by the High Court to do so.[236]

In January 2007, Finlay Geoghegan J struck out all claims against 11 of the 18 defendants, and limited the applicant's claims against another three. Later, claims were struck out concerning three further defendants. The applicant was thus required to submit a third statement of claims, accordingly.[237] This statement was submitted, though it was held by the High Court that it 'did not make sense and did not comply with the order at issue'.[238] Two further statements were submitted, but, due to the striking out of further claims, another was requested.[239] In April 2008, after further claims were struck out, yet another statement was ordered, and was delivered in May 2008. However, it was found to not be in compliance with the relevant order.[240] Another statement of claims was delivered in July 2008.[241] Proceeding on

---

230 ibid para 130.
231 Application no 72060/17.
232 ibid para 3.
233 ibid paras 7–14.
234 ibid para 15.
235 ibid para 16.
236 ibid para 17.
237 ibid para 18.
238 ibid para 19.
239 ibid para 20.
240 ibid paras 21–22.
241 ibid para 24.

the basis of this final statement, Feeney J held that the applicant had failed in all his claims, and the proceedings were dismissed.[242]

The applicant sought to appeal this decision, as well as various preceding orders, to the Supreme Court; however, he failed to lodge the proper books of appeal.[243] He was directed in February 2014 to submit the required documentation, and did so in March 2014.[244] The applicant filed the requisite documentation ahead of the hearing in March 2015, and filed his legal submissions on June 2015.[245] On one issue, the Supreme Court rejected his appeal outright, but on another directed the applicant to submit the proper books of appeal, which had not yet been completed. The applicant was directed in March 2016 to do so within six weeks in respect of one appeal and eight weeks in respect of the others. Nonetheless, this was not done until February 2017.[246] The Supreme Court rejected the remainder of the appeals in April 2017.[247]

Before the European Court of Human Rights, Keaney alleged that this process was unduly lengthy, and thus constituted an infringement of Article 6.1. It was submitted that numerous institutional factors resulted in the length of the proceedings, including the number of judges responsible for the administration of his case, the excessive workloads on the judiciary generally and how cases are prioritised to be heard before the superior courts.[248] The state, effectively, laid the blame solely on the applicant.[249]

The Court found that 'the applicant's litigation took on a scale incommensurate with the nature of the underlying legal claim'.[250] However, it did recognise that there were 'multiple occasions on which the applicant's failure to comply with court orders clearly resulted in further delays in the case'.[251] The Court did not hold the applicant responsible for the entire length of the proceedings,[252] but rather took considerable issue with how the applicant's appeals were permitted to simply lie dormant in the Supreme Court. Thus, it was held that there had been a breach of Article 6.1.[253]

Regarding Article 13, the Court put particular emphasis on the decisions in *Healy*[254] and *McFarlane*[255] in stressing Ireland's deficiencies regarding this issue. Reference was also made to the domestic decision in *Nash v DPP*,[256] wherein Clarke J held that damages may be awarded in instances where the constitutional right

---

[242] ibid para 25.
[243] ibid paras 26–27.
[244] ibid para 28.
[245] ibid para 29.
[246] ibid para 31.
[247] ibid para 32.
[248] ibid paras 74–77.
[249] ibid paras 78–84.
[250] ibid para 93.
[251] ibid para 95.
[252] ibid para 97.
[253] ibid paras 98 and 100.
[254] *Healey v Ireland*, Application no 27291/16.
[255] *McFarlane v Ireland*, Grand Chamber, Application no 31333/06.
[256] *Nash v DPP* [2015] IESC 32.

to a timely trial has been infringed. In considering this latter precedent, the Court took issue with the manner in which the exact parameters of such a claim were left undefined.[257] Although it recognised that subsequent litigation is necessary in a common law system for new doctrines and remedies to crystallise, it nonetheless reiterated the point made in *McFarlane* that 'the development of the constitutional remedy relied on, as well its scope and application, has to be sufficiently clearly set out for it to be considered effective'.[258]

The Court's overall conclusion on the issue of Article 13 hinged on the state's failure to sufficiently address the structural issues identified by the Grand Chamber in *McFarlane*. It noted that the considerable waiting times in the Supreme Court have largely been displaced into the newly formed Court of Appeal, and that the General Scheme of the European Convention on Human Rights (Compensation for Delays in Court Proceedings) Bill 2018 remains effectively in limbo.[259] Accordingly, the Court held Ireland to be in breach of Article 13.[260]

Interestingly, however, the Court refused to award the applicant damages:

> However, as indicated previously, the applicant's conduct throughout had a critical impact on the progress of his case, with the domestic courts at both levels indicating that his actions and the manner in which he had conducted his case bordered on an abuse of process. In finding, in particular, a violation of Articles 6 and 13 § 1 combined in the present case, the Court does not seek to provide a perverse incentive to applicants to pursue cases in an abusive manner at domestic level only to seek to secure a violation of Article 6 § 1 thereafter.[261]

Finally, it is noteworthy that Judge O'Leary rendered a separate concurring opinion. She criticised the Grand Chamber's decision in *McFarlane*, averring, interestingly, that the decision effectively ensured that the domestic remedy for delay would remain ineffective and undeveloped by signalling to prospective applicants that they were unlikely to be successful.[262] Thus, it is crucial that the state 'erect the appropriate "scaffolding" to support the efficient administration of justice'.[263] While Judge O'Leary appreciated that some such measures have been adopted, she maintained that it has been insufficient.[264]

The Judge closed her opinion emphatically:

> The judgment is not a victory for the applicant. It is, for the reasons explained therein, accompanied by no just satisfaction award due to the manner in which his case was conducted. It is instead a judgment of principle identifying a systemic problem of delay which in relation to some levels of the domestic court system may have since been remedied. It is also a judgment which requires the respondent State to act in relation to the provision of an effective domestic remedy in cases of delay. Not all sound legal principles find the appropriate champion.[265]

---

[257] *Keaney v Ireland* (n 231) para 121.
[258] ibid para 122.
[259] ibid paras 124–25.
[260] ibid para 127.
[261] ibid para 132.
[262] *Keaney v Ireland*, separate opinion of Judge O'Leary para 15.
[263] ibid para 17.
[264] ibid para 19.
[265] ibid para 26.

Ireland and International Law 2020

MICHAEL A BECKER*

THE COVID-19 PANDEMIC dominated 2020 and unleashed a wave of activity by governments and international organisations. As Ireland and other states undertook extraordinary measures in response to the public health emergency, the pandemic raised a wide array of international legal questions relating to human rights, state responsibility, international trade and transport, intellectual property and global inequality. At a more basic level, the pandemic provided a stark reminder of global interdependence and the importance of effective multilateral institutions and political leadership. As Dr Michael J Ryan, Executive Director of the World Health Organization's Health Emergencies Programme, told RTÉ's Sean O'Rourke in the early days of the crisis: 'None of us are safe until all of us are safe.'[1] Meanwhile, the long-running Brexit saga reached a historic milestone when the UK formally left the European Union on 31 January 2020. This hardly marked the end of Brexit, however, as the remainder of the year saw continuing fractious negotiations surrounding the future relationship between the UK and the European Union, including the status of Northern Ireland and the impact of Brexit on the Good Friday Agreement. Amidst these challenges, Ireland achieved a major triumph when it was elected in June 2020 to a two-year seat on the United Nations Security Council commencing 1 January 2021.

National elections in Ireland in February 2020 delivered an unprecedented tripartite coalition government of Fianna Fáil, Fine Gael and the Green Party – despite Sinn Féin winning the most votes of any party.[2] This domestic political transition did not lead to any major shift in Ireland's foreign policy, however, especially as Simon Coveney TD remained in place as Minister for Foreign Affairs and Trade, even as Micheál Martin TD succeeded Leo Varadkar TD as Taoiseach and other cabinet positions were reshuffled. Throughout 2020, government officials set forth Ireland's positions on matters with international legal implications and consistently emphasised the need for multilateralism and humanitarianism in global affairs.

I. COVID-19

Ireland enacted a wide range of emergency restrictions at home in response to COVID-19 and engaged broadly with international partners in attempts to alleviate the

---

* Trinity College Dublin.
[1] 'WHO's Dr Mike Ryan Calls for Global Solidarity to Fight Virus' *RTE News* (26 March 2020) www.rte.ie/news/2020/0326/1126519-whos-ryan-calls-for-global-solidarity-to-fight-virus/.
[2] 'FF, FG and Green Party Agree Historic Coalition Deal' *RTE News* (26 June 2020) www.rte.ie/news/politics/2020/0625/1149711-programme-for-government/.

worldwide public health crisis. On 11 March 2020, the World Health Organization (WHO) formally characterised the COVID-19 outbreak as a pandemic.[3] The next day, then-Taoiseach Leo Varadkar announced Ireland's first set of COVID-19 public health measures: restrictions on large gatherings and the closure of schools, universities and childcare facilities. Over the remainder of the year, the Irish government imposed further restrictions aimed at 'flattening the curve' to prevent the healthcare system collapsing. Measures included the closing of pubs, restaurants, retail shops and non-essential services; facemask mandates; limitations on public gatherings, sporting events and religious services; and travel restrictions.

From an international law perspective, one question was whether public health measures in Ireland and elsewhere complied with international human rights law. On 1 April 2020, Ireland and EU partners issued a joint statement to affirm the need for all public health measures to abide by principles of the rule of law, democracy and fundamental rights, and that all measures be strictly necessary, proportionate, temporary and subject to regular scrutiny.[4] Ireland reiterated that message at the UN Human Rights Council in September 2020.[5] Although Ireland placed limitations on various rights that find protection in international law, it notably did not seek to derogate formally from any of the international human rights treaties that provide for that possibility, such as the 1950 European Convention for the Protection of Human Rights and Fundamental Freedoms (Article 15) or the 1966 International Covenant on Civil and Political Rights (Article 4).[6] A study commissioned by the Irish Human Rights and Equality Commission concluded that 'the principal measures introduced to control the pandemic – restrictions on movement and home gatherings, obligations to wear face coverings' were justified under the circumstances but that 'significant human rights and equality concerns' remained.[7] The Irish government 'repeatedly blurred the boundary between legal requirements and public health guidance', which was contrary to the rule of law and in breach of international standards, including the rule of legality.[8] The study also found that restrictions 'disproportionately affected vulnerable and disadvantaged groups', including those subject to international legal protection.[9]

---

[3] WHO, 'WHO Director-General's Opening Remarks at the Media Briefing on COVID-19' (11 March 2020) www.who.int/director-general/speeches/detail/who-director-general-s-opening-remarks-at-the-media-briefing-on-covid-19---11-march-2020. The WHO had already declared COVID-19 a Public Health Emergency of International Concern on 30 January 2020. WHO, 'A Year Without Precedent: WHO's COVID-19 Response' (23 December 2020) www.who.int/news-room/spotlight/a-year-without-precedent-who-s-covid-19-response.

[4] DFAT, 'Joint Statement – Rule of Law in the Context of the Covid-19 Crisis', Statement (1 April 2020).

[5] Statement of Ireland, Human Rights Council, 45th Session, 'Enhanced Interactive Dialogue on the Impact of the COVID-19 Pandemic on Human Rights' (14 September 2020).

[6] A substantial minority of states worldwide formally derogated from their international human rights obligations; many more states restricted human rights based on public health or national security grounds as contemplated by the relevant treaties. See LH Helfer, 'Rethinking Derogations from Human Rights Treaties' (2021) 115 *American Journal of International Law* 20.

[7] C Casey, O Doyle, D Kenny and D Lyons, *Ireland's Emergency Powers During the Covid-19 Pandemic* (Irish Human Rights and Equality Commission, 2021) xii.

[8] ibid xii–xiii, 67–68.

[9] ibid xii–xiii. See also P Clancy, 'Human Rights in Ireland 2020' in this volume.

In terms of the global response, Ireland was the first country to fund the WHO's COVID-19 response plan, making an initial €1 million contribution.[10] Ireland subsequently contributed more than €17 million in direct funding to the UN Global Humanitarian Response Plan, with a specific focus on relief efforts in Ethiopia, Uganda, Tanzania and Malawi.[11] These amounts were in addition to a €10 million contribution to the UN Central Emergency Response Fund.[12] Ireland also quadrupled its funding to the WHO in 2020.[13] In August 2020, Minister of State for Overseas Development Aid and Diaspora Colm Brophy TD reported that Ireland had contributed €123 million to the international response to COVID-19[14] – a figure that had surpassed €150 million by the end of 2020.[15] Ireland also worked with EU partners on the COVAX initiative, which aimed to supply vaccines to the most vulnerable 20 per cent of people in every country.[16]

In July, Ireland expressed its support for UN Security Council Resolution 2532, which demanded a global ceasefire and 90-day 'humanitarian pause' to enable the provision of humanitarian assistance in armed conflict settings.[17] In commending the Security Council, Ireland emphasised the pandemic's potential to act as 'a multiplier of other risks and pressures', including the heightened vulnerability of women and girls and the risk that emergency measures might disproportionately affect certain groups, including 'older people, people living with disabilities, members of the LGBTQ+ community and ethnic minorities'.[18] At the UN Human Rights Council, Ireland stressed the need to balance efforts to prevent the rapid spread of disinformation about the virus against the risk of censorship and unjustified restrictions on free expression.[19]

COVID-19 also prompted 'the biggest repatriation effort in the history of the State'.[20] This included chartering flights to repatriate Irish citizens, as well as citizens from other EU Member States and the UK.[21] By the end of May 2020, the Irish government had assisted over 6000 Irish citizens to return from 126 different countries,[22] and had made use for the first time of the EU Civil Protection

---

[10] DFAT, 'Ireland Contributes €10 Million to UN Global Humanitarian Response Plan for COVID 19', Press Release (8 April 2020).

[11] ibid; DFAT, 'Ireland Supports International Covid-19 Response', Press Release (16 April 2020); DFAT, 'Tánaiste Statement to Dáil on Covid-19', Speech (4 June 2020).

[12] 'Ireland Contributes €10 Million' (n 10).

[13] 'Tánaiste Statement to Dáil' (n 11).

[14] DFAT, 'Irish Support for Global Responses to COVID-19 Reaches €123 Million', Press Release (17 August 2020).

[15] DFAT, 'Minister Simon Coveney Participates in UN General Assembly Special Session on COVID-19', Press Release (4 December 2020).

[16] ibid.

[17] DFAT, 'Ireland Statement to UN Security Council on Pandemic and Security' (2 July 2020). See UNSC Res 2532 (1 July 2020) UN Doc S/RES/2532. The call for a global ceasefire did not extend to military operations against terrorist groups. ibid para 3.

[18] 'Ireland Statement to UN Security Council' (n 17).

[19] Statement of Ireland, 44th Session, Human Rights Council, 'Interactive Dialogue on the Annual Report of the Special Rapporteur on the Promotion and Protection of the Right to Freedom of Opinion and Expression' (10 July 2020).

[20] DFAT, 'IIEA Webinar – The EU: Facing the Challenges of COVID-19', Speech (8 May 2020).

[21] ibid.

[22] 'Tánaiste Statement to Dáil' (n 11).

Mechanism, which partially reimburses repatriation costs in emergency situations.[23] Consular flights were organised throughout the year, including to bring Irish residents home from the UK at Christmas.[24]

II. BREXIT

The seismic shift marked by the 23 June 2016 referendum on Brexit came to fruition with the formal departure of the UK from the EU on 31 January 2020. This was preceded by a landslide victory by the Conservative Party in a 12 December 2019 snap election, which created the 80-seat majority at Westminster needed to pass the European Union (Withdrawal Agreement) Bill on 9 January 2020. That legislation implemented the agreement reached with EU negotiators in 2019, including the Northern Ireland Protocol, which was intended to avoid a 'hard border' on the island of Ireland.[25] Under the terms of the Protocol, the UK would leave the EU Customs Union but Northern Ireland would remain aligned to the EU single market – an arrangement subject to periodic review by the Northern Ireland Assembly.[26] The formal departure on 31 January 2020 started the clock running on negotiations for a comprehensive free trade agreement between the UK and the EU, as well as final agreement on certain modalities of the Protocol, with the formal transition period scheduled to end on 31 December 2020.

Notwithstanding the pandemic, negotiations on the future relationship, including implementation of the Northern Ireland Protocol, continued through the year, with the 15 October 2020 meeting of the European Council seen as an informal deadline.[27] Ireland remained closely involved as part of the EU27 and as a participant in the joint and specialised committees focused on the Protocol.[28] Negotiations were thrown into crisis in September, however, when the UK government brought forth the UK Internal Market Bill that, if adopted, would have authorised the UK to override parts of the Withdrawal Agreement by unilaterally interpreting rules on state aid and customs declarations in the Northern Ireland Protocol.[29] Prime Minister Boris Johnson defended the move to abrogate his own deal with Brussels on the ground that it would prevent the EU from interpreting the Withdrawal Agreement in 'an extreme and unreasonable' way.[30] Brandon Lewis, Northern Ireland Secretary, described it as a decision to 'break international law in a very

---

[23] ibid. The European Commission established the EU Civil Protection Mechanism in 2001.

[24] DFAT, 'Update on Covid Consular Flights and Ferry Access for Irish Residents Stranded in Britain', News (30 December 2020).

[25] DFAT, 'Minister Coveney Dáil Statement on Update on EU–UK Negotiations on Brexit', Speech (24 September 2020). The protocol, which replaced the 'Irish backstop', was designed to operate even without a broader EU–UK agreement. ibid.

[26] 'Brexit: EU and UK Reach Deal but DUP Refuses Support' *BBC News* (17 October 2019) www.bbc.com/news/uk-politics-50079385.

[27] 'EU–UK Negotiations on Brexit' (n 25).

[28] 'IIEA Webinar' (n 20).

[29] 'Johnson's Controversial Brexit Bill Clears First Commons Hurdle' *RTE News* (14 September 2020) www.rte.ie/news/brexit/2020/0914/1165013-brexit-politics/.

[30] ibid.

specific and limited way'.[31] The proposal met with considerable backlash, within and beyond the UK. Irish Minister for Foreign Affairs and Defence Simon Coveney described it as 'hugely problematic and illegal', adding that 'any unilateral departure from the terms of the Withdrawal Agreement ... could seriously erode and damage political trust, not only in the Brexit negotiations, but also within Northern Ireland at a time of real sensitivity'.[32] Meanwhile, then-US presidential candidate Joe Biden warned that any future US–UK trade deal would depend upon preserving the Good Friday Agreement and preventing the return of a hard border.[33]

Addressing the Dáil on 24 September 2020, Minister Coveney emphasised additional potential ramifications of the UK Internal Market Bill:

> Even if we get an agreement on a future relationship, I do not believe it will be ratified if there is still a threat by the UK to legislate to undermine the withdrawal agreement and break international law. Why would the EU ratify a new agreement with a country that is threatening to break an agreement that is not even 12 months old? As with everything in politics, trust and relationships are what matter in this context. I continue to try to remind the British Government in particular that, when all of this is done and we are on the other side of the transition at the end of this year, the relationship between the EU and the UK will be important for many of the global challenges that we face together and many of the mutual interests that we have and on which we need partnership.[34]

Minister Coveney also outlined the contingency plans being put in place in Ireland, including the Brexit Readiness Action Plan, efforts to ensure Irish access to the EU single market via the UK land bridge and the pursuit of EU financial support, including through the special Brexit adjustment reserve.[35] On 1 October, the European Commission launched infringement proceedings against the UK on the basis that advancing the proposed Internal Market Bill constituted a breach of the duty to act in good faith, and that its adoption would impede the implementation of the Withdrawal Agreement.[36]

As the end-of-year deadline approached without an agreement, Taoiseach Micheál Martin reiterated that a 'no-deal Brexit' would be 'very damaging to all concerned, to the Irish economy and indeed to the economies of the member states as well'.[37] State aid and level-playing-field rules remained key points of contention.[38] A partial breakthrough occurred on 8 December 2020, when the EU–UK Joint Committee announced an agreement-in-principle on the Northern Ireland Protocol, including

---

[31] D Staunton, 'UK Admits It Intends to Break International Law' *Irish Times* (8 September 2020).

[32] 'UK Plans to Break International Law "Hugely Problematic" – Coveney' *RTE* (8 September 2020) www.rte.ie/news/brexit/2020/0908/1163833-brexit/.

[33] 'Biden Says US Trade Deal Hinges on "Respect" for Good Friday Agreement' *BBC News* (17 September 2020) www.bbc.com/news/uk-politics-54171571.

[34] 'EU–UK Negotiations on Brexit' (n 25).

[35] ibid. See also Department of the Taoiseach, 'Brexit Readiness Action Plan' (9 September 2020) www.gov.ie/en/publication/849b3-the-brexit-readiness-action-plan/.

[36] European Commission, 'Withdrawal Agreement: European Commission Sends Letter of Formal Notice to the United Kingdom for Breach of its Obligations', Press Release (1 October 2020).

[37] C Kane, '"My Gut Instinct Is It's 50–50 Right Now" Taoiseach Says on Brexit Deal' *RTE News* (6 December 2020) www.rte.ie/news/2020/1206/1182652-brexit-trade-talks/.

[38] 'EU–UK Negotiations on Brexit' (n 25).

the criteria for goods moving from Great Britain to Northern Ireland to be considered 'not-at-risk' of entering the EU.[39] Crucially, the UK agreed to withdraw the controversial provisions of the Internal Market Bill that it had admitted would violate international law.[40] However, it was not until Christmas Eve, following intense negotiations focused on fishing rights in particular, that negotiators reached agreement.[41] This deal avoided a 'hard Brexit', but also confirmed a future relationship involving 'significant barriers to trade and an end to the seamless interchange between Britain and the continent'.[42] The Taoiseach described the deal as 'a good compromise and a balanced outcome ... the least bad version of Brexit possible, given current circumstances', but he acknowledged that Irish fisherman would be disappointed.[43] A year of hard-fought Brexit negotiations thus ended on a bittersweet note, with the worst-case scenario narrowly avoided but uncertainty looming over the direction that the new relationship – on the island of Ireland and beyond – would take.

III. UNITED NATIONS SECURITY COUNCIL ELECTIONS

On 17 June 2020, Ireland was elected to a two-year term on the 15-member UN Security Council, commencing 1 January 2021.[44] Ireland previously served on the Security Council in 1962, 1981–82 and 2001–02.[45] The Irish government had launched its campaign at a July 2018 event in New York headlined by former President Mary Robinson and U2's Bono, whose continuing involvement in the campaign was a vivid illustration of Irish 'soft power'.[46] The bid focused on themes of empathy, partnership and independence, and was part of the Global Ireland 2025 strategy to double 'the scope and impact of Ireland's global footprint'.[47]

---

[39] European Commission, 'Joint Statement by the Co-Chairs of the EU–UK Joint Committee' (8 December 2020) https://ec.europa.eu/commission/presscorner/detail/en/statement_20_2346.

[40] ibid. See DFAT, 'Minister Byrne Welcomes EU–UK Joint Statement on implementation of Withdrawal Agreement', Statement (9 December 2020).

[41] N O'Leary and D Staunton, 'Brexit Trade Deal Agree Between EU and UK After Intense Talks' *Irish Times* (24 December 2020).

[42] ibid.

[43] ibid. See also R Condon, 'Ireland and the European Union 2020' in this volume.

[44] DFAT, 'Ireland Wins Seat on United Nations Security Council', Press Release (18 June 2020). Ireland (128 votes) and Norway (130 votes) achieved the necessary two-thirds majority to be elected on the first ballot to the two seats allocated to their regional group, edging out Canada (108 votes). S Lynch and H McGee, 'Ireland Wins Seat on UN Security Council Following "Tough" Contest' *Irish Times* (17 June 2020).

[45] DFAT, 'Ireland Wins Seat' (n 44).

[46] S Carswell, 'How Pub Sing-Songs and Bono Brought Ireland to a Seat at the Highest Table' *Irish Times* (20 June 2020). UN diplomats were also given tickets to a U2 concert at Madison Square Garden. One can only speculate about the extent to which this gambit was more successful than Canada's subsequent invitation to a Céline Dion concert. See J Murphy, 'The Lengths Countries Go To for a Seat at UN Top Table' *BBC News* (15 June 2020) www.bbc.com/news/world-us-canada-52973244.

[47] DFAT, 'Tánaiste's Lecture to Ireland at Fordham Humanitarian Lecture Series', Speech (11 June 2020).

The Irish campaign recalled Ireland's own experience of colonisation, conflict, famine and mass migration, and emphasised eradicating poverty and hunger, assisting refugees and leading by example in responding to humanitarian emergencies.[48] It also underscored the Irish view that sustainable peace means addressing the root causes of conflict through inclusive, community-focused approaches.[49] To bolster its message of partnership and cooperation – values that the Irish government placed in contrast to policies of unilateralism, transactional diplomacy, protectionism and confrontation – Ireland referred to its leadership on the UN Sustainable Development Goals, climate justice, and efforts to promote and protect gender equality.[50] Prior to the election, then Tánaiste and Minister for Foreign Affairs Simon Coveney also made no secret of the Irish government's view that the Security Council was 'failing to meet its responsibilities' across a range of situations, including the conflict in Syria.[51] He stressed that an abiding faith in multilateralism – based on the 'principle of compromise' and the 'capacity to put ourselves in the language, thoughts, culture, and concerns of each other' – would guide Ireland's efforts to overcome these divisions, if elected.[52]

Following Ireland's election to the Security Council, then-Taoiseach Leo Varadkar said that the victory underpinned Ireland's place as 'a global island, with a clear and tangible ambition to play a central role on contributing to international peace and security'.[53] Minister Coveney lauded a 'fantastic result' that confirmed Ireland's international standing based on its 'almost 65 years of UN membership and a steadfast commitment to building peace and investing in conflict prevention', including its continuous contribution to UN peacekeeping operations since 1958.[54] He speculated that Ireland's humanitarian record and its position on issues including the Israeli–Palestinian conflict and climate change likely generated strong support across Africa and the Middle East, and among small island developing states.[55]

In a virtual address to the UN General Assembly on 26 September 2020, Taoiseach Micheál Martin stated that three principles – building peace, strengthening prevention and ensuring accountability – would underpin Ireland's approach on the Security Council.[56] The Taoiseach emphasised that peacekeeping operations must be 'adequately resourced, have access to appropriate training and be sensitive to local needs', and that more UN resources should be put towards preventive diplomacy and early intervention, including efforts to identify human rights abuses and the root causes of conflict.[57] He emphatically rejected the argument that climate change, food

---

[48] DFAT, 'Ireland: United Nations Security Council 2021–2022', Campaign Brochure (July 2018) www.dfa.ie/media/dfa/ourrolepolicies/unitednations/Campaign-Brochure-July-2018.pdf.
[49] ibid; 'Tánaiste's Lecture to Ireland at Fordham' (n 47).
[50] ibid.
[51] DFAT, 'UN Security Council Open Debate on the UN Charter', News (9 January 2020).
[52] ibid.
[53] DFAT, 'Ireland Wins Seat' (n 44).
[54] ibid.
[55] Carswell (n 46).
[56] UNGA (75th Session), 'General Debate' (26 September 2020) UN Doc A/75/PV12, Annex XVIII (Statement of Mr Micheál Martin, Taoiseach of Ireland).
[57] ibid.

insecurity or human rights were beyond the Council's remit, describing this as 'not a case of either/or':

> We know that climate change not only impedes sustainable development but also contributes to conflict. We know that human rights abuses and the denial of justice can fuel radicalisation and extremism. We know that poverty, hunger and resource deprivation fuel insecurity and violence. We know that rising oceans pose an existential threat to some Small Island Developing States. We know that without a firm commitment to supporting the poorest and most vulnerable countries on their development pathways, we will never adequately address insecurity and conflict ... What we do not yet have is a Security Council ready and able to take on its responsibilities to address these issues.[58]

The Taoiseach also called for Security Council reform and expressed support for the Code of Conduct Regarding Security Council Action against Genocide, Crimes against Humanity or War Crimes and the 2015 French–Mexican initiative on restricting the use of the veto in cases of mass atrocity.[59] Failing to reform Security Council practices and procedures, including by enhancing the representation of African countries, posed a threat to the legitimacy of the Council itself.[60] The Taoiseach also emphasised that accountability extended to respecting Security Council resolutions and that 'States cannot unilaterally decide which aspects of international law to adhere to, and which to set aside when politically inconvenient'.[61]

IV. INTERNATIONAL AGREEMENTS

This section sets out the international agreements that entered into force for Ireland during 2019, the last year for which full information is available. These agreements demonstrate Ireland's engagement across a range of issues, including environmental protection, public health, international security, human rights, and transnational and international criminal law. For example, amendments to the 1987 Montreal Protocol on Substances that Deplete the Ozone Layer (placing further limits on production and use of hydrofluorocarbons) and to the 1989 Basel Convention on the Control of Transboundary Movements of Hazardous Wastes and their Disposal (placing restrictions on the destinations to which hazardous waste can be sent) entered into force for Ireland in 2019, as did the 2013 Minamata Convention on Mercury, which seeks to phase out mercury use in many products. Ireland also became a party to the 2011 Council of Europe Convention on Preventing and Combating Violence against Women and Domestic Violence; this treaty requires states to criminalise a range of conduct and to exercise due diligence in the prevention of gender-based violence. The Second Additional Protocol to the European

---

[58] ibid.

[59] ibid. Adherents to the Code of Conduct pledge not to vote against 'a credible draft resolution before the Security Council on timely and decisive action to end the commission of genocide, crimes against humanity or war crimes, or to prevent such crimes'. See UN Doc A/70/621-S/2015/978 (14 December 2015). On the political statement organised by France and Mexico: www.globalr2p.org/resources/political-declaration-on-suspension-of-veto-powers-in-cases-of-mass-atrocities/.

[60] Statement of Mr Micheál Martin (n 56).

[61] ibid.

Convention on Extradition, relating to tax and other fiscal offences, also entered into force for Ireland in 2019,[62] as did the Kampala Amendment to the Rome Statute of the International Criminal Court (ICC), which brought the crime of aggression under ICC jurisdiction.

Table 1 lists the multinational agreements that entered into force for Ireland in 2019.[63]

Table 1. List of Multilateral Agreements that Entered into Force during 2019

ITS Number	Title of Agreement
No 1 of 2019	Amendment to the Montreal Protocol on Substances that Deplete the Ozone Layer *Ireland's Instrument of Ratification deposited on 12 March 2018, entered into force on 1 January 2019, except for the changes to Article 4 of the Protocol set out in article I of the Amendment*
No 2 of 2019	Convention on Centralised Customs Clearance Concerning the Allocation of National Collection Costs Retained When Tradition Own Resources Are Made Available to the EU Budget *Ireland's notification of the completion of procedures necessary for the entry into force of this Agreement deposited on 16 June 2017, entered into force on 16 January 2019*
No 4 of 2019	Agreement between the Member States of the European Union concerning the status of military and civilian staff seconded to the institutions of the European Union, of the headquarters and forces which may be made available to the European Union in the context of the preparation and execution of the tasks referred to in Article 17(2) of the Treaty on European Union, including exercises, and of the military and civilian staff of the Member States put at the disposal of the European Union to act in this context *Ireland's notification of the completion of the procedures necessary for the entry into force of this Agreement, with modification of reservation, deposited on 22 February 2019, entered into force on 1 April 2019*
No 5 of 2019	Protocol to the Euro-Mediterranean Agreement establishing an Association between the European Communities and their Member States, of the one part, and the Hashemite Kingdom of Jordan, of the other part, to take account of the accession of the Republic of Bulgaria and Romania to the European Union *Approved on behalf of the European Union and its Member States on 18 March 2019 and by Jordan on 1 July 2010, entered into force on 1 April 2019*

(continued)

---

[62] Ireland entered a reservation to the Second Additional Protocol to exclude provisions on amnesties and judgments *in absentia*.

[63] Full details of multilateral agreements that entered into force in 2020 are not yet available.

ITS Number	Title of Agreement
No 6 of 2019	Multilateral Convention to Implement Tax Treaty Related Measures to Prevent Base Erosion and Profit Shifting *Ireland's Instrument of Ratification, with reservations and notifications, deposited on 29 January 2019, entered into force with respect to Ireland on 1 May 2019*
No 7 of 2019	Agreement Among the States Parties to the North Atlantic Treaty and the Other States Participating in the Partnership for Peace Regarding the Status of Their Forces *Ireland's signature, with reservation, on 28 February 2019. Ireland's Instrument of Ratification, with confirmation of reservation, deposited on 9 April 2019, entered into force with respect to Ireland on 9 May 2019*
No 9 of 2019	Agreement on Air Transport between Canada and the European Community and its Member States *Ireland's notification of the completion of the procedures necessary for the entry into force of this Agreement deposited on 20 February 2015, entered into force on 16 May 2019*
No 10 of 2019	Protocol amending the Agreement on Air Transport between Canada and the European Community and its Member States, to take account of the accession to the European Union of the Republic of Croatia *Approved on behalf of the European Union and its Member States on 16 April 2019 and by Canada on 20 June 2018, entered into force on 16 May 2019*
No 11 of 2019	Protocol amending the Agreement on maritime transport between the European Community and its Member States, of the one part, and the government of the People's Republic of China, of the other part *Approved on behalf of the European Union and its Member States on 8 April 2019 and by China on 24 May 2019, entered into force on 24 May 2019*
No 12 of 2019	Minamata Convention on Mercury *Ireland's Instrument of Ratification deposited on 18 March 2019, entered into force with respect to Ireland on 16 June 2019*
No 13 of 2019	Second Additional Protocol to the European Convention on Extradition *Ireland's Instrument of Ratification, with reservations pursuant to Article 9(2) of the Protocol, deposited on 22 March 2019, entered into force with respect to Ireland on 21 June 2019*
No 14 of 2019	Council of Europe Convention on Preventing and Combating Violence against Women and Domestic Violence *Ireland's Instrument of Ratification, with reservations pursuant to Article 78(2) of the Convention, deposited on 8 March 2019. Entered into force with respect to Ireland on 1 July 2019*

(continued)

ITS Number	Title of Agreement
No 15 of 2019	Third Additional Protocol to the Agreement establishing an association between the European Community and its Member States, of the one part, and the Republic of Chile, of the other part, to take account of the accession of the Republic of Croatia to the European Union *Approved on behalf of the European Union and its Member States on 6 November 2017 and by Chile on 16 May 2019, entered into force on 1 July 2019*
No 16 of 2019	Council of Europe Convention on Cinematographic Co-production (revised) *Signed, without reservation as to ratification, on behalf of Ireland on 16 May 2019, entered into force with respect to Ireland on 1 September 2019*
No 18 of 2019	Amendments to the Rome Statute of the International Criminal Court on the Crime of Aggression *Ireland's Instrument of Ratification deposited on 27 September 2018, entered into force with respect to Ireland on 27 September 2019*
No 19 of 2019	Convention drawn up on the basis of Article K.3 of the Treaty on European Union, relating to extradition between the Member States of the European Union *Ireland's notification of the completion of the procedures necessary for the entry into force of this Convention deposited on 28 June 2002, entered into force on 5 November 2019*
No 21 of 2019	Amendment to the Basel Convention on the Control of Transboundary Movements of Hazardous Wastes and their Disposal *Ireland's Instrument of ratification deposited on 13 November 2009, entered into force on 5 December 2019*

Table 2 lists the bilateral agreements that entered into force for Ireland in 2019.[64]

Table 2. List of Bilateral Agreements that Entered into Force during 2019

ITS Number	Title of Agreement
No 3 of 2019	Agreement between Ireland and the Argentine Republic Concerning the Employment of Dependants of Employees Assigned to Official Duty in the State of the Other Party *Entered into force upon signature on 14 February 2019*

(continued)

---

[64] Full details of bilateral agreements that entered into force in 2020 were not yet available at time of writing.

ITS Number	Title of Agreement
No 8 of 2019	Protocol amending the Convention between Ireland and Belgium for the Avoidance of Double Taxation and the Prevention of Fiscal Evasion with respect to Taxes on Income, signed at Brussels on 24 June 1970 *Notifications of the completion of the procedures necessary for the entry into force of the Protocol exchanged on 23 December 2014 and 14 May 2019, entered into force on 14 May 2019*
No 17 of 2019	Agreement amending the Agreement between the Government of Ireland and the Government of the United States of America on Air Transport Preclearance *Notifications of the completion of the procedures necessary for the entry into force of this Agreement exchanged on 5 September 2019, entered into force on 5 September 2019*
No 20 of 2019	Host Country Agreement between the Government of Ireland and the Permanent Court of Arbitration *Ireland's notification of the completion of the procedures necessary for the entry into force of this Agreement deposited on 5 November 2019, entered into force on 5 November 2019*

V. FOREIGN CONFLICTS AND CONTROVERSIES

A wide range of foreign conflicts and international legal controversies drew the attention of the Irish government in 2020. This section highlights the state practice of Ireland with respect to situations involving Belarus, China, Ethiopia, Israel and Palestine, Morocco and Western Sahara, Myanmar, Russia, Syria, the USA and Yemen.

Belarus. On 9 August 2020, Belarus held a presidential election. According to the Belarus government, incumbent president Aleksander Lukashenko prevailed, with 80 per cent of the vote. Prior to the election, Lukashenko's main challenger, Sergei Tikhanovksy, was arrested; his wife, Svetlana Tikhanovsky (who spent her childhood summers in Roscrea, Co Tipperary in connection with Irish programmes supporting children affected by the 1986 Chernobyl disaster), became Lukashenko's sole challenger, as other opposition figures faced harassment, intimidation and arrest.[65] The announcement of Lukashenko's victory was met with mass demonstrations that police and security forces violently repressed. The Organisation for Security and Cooperation in Europe (OSCE) confirmed widespread human rights violations, including arbitrary detention, torture, forced disappearances and unlawful restrictions on freedom of expression and assembly.[66]

---

[65] D Dean, 'The Breaking Point in Belarus Has Been Made Flesh in Svetlana Tikhanovsky' *Irish Times* (5 August 2020).

[66] OSCE Rapporteur's Report under the Moscow Mechanism on Alleged Human Rights Violations Related to the Presidential Elections of 9 August 2020 in Belarus (29 October 2020) www.osce.org/files/f/documents/2/b/469539.pdf.

During the initial wave of protests, Minister for Foreign Affairs and Defence Simon Coveney declared that Ireland did not accept the election result 'as a true reflection of the democratic will of the Belarussian people' and condemned the human rights violations.[67] Noting Ireland's strong connections with the people of Belarus, Minister Coveney expressed support for the imposition of EU sanctions.[68] Taoiseach Micheál Martin spoke directly with Svetlana Tikhanovsky to express Ireland's solidarity with her and the people of Belarus, and Minister of State for European Affairs Thomas Byrne TD declared Ireland's support for the redirection of EU assistance to civil society groups.[69] In September, Minister Coveney reiterated Ireland's concerns about the situation, including attacks on media freedom and arbitrary detention, during an informal UN Security Council meeting.[70] Similar messages were delivered to the UN Human Rights Council and to the European Council as Ireland urged the EU to 'act quickly and with unity to impose sanctions against individuals responsible for falsifying the election result and for the use of State violence in Belarus'.[71] On 1 October 2020, the EU imposed sanctions against high-level officials in Belarus; two further rounds followed and by year's end the EU had sanctioned 88 individuals and seven entities, including companies working with the Lukashenko regime.[72] On the occasion of the Universal Periodic Review of Belarus at the Human Rights Council in November 2020, Ireland urged Belarus to 'Immediately, and unconditionally, release all political prisoners and human rights defenders and refrain from such detentions in the future', and to 'Allow independent journalists and media to conduct their work free from harassment, intimidation and fear'.[73] Ireland continued to condemn further violent crackdowns against protestors and called for an 'inclusive national dialogue' aimed at 'a peaceful and democratic resolution of the current crisis'.[74]

China. In June 2020, China adopted a new national security law for Hong Kong.[75] The law was set to enable authorities 'to crack down on subversive and secessionist activity' and to establish 'special state security and prosecution units' in the territory.[76] Minister Coveney criticised the adoption of the law 'without any meaningful

---

[67] DFAT, 'Statement by Minister Simon Coveney, TD, on the Belarus Presidential Election', Press Release (17 August 2020).

[68] ibid.

[69] DFAT, 'Statement on Belarus by the Minister for European Affairs, Thomas Byrne TD', Statement (24 August 2020).

[70] DFAT, 'Minister Coveney Addresses UN Security Council Meeting on Belarus', Press Release (4 September 2020).

[71] DFAT, 'Statement by Minister Simon Coveney on Human Rights Violations in Belarus', Press Release (21 September 2020).

[72] Council of the EU, 'Belarus: EU Imposes Third Round of Sanctions over Ongoing Repression', Press Release (17 December 2020).

[73] Statement of Ireland, 36th Session of the UPR Working Group, 'Review of Belarus' (2 November 2020).

[74] DFAT, 'Statement by Minister of State for European Affairs, Thomas Byrne TD on Belarus', Statement (17 November 2020).

[75] DFAT, 'Statement by Minister Coveney on National Security Law in Hong Kong', Statement (7 July 2020).

[76] P Goff, 'Fears of "Reign of Terror" as China Passes Hong Kong National Security Law' *Irish Times* (30 June 2020).

consultation' with Hong Kong's legislative council or civil society, noting its threat to the 'One Country, Two Systems' principle.[77] Aligning itself with the EU, Ireland called upon China to respect the right to peaceful assembly in Hong Kong.[78] Ireland also supported a cross-regional joint statement at the UN Human Rights Council that highlighted the law's potential to undermine international human rights protections in Hong Kong.[79]

China also faced continuing scrutiny for its treatment of the Muslim-minority Uyghur population in the north-western province of Xinjiang – conduct alleged to include mass detention and indoctrination, involuntary labour, torture, family separation and forced sterilisations.[80] On 6 October 2020, Ireland joined 38 other states at the UN General Assembly to express 'grave concern' at credible reports of gross human rights violations in Xinjiang.[81] Ireland also called on China to grant unrestricted access to the region to the UN High Commissioner for Human Rights.[82] On 8 October 2020, Seanad Éireann held a debate on a motion proposed by Senator Rónán Mullen and seconded by Senator Michael McDowell on human rights violations against the Uyghur Muslim population and other minority groups in China.[83] The motion, which passed unanimously with cross-party support, noted with concern the reports of systematic human rights violations against the Uyghur minority in Xinjiang, demanded that the Irish government condemn such practices unreservedly, and called upon China to end such practices and allow UN human rights monitors to access detention centres in the region.[84] The motion also called upon the Irish government to use 'all available trade and diplomatic channels' to insist on the observance of basic human protections for the Uyghurs.[85] During the debate, which also touched on China's policies in Tibet and Ireland's approach to Taiwan, Senator Mullen and others stressed the need for Ireland to prevent economic and trade considerations from undermining its human rights agenda.[86] Senator Malcolm Byrne specifically noted with concern that China was currently a member of the UN Human Rights Council and that Ireland should in the future support only those countries 'committed to protecting and defending human rights' for membership.[87]

---

[77] DFAT, 'Statement by Minister Coveney on National Security Law in Hong Kong', Press Release (1 July 2020).
[78] ibid. See also European Council, 'Declaration of the High Representative on behalf of the European Union on Adoption by China's National People's Congress of a National Security Legislation on Hong Kong', Press Release (1 July 2020).
[79] Foreign and Commonwealth Office (UK), 'UN Human Rights Council 44: Cross-regional Statement on Hong Kong and Xinjiang', Speech (30 June 2020).
[80] See Y Murray, 'Inside Xinjiang: China Cracks Down on Uighur Population' *RTE News* (1 October 2020) www.rte.ie/news/world/2020/0929/1168302-china-xianjiang/.
[81] UNGA Third Committee (75th Session), 'General Debate' (6 October 2020) UN Doc A/C.3/75/SR.3, paras 11–14 (Statement by Germany).
[82] Statement of Ireland, 45th Session, Human Rights Council, 'General Debate' (25 September 2020).
[83] Seanad Deb 8 October 2020, vol 271 no 9, www.oireachtas.ie/en/debates/debate/seanad/2020-10-08/11/.
[84] ibid.
[85] ibid.
[86] ibid.
[87] ibid.

Addressing the Seanad, Minister of State for Overseas Development and Trade Colm Brophy TD emphasised Ireland's 'positive and growing' relationship with China and expressed disappointment that the situation in Xinjiang was 'impacting negatively' on that relationship.[88] Alluding to the need to engage strategically, he asserted that Ireland must ensure that 'in seeking to challenge Chinese policy in Xinjiang, we make it clear that we do not, in any way, seek to undermine Chinese sovereignty … We are pro-human rights, not anti-China'.[89] Minister Brophy also noted China's official justification for its policies in Xinjiang – the threat posed by Islamic extremism. He acknowledged, however, that China's policies must be appropriate, proportionate and respectful of the human rights of the Uyghur people, and that existing reports 'suggest this is not the case'.[90] Overall, Minister Brophy asserted that the best approach required Ireland to express its views on Xinjiang through diplomatic channels, working in concert with like-minded states and EU partners.[91] He also recalled that Ireland had consistently supported calls for 'immediate, meaningful and unfettered access to Xinjiang for independent observers'.[92] However, Minister Brophy expressly disassociated the Irish government from the element of the motion calling for the use of all available trade channels. Noting that external trade was an EU competence, he stated that it was beyond the power of the Irish government 'to prohibit or sanction the importation of goods and services at Member State level' and that no European consensus for such a policy yet existed.[93]

Ethiopia. In November 2020, fighting erupted in the Tigray region of Ethiopia as federal troops responded forcefully to an insurrection by the Tigrayan People's Liberation Front.[94] Minister Coveney expressed Ireland's deep concern over reported atrocities and ethnic profiling, and called on all parties to 'cease hostilities, respect international humanitarian law, and begin dialogue', while Minister Brophy reiterated Ireland's long-standing relationship with Ethiopia and Ireland's 'continuing solidarity with the people of Ethiopia', including refugees and internally displaced people.[95]

Israel/Palestine. In January 2020, the US administration of President Donald J Trump unveiled a Middle East peace plan that was described as giving Israel 'most of what it has sought over decades of conflict while offering the Palestinians the

---

[88] DFAT, 'Minister Brophy Speech to Seanad Private Members Motion on Xinjiang', Speech (9 October 2020).

[89] ibid. In response, Senator Mullen asserted that 'what is being challenged is not the sovereignty of the country but the failure of the country to comply with international norms of human rights and human dignity'. Seaned Deb (n 83).

[90] ibid.

[91] ibid.

[92] ibid.

[93] 'Minister Brophy Speech' (n 88). Senator Mullen noted that Ireland plays a role in developing EU trade policy and that Irish ministers had participated in trade missions to China. Seaned Deb (n 83).

[94] A Schipani and D Pilling, 'Clashes in Ethiopia after Federal Troops Sent to Quell Rebellion' *Irish Times* (4 November 2020).

[95] DFAT, 'Minister Coveney Announces €2.4 Million Irish Aid Response to Ethiopia Humanitarian Crisis', Press Release (4 December 2020).

possibility of a state with limited sovereignty' – a proposal that the Palestinian Authority rejected immediately.[96] Minister Coveney expressed Ireland's support for 'any peace initiative that respected the international parameters for a two-state solution and UN Security Council resolutions' – a threshold that the US proposal, he noted, did not appear to meet.[97] He further emphasised that 'No solution can be imposed'.[98] In response to Israel's announcement that it planned to continue with annexation plans, Minister Coveney stated that 'annexation of territory by force is prohibited under international law, including by the UN Charter', and 'would be a decisive step away from the Oslo Accords'.[99] He later condemned the decision by Israel in February 2020 to proceed with settlement construction in parts of East Jerusalem and reiterated Ireland's position that 'All settlement activity in the occupied Palestinian territory is very clearly illegal under international law'.[100] The same message was delivered to the UN Human Rights Council, where Minister Coveney emphasised the need for a 'negotiated and agreed two-state solution' and decried the provocation of unilateral and unlawful annexation.[101] Ireland also expressed concern about the lack of accountability for alleged violations of international law by Israel against Palestinian civilians and condemned both 'indiscriminate rocket fire from Gaza that recklessly endangers Israeli civilians, and acts of settler violence against Palestinians'.[102]

Morocco/Western Sahara. During 2020, Israel normalised its relations with Bahrain, Morocco, Sudan and the United Arab Emirates in a series of agreements brokered by the USA.[103] In a related development, the USA agreed to recognise Morocco's sovereignty over Western Sahara, which the UN considers a non-self-governing territory whose status remains to be determined.[104] Ireland welcomed the agreement between Israel and Morocco, but affirmed that it continued to support

---

[96] M Crowley and D Halbfinger, 'Trump Releases Mideast Peace Plan That Strongly Favors Israel' *New York Times* (28 January 2020).

[97] DFAT, 'Statement by Tánaiste on the US Middle East Peace Initiative', Statement (28 January 2020).

[98] ibid.

[99] ibid. On Ireland's historic support for the Palestinian people, see J Doyle, 'Irish Nationalism and the Israel–Palestinian Conflict' in R Miller (ed), *Ireland and the Middle East: Trade, Politics and Diplomacy* (Newbridge, Irish Academic Press, 2007) 87–100.

[100] DFAT, 'Statement by Tánaiste on Settlement Announcements in East Jerusalem', Statement (21 February 2020).

[101] DFAT, 'Tánaiste's Address to the Forty-Third Session of the Human Rights Council', News (25 February 2020). See also Statement of Ireland, Human Rights Council, 43rd Session, 'Human Rights Situations that Require the Council's Attention' (10 March 2020); DFAT, 'Statement by Tánaiste on Developments in Israel', Statement (23 April 2020); DFAT, 'Statement by the Minister Simon Coveney on Settlement Announcements in the West Bank', Statement (16 October 2020); DFAT, 'Statement by Minister for Foreign Affairs Simon Coveney on Settlement Announcements in the West Bank' (17 November 2020).

[102] Statement of Ireland, 43rd Session of the Human Rights Council, 'Human Rights Situation in Palestine and Other Occupied Arab Territories' (15 June 2020).

[103] J Singer, 'The Abraham Accords: Normalization Agreements Signed by Israel with the UAE, Bahrain, Sudan, and Morocco' (2021) 60 *International Legal Materials* 448. These agreements upended the long-held position among Arab League states that normalisation of relations with Israel required prior resolution of Palestine's status.

[104] ibid 450–51.

self-determination for the people of Western Sahara and its position that UN-led talks should swiftly resume.[105]

Myanmar. During 2016–17, Myanmar's military undertook 'clearance operations' in the country's northwest that caused more than 700,000 members of the Rohingya group, a Muslim ethnic minority, to flee to Bangladesh.[106] The International Independent Fact-Finding Mission on Myanmar (IIFFMM) established by the UN Human Rights Council in March 2017 documented a range of gross violations of human rights and international humanitarian law and asserted that 'factors allowing the inference of genocidal intent are present'.[107] In January 2020, the International Court of Justice (ICJ) indicated provisional measures against Myanmar in a case alleging violations of the 1948 Convention on the Prevention and Punishment of Genocide.[108] As Ireland pledged to assist continuing relief efforts for Rohingya refugees, Minister Brophy acknowledged that humanitarian aid could help to allay 'the very worst consequences of political crisis' but also that 'Only by comprehensively addressing the human rights violations committed against the Rohingya can we create the conditions necessary for their safe, voluntary, dignified, and sustainable return to their places of origin'.[109] He affirmed that 'Ireland stands ready to play its role in that process'.[110] Ireland also urged Myanmar to implement the recommendations of the IIFFMM and the 2017 Kofi Annan-led Advisory Commission on Rakhine State.[111]

Russia. In August 2020, Russian opposition leader Alexei Navalny, a fierce critic of the Kremlin and Russian president Vladimir Putin, fell ill, following a suspected poisoning.[112] Germany authorities later confirmed the use of a 'Novichok' nerve agent.[113] Minister Coveney condemned the assassination attempt as 'abhorrent to

---

[105] DFAT, 'Statement on Normalisation of Relations Between Israel and Morocco', Statement (12 December 2020).

[106] The Rohingya have faced decades of discrimination and persecution in Myanmar; there is a small Rohingya refugee community in Ireland. S Pollak, 'Despite Barriers, Rohingya Resettlement in Carlow Deemed Success' *Irish Times* (24 August 2019).

[107] 'Report of the Detailed Findings of the Independent International Fact-Finding Mission on Myanmar' (17 September 2018), UN Doc A/HRC/39/CRP.2 para 1441.

[108] 'Application of the Convention on the Prevention and Punishment of the Crime of Genocide (The Gambia v Myanmar) (Provisional Measures)' (23 January 2020) International Court of Justice, General List No 178.

[109] DFAT, 'Minister Brophy Pledges €1 million in Humanitarian Assistance to Rohingya Refugee Crisis', Press Release (25 October 2020).

[110] ibid. Canada, Maldives and the Netherlands expressed plans to intervene in the ICJ case; there was no similar indication from Ireland. See P Pillai, 'Intervention in *The Gambia v Myanmar* at the International Court of Justice' (*OpinioJuris*, 3 September 2020) http://opiniojuris.org/2020/09/03/canada-and-the-netherlands-new-intervention-in-the-gambia-v-myanmar-at-the-international-court-of-justice/.

[111] Statement of Ireland, Human Rights Council, 43rd Session, 'Interactive Dialogue on the Report of the High Commissioner on the Situation of Human Rights of Rohingya Muslims and Other Minorities in Myanmar' (27 February 2020). See also Advisory Commission on Rakhine State, 'Towards a Peaceful, Fair and Prosperous Future for the People of Rakhine: Final Report of the Advisory Commission on Rakhine State' (August 2017) https://reliefweb.int/report/myanmar/towards-peaceful-fair-and-prosperous-future-people-rakhine-final-report-advisory.

[112] A Roth and M Farrer, 'Russian Opposition Activist Alexei Navalny Fights for Life after "Poisoning"' *Irish Times* (20 August 2020).

[113] DFAT, 'Min Coveney Condemns Poisoning of Russian Opposition Leader Alexei Navalny', News (3 September 2020).

all those who value the fundamental principles of democracy and respect for human rights as enshrined in the European Convention on Human Rights'.[114] He described the use of a chemical weapon as a 'completely unacceptable' breach of international law and called for those responsible to be held accountable.[115] Ireland also reiterated in October 2020 its unwavering support for Ukraine's territorial integrity and its non-recognition of Russia's 2014 purported annexation of Crimea.[116]

Syria. In March 2020, Ireland expressed grave concern about reports of flagrant breaches of international humanitarian law by Syrian forces, as well as human rights violations against the Kurdish community, and reiterated support for a Security Council referral of the situation in Syria to the ICC.[117] On 8 April 2020, the Investigation and Identification Team established by the Organisation for the Prohibition of Chemical Weapons to identify the perpetrators of chemical weapon attacks in Syria attributed three such attacks from March 2017 to the Syrian Air Force.[118] Minister Coveney welcomed the report as 'an important step in tackling impunity for the use of chemical weapons'.[119] He also lamented the suffering that the Syrian people had endured over nine years of war, including 'unconscionable' attacks on hospitals and health facilities.[120] At a donor conference in June 2020, Ireland pledged a further €25 million to the humanitarian crisis in Syria.[121] On that occasion, Minister Coveney called for the perpetrators of appalling violence to be held accountable while asserting that the 'vast human tragedy' in Syria could be ended only through negotiation.[122] Ireland also criticised UN Security Council Resolution 2254 (2020) for authorising only one crossing point for humanitarian assistance to Syria, notwithstanding urgent challenges posed by COVID-19.[123]

USA/International Criminal Court. In June 2020, US President Trump issued an Executive Order that threatened sanctions against parties associated with the ICC, including individuals or entities providing material support to the institution.[124] On 2 September 2020, the Trump administration followed through on that threat and imposed sanctions on the ICC prosecutor, Fatou Bensouda, and other personnel.[125]

---

[114] ibid.

[115] ibid.

[116] Statement of Ireland, Human Rights Council, 45th Session, 'ID High Commissioner Oral Update on Ukraine' (1 October 2020).

[117] Statement of Ireland, Human Rights Council, 43rd Session, 'Interactive Dialogue with the Commission of Inquiry on the Syrian Arab Republic' (9 March 2020).

[118] 'First Report of the OPCW IIT Pursuant to Paragraph 10 of Decision C-SS-4/Dec.3', Doc No S/1867/2020.

[119] DFAT, 'Statement by Tánaiste Simon Coveney, TD on the Investigation into the Use of Chemical Weapons in Syria', Press Release (9 April 2020).

[120] ibid.

[121] DFAT, 'Ireland Pledges €25m to the Syria Crisis in 2020', Press Release (30 June 2020). This brought Ireland's contribution since 2012 to over €168 million. ibid.

[122] ibid.

[123] Statement of Ireland, Human Rights Council, 44th Session, 'Interactive Dialogue with the Commission of Inquiry on the Syrian Arab Republic' (14 July 2020).

[124] See Executive Order 13928 of 11 June 2020 (Blocking Property of Certain Persons Associated with the International Criminal Court) https://trumpwhitehouse.archives.gov/presidential-actions/executive-order-blocking-property-certain-persons-associated-international-criminal-court/.

[125] US Department of the Treasury, 'Blocking Property of Certain Persons Associated with the International Criminal Court Designations' (2 September 2020) https://home.treasury.gov/policy-issues/financial-sanctions/recent-actions/20200902.

Minister Coveney expressed deep regret over the US action and affirmed Ireland's continuing support for the ICC – 'an independent and impartial institution with a key role in the fight against impunity'.[126] Earlier in the year, Minister Coveney had emphasised the responsibility of UN Security Council members to call out breaches of international humanitarian law – 'no matter how uncomfortable the politics' – and to refer situations, where appropriate, to the ICC.[127] Taoiseach Micheál Martin reiterated Ireland's support for the ICC in his virtual address to the UN General Assembly and expressed deep concern over 'any measures taken against the Court, and against its officials and staff'.[128] Ireland made its annual €200,000 contribution to the ICC's Trust Fund for Victims in December 2020, with the Irish Ambassador to the Netherlands, HE Kevin Kelly, reaffirming Ireland's 'continued support and engagement with the ICC and the Rome Statute'.[129]

USA/Iran/Iraq. The beginning of 2020 was marked by a series of events concerning the USA, Iran and Iraq. On 27 December 2019, an Iran-backed militia in Iraq launched a rocket attack against an Iraqi military base in Kirkuk, killing a US contractor and injuring US and Iraqi military personnel.[130] The USA retaliated two days later with strikes against sites in Iraq and Syria that killed up to 25 militia fighters. On 31 December 2019, pro-Iran paramilitary groups in Iraq attacked and penetrated the US embassy site in Baghdad. Ireland condemned the attacks on the US embassy and called upon the Iraqi authorities 'to guarantee the safety of all diplomatic missions and their personnel'.[131]

On 3 January, the USA carried out an aerial attack against two vehicles at Baghdad's international airport. The victims included General Qasem Soleimani, a high-ranking member of Iran's leadership and the head of the elite Quds Force.[132] The USA defended the strike as a means to deter future attacks by Iran, but provided scant evidence of any imminent threat.[133] Following several days of escalating rhetoric on both sides – including Iran's announcement that it would no longer abide by

---

[126] DFAT, 'Statement by Minister Coveney on the International Criminal Court & US Measures', Statement (4 September 2020).

[127] 'Tánaiste's Lecture to Ireland at Fordham' (n 47). He further stated that arrest warrants issued by the ICC must be executed and that failure to give effect to ICC decisions cannot be met with silence. ibid.

[128] Statement of Mr Micheál Martin (n 56). During the Universal Periodic Review of the United States by the Human Rights Council, Ireland urged the United States to 'Reverse all measures against the ICC, its officials and staff'. Statement of Ireland, 36th Session of the UPR Working Group, 'Review of the United States' (9 November 2020).

[129] ICC, 'Ireland Continues Its Support of €200,000 to Ensure Reparative Justice Becomes a Meaningful Reality', Press Release (14 December 2020).

[130] C Smith, 'United States Killed Iraqi Military Official and Iraqi Military Personnel in the Two Recent Attacks' (*Just Security*, 5 January 2020) www.justsecurity.org/67917/united-states-killed-iraqi-military-official-and-iraqi-military-personnel-in-the-two-recent-attacks/.

[131] DFAT, 'Ireland Condemns the Recent Attacks on the US Embassy in Baghdad', News (2 January 2020).

[132] 'Qasem Soleimani: US Kills Top Iranian General in Baghdad Air Strike' *BBC News* (3 January 2020) www.bbc.com/news/world-middle-east-50979463. An Iraqi military commander, Abu Mahdi al-Muhandis, was also killed. See Smith (n 130).

[133] M Milanovic, 'The Soleimani Strike and Self-Defence against an Imminent Armed Attack' (*EJIL:Talk!*, 7 January 2020) www.ejiltalk.org/the-soleimani-strike-and-self-defence-against-an-imminent-armed-attack/.

enrichment limits in the 2015 Joint Comprehensive Plan of Action (JCPOA) – Iran launched missile attacks on 8 January 2020 against two Iraqi military bases used by US forces and coalition partners in the campaign against the Islamic State.[134] Ireland condemned the missile strikes against the Iraqi bases and urged all parties to de-escalate.[135] Ireland also repeated its regret over the Trump administration's 2018 decision to withdraw from the JCPOA, but stated that Iran's non-compliance with the agreement, which remained operative, would further destabilise the region.[136] Notably, Ireland did not appear to take a public position on the US strike in Iraq that killed Soleimani, including whether such action was in accordance with international law.[137]

Yemen. The conflict in Yemen, described as the largest humanitarian crisis in the world, entered its sixth year in 2020 as the Saudi-led coalition continued to fight Iran-backed Houthi rebels.[138] All parties to the conflict were accused of war crimes, including attacks that killed and injured civilians or targeted civilian objects.[139] Ireland responded specifically to two attacks attributed to Houthi forces during 2020. On 28 March 2020, Houthi forces launched ballistic missiles at Riyadh and certain border areas. Ireland condemned that action and reminded the parties that 'Indiscriminate attacks against civilians and civilian areas are completely unacceptable, and are contrary to international law'.[140] Ireland also encouraged the parties to abide by the UN Secretary-General's call for a ceasefire in light of the COVID-19 pandemic.[141] In December 2020, a new 'unity cabinet' drawn from opposing Yemeni factions (but united by opposition to the Houthi insurgents) was attacked by Houthi forces at the airport in Aden, resulting in at least 22 deaths.[142] Minister Coveney condemned the 'cowardly attack on the returning Yemeni government' and urged engagement with the UN-led political process.[143]

VI. INTERNATIONAL HUMAN RIGHTS MECHANISMS

Following its review by the Committee on the Elimination of Racial Discrimination in December 2019, Ireland was not reviewed by any of the UN human rights treaty

---

[134] S Lynch, 'Iran Launches Missiles at US Military Bases in Iraq' *Irish Times* (8 January 2020). Iran also mistakenly shot down a Ukrainian passenger jet over Tehran, killing 176 people, within hours of the missile attack.

[135] DFAT, 'Statement by Ireland on Developments in Iran & Iraq', News (8 January 2020).

[136] ibid.

[137] M Anssari and B Nussberger, 'Compilation of States' Reactions to US and Iranian Uses of Force in Iraq in January 2020' (*Just Security*, 22 January 2020) www.justsecurity.org/68173/compilation-of-states-reactions-to-u-s-and-iranian-uses-of-force-in-iraq-in-january-2020/#ReactionsLegalitiyUSStrike.

[138] Human Rights Watch, 'World Report 2021: Yemen, Events of 2020' (2021) www.hrw.org/world-report/2021/country-chapters/yemen.

[139] ibid.

[140] DFAT, 'Statement on Missile Attacks in Saudi Arabia', Statement (30 March 2020).

[141] ibid.

[142] 'Yemen War: Deadly Attack at Aden Airport as New Government Arrives' *BBC News* (31 December 2020) www.bbc.com/news/world-middle-east-55484436.

[143] DFAT, 'Statement by Minister Coveney on Yemen Attack', Press Release (30 December 2020). Ireland played a significant role in driving forward the September 2017 resolution by the UN Human Rights Council that established the Group of Eminent International and Regional Experts on Yemen. See Dáil Deb 31 January 2018, www.oireachtas.ie/en/debates/question/2018-01-31/130/.

monitoring bodies in 2020.[144] Ireland was scheduled to appear before the Human Rights Committee in October 2021, and Ireland's third cycle through the Universal Periodic Review (UPR) of the UN Human Rights Council was set for November 2021.

Although not a member of the 47-member state UN Human Rights Council during 2020 (Ireland last held a seat during 2013–15), Ireland took part in the three regular sessions held in 2020. This included interactive dialogues with country-specific and thematic special rapporteurs and experts, and the commissions of inquiry and fact-finding missions for Burundi, Libya, South Sudan and Syria.[145] Ireland's submissions highlighted its implementation of international human rights standards at home – for example, with respect to the prevention of human trafficking, domestic violence and discrimination against LGBTI+ people – alongside its efforts to promote human rights abroad, including its commitment to the protection of civil society actors and calls to facilitate humanitarian relief and to investigate and prosecute perpetrators of human rights violations and abuses.[146]

Ireland also made statements with respect to each of the 28 states that were subject to the UPR during 2020.[147] Those statements and recommendations highlighted human rights priorities in Irish foreign policy, including:

— the abolition of the death penalty (mentioned in eight statements);
— the adoption or implementation of legislation to combat sexual- and gender-based violence (mentioned in 11 statements);
— the adoption or implementation of anti-discrimination measures for gender and/or sexual orientation (mentioned in 12 statements), including the decriminalisation of consensual same-sex conduct (mentioned in four statements);
— the need to uphold the rights of human rights defenders (mentioned in seven statements); and
— the need to protect freedom of assembly, association and expression (mentioned in six statements).

---

[144] Committee on the Elimination of Racial Discrimination, 'Concluding Observations on the Combined Fifth to Ninth Reports of Ireland' (12 December 2019), UN Doc CERD/C/IRL/CO/5-9. Several human rights treaty-monitoring bodies suspended or postponed their scheduled work during 2020 due to COVID-19.

[145] Ireland's statements to the 43rd, 44th, and 45th Sessions of the Human Rights Council are available at www.dfa.ie/our-role-policies/international-priorities/human-rights/ireland-and-the-human-rights-council/irelandsstatementatthehrc/. Several of Ireland's statements are referenced elsewhere in this report.

[146] Statements of Ireland, 44th Session, Human Rights Council, 'Interactive Dialogue with the Special Rapporteur on Trafficking in Persons, Especially Women and Children' (3 July 2020); 'Interactive Dialogue on the Report of the Special Rapporteur on Violence against Women, Its Causes and Consequences' (7 July 2020); 'Interactive Dialogue on the Independent Expert on Protection against Violence and Discrimination Based on Sexual Orientation and Gender Identity' (8 July 2020); 'Interactive Dialogue on the Report of the Special Rapporteur on the Rights of Peaceful Assembly and of Association' (9 July 2020).

[147] The states reviewed were Andorra, Armenia, Belarus, Bulgaria, Croatia, Grenada, Guinea, Guinea-Bissau, Guyana, Honduras, Jamaica, Kenya, Kiribati, Kuwait, Kyrgyzstan, Laos, Lesotho, Liberia, Libya, Malawi, Maldives, Marshall Islands, Mongolia, Panama, Spain, Sweden, Turkey and the USA. Ireland's statements are available at www.dfa.ie/our-role-policies/international-priorities/human-rights/ireland-and-the-human-rights-council/irelandsstatementsattheupr/.

Three Irish nationals were appointed as Special Procedure Mandate Holders during 2020. In April, Professor Mary Lawlor, the founder of Dublin-based Front Line Defenders and adjunct professor at Trinity College Dublin, became UN Special Rapporteur on the Situation of Human Rights Defenders.[148] In July, Professor Siobhán Mullaly, the Director of the Irish Centre for Human Rights at NUI Galway (and the founding editor of the *Irish Yearbook*), was appointed the UN Special Rapporteur on Trafficking in Persons, Especially Women and Children.[149] Finally, Professor Gerard Quinn, formerly of the Centre on International Disability Law & Policy at NUI Galway, was appointed UN Special Rapporteur on the Rights of Persons with Disabilities in October 2020.[150] Ireland called on all states to issue standing invitations to all Special Procedure Mandate Holders and condemned 'acts of intimidation and reprisal against those seeking to cooperate with the mandates'.[151]

VII. INTERNATIONAL DISARMAMENT

Ireland deposited its ratification of the Treaty on the Prohibition of Nuclear Weapons (TPNW) on 6 August 2020 – the seventy-fifth anniversary of the bombing of Hiroshima.[152] The TPNW gives effect to the obligation upon states parties under Article VI of the 1968 Treaty on the Non-proliferation of Nuclear Weapons (NPT)

> to pursue negotiations in good faith on effective measures relating to cessation of the nuclear arms race at an early date and to nuclear disarmament, and on a treaty on general and complete disarmament under strict and effective international control.[153]

Ireland was part of the core group of states, alongside Austria, Brazil, Mexico, Nigeria and South Africa, that initiated the process leading to adoption of the TPNW.[154] Minister for Foreign Affairs and Defence Simon Coveney described broad support for the treaty, which was set to enter into force in January 2021, as 'a clear indication of the will of the majority of countries to add fresh momentum to achieve the goal of a world free of nuclear weapons'.[155] He added that the TPNW

---

[148] DFAT, 'Tánaiste Congratulates Mary Lawlor on Appointment as UN Special Rapporteur on Human Rights Defenders', Statement (30 April 2020).

[149] Irish Centre for Human Rights, 'Professor Siobhán Mullally Appointed as UN Special Rapporteur', Press Release (17 July 2020).

[150] Raoul Wallenberg Institute, 'The Next UN Special Rapporteur on the Rights of Persons with Disabilities', Press Release (7 October 2020).

[151] Statement of Ireland, Human Rights Council, 44th Session, 'Human Rights Bodies and Mechanisms' (15 June 2020).

[152] Treaty on the Prohibition of Nuclear Weapons (adopted 7 July 2017, entered into force 22 January 2021); UN Secretary-General, Depository Notification No C.N.330.2020.TREATYIES-XXVI.9 (6 August 2020) (Ireland).

[153] Treaty on the Non-Proliferation of Nuclear Weapons (adopted 1 July 1968, entered into force 5 March 1970) 729 UNTS 161, Art VI.

[154] DFAT, 'Statement by Minister of State for the Diaspora and International Development, Ciarán Cannon, TD – Prohibition of Nuclear Weapons Bill 2019', Statement (19 September 2019).

[155] DFAT, 'Statement by Minister on the 50th Ratification of the Treaty on the Prohibition of Nuclear Weapons', News (25 October 2020). By the end of 2020, however, no states known or believed to possess nuclear weapons had joined the TPNW.

'challenges us to think about the enormity of the threat posed by these weapons, and by stigmatizing and prohibiting nuclear weapons, it makes a statement that these weapons are no longer acceptable'.[156]

The Tenth Review Conference of the NPT, scheduled for April–May 2020, was postponed to August 2021 due to COVID-19.[157] At an event marking the fiftieth anniversary of the NPT's entry into force, Minister Coveney recalled the urgency of working towards full implementation and stated that it was an Irish priority to see further consideration given to 'the humanitarian consequences of a nuclear weapons explosion, whether deliberately, by accident or miscalculation'.[158] He also emphasised Ireland's support for a nuclear weapons-free zone in the Middle East and its efforts to promote the 'equal and meaningful participation of women' on the issue.[159] Minister Coveney also addressed the UN Conference on Disarmament and expressed Ireland's regret that the Conference remained unable to adopt a programme of work or reach agreement on new membership applications.[160] He noted Ireland's deep concern over repeated incidents of chemical weapons use in recent years.[161] At a UN Security Council debate in May 2020 on the protection of civilians in armed conflict, Ireland welcomed the priority attached by the UN Secretary-General to the problem posed by the use of explosive weapons in densely populated areas, and Ireland took the lead in driving forward a proposed political declaration on the humanitarian consequences of such tactics.[162] Finally, in his virtual address to the UN General Assembly, Taoiseach Micheál Martin conveyed Ireland's position that North Korea must abandon all nuclear weapons, other weapons of mass destruction and ballistic missile programmes, and that full implementation of the JCPOA must be pursued to prevent Iran from developing nuclear weapons.[163]

VIII. CLIMATE CHANGE

In an address to the Ireland at Fordham Humanitarian Lecture Series setting out Ireland's priorities for the UN Security Council, then-Tánaiste and Minister for Foreign Affairs and Trade Simon Coveney invoked climate change in making the case for multilateralism:

> No country on its own can stop climate change. However, acting together, we can ensure that our children and grandchildren inherit a better world – and we know what we need to do. We have a map. We have a process. We have targets. Working in partnership, we can

[156] ibid.
[157] DFAT, 'Min Coveney Remarks on the Treaty on the Non-Proliferation of Nuclear Weapons', News (15 December 2020).
[158] ibid.
[159] ibid.
[160] DFAT, 'Tánaiste's Statement to the Conference on Disarmament', Speech (24 February 2020).
[161] ibid.
[162] DFAT, 'Ireland National Statement at the Security Council Open Debate on "Protection of Civilians in Armed Conflict"', News (27 May 2020).
[163] Statement of Mr Micheál Martin (n 56).

achieve these targets. Failure to do so is frightening. There is, as I said, the risk of increased conflict. There are island states facing existential threats, which might literally be underwater in our lifetimes. Food systems will need to change, fast. There will be increased demand on the humanitarian system. In addition to our efforts to do better at home, climate action is a cornerstone of Ireland's international development policy. I see delivery on climate change not just as enlightened humanitarianism but, fundamentally, as part of our future national security.[164]

On the domestic front, the Irish government published the Climate Action and Low Carbon Development (Amendment) Bill 2020, which sought to put Ireland on track to meet its international obligations and the goal of net zero emissions by 2050.[165] This remained no small task, given Ireland's poor record on emissions within the EU, notwithstanding a 5.9 per cent decline in 2020 due to COVID-19.[166] Meanwhile, in July, the Supreme Court of Ireland in *Friends of the Irish Environment v Ireland* unanimously quashed a part of Ireland's existing climate strategy – the 'national mitigation plan' required by the Climate Action and Low Carbon Development Act 2015 – on the ground that the plan failed to adequately specify how it would achieve the statutory objectives.[167] The plan lacked the necessary detail to allow 'a reasonable and interested member of the public' to form a view on whether the policy could be considered 'effective and appropriate'.[168] The UN Special Rapporteur on Human Rights and the Environment lauded the decision as a 'landmark' even as the Court declined to find an unenumerated or derived right to a healthy environment under the Irish Constitution.[169] The judgment placed further pressure upon the Irish government to commit to meaningful climate action. It also signalled broadly that government climate policies aimed at meeting international standards may properly be subject to domestic judicial review.

IX. PEACE SUPPORT OPERATIONS

During 2020, members of the Irish Defence Forces (IDF) contributed 569 personnel to 10 overseas missions across Africa, the Middle East and the Balkans.[170] Ireland's

---

[164] DFAT, 'Tánaiste's Lecture to Ireland at Fordham' (n 47).

[165] Department of the Taoiseach, 'Government Publishes New Climate Law Which Commits Ireland to Net-Zero Carbon Emissions by 2050', Press Release (7 October 2020).

[166] K O'Sullivan, 'Ireland's Carbon Emissions Decline by Almost 6% in 2020 Due To Pandemic' *Irish Times* (29 January 2021); K O'Sullivan, 'Ireland Has Third Highest Emissions of Greenhouse Gas in EU' *Irish Times* (26 August 2019).

[167] [2020] IESC 49.

[168] ibid s 6.37.

[169] See O Kelleher, 'The Supreme Court of Ireland's Decision in Friends of the Irish Environment v Government of Ireland ("Climate Case Ireland")' (*EJIL:Talk!*, 9 September 2020) www.ejiltalk.org/the-supreme-court-of-irelands-decision-in-friends-of-the-irish-environment-v-government-of-ireland-climate-case-ireland/.

[170] Dáil Deb 17 November 2020, www.oireachtas.ie/en/debates/question/2020-11-17/437/. At the time of writing, the IDF 2020 annual report was not yet available.

largest commitments remained with the UN Interim Force in Lebanon (UNIFIL) (340 personnel) and the UN Disengagement Observer Force (UNDOF) in Syria (137 personnel).[171] Brigadier General Maureen O'Brien continued to serve as the UNDOF Acting Force Commander.[172] Table 3 shows the number of permanent IDF personnel deployed overseas annually since 2015.

Table 3. Irish Participation in Overseas Peace Support Operations (2015–20)

	Year					
	2015	2016	2017	2018	2019	2020
Numbers deployed overseas	426	423	603	589	678	589

Table 4 shows the breakdown of IDF personnel across UN and UN-mandated missions during 2020, accounting for 95 per cent of overseas deployment.

Table 4. IDF Personnel Serving Overseas in UN and UN-Mandated Missions in 2020 (as of 4 November 2020)

Mission	IDF personnel
UNIFIL (UN Interim Force in Lebanon)	340
UNTSO (UN Treaty Supervision Organisation) (Israel and Syria)	12
MINUSMA (UN Mission in Mali)	14
MINURSO (UN Mission for the Referendum in Western Sahara)	2
MONUSCO (UN Stabilisation Mission in the DRC)	3
UNDOF (UN Disengagement Observer Force) (Syria)	137
EUFOR (EU-Led Operation in Bosnia and Herzegovina)	5
EUTM Mali (EU-Led Training Mission)	13
KFOR (NATO-Led Security Presence in Kosovo)	13
EU Naval Service (Operation Irini) (Libya arms embargo)	3
Total	542

In March 2020, Vice Admiral Mark Mellet, IDF Chief of Staff, delivered remarks as part of the Ireland at Fordham Humanitarian Lecture Series in which he

---

[171] ibid. On the day-to-day operations of various IDF peacekeeping contingents, see S O'Riordan, 'Spare a Thought for Ireland's Peacekeepers Away From Home at Christmas' *Irish Examiner* (2 January 2021).
[172] DOD, 'An Taoiseach and Minister Kehoe Pay Tribute to Irish Peacekeepers on International Day of UN Peacekeepers', Press Release (29 May 2020).

stressed Ireland's long commitment to peacekeeping operations and the current focus on 'systematically integrating protection of civilians and gender based violence initiatives into policy and practice to protect the most vulnerable, especially women and girls'.[173] Vice Admiral Mellet highlighted the Irish Navy's contribution in recent years to rescue operations in the Mediterranean, ongoing participation in missions in Mali and Syria, and Ireland's leadership on promoting the link between gender equality and peace, including efforts 'to institutionalise a gender perspective' amongst Irish forces.[174]

On the occasion of the International Day of UN Peacekeepers, then-Minister of State with Responsibility for Defence Paul Kehoe TD also highlighted Ireland's proactive role in advancing the Women, Peace and Security agenda in peacekeeping operations and commended the Irish women and men serving in such operations.[175] Then-Taoiseach and Minister for Defence Leo Varadkar remarked that Ireland, with its continuous participation in UN peacekeeping since 1958, was 'as proud of the blue helmet as we are of the harp or the shamrock' – and that Ireland would bring its experience to bear at the UN Security Council.[176]

On 21 December 2020, a Lebanese Military Tribunal convicted Mr Mahmoud Bazzi of the 1980 murders of Privates Thomas Barrett and Derek Smallhorne, Irish personnel then deployed to UNIFIL.[177] Another Irish soldier, Private John O'Mahony, survived serious injuries from the incident and participated in the proceedings against Mr Bazzi.[178] Irish officials, who had impressed upon Lebanese officials the importance of obtaining justice for the victims, expressed satisfaction that a conviction was finally obtained.[179]

X. INTERNATIONAL DEVELOPMENT AND DIASPORA AFFAIRS

Ireland's Overseas Development Assistance (ODA) totalled €869.87 million in 2019,[180] a 10 per cent increase over its ODA in 2018.[181] This amounted to 0.32 per cent of the Irish Gross National Product (GNP) – a figure broadly in line with ODA as a percentage of GNP since 2015, but significantly lower than the high of 0.59 per cent achieved in 2008 and the long-standing goal to allocate 0.7 per cent of Gross National Income to ODA by 2030.[182] The breakdown of Irish ODA for the period 2014–19 is set out in Table 5.

---

[173] Vice Admiral Mark Mellett, 'The Sustainable Development Goas and Common Values – A Vital Framework for Humanitarian Action' Speech (Fordham University, 2 March 2020).
[174] ibid.
[175] 'International Day of UN Peacekeepers' (n 172).
[176] ibid.
[177] DOD, 'Minister for Defence Mr Simon Coveney, TD, Notified by the Lebanese Authorities of the Convention of Mr Mahmoud Bazzi, the Alleged Perpetrator of the Murder of Two Irish Soldiers in 1980' Press Release (21 December 2020).
[178] ibid.
[179] ibid.
[180] The equivalent figures for 2020 were not available at time of writing.
[181] Government of Ireland, 'Overseas Development Assistance: Annual Report 2019', 74.
[182] ibid 8, 75.

Table 5. Irish ODA, 2014–19

	Year					
	2014	2015	2016	2017	2018	2019
Total ODA Budget (€ millions)	614.86	647.56	725.78	743.42	791.63	869.87
per cent of GNP	0.39	0.32	0.32	0.32	0.31	0.32

ODA in 2019 was guided by Ireland's current strategy for international development – A Better World – which prioritises gender equality, climate action, good governance and combating global poverty. The 2019 Annual Report, published on 10 November 2020, highlighted Ireland's attention to gender equality and women's empowerment.[183] Minister of State for the Diaspora and International Development Colm Brophy TD explained how changes within Ireland helped to explain that focus when it came to ODA:

> Gender equality is a fundamental human right. It is an essential driver of sustainable development. However, there are those who are pushing back against gender equality. We in Ireland have over our lifetimes travelled a journey on gender equality. Our story resonates with others. Our journey has helped make Irish Aid a global champion on gender equality and development, with the proportion of Irish Aid targeting gender equality consistently among the highest in the OECD.[184]

ODA was also guided by two additional initiatives launched in 2019: Global Ireland's Strategy for Africa to 2025 and the Strategy for Partnership with Small Island Developing States.[185] Among the achievements detailed in the 2019 Annual Report are:

— Irish NGOs funded by Irish Aid provided life-saving assistance to more than 300,000 people affected by humanitarian emergencies in 23 countries;
— Humanitarian experts from Ireland's Rapid Response Corps supported UN crisis operations in 16 different countries; and
— Irish Aid provided emergency supplies to more than 30,000 households across Nigeria, Mozambique, Ethiopia and Burkina Faso.[186]

2019 also saw more than 150 high-level visits between Ireland and African countries, including a visit by then-Taoiseach Leo Varadkar to Mali and Ethiopia, and extensive efforts to deepen bilateral development cooperation with Mozambique.[187] Ireland launched the Domestic Resource Mobilisation initiative to support tax administrative capacity in developing countries.[188]

---

[183] DFAT, 'Ireland's Official Development Assistance Annual Report 2019', Press Release (10 November 2020).
[184] ibid.
[185] ibid 8.
[186] ibid 10–11.
[187] ibid 11–12.
[188] ibid 12.

The Irish government also found itself on the receiving end of praise in 2020 for its international development work. In May, the Organisation for Economic Cooperation and Development (OECD) described Ireland's programme as 'strong, with many areas of excellence', and found that Ireland 'walks the talk' in terms of prioritising the furthest behind and advocating for multilateralism.[189] In November, the Overseas Development Institute gave Ireland top ranking in its 'Principled Aid Index 2020'.[190] In reflecting on this recognition, Minister Brophy expressed Ireland's plans to deepen its engagement on climate change, global health and the needs of those in crisis.[191]

Ireland allocated more than €150 million in funding to the battle against COVID-19 in 2020.[192] Other development aid and humanitarian relief was directed to a variety of conflicts and disasters around the world. Ireland provided €7 million to the United Nations Relief Works Agency for Palestine Refugees in the Near East (UNRWA), noting the magnifying impact of the pandemic on the long-standing vulnerabilities and needs of 5.6 million Palestinian refugees.[193] At a June 2020 donor conference, Ireland pledged an additional €25 million to the humanitarian crisis in Syria.[194] In August 2020, a massive warehouse explosion in the port of Beirut – attributed to the negligent safeguarding of explosive materials – resulted in hundreds of deaths, thousands wounded and wide-scale property destruction that left many more thousands homeless.[195] Ireland dispatched medical equipment and personal protective equipment to assist the health response to the disaster.[196] In October, Ireland pledged €1 million to support the needs of Bangladesh and other states hosting Rohingya refugees[197] and allocated €500,000 to the International Committee of the Red Cross for relief efforts in the Central Sahel, increasing Ireland's total funding to that region to €5 million for 2020.[198] Ireland also contributed €200,000 in response to flooding in Sudan in November 2020,[199] pledged €2.4 million to support the humanitarian response to the Tigray crisis in Ethiopia[200] and contributed €4 million in

---

[189] DFAT, 'Irish Aid "Walks the Talk" Says OECD', Press Release (20 May 2020). The OECD report is available at www.dfa.ie/media/missions/prepparis/OECD-DAC-Peer-Review-Ireland-2020.pdf.

[190] DFAT, 'Ireland Ranks No 1 in How it Delivers Foreign Aid', Press Release (10 November 2020).

[191] ibid.

[192] DFAT, 'Minister Simon Coveney Participates in UN General Assembly Special Session on COVID-19', Press Release (4 December 2020).

[193] DFAT, 'Tánaiste Simon Coveney Pledges Support to the UN Agency for Palestine Refugees', Press Release (23 June 2020).

[194] DFAT, 'Ireland Pledges €25m to the Syria Crisis in 2020', Press Release (30 June 2020).

[195] 'Beirut Explosion: At Least 135 Killed as Port Officials Put Under House Arrest' *Irish Times* (5 August 2020).

[196] DFAT, 'Support for Lebanon', Press Release (16 August 2020).

[197] 'Rohingya Refugee Crisis' (n 109).

[198] DFAT, 'Min Brophy Announces Additional €500,000 Funding for Red Cross in Central Sahel', Press Release (22 October 2020).

[199] DFAT, 'Irish Aid Announces €200,000 Fund to Support Sudan Flood Relief', Press Release (3 November 2020

[200] DFAT, 'Minister Coveney Announces €2.4 Million Irish Aid Response to Ethiopia Humanitarian Crisis', Press Release (4 December 2020).

Irish Aid assistance to displaced persons in Mozambique, where the government was grappling with an Islamic militant-led insurgency.[201]

In terms of diaspora affairs, Ireland announced a new Diaspora Strategy for 2020–25, which included five key commitments:

— to ensure that vulnerable overseas Irish communities receive support;
— to hold a referendum to extend the right to vote in presidential elections to Irish citizens abroad;
— to seek solutions for undocumented Irish citizens in the USA;
— to promote work and study opportunities in Ireland to diaspora communities; and
— to facilitate emigration back to Ireland.[202]

Ireland also launched a new government strategy for the Asia-Pacific region, which aimed to create new opportunities for strategic engagement, increase economic and commercial engagement up to €100 billion in trade by 2025 (up from €56 billion in 2018) and provide support to the more than 100,000 Irish-born people in the region.[203] Closer to home, Irish Aid launched the Saolta programme, an initiative aimed at increasing 'awareness and understanding of global development issues' across the adult and community education sector in Ireland, with the broader goal of strengthening local engagement on global issues such as poverty, gender equality and migration.[204]

---

[201] DFAT, 'Minister Brophy Announces Further Assistance of €1m to Humanitarian Crisis in Northern Mozambique', Press Release (10 December 2020).
[202] DFAT, 'Launch of Diaspora Strategy 2025', Press Release (4 December 2020).
[203] DFAT, 'Launch of Asia Pacific Strategy: "Global Ireland: Delivering in the Asia Pacific Region to 2025"', Speech (9 January 2020).
[204] Irish Aid, 'Launch of Saolta', News (31 January 2020).

Irish State Practice on the Law of the Sea 2020

RÍAN DERRIG*

I. INTRODUCTION

TWO LEITMOTIFS FEATURE prominently in this survey of Ireland's practice on law-of-the-sea-related topics in 2020: the state's efforts to respond to consequences of the UK's exit from the EU; and effects of the COVID-19 pandemic on government, and on maritime- and ocean-related activities. Both themes recur in the report's analysis of state practice on different topics. Concerning Brexit, significant negative consequences for Irish fishers were concretised in the terms negotiated between the EU and the UK in the Trade and Cooperation Agreement, finalised on 24 December 2020. Brexit has also strained territorial and maritime disputes that have persisted since the formation of the Irish Free State and the partition of the island in the form of standing, if infrequently articulated and studiously avoided, claims maintained by both Ireland and the UK. Containment of the material stakes attached to these disputes – in relation to Lough Foyle and Rockall – has been made more challenging by the removal of the mediating influence of EU law frameworks and the necessity of reattaching material costs to the existence of territorial and maritime borders between the EU and the UK.

Concerning COVID-19, an obvious consequence of the public health measures required by the pandemic has been a delay in the work of government departments. This has affected Ireland's development of a National Marine Planning Framework, an important legislative project that implements principles of Marine Spatial Planning established at the EU and international levels. The new planning processes established under this framework will have significant consequences for the development of renewable energy projects in Irish waters, which is an area of interest in government and across Irish political parties. Redeployment of naval service personnel to support health professionals operating COVID-19 test centres meant fewer vessels and personnel were available to enforce fisheries regulations in Irish waters. Ongoing negotiations at the UN level in the context of the Intergovernmental Conference on an international legally binding instrument under the United Nations Convention on the Law of the Sea (UNCLOS) on the conservation and sustainable use of marine biological diversity of areas beyond national jurisdiction (the BBNJ process), in which Ireland is participating, were significantly delayed by

* I am grateful to Lt Cdr Claire Murphy, Lt Gillian Power and Capt Patrick Burke of the Irish Naval Service, and to Eleanor Buckley of the SFPA for providing me with statistics that appear in this report.

the COVID-19 pandemic. Among other topics, these negotiations pertain to regulating the use of marine genetic resources in ocean areas beyond national jurisdiction. It has become clear that such resources are of much importance in developing medical products, including test kits used to identify the COVID-19 virus.

The UN Secretary-General's Report on Oceans and the Law of the Sea 2020 noted the significance of the United Nations Decade of Ocean Science for Sustainable Development 2021–2030 as a convening framework for activities intended to support states in achieving the 2030 Agenda for Sustainable Development. The 'Ocean Decade', seeking to facilitate 'science we need for the ocean we want', will promote the development of marine science and technology with the aim of facilitating the achievement of targets specified under the 2030 Agenda for Sustainable Development, Goal 14 (Sustainable Development Goal 14) on life below water. The Ocean Decade was a proposal of the Intergovernmental Oceanographic Committee of UNESCO in 2017, which coordinates the initiative.

II. MARINE SPATIAL PLANNING

Directive 2014/89/EU of the European Parliament and of the Council of 23 July 2014 establishing a framework for maritime spatial planning (the MSP Directive) required Member States to establish a maritime planning process, and through this process to produce a maritime spatial plan or plans.[1] Acting on a legal basis found in Articles 43(2), 100(2), 192(1), and 194(2) of the Treaty on the Functioning of the European Union (TFEU), which relate to agriculture and fisheries; transport; environment; and energy respectively, this directive was prompted by a recognition of the increasing demands being made for maritime space for different, overlapping and at times competing uses, all of which place pressures on marine environments and are interrelated with activities on land, having social and economic consequences for communities relying on coastal resources.[2] The aim of marine spatial planning (MSP), as outlined in the MSP Directive, is to promote sustainable development by identifying and managing the use of marine spaces for different purposes. This should have the consequence of possible conflicts over such spaces being better managed, multipurpose uses being facilitated and the growth of marine economies being sustainably developed based on an ecosystem approach. The Directive emphasises the importance of taking into account land–sea interactions, an emphasis reflected in Irish legislation and policy documents, which frequently note connections between the state's National Marine Planning Framework (NMPF) and the terrestrial National Planning Framework.[3]

---

[1] Directive 2014/89/EU of the European Parliament and of the Council of 23 July 2014 establishing a framework for maritime spatial planning [2014] OJ L257/135. Different practices exist concerning the use of 'maritime' or 'marine'. In recent official publications, Irish government departments have usually used 'marine'. Both terms appear in this report and are used interchangeably.

[2] ibid recitals 1, 14 and 16. Consolidated version of the Treaty on the Functioning of the European Union [2012] OJ C326/1.

[3] Department of Housing, Planning and Local Government, 'Marine Planning Policy Statement (Consultation Draft)' (2019).

At the EU level, EU legislation concerning MSP is situated in relation to the Union's Integrated Maritime Policy (IMP), first launched in a Communication from the Commission in 2007.[4] The legal framework for the IMP is found in Regulation No 508/2014 of the European Parliament and of the Council of 15 May 2014 on the European Maritime and Fisheries Fund, with a legal basis in Articles 42, 43(2), 91(1), 100(2), 173(3), 175, 188, 192(1), 194(2) and 195(2) TFEU, relating to agriculture and fisheries; transport; industry; economic, social and territorial cohesion; environment; energy; and tourism.[5] The IMP articulates an approach to all sea-related EU policies based on the premise that the Union can extract more benefit from its maritime spaces by coordinating uses of those spaces, and was motivated by an awareness that existing regulation of maritime spaces was fragmented, often subject to varying sector-specific regulation. The policy is part of Union efforts to strengthen what it calls the 'blue economy' and achieve 'blue growth', terms first employed by the Commission in 2012.[6] At the international level, initiatives that aim to encourage and facilitate states employing principles of MSP are widespread. In 2017, the International Oceanographic Commission of UNESCO, with the European Commission, adopted the Joint Roadmap to accelerate Marine Spatial Planning (MSP) Processes Worldwide.[7] This resulted in the establishment of the international MSPforum and the MSPglobal Initiative, which are intended to contribute to the Ocean Decade, and to Sustainable Development Goal 14 on life below water.

Ireland has worked towards implementing the requirements of the MSP Directive through a series of legislative actions since 2014.[8] The report period was one of consultation and some delay, bookended by important developments. In November 2019, the government approved the Marine Planning Policy Statement and the draft NMPF. Public consultation on the draft NMPF took place over 2020, moving online after April 2020 due to public health guidelines concerning the COVID-19 pandemic and constituting the first civil-service-led online public consultation.[9] At the end of the report period, the draft NMPF was due to be approved by the government, followed by the Dáil and Seanad (the lower and upper houses of the Irish Parliament respectively) in the first half of 2021. Over the course of the report period, an important piece of legislation was being developed in support of Ireland's MSP. The general scheme of the Maritime Planning

---

[4] Commission, 'An Integrated Maritime Policy for the European Union' (Communication) COM (2007) 0575.

[5] Regulation (EU) No 508/2014 of the European Parliament and of the Council of 15 May 2014 on the European Maritime and Fisheries Fund and repealing Council Regulations (EC) No 2328/2003, (EC) No 861/2006, (EC) No 1198/2006 and (EC) No 791/2007 and Regulation (EU) No 1255/2011 of the European Parliament and of the Council [2014] OJ L149/1.

[6] Commission, 'Blue Growth Opportunities for Marine and Maritime Sustainable Growth' (Communication) COM (2012) 0494.

[7] Conference Conclusions: 2nd International Conference and Marine/Maritime Spatial Planning, 'Joint Roadmap to Accelerate Maritime/Marine Spatial Planning Processes Worldwide' (UNESCO, 2017) www.mspglobal2030.org/wp-content/uploads/2019/03/Joint_Roadmap_MSP_v5.pdf.

[8] European Union (Framework for Maritime Spatial Planning) Regulations 2016, SI No 352/2016; Planning and Development (Amendment) Act 2018, pt 5.

[9] Department of Housing, Local Government and Heritage, 'Project Ireland 2040: National Marine Planning Framework' (2021) 6.

and Development Management (MPDM) Bill was published in December 2019.[10] Significant changes were subsequently made to the text and title of the bill, which has proceeded as the Marine Area Planning Bill 2021 (MAP Bill). This Bill restated and added to the legislative basis set out for the NMPF in Part 5 of the Planning and Development (Amendment) Act 2018.[11] The primary purpose of the MAP Bill is to create a single planning regime that will apply to the entirety of Ireland's maritime area. This regime will replace the processes by which development and activities are currently regulated under the Foreshore Act of 1933.[12] The process laid out in the new Bill will operate on the basis of one consent being granted to permit occupation of a marine area (identified as Maritime Area Consent) and one consent being granted to develop (identified as planning permission), subject to a single environmental impact assessment. While, under the Foreshore Act, regulated activities were in practice led by those wishing to undertake them, ie developers, the MAP Bill conceives of such activities as being subject to planning undertaken in line with the NMPF, and so being 'plan-led'. An important difference between the regime under the Foreshore Act and that outlined in the MAP Bill is that while the former covered the 'foreshore', defined as the bed and shore of the sea, tidal rivers and estuaries to the outer limit of the territorial sea, the MAP Bill will cover Ireland's entire maritime area to a distance of 200 nautical miles, ie its territorial seas, its exclusive economic zone (EEZ) and most areas of continental shelf.[13] This legislative work is being undertaken in a context of heightened interest in the development of renewable energy projects in Irish waters, which are anticipated to make a large contribution to the achievement of the state's decarbonisation goals, as well in the possibility of undertaking carbon capture and sequestration projects.[14]

III. MARINE LIVING RESOURCES

Depletion of fish stocks and continuing (in some cases, dramatic) loss of biodiversity in the world's oceans is increasingly recognised as a topic that must be addressed through international cooperation, potentially on the basis of binding multilateral treaty commitments. Ireland is party to a number of international instruments adopted with the aim of slowing loss of biodiversity, including ocean biodiversity. In 2010, the Conference of the Parties to the Convention on Biological Diversity (CBD) adopted the Strategic Plan for Biodiversity 2011–2020. The Plan included a set of targets – the Aichi Biodiversity Targets – which sought to increase awareness of the importance of maintaining biodiversity and specify actions that should

---

[10] Department of Housing, Planning and Local Government, 'Marine Planning and Development Management Bill (MPDM): General Scheme' (2019).

[11] Planning and Development (Amendment) Act, 5.

[12] Foreshore Act 1933. On case law clarifying the meaning of the foreshore in Irish law, see R Long, 'Irish State Practice on the Law of the Sea 2015 and 2016' (2016) 11–12 *Irish Yearbook of International Law* 107, 112–13; R Long, *Marine Resource Law* (Dublin, Round Hall, 2007) para 2-09.

[13] Long, *Marine Resource Law* (n 12) 67–68.

[14] 'Project Ireland 2040' (n 9) 115–26.

be taken by national governments to support its protection. Target 6 specified that by 2020 all fish and invertebrate stocks and aquatic plants should be

> harvested sustainably, legally and applying ecosystem based approaches so that overfishing is avoided, recovery plans and measures are in place for all depleted species, fisheries have no significant adverse impacts on threatened species and vulnerable ecosystems and the impacts of fisheries on stocks, species and ecosystems are within safe ecological limits.[15]

Ireland, like all coastal states, was required by Target 11 to designate at least 10 per cent of its coastal and marine areas as marine protected areas (MPAs), or as areas subject to other effective area-based conservation measures (OECMs), by 2020. A similar goal was included as Target 14.5 of Sustainable Development Goal 14 on life below water.

In December 2019, the Minister for Housing, Planning and Local Government established the MPA Advisory Group, comprising independent experts tasked with producing a report on the expansion of Ireland's network of MPAs. The report of this group was published in October 2020. Consultation with the public and stakeholders took place through 2020, further public consultation was initiated after the report's publication and the government was expected to propose legislation based on the recommendations of the expert group in 2021. The report noted Ireland's obligations with respect to conservation and sustainable management of the marine environment not only under the CBD, but also under the Convention for the Protection of the Marine Environment of the North-East Atlantic (the OSPAR Convention), the EU Marine Strategy Framework Directive and existing area-based protection established under the EU Birds and Habitats Directives (the Natura 2000 network).[16] The advisory group summarised the report's conclusions about Ireland's fulfilment of these obligations in the following terms:

> At this point, Ireland's network of protected areas cannot be considered coherent, representative, connected or resilient or to be meeting Ireland's international commitments and legal obligations. There is no definition of MPA in Irish law and this is a gap which needs to be addressed. The provisions of the Wildlife Acts, as amended, are limited in terms of their geographic scope, applying only to the foreshore. This means that currently protection in marine areas beyond 12 nautical miles is limited to measures taken under the EU Birds and Habitats Directives or the OSPAR Convention.[17]

---

[15] COP 10 Decision X/2, 'Strategic Plan for Biodiversity 2011–2020', Convention on Biological Diversity (2010).

[16] Department of Housing, Local Government and Heritage, 'Expanding Ireland's Marine Protected Area Network: A Report by the Marine Protected Area Advisory Group' (2020); Convention for the Protection of the Marine Environment of the North-East Atlantic (opened for signature on 22 September 1992, entered into force 25 March 1998) 2354 UNTS 67 (OSPAR); Directive 2008/56/EC of the European Parliament and of the Council of 17 June 2008 establishing a framework for community action in the field of marine environmental policy (Marine Strategy Framework Directive) [2008] OJ L164/19; Council Directive 92/43/EEC of 21 May 1992 on the conservation of natural habitats and of wild fauna and flora [1992] OJ L206/7; Directive 2009/147/EC of the European Parliament and of the Council of 30 November 2009 on the conservation of wild birds [2010] OJ L20/7.

[17] 'Expanding Ireland's Marine Protected Area Network' (n 16) vii.

The report of the expert group proposed an operational definition of an MPA for MPAs in Ireland, made detailed recommendations about how MPAs should be designated and interconnected, and examined the premises underpinning designation of MPAs – addressing in quite substantive detail the social and economic consequences of managing activities in such areas in this way.[18] The 2020 Stock Book, a report published annually by the Marine Institute, identified a decline in the number of sustainably fished stocks in 2020, to 33 out of 74 (45 per cent), compared to 35 out of 74 (47 per cent) in 2019.[19] The percentage of stocks overfished remained the same as the previous year, at 18 per cent, while the percentage of stocks of unknown status increased to 38 per cent. As can be seen in the survey of case law from the superior courts below, examination of pertinent case law from Irish courts in 2020 offers a snapshot of the challenges faced in attempting to sustainably manage fishing resources in Irish waters.

At the international level, the UN Secretary-General's Report on Oceans and the Law of the Sea 2020 noted that of the four ocean-related targets under the Sustainable Development Goals maturing in 2020, only Target 14.5, concerning protected areas, seemed attainable.[20] The Secretary-General specified that as of December 2019, 17 per cent of marine areas under national jurisdiction were covered by protected areas, but only 7.4 per cent of the world's oceans were similarly covered. Many areas of important marine biodiversity had partial or no coverage, and in some cases implementation problems arose after areas were designated as protected. The importance of marine living resources, biodiversity and ecological integrity of marine environments to human health has recently received heightened attention due to the use of marine microbes in medical test kits, including for the COVID-19 virus, and due to their potential uses in the development of new antibiotic drugs.[21]

Marine microbes such as these are widely referred to as marine genetic resources (MGRs). They are increasingly being considered a valuable commodity, especially for pharmaceutical purposes. The ways in which they can be collected and used when found in ocean areas beyond national jurisdiction (ABNJ) is currently one of four principal topics of negotiation in the context of the BBNJ process. The first session of the BBNJ process was held in September 2018, the second in April 2019 and the third in August 2019. Intersessional discussions have proceeded online and the fourth session, postponed due to the COVID-19 pandemic, is scheduled to take place in March 2022. While this was intended to be the final and concluding session,

[18] With respect to what distinguishes an MPA from an OECM, the report of the expert group report noted, drawing on a decision adopted by the COP of the CBD in 2018, that 'The main distinguishing criterion between a protected area and an OECM [other effective area-based conservation measures] is that the primary objective for protected areas must be nature conservation, whereas OECMs may have other primary objectives, such as the restoration of a sustainable fishery or the conservation of historic features, but also deliver effective in-situ conservation of biodiversity'. ibid 33.

[19] *The Stock Book 2020: Annual Review of Fish Stocks in 2020 with Management Advice for 2021* (Marine Institute, 2020) 17.

[20] UNGA, 'Report of the Secretary-General on Oceans and the Law of the Sea 74/19' (2020) UN Doc A/75/340 para 59.

[21] ibid para 61; H Scales, 'Covid Tests and Superbugs: Why the Deep Sea Is Key to Fighting Pandemics' *The Guardian* (London, 29 September 2021) www.theguardian.com/environment/2021/sep/29/covid-tests-and-superbugs-how-the-deep-sea-could-help-us-fight-pandemics.

at the time of writing the likelihood of a text being agreed at that point is considered unlikely, and a fifth session may be required. Alongside the regulation of MGRs, the overall package that is intended to constitute the treaty instrument consists of three other significant parts: the regulation of area-based management tools, including MPAs; the regulation of the conduct of environmental impact assessments; and capacity building and transfer of marine technology. The first and fourth parts – on MGRs, including questions of benefit sharing, and on capacity building and technology transfer – are the subjects of particularly strong disagreement broadly divided along global north/global south lines. Put simply, these parts engage significant financial stakes: in the case of MGRs, attaching to the degree of freedom to use such resources without committing to transfer benefits derived from their use to least-developed states; and in the case of capacity building and technology transfer, attaching to the extent to which such activities are voluntary or mandatory.[22] On the above parts, the Irish position is advanced as part of the EU's common position, and it coheres with the general approach of global north, industrialised states.[23]

As has been observed in previous reports by Ronán Long, the BBNJ process is of significant importance to Ireland as the new instrument will apply to the high seas over areas of Irish continental margin beyond 200 nautical miles from the baselines. Ireland also has been involved in deep ocean research projects relating to ABNJ, including the ATLAS and MERCES projects. The ATLAS project worked across the North Atlantic to better understand how area-based management approaches can be applied to deep-sea ecosystems and MGRs, concluding in 2020. The iAtlantic project now continues this work. The MERCES project focused on the restoration of degraded marine habitats.

At the third session of the BBNJ process, on 30 August 2019, the Irish Department of Foreign Affairs supported a side event entitled 'Capacity-Building, Gender Empowerment and the BBNJ Agreement', along with the World Maritime University, the government of the Republic of Palau and The Nippon Foundation. The event examined initiatives underway in particular multilateral organisations to promote gender equality and the empowerment of women in ocean affairs.

IV. FISHERIES

A. EU–UK Trade and Cooperation Agreement

The EU and the UK concluded the Trade and Cooperation Agreement (TCA) on 24 December 2020. The EU–UK Withdrawal Agreement had been concluded

---

[22] V de Lucia, 'The Question of the Common Heritage of Mankind and the Negotiations towards a Global Treaty on Marine Biodiversity in Areas beyond National Jurisdiction: No End in Sight?' [2020] *McGill International Journal of Sustainable Development Law and Policy* 138; R Long and MH Nordquist, *Marine Biodiversity of Areas beyond National Jurisdiction*, vol 24 (Leiden, Brill/Nijhoff, 2021).

[23] Statement of the European Union and its Member States at the Intergovernmental Conference on an internationally binding instrument under the United Nations Convention of the Law of the Sea on the conservation and sustainable use of marine biological diversity of areas beyond national jurisdiction 2018. http://statements.unmeetings.org/media2/19407932/eu-general-statement-written-version.pdf.

on 17 October 2019 and entered into force on 1 February 2020. As noted above, the report period was dominated by media coverage of the negotiations that culminated in the TCA, with fishing frequently gaining much attention as a source of particularly acute disagreement. In substance, the TCA is a bilateral agreement between the EU and the UK, addressing trade issues and cooperation on specified subject matters.[24] Heading Five of the TCA addresses fisheries, establishing a framework whereby the EU and the UK will cooperate to manage fish stocks and fishing in their waters. Under this new framework, access will be granted to UK and EU Member State vessels to the 'waters' of each party, subject to being granted licences determined by reference to total allowable catch (TAC) levels agreed between the EU and the UK on an annual basis.[25] As a legal framework intended to permit several parties to collectively manage and distribute a natural resource between themselves, the structure, language and concepts of Heading Five resemble the Common Fisheries Policy (CFP), with the caveat that distribution is skewed somewhat more in the UK's favour than had been the case under the CFP. Changes to shares of the TACs allotted to the UK will be phased in over a five-year period from 2021 to 2026, with these shares being negotiated annually thereafter through a process outlined in Heading Five. Each fish stock has its own TAC; however, the UK share of the TAC for 55 stocks will increase from 2021 onwards, with corresponding decreases in Union shares. Due to the variegated nature of these transfers from Union to UK vessels, different Member States are affected differently. The value of these changes has yet to be realised, but by 2026 the total final transfer made by Ireland due to these changes is estimated to amount to a 15 per cent reduction in the overall value of Irish quotas in 2020, which means Ireland is one of the most seriously affected Member States.[26]

B. Law Enforcement and Compliance

The Naval Service and the Sea Fisheries Protection Authority (SFPA) are charged with tasks relating to the enforcement of the EU law framework of the CFP and

---

[24] T Bickl, 'EU–UK Collaborative Dispute Resolution – Why Are Northern Ireland Issues So Cumbersome?' (*OpinioJuris*, 24 July 2021) http://opiniojuris.org/2021/07/24/EU-UK-collaborative-dispute-resolution-why-are-northern-ireland-issues-so-cumbersome/.

[25] Trade and Cooperation Agreement between the European Union and the European Atomic Energy Community, of the one part, and the United Kingdom of Great Britain and Northern Ireland, of the other part [2021] OJ L149/2, Art 495(1)(g). The definition of 'waters' in the TAC includes territorial waters, with special arrangements applying in respect of the UK to 'the territorial sea adjacent to the Bailiwick of Guernsey, the Bailiwick of Jersey and the Isle of Man'. It is notable that under the CFP, Member States have the possibility, until 31 December 2022, of restricting fishing in territorial waters 'to fishing vessels that traditionally fish in those waters from ports on the adjacent coast': Regulation (EU) No 1380/2013 of the European Parliament and of the Council of 11 December 2013 on the Common Fisheries Policy, amending Council Regulations (EC) No 1954/2003 and (EC) No 1224/2009 and repealing Council Regulations (EC) No 2371/2002 and (EC) No 639/2004 and Council Decision 2004/585/EC [2013] OJ L354/22, Art 5(2).

[26] 'Report of the Seafood Task Force: Navigating Change. The Way Forward for Our Seafood Sector and Coastal Communities in the Wake of the EU/UK Trade and Cooperation Agreement' (2021). This task force was established by the Irish Minister for Agriculture, Food and the Marine.

international fisheries law. These bodies undertake these tasks on behalf of Ireland, acting in its legal capacity as a flag, coastal and port state.[27] The statistics presented in Table 1 show the Naval Service undertook 309 inspections of the 1169 vessels sighted in 2020, cited 15 for infringements and detained 16. The vessels detained were flagged in Ireland (10), France (5) and Germany (1).

Table 1. Fisheries Vessels Boarded, Inspected and Detained by the Naval Service in 2020

Nationality	Sightings	Boardings	Infringements	Detentions
Ireland	632	145	4	10
Spain	218	52	4	0
UK	91	32	2	0
France	207	68	5	5
Belgium	7	4	–	–
Germany	2	2	0	1
Netherlands	9	4	–	–
Russian Federation	2	1	–	–
Poland	1	1	–	–
Total	**1169**	**309**	**15**	**16**

Source: Information provided to the author by the Naval Service.

These statistics represent a significant drop in the number of boardings relative to sightings when compared to the same figures for 2019, as seen in Table 2. Responding to media discussion of problems enforcing fisheries regulations in Irish waters, a spokesperson for the Naval Service attributed this drop in boardings to the redeployment of Naval Service ships and personnel to support the Health Service Executive and the National Ambulance Service in running COVID-19 test centres in Dublin, Cork and Galway.[28]

Table 2. Fisheries Vessels Boarded, Inspected and Detained by the Naval Service in 2019

Nationality	Sightings	Boardings	Infringements	Detentions
Ireland	606	339	6	5
Spain	276	255	–	2
UK	96	70	2	2
France	119	86	–	1

(continued)

---

[27] United Nations Convention on the Law of the Sea (opened for signature 10 December 1982, entered into force 16 November 1994) 1833 UNTS 396, Art 73(1) (UNCLOS).

[28] M Delaney, 'Significant Enforcement Problems Prevail in Irish Industry: Fishing's Control Issues' (*Noteworthy*, 7 April 2021) www.noteworthy.ie/net-loss-pt2-enforcement-5401709-Apr2021/.

Nationality	Sightings	Boardings	Infringements	Detentions
Belgium	10	4	–	1
Germany	5	4	–	–
Netherlands	14	7	–	–
Russian Federation	4	3	–	–
Norway	0	0	–	–
Lithuania	0	0	–	–
Denmark	0	0	–	–
Portugal	2	2	–	1
Greenland	1	1	–	–
Estonia	1	1	–	–
Total	1134	772	8	12

Source: Information provided to the author by the Naval Service.

Table 3 shows the SFPA undertook a total of 1808 inspections in 2020. While most inspected boats were Irish-flagged, French-, Spanish- and UK-flagged boats comprised a significant portion of vessels inspected.

Table 3. Fisheries Vessels Inspected by the SFPA in 2020

Nationality	SFPA inspections
Denmark	27
Faroe Islands	10
France	120
Germany	6
Iceland	1
Ireland	1435
Norway	19
Poland	1
Spain	107
UK	82
Total	1808

Source: Information provided to the author by the SFPA.

C. Penalty Point System

On 28 August 2020, the Taoiseach (Irish Prime Minister) Micheál Martin, acting as Minister for Agriculture, Food and the Marine, made Statutory Instrument (SI)

No 318 of 2020, the European Union (Common Fisheries Policy) (Point System) Regulations 2020.[29] SI 318 transposed into Irish law requirements specified in Article 92 of Council Regulation (EC) No 1224/2009 of 20 November 2009 (the Control Regulation) and Articles 125–34 (Title VII) of Commission Implementing Regulation (EU) No 404/2011 of 8 April 20113 (the Commission Regulation).[30] These articles of the Control Regulation and the Commission Regulation required Member States to establish a system, through national legislation, whereby penalty points can be assigned to holders of fishing licences for serious infractions of regulations specified by the EU law framework of the CFP. This order was the Irish government's fourth attempt to instate such a system. Previous statutory instruments made with the same aim in 2014, 2016 and 2018 were all subjected to challenge and struck down by decisions of the High Court and the Supreme Court.[31] On 2 July 2020, the European Commission had sent a reasoned opinion to Ireland in accordance with the process established in Article 258 TFEU due to its failure to fulfil its obligations under the Control Regulation, stating that:

> Ireland has failed to comply with European Union rules on establishing a point system for fisheries-related serious infringements committed by masters and licence holders of vessels flying the flag of Ireland. The Commission considers that Ireland has not established a system that assigns an appropriate number of points to masters of fishing vessels who commit serious violations of the common fisheries policy rules. It has also failed to put into operation the current national legislation implementing the point system for licence holders.[32]

The Commission has also withheld European and Maritime Fisheries Funds from Ireland due to the state's failure to successfully instate such a points system.[33] SI 318 provides for the establishment of a Determination Panel composed of '3 independent legal professionals' appointed by the SFPA upon the nomination of the Attorney General. If requested by a licence holder, the Panel will hold an oral hearing to determine the assignment of penalty points, and a determination can be appealed to an Appeals Officer, appointed by the Minister for Agriculture, Food and the Marine (the Minister) upon the nomination of the Attorney General, who will be a practising barrister or solicitor of at least five years' standing.

---

[29] European Union (Common Fisheries Policy) (Point System) Regulations 2020, SI 318/2020.

[30] Council Regulation (EC) No 1224/2009 of 20 November 2009 establishing a Community control system for ensuring compliance with the rules of the common fisheries policy, amending Regulations (EC) No 847/96, (EC) No 2371/2002, (EC) No 811/2004, (EC) No 768/2005, (EC) No 2115/2005, (EC) No 2166/2005, (EC) No 388/2006, (EC) No 509/2007, (EC) No 676/2007, (EC) No 1098/2007, (EC) No 1300/2008, (EC) No 1342/2008 and repealing Regulations (EEC) No 2847/93, (EC) No 1627/94 and (EC) No 1966/2006 [2009] OJ L343/1; Commission Implementing Regulation (EU) No 404/2011 of 8 April 2011 laying down detailed rules for the implementation of Council Regulation (EC) No 1224/2009 establishing a Community control system for ensuring compliance with the rules of the Common Fisheries Policy [2011] OJ L112/1.

[31] For background and analysis of this case law, see Long, 'Irish State Practice' (n 12) 125–26.

[32] 'Maritime Affairs and Fisheries: Commission Sends Reasoned Opinion to IRELAND over Compliance with Point System Rules' (2 July 2020) https://Ec.Europa.Eu/Commission/Presscorner/Detail/EN/INF_20_1212.

[33] On the EMFF and Ireland, see Long, 'Irish State Practice' (n 12) 111; Editorial, 'Taoiseach to Reconsider Irish Penalty Points System after Flaws Unveiled' *The Fishing Daily* (30 August 2020) https://thefishingdaily.com/featured-news/taoiseach-to-reconsider-irish-penalty-points-system-after-flaws-unveiled/; Regulation (EU) No 508/2014 (n 5).

D. High Court and Supreme Court Cases

In *Tom Kennedy and Neil Minihane v The Minister for Agriculture, Food and the Marine*,[34] the Irish High Court delivered its judgment on an action for judicial review of a policy directive made by the Minister in 2019 brought by two holders of commercial sea fishing licences. The case raised interesting questions concerning the nature of the right or interest conferred by the state upon a holder of a sea fishing licence. It also raised issues relating to the extent to which individuals particularly affected by a legislative instrument or ministerial order are entitled to be consulted and informed during the process of adopting that instrument or order. These latter issues were ultimately given greatest consideration and were determinative of the court's judgment in favour of the applicants. The judgment contains some holdings that are of significance in clarifying consultation obligations the state must fulfil when regulating sea fishing, and concerning the extent of the Minister's power to effect regulation of this sector using policy directives. In November 2020, the state appealed the High Court's judgment to the Court of Appeal and sought a stay on the orders made by the High Court.[35] These proceedings remain pending at the time of writing.

The directive challenged, Policy Directive 1 of 2019, excluded vessels over 18 metres in length from fishing with trawl or seine nets within six nautical miles of the baselines, including waters within the baselines, with the exception that fishing for sprat in this zone using such gear would be phased out over two years from 1 January 2020. The applicants operated three vessels from their respective bases in Dingle in County Kerry and Castletownbere in County Cork. They had developed a model of fishing whereby for three months of each year they fished within six nautical miles of the baselines for herring, bull mackerel and sprat. As their vessels were over 18 metres in length, this directive would prohibit them from fishing from herring and mackerel in this zone, and would require them to phase out fishing for sprat. The applicants challenged the directive on two main grounds: that it was ultra vires the powers conferred on the Minister by the Fisheries (Amendment) Act 2003 as amended by the Sea Fisheries and Maritime Jurisdiction Act 2006; and that the directive was adopted by a method inconsistent with the applicant's rights to fair procedures and to be given adequate reasons for the decision taken.

Considering each of these grounds in turn, the applicants' ultra vires argument had two components. First, that while section 3(2) of the Fisheries (Amendment) Act 2003 made the Registrar General of Fishing Boats independent in the performance of their functions subject to 'such policy directives in relation to sea-fishing boat licensing as the Minister may give in writing from time to time', section 3(3) of the same act as amended by section 99(3) of the Sea Fisheries and Maritime Jurisdiction Act 2006 limited the Minister's powers in ways that the directive contravened. Section 3(3) reads:

A policy directive given under subsection (2)(b) may provide for measures to control and regulate the capacity, structure, equipment, use and operation of sea fishing boats for the

---

[34] [2020] IEHC 497.
[35] Department of Agriculture, Food and the Marine, 'McConalogue Lodges Legal Appeal against Court Decision to Allow Large Trawlers Fish inside Ireland's Six Mile Zone', Press Release (11 November 2020).

purpose of protecting, conserving or allowing the sustainable exploitation of living marine aquatic species or the rational management of fisheries, in furtherance of national policy objectives and to comply with requirements of the common fisheries policy of the European Communities or other international obligations which are binding on the State.

Laying stress on the subsection's linking of ministerial policy directives to the purpose of conserving and sustainably using living marine aquatic species or rationally managing fishing, the applicants maintained that Policy Directive 1 had no connection to such aims, but was instead intended to redistribute resources and income from larger to smaller vessels.[36] The court and the applicants made reference to the fact that one of the aims of the directive stated in documents published by the Minister was 'to facilitate the further sustainable development of the small scale inshore and the sea-angling sectors which strongly rely on inshore waters'.[37] A consultation document prepared by the Minister's department elaborated that exclusion of larger vessels from inside the six nautical mile zone would cohere with the aims of the MSP Directive by seeking to strengthen connections between local, small-scale inshore fishers and the economies and resources of this zone.[38] The measure was envisaged as contributing to localising fishing resources and as potentially strengthening the inshore fisheries sector, currently an occupation with an ageing profile.[39] MacGrath J did not accept the applicants' argument that section 3(3) of the Act of 2003 required ministerial policy directives to pursue both conservation aims *and* aims of rational management, and found that Policy Directive 1 challenged did seek to rationally manage sea fisheries. He also found that even were this finding incorrect and the subsection should be read to require that policy directives pursue aims of both kinds, the directive did in fact pursue conservation and sustainability aims.[40] This portion of the judgment is notable for the support it offered, if indirectly, to ministers seeking to pursue aims like redistributing marine resources in accordance with goals of national policy and of EU law.

The second component of the ultra vires argument was that the Minister had acted outside the powers conferred by section 3(2) of the Act of 2003 (subsection 2(a) of which noted the necessity of compliance with obligations of the state under EU law), because Policy Directive 1 contravened provisions of the CFP regulations. This argument was made possible by the fact that the Sea Fisheries (Amendment) Act 2019 permits sea-fishing boats owned and operated in Northern Ireland to fish in the 0–6 nautical mile zone adjacent to the coasts of Ireland provided they comply with obligations that would apply to Irish fishing boats in the same zone.[41] The applicants argued that as a result, the directive contravened the provisions of

---

[36] [2020] IEHC 497 (n 34) paras 18 and 20–21.
[37] ibid para 20.
[38] ibid paras 44 and 55.
[39] ibid para 59.
[40] ibid para 87–92.
[41] On the background to this being the 'voisinage arrangement' agreed between civil servants in Northern Ireland and the Republic of Ireland in 1964–65, subsequently challenged in *Barlow & others v Minister for Agriculture, Food and the Marine & others* [2016] IESC 622, found not to constitute a legal arrangement by the Supreme Court and to thus require legislation in order to continue to operate, see Long, 'Irish State Practice' (n 12) 128–29.

Articles 19 and 20 of Regulation 1380/2013 (the CFP Regulation). Article 19(1) of the CFP Regulation requires that where a Member State adopts national measures for the conservation of fish stocks in Union waters, those measures must apply solely to vessels flying the flag of that Member State. Article 20(2) specifies that where a Member State adopts conservation and management measures liable to affect vessels of other Member States, those measures should only be adopted after consultation with the Commission, the relevant Member States and the relevant Advisory Councils. The applicants argued that Policy Directive 1 was a measure that had the effect of conserving and managing fish stocks, and that, as it would in practice apply to Northern Ireland-registered boats fishing in the 0–6 nautical mile zone of waters off the coast of Ireland, the state was required to fulfil the consultation requirements of Article 20(2), which it did not. The court accepted the respondent's argument that the directive was not in fact one that had been adopted for the conservation of fish stocks in Union waters as envisaged in Article 19, nor was it a non-discriminatory measure for the conservation and management of fish stocks and the maintenance or improvement of the conservation status of marine ecosystems within 12 nautical miles of the state's baselines as specified in Article 20, with the consequence that these provisions of the CFP Regulation were not engaged. Essentially, the court accepted that rather than being a conservation and management measure with respect to fish stocks, the directive was an environmental measure with ecosystem and economic benefits, as argued by the Minister.[42] This distinction 'between a conservation measure and a measure which may have conservation effects' allowed MacGrath J to dispatch the applicants' argument with relative brevity. However, the judgment's analysis of this point highlights a web of relationships, agreements of varying formality, instruments of Irish, UK and EU law that have structured interactions, and use of resources in waters around the island of Ireland. Of some intricateness and delicacy, these relationships and agreements have been strained by Brexit.

The applicants' second main basis for challenging the directive was that, given the nature of the rights infringed, which they understood to be their constitutional rights to pursue a livelihood and to property, the state was required to satisfy a high standard of reasonableness, proportionality and fair procedures, and to give adequate reasons for the decision taken.[43] Ultimately, MacGrath J found that the Minister had outlined the terms of how the consultation process pertaining to the directive would proceed, without then fulfilling those terms. Specifically, given that the directive would impinge on the interests of a narrow and easily identifiable number of fishers, these affected stakeholders should have been made aware of the preferred decision before a final decision was taken. While the applicants were given, and did take, the opportunity to make submissions during a consultation process prior to the publication of the directive, they were not made aware of the option preferred by the Minister before that option was taken.[44] The judgment caveated this holding

---

[42] [2020] IEHC 497 (n 34) para 104.
[43] ibid para 118.
[44] ibid paras 178 and 189–92.

by emphasising the specific facts of the case, amounting to the conclusion that the respondent had committed to doing something they did not in fact do, not that they failed to do something they would otherwise have been legally obliged to do. A noteworthy part of the court's analysis of this point was that Irish sea fishing boat licences are not in themselves a tradable commodity; fishing quotas and opportunities are under the management of the Minister and are not privately owned; and that while a change in the terms on which a fishing licence is granted 'may, as a matter of fact, have financial implications for the holder of the licence, it does not necessarily follow that such a consequence renders that measure unlawful, nor does it necessarily constitute an attack on property rights'.[45] MacGrath J held it had not been established that there was significant interference with any fundamental right of the applicants, and that consequently the duty of the Minister to give reasons did not 'lie at the higher end of the scale'.[46] This portion of the judgment clarified and affirmed an aspect of Irish state practice with respect to fishing resources and opportunities that is not universally shared, which is that fish stocks are not something with respect to which licensed fishers have property rights, but are instead a natural resource belonging to the state.[47] It also contained useful discussion of the distinction between being required by the state to alter a business model in ways likely to cause financial loss, in this case based on a particular fishing practice, and having a fundamental right infringed.

In *Pat Fitzpatrick and Michael Flannery v Minister for Agriculture, Food and the Marine and the Sea Fisheries Protection Authority*,[48] the Supreme Court delivered a judgment which considered a challenge to the interpretation of some specific terms used in the EU law instruments that structure the CFP. These interpretations were relied upon by Irish state authorities to fulfil the state's obligations under those instruments. The applicants were sea fishers who brought an action in the High Court for judicial review of a decision made by the Minister to close a lucrative nephrops (also known as Norway lobster, Dublin Bay prawns, prawns and scampi) fishery to Irish fishers in autumn 2017, and of the decision made by the SFPA to communicate statistics showing the exhaustion of the 2017 national quota for nephrops in that area not based on the fishers' own logbook records.

Normally, fishers maintain an 'electronic logbook', into which quantities of fish caught are manually inputted and transmitted to the SFPA at least once a day. This is a requirement of the Control Regulation, which, along with the Commission Regulation, provides detailed criteria for implementation of the CFP. The applicants were operating in an area of the Irish EEZ off the west coast of Ireland known as the Porcupine Bank, in which particularly large nephrops can be caught. In 2008 and 2009, the nephrops stock in this area was heavily depleted, in response to which provisions of the CFP were used to designate the Porcupine Bank a sub-area of the larger Area VII as designated under the system employed

---

[45] ibid para 149.
[46] ibid para 152.
[47] ibid paras 127 and 132–47. The court examined the complexity introduced by the possibility of trading vessel tonnage, which had the consequence of commodifying the tonnage of a vessel.
[48] [2020] IESC 13.

by the International Council for the Exploration of the Sea (ICES), and to subject it to special regulations. This sub-area is called Functional Area 16 (FU16) and is approximately 68,000 square kilometres in size. Like other EU Member States, Ireland has a national TAC for nephrops in Area VII, of which a particular proportion can be caught in FU16. In July 2017, the SFPA became concerned that Irish fishers were catching nephrops in FU16 but misreporting that catch as having been caught outside FU16, perhaps on their way to or from FU16. At that point, the catch for nephrops in FU16 based on data from fishers' logbooks was 733 tonnes, whereas the SFPA believed the true figure to be closer to 1991 tonnes – more than Ireland's TAC in that area for all of 2017. The SFPA came to this figure by using a 'time spent' methodology. For example, if 75 per cent of the total duration of a fishing trip was spent in FU16, 75 per cent of the nephrops reported to have been caught were concluded to have been caught in FU16.[49] The SFPA illustrated the necessity of using this method by presenting suspicious logbook data to the High Court – cases where huge proportions of a total catch were reported to have been obtained during short periods spent in improbably bountiful sea areas close to the coast, while tiny proportions of the total catch from the same trip were reported to have been obtained during long periods spent in FU16. At the same time, UK vessels operating in FU16 were logging higher (in some cases up to 10 times higher), and historically more typical, catches of nephrops.

The judgment circled around the challenge made by the applicants to the SFPA's use of this 'time-spent' method. The central question was whether the terms 'data' and 'information', used in the Control Regulation to refer to the information Member State authorities (in this case, the SFPA) must collect and report to the Commission for the purpose of administering the CFP, excluded the use of such a method. The applicants argued the SFPA was bound by the terms of the Control Regulation to submit only information obtained from logbooks, and if they doubted the veracity of this information, the Control and Commission Regulations specified enforcement measures available to them, such as inspections of individual fishing vessels. The respondents argued that the wording of the provisions of the Control Regulation relied on by the applicants did not exclude the possibility of employing another method for the ascertainment of information that the authority deemed more accurate than logbook data, and that the applicants' argument in effect demanded Ireland report information to the Commission which the SFPA strongly believed to be inaccurate. The Supreme Court held that this issue was an interpretative one requiring guidance from the European Court of Justice (ECJ), and referred two questions to the ECJ under the preliminary ruling procedure established by Article 267 TFEU. Those two questions were:

(i)   Is the Single Control Authority in a Member State in notifying and certifying to the European Commission under Article 33(2)(a) and Article 34 of the Control Regulation limited to notifying the data as to catch in a particular fishing ground logged by fishers under Articles 14 and 15 of the Regulation when the Single Control Authority for good reason believes the logged data to be grossly unreliable or is it entitled to employ reasonable, scientifically valid methods to treat and certify the logged data so as to achieve more accurate outtake figures for notification to the European Commission?

---

[49] ibid para 9.

(ii)   Where the Authority is so satisfied, based on reasonable grounds, can it lawfully uti-
lise other data flows such as fishing licenses, fishing authorisations, vessel monitoring
system ('VMS') data, landing declarations, sales notes and transport documents?[50]

The ECJ was expected to respond to this preliminary ruling request in early 2022.

E. Labour Conditions on the Irish Fishing Fleet

In addressing the topic of labour at sea, the 2020 Report of the UN Secretary-General
noted that fishing is one of the most dangerous occupations in the world, a fact exacerbated by the COVID-19 pandemic. Regulatory responses to the pandemic have caused
many serious difficulties for seafarers seeking to join or leave vessels, in some cases
being unable to do so and subjected to unilateral extensions of periods of service or
confined on ships ordered to anchorage or remote berths in the conditions of their
everyday work, including with regard to protective clothing and in obtaining urgent
medical help, or due to other social and economic hardships imposed by the pandemic.

The Secretary-General's report noted that with the aim of improving safety
standards and working conditions of fishers, and combating illegal, unreported
and unregulated (IUU) fishing, in October 2019, 48 states, including Ireland,
signed the Torremolinos Declaration on the Cape Town Agreement of 2012 on the
Implementation of the Provisions of the Torremolinos Protocol of 1993 relating to
the Torremolinos International Convention for the Safety of Fishing Vessels, 1977.[51]
This declaration signals an intention to ratify the Cape Town Agreement of 2012
by the tenth anniversary of its adoption – 11 October 2022. The Cape Town Agreement
was adopted by the International Maritime Organization (IMO) as neither the 1993
Torremolinos Protocol nor the 1977 Torremolinos International Convention for the
Safety of Fishing Vessels, which the 1993 Protocol had modified, had come into
force. The Cape Town Agreement sets out standards for the construction and safety
of fishing vessels over 24 metres in length or equivalent in gross tons; includes regulations intended to improve the safety of crews and observers; and, by including
regulations related to port state inspections, is expected to help combat IUU fishing.
Currently, fishing vessels are frequently exempted from safety standards established
under other international maritime agreements. The agreement will enter into force
12 months after at least 22 states with an aggregate 3600 fishing vessels of at least
24 metres in length operating on the high seas have consented to be bound by it. So far,
16 states have ratified the Cape Town Agreement. In March 2020, during an EU High
Level Ministerial Maritime Conference in Opatija, Croatia, a further three states –
Bulgaria, Poland and Portugal – signed the Torremolinos Declaration.[52] The IMO
held webinars in Latin America and the Caribbean in October and November 2020
to encourage further states to ratify the Cape Town Agreement.[53]

---

[50] ibid para 130.
[51] UNGA (n 20) para 33.
[52] 'Three States Sign Torremolinos Declaration' *The Maritime Executive* (11 March 2020)
www.maritime-executive.com/article/three-states-sign-torremolinos-declaration.
[53] 'IMO Webinars Put Fishing Vessel Safety High on Agenda', Press Release (IMO, 23 October 2020)
www.imo.org/en/MediaCentre/PressBriefings/Pages/37-fishing-safety.aspx.

Labour conditions in the Irish fishing fleet have been the object of particularly strong international scrutiny and criticism since 2015. The results of an investigation conducted by *The Guardian* newspaper were published in November 2015, documenting employment of undocumented Asian and African migrant workers on boats operating from Irish ports in extremely poor working conditions, including sleep deprivation and confinement on boats, receiving pay far below the Irish minimum wage, and being subjected to trafficking and debt practices characterised by many commentators as a form of modern slavery.[54] The Irish government responded by establishing a dedicated permit scheme (the Atypical Workers Scheme for Sea-Fishers) for non-European Economic Area (EEA) migrants entering the state to work on fishing vessels, which was subsequently the object of strong criticism from the International Transport Workers' Federation (ITF), a labour union. A legal challenge launched by the ITF was settled by the state in 2019, and agreement was reached with the union on proposals to reform the way such workers are regulated and protected. Prior to this settlement, four UN Special Rapporteurs – on the human rights of migrants; on contemporary forms of racism, racial discrimination, xenophobia and related intolerance; on contemporary forms of slavery, including its causes and consequences; and on trafficking in persons, especially women and children – took the very significant step of publishing a detailed letter outlining concerns about the scheme and drawing the state's attention to a series of international instruments concerning the prohibition of slavery, racial discrimination and human trafficking, and establishing obligations binding on the state under international human rights and labour law.[55] The US State Department had also downgraded Ireland from a Tier 1 to a Tier 2 country in its annual 2018 Trafficking in Persons (TIP) Report. Downgrading can have consequences for a state's preferential trading status with the USA, and in 2019 there was anticipation that Ireland would be downgraded yet again. Ireland remained at Tier 2 in the 2019 TIP Report, but was downgraded to the Tier 2 Watch List in the 2020 TIP Report. The state's continuing lack of effective action to protect vulnerable migrant sea fishers, among other failings, was identified as a reason for this further downgrading.[56] Ireland is the only state in Western Europe to have received this ranking.

Looking to other related rankings, in 2020 Ireland remained on the White List published in the Paris Memorandum of Understanding on Port State Control

---

[54] F Lawrence et al, 'Revealed: Trafficked Migrant Workers Abused in Irish Fishing Industry' *The Guardian* (London, 2 November 2015) www.theguardian.com/global-development/2015/nov/02/revealed-trafficked-migrant-workers-abused-in-irish-fishing-industry.

[55] F González Morales et al, 'Mandates of the Special Rapporteur on the Human Rights of Migrants; the Special Rapporteur on Contemporary Forms of Racism, Racial Discrimination, Xenophobia and Related Intolerance; the Special Rapporteur on Contemporary Forms of Slavery, Including Its Causes and Consequences; and the Special Rapporteur on Trafficking in Persons, Especially Women and Children, OL IRL 1/2019' (12 February 2019) https://spcommreports.ohchr.org/TMResultsBase/DownLoadPublicCommunicationFile?gId=24331. See the article by Dr Maria Grazia Giammarinaro, Special Rapporteur on trafficking in persons, especially women and children: MG Giammarinaro, 'A Human Rights-Based Approach to Trafficking in Persons in Conflict Situations' (2019) 14 *Irish Yearbook of International Law* 7.

[56] 'Trafficking in Persons Report' (US Department of State 2020) 55 and 269–72.

(the Paris MoU) Annual Report.[57] The Paris MoU is an agreement between the maritime authorities of 27 states that establishes an information system assigning 'risk profiles' to individual ships based on past performance with respect to international instruments concerning safety, pollution, labour and maintenance standards, and commits participating authorities to exercise port state control to carry out inspections on ships with high-risk profiles entering ports under their authority. The White List identifies flag states whose ships have performed well, based on records of the total number of inspections and detentions of vessels in a given three-year period. While the Maritime Labour Convention (MLC) is an important international instrument regulating working conditions of seafarers cited by the Paris MoU as relevant to the agreement, the MLC excludes fishers.

V. TERRITORIAL AND MARITIME DELIMITATION DISPUTES

Two territorial disputes with consequences for maritime delimitations have prompted Ireland to articulate its position with respect to each during the report period. The first, concerning Rockall, was frequently noted as a point of contention and ambiguity in Brexit negotiations throughout 2020 by EU sources and representatives of the Irish and Scottish fishing industries. A brief outline of this long-standing dispute is warranted. The dispute straddles several legal regimes – the law of the sea; customary international law on the acquisition of territory; and the EU law framework of the CFP – and involves four protagonists – Ireland; the UK; Denmark (on behalf of the Faroe Islands); and Iceland. The core of the dispute comprises a claim made by the UK in 1955 to territorial sovereignty over Rockall rock, effected by an annexation carried out by the Royal Navy and with the aim of facilitating test-firing of tactical nuclear missiles.[58] The UK's asserted legal basis for this claim has appeared to be that the territory was *res nullius* (the terms *terra nullius* or *territorium nullius* are also used in practice, notwithstanding their legal meanings not necessarily being synonymous) at the date of annexation.[59] This claim has not been recognised by any of the other parties to the dispute. While, before 1997, the UK claimed jurisdiction over extensive areas of continental shelf and EEZ on the basis of its assertion of territorial sovereignty over Rockall, since 1997 it has resiled from this position and asserted that Rockall generates a 12 nautical mile territorial sea, as a 'rock' within

---

[57] 'Paris MoU on Port State Control: White, Grey and Black List' (2020) www.parismou.org/detentions-banning/white-grey-and-black-list.

[58] F MacDonald, 'The Last Outpost of Empire: Rockall and the Cold War' (2006) 32 *Journal of Historical Geography* 627.

[59] On this dispute, see R Derrig, 'Was Rockall Conquered? An Application of the Law of Territory to a Rock in the North Atlantic Ocean' (2019) 14 *Irish Yearbook of International Law* 56; ED Brown, 'Rockall and the Limits of National Jurisdiction of the UK: Part I' (1978) 2 *Marine Policy* 3, 181; ED Brown, 'Rockall and the limits of National Jurisdiction of the UK: Part II' (1978) 2 *Marine Policy* 4, 275; CR Symmons, 'Ireland and the Rockall Dispute: An Analysis of Recent Developments' (1998) *IBRU Boundary and Security Bulletin* 78; R Collins, 'Sovereignty Has "Rock-All" to Do with It ... or Has It? What's at Stake in the Recent Diplomatic Spat between Scotland and Ireland?' (*EJIL: Talk!*, 8 July 2019); J Harrison, 'Guest Blog – Unpacking the Legal Disputes over Rockall' (*Scottish Parliament Information Centre*, 18 June 2019).

the meaning of Article 121(3) UNCLOS. Responding to the UK's earlier continental shelf claims, Denmark (on behalf of the Faroe Islands), Iceland and Ireland had made claims to overlapping areas of continental shelf in the region around Rockall. Ireland and the UK concluded a bilateral delimitation of their continental shelves and EEZs with respect to each other in 1988. Iceland and Denmark object to this agreement and note it has no effect with respect to them. Ireland has made a partial submission concerning an area of continental shelf beyond 200 nautical miles it considers not to be the subject of any dispute, and the UK and Denmark have submitted full details of their claims to continental shelf to the UN Commission on the Limits of the Continental Shelf (CLCS). Iceland has objected to these submissions and to their being considered by the CLCS. This objection, and the fact that the rules of procedure of the CLCS prevent it from considering submissions concerning an area where a land or maritime dispute exists, mean the CLCS has not made any recommendations in response to these submissions.[60] Ireland has consistently rejected the UK claim to territorial sovereignty over Rockall rock, without articulating a counter-claim. Irish fishers, supported by the state, have continued to articulate the view that they are entitled to fish within 12 nautical miles of Rockall on the basis of long-standing ties to the rock and its seas.

Discussion of the dispute during the report period is bookended by two joint statements made by the Irish Ministers for Foreign Affairs and for Agriculture, Food and the Marine. On 7 June 2019, the Tánaiste (Deputy Head of the Irish Government) and Minister for Foreign Affairs and Trade, Simon Coveney, and the Minister for Agriculture Food and the Marine, Michael Creed, responded to a 'formal letter of notice' from the Scottish Cabinet Secretary for External Affairs, Fiona Hyslop, that communicated that Scotland intended to deploy vessels to prevent Irish vessels from fishing within 12 nautical miles of Rockall. The Tánaiste stated: 'the longstanding position of the Irish Government is that Irish vessels are entitled to access to Rockall waters. We have never recognised UK sovereignty over Rockall and accordingly we have not recognised a territorial sea around it either'.[61] Speaking in the Dáil on 3 July 2019, the Minister for Agriculture, Food and the Marine stated:

> Ireland does not recognise the United Kingdom's claim to sovereignty over Rockall. The waters around Rockall, including within 12 nautical miles, are part of sea area 6b, within which Irish vessels, like those of other EU Member States, have a right of access under the Common Fisheries Policy.[62]

---

[60] On these submissions, see CR Symmons, 'The Irish Partial Submission to the Commission on the Limits of the Continental Shelf in 2005: A Precedent for Future Such Submissions in the Light of the "Disputed Areas" Procedures of the Commission?' (2006) 37 *Ocean Development and International Law* 299; C Yiallourides, 'It Takes Four to Tango: Quadrilateral Boundary Negotiations in the North-East Atlantic' (2018) 87 *Marine Policy* 78.

[61] Department of Agriculture, Food and the Marine, 'Coveney and Creed Reject Scottish Government's Unilateral Threat of Enforcement Action against Irish Fishing Vessels Fishing within 12 Miles of Rockall', Press Release (7 June 2019) www.gov.ie/en/press-release/1cf306-coveney-and-creed-reject-scottish-governments-unilateral-threat-of-e/.

[62] Dáil Deb 3 July 2019. 'Sea area 6b' (properly VIb) refers to geographical areas fixed by the International Council for the Exploration of the Sea and incorporated into the framework for statistical reporting under the CFP, defined in Council Regulation (EC) 218/2009 of 11 March 2009 on the submission of nominal catch statistics by Member States fishing in the north-east Atlantic (recast) [2009] OJ L87/70.

The second joint statement was made on 8 January 2021 in response to reports that on 4 January 2021 a Marine Scotland patrol boat stopped and boarded an Irish fishing trawler, forcing it to leave waters within 12 nautical miles of Rockall. The Ministers for Foreign Affairs and for Agriculture, Food and the Marine stated:

> Through this engagement [with Scottish and UK authorities], the Irish Government is seeking to address the issues involved, reflecting the longstanding fisheries tradition in the area. Taking account of the new EU–UK Trade and Cooperation Agreement, this may also require contact with the European Commission. In addressing these issues, the Minister for Foreign Affairs and the Minister for Agriculture, Food and the Marine, as well as their respective officials, are considering all options for further engagement on the issues involved and are continuing to work closely together. While engagement continues, there remains an increased risk of enforcement action being taken by Scottish fisheries control authorities against Irish vessels operating in the waters around Rockall at present.[63]

As this statement notes, this dispute now engages provisions of the TCA.[64]

The second territorial and maritime delimitation dispute that has elicited a statement of Ireland's position concerns Lough Foyle. Lough Foyle is the estuary of the River Foyle, forming a bay that straddles the Irish border, with its western shore in County Donegal (Ireland) and its eastern shore in County Derry/Londonderry (Northern Ireland, part of the UK). Since the island of Ireland was partitioned, with the six counties that now comprise Northern Ireland seceding from the briefly unitary Irish Free State in December 1922, jurisdiction over Lough Foyle has been disputed. The same has been true of the bay straddling the border at its point of entry to the sea on the south-east coast, Carlingford Lough, although in practice a line roughly equidistant from each coast seems to have been frequently accepted by both the Irish and UK authorities at least for administrative purposes.[65]

From the perspective of Ireland, dispute over both bays stems from the state's long-standing claim to the territorial waters around Northern Ireland. There have been two separate legal bases for this claim. The first was found in Article 2 of the 1937 Constitution of Ireland. This article stated: 'The national territory consists of the whole island of Ireland, its islands and the territorial seas.'[66] This was based on the view that the island of Ireland had historically been a unitary territory, during British colonial rule and before, and was forcibly partitioned by the British government in the context of a war of independence, which concluded with the negotiation of the Articles of Agreement for a Treaty Between Great Britain and Ireland 1921 (the 1921 Treaty). In fulfilment of its obligations under the 1998 Belfast Agreement (widely known as the Good Friday Agreement, a peace agreement between Ireland

---

[63] Department of Agriculture, Food and the Marine and Department of Foreign Affairs, 'Joint Statement by the Ministers for Foreign Affairs and Agriculture, Food and the Marine on Rockall', Press Release (8 January 2021) www.gov.ie/en/press-release/b084f-joint-statement-by-the-ministers-for-foreign-affairs-and-agriculture-food-and-the-marine-on-rockall/.

[64] See above n 24. Noting the possibility of the Rockall dispute being pursued through the dispute settlement procedures of the TCA, see Bickl (n 24).

[65] On these disputes, see CR Symmons, 'The Maritime Border Areas of Ireland, North and South: An Assessment of Present Jurisdictional Ambiguities and International Precedents Relating to the Determination of "Border Bays"' (2009) 24 *International Journal of Marine and Coastal Law* 457.

[66] Bunreacht na hÉireann 1937.

and the UK that involved representatives of the unionist and nationalist communities in Northern Ireland), the Irish government held a referendum, with the result that Articles 2 and 3 of the Constitution were replaced. The current Article 2 does not make a unilateral territorial claim to the entire island.[67]

The second basis for Ireland's claim to the territorial seas of the entire island relies on wording that remains in the current Article 3 of the Constitution of Ireland, and on an interpretation of the Government of Ireland Act 1920 (the Act of 1920), which was the act of the UK Westminster Parliament that established Northern Ireland as a quasi-autonomous entity, as well as establishing a territory known as Southern Ireland, constituting what remained of the entire island territory when Northern Ireland was removed.[68] This interpretation noted that the entity identified as Northern Ireland in that act was defined as the aggregation of six parliamentary counties, and that under British legal custom parliamentary counties constitute landmasses ending at the high-water mark. A historically aware plain reading of the Act of 1920 supports the view that at that time the Westminster Parliament did not intend Northern Ireland or Southern Ireland to have jurisdiction over territorial waters, as both entities were intended by the British government to remain within the Union of the (then) United Kingdom of Great Britain and Ireland. This would have entailed jurisdiction of territorial waters around the island of Ireland being exercised by the Westminster Parliament. However, the terms of the 1921 Treaty reproduced the territorial definitions of Northern Ireland and Southern Ireland contained in the 1920 Act, while recognising Southern Ireland as the Irish Free State, and granting it the 'same constitutional status in the Community of Nations known as the British Empire as the Dominion of Canada, the Commonwealth of Australia, the Dominion of New Zealand, and the Union of South Africa'.[69] This made it a dominion of the British Empire, entailing jurisdiction over territorial waters. The territorial definition of Northern Ireland remained as defined by the Act of 1920, while under the 1921 Treaty it was given the possibility of seceding from the Irish Free State and retaining the legal status it was granted under that act, which it exercised. As per the terms of the Act of 1920, the Irish Free State would then constitute the island territory less the entity defined as Northern Ireland.

---

[67] Arts 2 and 3 now read: 'Article 2. It is the entitlement and birthright of every person born in the island of Ireland, which includes its islands and seas, to be part of the Irish Nation. That is also the entitlement of all persons otherwise qualified in accordance with law to be citizens of Ireland. Furthermore, the Irish nation cherishes its special affinity with people of Irish ancestry living abroad who share its cultural identity and heritage. Article 3(1). It is the firm will of the Irish nation, in harmony and friendship, to unite all the people who share the territory of the island of Ireland, in all the diversity of their identities and traditions, recognising that a united Ireland shall be brought about only by peaceful means with the consent of a majority of the people, democratically expressed, in both jurisdictions in the island. Until then, the laws enacted by the Parliament established by this Constitution shall have the like area and extent of application as the laws enacted by the Parliament that existed immediately before the coming into operation of this Constitution. Article 3(2). Institutions with executive powers and functions that are shared between those jurisdictions may be established by their respective responsible authorities for stated purposes and may exercise powers and functions in respect of all or any part of the island.' ibid (amended).
[68] Government of Ireland Act 1920.
[69] Articles of Agreement for a Treaty Between Great Britain and Ireland 1921, Art 1.

Consequently, the Irish Free State and later Ireland has consistently claimed that all territorial waters around the island of Ireland remained under its jurisdiction after the six parliamentary counties constituting Northern Ireland seceded.[70]

The territorial definitions created by the Act of 1920 have subsequently been replicated in iterations of legislation of both the UK and Irish Parliaments.[71] This claim has also remained congruent with the position specified in the Constitution of Ireland by virtue of the wording of Article 3, the relevant portion of which remained unchanged by amendments made after the Good Friday Agreement:

> Article 3(1). It is the firm will of the Irish Nation, in harmony and friendship, to unite all the people who share the territory of the island of Ireland, in all the diversity of their identities and traditions, recognising that a united Ireland shall be brought about only by peaceful means with the consent of a majority of the people, democratically expressed, in both jurisdictions in the island. *Until then, the laws enacted by the Parliament established by this Constitution shall have the like area and extent of application as the laws enacted by the Parliament that existed immediately before the coming into operation of this Constitution.* (emphasis added)[72]

The final highlighted sentence maintains a formulation similar to the prior Article 3, which provides for continuity in the extent of jurisdiction claimed by the Parliament of the Irish Free State. One difference between these formulations is that the prior Article 3 referred to Saorstát Éireann (the Irish Free State) by name, while the amended Article 3 avoids doing so. Nor does the Good Friday Agreement refer to the portion of the island of Ireland that is not Northern Ireland by name, continuing the practice established in the Act of 1920 of defining that portion of the territory by reference to what-is-not-Northern-Ireland. It is this history that implicates the current dispute over Lough Foyle because as border bays, the mouths of which have not been closed by straight baselines, both Lough Foyle and Carlingford Lough can be considered territorial waters, and the Irish position has treated them as such.

While the first basis for the Irish claim no longer persists due to the state's changed position after the Belfast Agreement, the status of the second is less clear. As noted, the position expressed in the amended Articles 2 and 3 of the Constitution of Ireland does not preclude the persistence of this second separate basis, and the state has made no statement resiling from this position, maintaining a practice of reiterating its rejection of the UK's claim to the bay. Prompted by problems regulating aquaculture on Lough Foyle due to jurisdictional ambiguities as a consequence of no maritime delimitation having been agreed, and due to the cross-border Loughs Agency being given inadequate legislative basis to operate by both the UK and Irish

---

[70] For two views on this long-standing claim, see the exchange: CR Symmons, 'Who Owns the Territorial Waters of Northern Ireland? A Note on DPP for Northern Ireland v McNeill' (1976) 27 *Northern Ireland Legal Quarterly* 48; T Towey, 'Who Owns the Territorial Waters of Northern Ireland? The McNeill Case: Another View' (1983) 32 *International & Comparative Law Quarterly* 1013; CR Symmons, 'Who Owns the Territorial Waters of Northern Ireland? A Rejoinder' (1984) 33 *International & Comparative Law Quarterly* 1064.

[71] For a detailed account of these iterations, see Towey (n 70).

[72] Bunreacht na hÉireann 1937 (n 66) (amended).

Parliaments, in October 2020 Minister for Agriculture, Food and the Marine Charlie McConalogue stated:

> The disputed ownership of Lough Foyle, between the Irish and British Governments, has caused very significant problems over the years. It has meant the regulation, particularly of aquaculture, on Lough Foyle, has not been possible because there is no legal clarity or agreement in relation to responsibilities for oversight. There has been ongoing engagement between the Irish Government and the British Government for a number of years now to try and resolve the situation. A committee has been established, under the jurisdiction of the Minister for Foreign Affairs, and is meeting at Irish Government level to move the issue forward in terms of engagement with the British Government. However, there has been very limited progress in recent times. The situation is something that, as Minister for Agriculture, Food and the Marine, I will be pressing and trying to ensure we do all we can within our power to try and progress. Obviously, it is not something that can be done uni-laterally. It is going to require agreement with the British Government. Obviously, it is also complicated at the moment by the Brexit talks. There was a similar situation in Carlingford Lough but there has been long-standing agreement there that each state has responsibility for oversight on its own side of the midway line. Such an agreement has never been pos-sible to achieve in the Foyle. The situation remains that there is no clarity or jurisdiction for either the Irish Government or the British Government to oversee aquaculture, in particular. The matter needs to be clarified in order for the appropriate, standard regulation and over-sight of aquaculture to be in place.[73]

The UK position has been to claim sovereignty over the entirety of Lough Foyle, to the high-water mark on the Donegal coast. This position was clarified as recently as 2016, when Secretary of State for Northern Ireland James Brokenshire responded to a question about Lough Foyle in the UK House of Commons by saying: 'The [UK] Government's position remains that the whole of Lough Foyle is within the UK'.[74] This position was confirmed by a spokesperson for the Northern Ireland Office:

> The UK maintains its formal claim to the whole of Lough Foyle, based on a 1662 charter of Charles II, which granted the waters and bed (as well as the fisheries) of Lough Foyle to the Irish Society, and included them as part of County Londonderry ... With regard to Carlingford Lough, the UK claims the northern part of the lough.[75]

---

[73] C McGinty, 'Disputed Ownership of Lough Foyle Causing Major Problems' *Donegallive* (1 October 2020) www.donegallive.ie/news/inishowen/577780/disputed-ownership-of-lough-foyle-causing-major-problems.html. In 2011, the UK and Irish governments concluded a Memorandum of Understanding delineating lines beginning outside the mouths of Lough Foyle and Carlingford Lough for the purpose of allocating responsibilities for granting leases to developers seeking to under-take offshore renewable energy projects. The MoU was concluded 'without prejudice to the nego-tiation of territorial sea boundaries'. P Baker, 'Without Prejudice to the Negotiation of Territorial Sea Boundaries ...' (*Slugger O'Toole*, 15 December 2011) https://sluggerotoole.com/2011/12/15/without-prejudice-to-the-negotiation-of-territorial-sea-boundaries/.

[74] HC Deb 16 November 2016, UIN 52620W. The Irish Department of Foreign Affairs responded by stating that 'Ireland has never accepted the UK's claim to the whole of Lough Foyle'. S Murray, 'Irish and UK Governments Reassert Their Claims over Lough Foyle' (*thejournal.ie*, 17 November 2016) www.thejournal.ie/lough-foyle-ownership-3086385-Nov2016/.

[75] J Manley, 'Labour MP Who Reignited Territorial Row Says UK Has No Lough Foyle Claim' *The Irish News* (23 November 2016) www.irishnews.com/news/2016/11/23/news/labour-mp-who-reignited-territorial-waters-row-says-uk-has-no-claim-to-lough-foyle-797369/.

VI. MARINE SCIENTIFIC RESEARCH

Under Part XIII of UNCLOS, research vessels flagged to states other than Ireland seeking to undertake marine scientific research within waters under Ireland's sovereignty and jurisdiction must seek consent from the state before undertaking this research. Part XIII lays out a scheme for the granting of such consents, known as the 'consent regime'. While the coastal state (in this case, Ireland) has exclusive discretion to grant or deny consent within territorial waters, the state's ability to deny consent in the EEZ or on the continental shelf is caveated by the expectation that it will be granted 'in normal circumstances', and by the enumeration of a specified set of circumstances that permit the coastal state to withhold consent.[76] Details of foreign-flagged research vessels undertaking marine scientific research in waters under the state's sovereignty and jurisdiction are outlined in Table 4. When compared to the same figures for 2019, a considerable decrease in such research activity is apparent.

Table 4. 2020 Foreign Vessel Activity in Irish Waters

Country	Vessel name	Survey name/ code	Discipline	No of days in Irish waters	Location
UK	Scotia	Bottom trawl survey targeting juvenile gadoid species. Trawl and CTD sampling	Fisheries	7	ICES management area VIA
UK	Cefas Endeavour	Groundfish survey	Fisheries	20	Celtic Sea, Bristol Channel and Western Channel
UK	Achilles	Agri-Food and Biosciences Institute Irish Sea Cod and Round Fish Survey 2019 – Fishery Science Partnership	Fisheries	25	Area Vlla – Irish Sea

(continued)

[76] UNCLOS, Art 246; L Fernandes Coelho, 'Marine Scientific Research and Small Island Developing States in the 21st Century: Appraising the International Legal Framework' (World Maritime University, 2021).

Country	Vessel name	Survey name/ code	Discipline	No of days in Irish waters	Location
Norway	Morten Einar	To test catch regulation devices for limiting catch sizes and conduct underwater observations of the fishing gear	Fisheries	10	North of the PAP site
Norway	Fiskebas	Tagging and biological sampling of mackerel West of Scotland and Ireland	Fisheries	20	Atlantic Ocean, west of Ireland and Scotland
Germany	Meteor	To study the variability of water masses and transports in the eastern basin of the subpolar North Atlantic and in the Eastern Boundary Current located off the European continental shelf (moorings, CTDO/LADCP, vm-ADCP, tracers)	Oceanographic	7	Subpolar North Atlantic stretching from Goban Spur at the Irish shelf break to Flemish Pass at the Canadian shelf break and from about 47°N to about 52°30'N at the Mid-Atlantic Ridge
Netherlands	Pelagia	The unknown role of submarine canyons – pathways or sinks for organic carbon	Oceanographic/ marine biology	3	Whittard Canyon Complex

(continued)

Country	Vessel name	Survey name/ code	Discipline	No of days in Irish waters	Location
UK	Scotia	Demersal trawling survey to assess pre-recruit year class strengths of cod, haddock, whiting, Norway pout, mackerel and herring	Fisheries	15	Irish and Scottish west coast
UK	RSS Discovery	The objective of the PAP-SO is to provide high temporal resolution (hours) data for an increasing number of essential ocean variables (EOVs)	Oceanographic/ geophysics	7	PAP site
Spain	Vizconde de Eza	Abundance estimations and distribution patterns of demersal–benthic species	Fisheries	30	Porcupine Bank
UK	Scotia	Bottom trawl survey targeting juvenile gadoid species on Rockall bank	Fisheries	8	Rockall Bank
UK	Scotia	Camera survey of seapen beds on upper Rockall Bank combined with a bottom trawl survey looking at changes in fish composition and abundance with depth	Fisheries	8	Rockall bank/ Hatton Bank

(continued)

Country	Vessel name	Survey name/ code	Discipline	No of days in Irish waters	Location
France	Thalassa	EVHOE Survey	Fisheries	15	North Eastern Atlantic

Source: Information provided to the author by the Marine Institute.

Concerning research in which Ireland is involved, in February 2020 a project titled 'Joint European Research Infrastructure of Coastal Observatories: Science, Service, Sustainability' (JERICO-S3) began. The Marine Institute will undertake a work package of this large project comprising 39 partners, which focuses on providing environmental data on European coastal and shelf seas, as well as supporting research infrastructure. Two projects funded under the Government of Ireland's ObSERVE Programme were completed in 2020 – ObSERVE Aerial and ObSERVE Acoustic. The ObSERVE Programme was established in 2014 by the Department of Communications, Climate Action & Environment in partnership with the Department of Culture, Heritage and the Gaeltacht, with the aim of improving understanding of protected offshore species and sensitive habitats through data collection across Ireland's EEZ. A departmental press release notes that the Atlantic Margin, where Ireland's continental shelf merges with deeper basins, has been a focus of the project due to it being of 'growing interest to marine industry', and being an area poorly understood in the past. ObSERVE Aerial involved conducting aerial surveys of whales, dolphins, seabirds and other marine life, while ObSERVE Acoustic recorded underwater sounds made by whales, dolphins and porpoises to learn about their occurrence, distribution, abundance and migration habits.

VII. INTERNATIONAL WHALING COMMISSION

A whaling station existed in Ireland in the early twentieth century, established by Norwegian whalers and based in County Mayo, but this activity faltered by the late 1920s and commercial whaling was prohibited by the Whale Fisheries Act of 1937.[77] Ireland has been a party to the 1946 International Convention for the Regulation of Whaling since 1985.[78] The International Whaling Commission (IWC), established under the auspices of the Convention, is a body that has responsibility for the conservation of whale stocks with the aim of making possible the development of the whaling industry. In practice, the IWC has placed a moratorium on commercial whaling. Ireland has supported the IWC moratorium and is among the states that oppose scientific programmes that involve killing whales, such as

---

[77] Whale Fisheries Act 1937. A film directed by Robert W Paul documenting activity at the Inishkea whaling survives: RW Paul, *Whaling Afloat and Ashore* (1908) https://www.youtube.com/watch?v=X3TUY-0lVvY.

[78] International Convention for the Regulation of Whaling 1946 (adopted 2 December 1946) 161 UNTS 72.

the programme conducted by Japan in the Southern Ocean Whale Sanctuary prior to its 2018 announcement that it would leave the IWC and resume commercial whaling within its territorial waters and EEZ. Since 2012 the IWC has met biennially. The sixty-eighth such meeting was scheduled for 2020, but was postponed to autumn 2021 due to the COVID-19 pandemic. The Conservation Committee of the IWC met virtually from 28 September to 2 October 2020, considering issues requiring decision in 2020.[79]

VIII. MERCHANT SHIPPING (INVESTIGATION OF MARINE CASUALTIES) (AMENDMENT) BILL 2020

In November 2020, the government published the General Scheme of the Merchant Shipping (Investigation of Marine Casualties) (Amendment) Bill 2020. The purpose of this Bill was to make a series of amendments to the Merchant Shipping (Investigation of Marine Casualties) Act 2000 (the Act of 2000). These amendments responded to the July 2020 judgment of the ECJ in an infringement action taken by the Commission against Ireland.[80] The Act of 2000 had established the Marine Casualty Investigation Board (MCIB) in order to create a body charged with conducting technical safety investigations of marine casualties and producing reports on those incidents with the aim of preventing future casualties. A requirement of Council Directive 1999/35/EC of 29 April 1999 on a system of mandatory surveys for the safe operation of regular ro-ro ferry and high-speed passenger craft services had been that Member States define such a body within their legal systems, capable of investigating accidents involving specified types of vessels.[81] This requirement was broadened by Directive 2009/18/EC of the European Parliament and of the Council of 23 April 2009 establishing the fundamental principles governing the investigation of accidents in the maritime transport sector and amending Council Directive 1999/35/EC and Directive 2002/59/EC of the European Parliament and of the Council. Importantly, Article 8(1) of the 2009 Directive specified a criterion of independence applicable to the investigative body (in Ireland, the MCIB):

> Member States shall ensure that safety investigations are conducted under the responsibility of an impartial permanent investigative body, endowed with the necessary powers, and by suitably qualified investigators, competent in matters relating to marine casualties and incidents.

> In order to carry out a safety investigation in an unbiased manner, the investigative body shall be independent in its organisation, legal structure and decision-making of any party whose interests could conflict with the task entrusted to it.[82]

---

[79] 'Report of the Conservation Committee' (International Whaling Commission, 2020).
[80] Case C-257/19 *Commission v Ireland* ECLI:EU:C:2020:541.
[81] Council Directive 1999/35/EC of 29 April 1999 on a system of mandatory surveys for the safe operation of regular ro-ro ferry and high-speed passenger craft services [1999] OJ L138/1.
[82] Directive 2009/18/EC of the European Parliament and of the Council of 23 April 2009 establishing the fundamental principles governing the investigation of accidents in the maritime transport sector and amending Council Directive 1999/35/EC and Directive 2002/59/EC of the European Parliament and of the Council [2009] OJ L131/114, Art 8(1).

Notwithstanding a declaration in section 8 of the Act of 2000 characterising the MCIB's independence in terms similar to those of Article 8 of the 2009 Directive, section 9(1) of the same Act specified that the MCIB would consist of the Chief Surveyor in the Marine Survey Office of the Department of the Marine and Natural Resources, the Secretary-General of the same department or their nominee and three other persons appointed by the Minister of the same department.

In 2015, the Commission sent a letter to Ireland asking the state to clarify the rules under Irish law by which the independence and impartiality required of the MCIB under Article 8 of the 2009 Directive were ensured, and noting that the Chief Surveyor and Secretary-General (by then of the Department of Transport, Tourism and Sports, which had assumed some responsibilities of the Department of the Marine and Natural Resources) also had other regulatory and enforcement responsibilities in the fields of maritime transport and fisheries. The Commission's concern was that the extent to which the MCIB's personnel were interwoven with senior departmental office holders meant that the MCIB was not 'independent in its organisation, legal structure and decision-making of any party whose interests could conflict with the task entrusted to it', as required by the 2009 Directive. Ireland rejected this concern, referring to the principle of independence referred to in section 8 of the Act of 2000; the Commission did not accept this response and responded with a formal letter of notice reiterating its concerns; Ireland again rejected this argument and charged the Commission with not having produced evidence of any conflict of interests of members of the MCIB or infringement in practice of the requirements of the 2009 Directive; the Commission responded by sending a reasoned opinion to Ireland; which Ireland again disputed; and the Commission then brought an infringement action before the ECJ. The Court agreed with the Commission that the

> presence within that investigative body of two civil servants who are respectively responsible for the DTTS [the department] and the Marine Survey Office, public authorities whose interests could conflict with the task entrusted to the MCIB, has the consequence that independence in that body's organisation and decision-making is not guaranteed.[83]

The court accordingly found that Ireland had not complied with its obligations under Article 8(1) of the 2009 Directive.

Ireland first responded to this judgment by making regulations under the European Communities Act 1972 providing for a revised MCIB structure whereby the Secretary-General and Chief Surveyor would not be members of the board 'for the purpose of decisions relating to investigations that fall within the scope of Directive 2009/18/EC'.[84] The general scheme of the proposed Bill responds to this judgment in a more comprehensive way by removing references to the Secretary-General and Chief Surveyor from section 9 of the Act of 2000, providing for a board of at least five and a maximum of seven members appointed by the Minister, and specifying that no serving or former officer of the Department

---

[83] *Commission v Ireland* (n 81) para 73.
[84] European Communities (Merchant Shipping) (Investigation of Accidents) (Amendment) Regulations 2020, SI 444/2020.

of Transport will be a member of the board. The general scheme also introduces a requirement that at least 40 per cent of the board be men and 40 per cent women.[85]

IX. SEA LEVEL RISE IN RELATION TO INTERNATIONAL LAW

At the twenty-ninth meeting of the Sixth Committee of the UN General Assembly (UNGA) in November 2019, James Kingston, Legal Advisor to the Department of Foreign Affairs (DFA), made a statement on behalf of Ireland on the report of the International Law Commission (ILC) on the work of its seventy-first session. Among other topics, the statement welcomed the inclusion of the topic of 'Sea-level rise in relation to international law' on the ILC's programme of work, and the initiation of an open-ended Study Group on the topic.[86] Climate-change-induced sea-level rise is widely recognised as an existential threat in low-lying coastal regions around the world, and particularly for small island states. In February 2020, a first issues paper was published on the topic, authored by Bogdan Aurescu and Nilüfer Oral, Co-Chairs of the Study Group. The paper surveyed scientific literature on sea-level rise, and laid out a plan to examine 'possible legal effects or implications of sea-level rise in three main areas: (a) law of the sea; (b) statehood; and (c) protection of persons affected by sea-level rise'.[87] A methodology by which the Study Group would conduct its work was explained, significant issues requiring further examination were identified and preliminary observations were made on many of those issues, drawing on case law and legal academic literature. The ILC is a body of 34 international law experts established under the UN Charter and charged with promoting the development and codification of international law. Its members are elected by the UNGA every five years. Mahon Hayes, a former legal advisor to the DFA and member of the Irish delegation to the Third UN Conference on the Law of the Sea, has been the only Irish member of the ILC, serving from 1987 to 1991.[88]

X. ACHILL ISLAND SEA SALT

In December 2020, the Department of Agriculture, Food and the Marine published an application to the European Commission under Regulation (EU) No 1151/2012 of the European Parliament and of the Council of 21 November 2012 on quality

---

[85] General Scheme Merchant Shipping (Investigation of Marine Casualties) (Amendment) Bill 2020.

[86] UNGA Sixth Committee (74th Session), 'Report of the International Law Commission on the Work of Its Seventy-first Session' (26 October 2019) UN Doc A/C.6/74/SR.29, para 43; D Cubie, 'Ireland and International Law 2019' (2019) 14 *Irish Yearbook of International Law* 108, 116.

[87] ILC, 'First Issues Paper by Bogdan Aurescu and Nilüfer Oral, Co-Chairs of the Study Group on Sea-Level Rise in Relation to International Law' (28 February 2020) UN Doc A/CN.4/740, para 44.

[88] See the recently published overview of the history of the ILC and accompanying photographic exhibition, supported by Ireland among other states and organisations: *70 Years of the ILC* (United Nations, Office of Legal Affairs, 2020) 143 (M Hayes). For Hayes's account of the role of the Irish delegation at UNCLOS III, see M Hayes, *The Law of the Sea: The Role of the Irish Delegation at the Third UN Conference* (Dublin, Royal Irish Academy, 2011).

schemes for agricultural products and foodstuff, for registration of the name 'Achill Island Sea Salt' as a protected designation of origin (PDO). Such a designation of origin identifies a product originating in a specific place, 'whose quality or characteristics are essentially or exclusively due to a particular geographical environment with its inherent natural and human factors'.[89] Well known PDOs are Greek feta cheese and French champagne.

---

[89] Regulation (EU) No 1151/2012 of the European Parliament and of the Council of 21 November 2012 on quality schemes for agricultural products and foodstuffs [2012] OJ L343/1, Art 5.

Ireland and the European Union 2020

RÓNÁN R CONDON

I. OVERVIEW

A. The Coronavirus Crisis

2020 WAS INDELIBLY marked by COVID-19, an unprecedented global pandemic, which posed a serious health risk to EU citizens and demanded a concerted health and economic response. The short-term response included a €2.7 billion Emergency Support Instrument, which to a large extent financed the EU's vaccine initiative.[1] Other initiatives included relaxing state aid and budgetary rules due to the severe economic impact of the pandemic and associated 'lockdowns';[2] redirecting cohesion, structural and investment funds towards supporting small and medium enterprises, vulnerable groups and temporary employment schemes; and support for the health sector.[3] Significant sums of money were directed into the newly created SURE (Support to Mitigate Unemployment Risks in an Emergency) scheme, under which by the end of 2020 €39.5 billion had been disbursed[4] in the form of loans provided to Member States from moneys borrowed by the EU on the financial markets on behalf of Member States.[5] The EU also negotiated with pharmaceutical companies for the provision of vaccines, and by the end of 2020, 2.3 billion vaccine doses had been secured.[6] All these measures were aimed at combating and cushioning the immediate and severe economic shock of the pandemic as well as the pressing public health crisis.[7] By the end of 2020, some 350,000 Europeans had lost their lives to the virus, but by December 2020 the European Medicines Agency had approved several vaccines, which would be rolled out progressively over the course of 2021.

---

[1] See European Commission, 'The EU in 2020: General Report on the Activities of the European Union' (Luxembourg, Publications Office of the European Union, 2021) 16.

[2] ibid 18. More precisely, the 'escape clause' in the Stability and Growth Pact was activated, and the State Aid Temporary Framework was adopted. The latter measure enabled the release of some €3 trillion in state aids.

[3] ibid, ie the Coronavirus Response Investment Initiative.

[4] ibid 19: €90.3 billion had been approved.

[5] ibid. €2.5 billion in loans were approved in respect of Ireland.

[6] ibid 20. Albeit not without controversy, ie the EU's dispute with AstraZeneca over vaccine delivery. For an overview, see T Connolly, 'AstraZeneca, EU Reach Settlement on Vaccine Delivery' (3 September 2021) www.rte.ie/news/coronavirus/2021/0903/1244484-coronavirus-vaccine/.

[7] Almost all EU27 Member States' economies severely contracted in 2020, the exceptions being Ireland and Romania.

Ireland was the only EU27 Member State to record GDP growth in 2020, largely buoyed by the pharmaceutical and information technology sectors' exports.[8] However, this growth largely disguised the large number of citizens who became unemployed due to the pandemic and who were dependent on the COVID-19 Pandemic Unemployment Payment.[9] Nonetheless, the Irish economy grew by 5.9 per cent in 2020.[10] The debt-to-GDP ratio in 2020 remained relatively steady, at 51.2 per cent, but the government ran a €18.4 billion budget deficit.[11] Because of distorting effects of transnational corporation activity, a truer understanding of national indebtedness, perhaps, is reflected in the debt-to-GNI ratio, which was projected to reach 108 per cent in 2020.[12] This means that Ireland has the highest public debt per capita in the European Union.[13]

B. Budgetary Impasse

The approval of the EU's ambitious €1.8 trillion budget (2021–27) and €750 billion Next Generation EU (Pandemic) Recovery Package (NGEU) suffered a setback in November 2020, when Poland and Hungary vetoed it because it attempted to link the disbursement of funds to the rule of law. Poland and Hungary lifted their veto in early December, claiming victory in having achieved some concessions.[14] The most important concession was that the rule of law sanctions could not be triggered until the Court of Justice of the European Union (CJEU) ruled on the legality of the rule of law mechanism. Relatedly, 2020 was the first year in which the European Commission issued rule of law reports on each EU27 Member State.[15] In the cases of Poland and Hungary, concerns were expressed in respect of judicial independence, corruption, media pluralism, the legislative process and with respect to civil society.[16] In Ireland's case, some concern was expressed about the funding of the

---

[8] See Eurostat, 'Real GDP Growth Rate – Volume' (updated on 15 May 2022) https://ec.europa.eu/eurostat/databrowser/view/tec00115/default/table?lang=en.

[9] According to the ESRI, the average monthly unemployment rate in 2020 was 18.7%. ESRI, 'Irish Economy to Recover Quite Strongly from Restrictions but Unemployment Unlikely to Return to Pre-pandemic Levels until 2023 at the Earliest', Press Release (21 March 2021) www.esri.ie/news/irish-economy-to-recover-quite-strongly-from-restrictions-but-unemployment-unlikely-to-return.

[10] See Eurostat (n 8).

[11] See CSO, 'Government Finance Statistics – Annual' (21 April 2021) www.cso.ie/en/statistics/governmentaccounts/governmentfinancestatisticsa/.

[12] See Department of Finance, 'Minister Donohoe Publishes Annual Report on Public Debt in Ireland 2020' (28 January 2021) www.gov.ie/en/press-release/a5c79-minister-donohoe-publishes-annual-report-on-public-debt-in-ireland-2020/.

[13] See F Reddan, 'Ireland to Have Highest Debt Per Head in Europe this Year' *Irish Times* (8 March 2021) www.irishtimes.com/business/economy/ireland-to-have-highest-debt-per-head-in-europe-this-year-1.4503652.

[14] See D McLaughlin, 'Cheers and Jeers as Poland and Hungary lift Veto on EU Funds' *Irish Times* (11 December 2020) www.irishtimes.com/news/world/europe/cheers-and-jeers-as-poland-and-hungary-lift-veto-on-eu-funds-1.4434424.

[15] European Commission, '2021 Rule of Law Report – Communication and Country Chapters' (30 September 2020) https://ec.europa.eu/info/publications/2020-rule-law-report-communication-and-country-chapters_en.

[16] ibid. For the Hungarian report, see European Commission, '2020 Rule of Law Report – Country Chapter Hungary' (30 September 2020) https://ec.europa.eu/info/sites/default/files/2021_rolr_country_chapter_hungary_en.pdf; for Poland, see European Commission, '2020 Rule of Law Report – Country Chapter Poland' (30 September 2020) https://ec.europa.eu/info/sites/default/files/2021_rolr_country_chapter_poland_en.pdf.

judiciary, judicial appointments and the procedures in place for sanctioning judicial misconduct.[17] The NGEU was particularly significant because for the first time Eurobonds were issued on the financial markets to fund this initiative. It also embedded green transition and digital transformation requirements into its conditions. Each Member State was required to submit a National Recovery and Resilience Plan (NRRP) detailing how it would meet the objectives of the NGEU. In Ireland's case, the Recovery and Resilience Facility will disburse €915 million in grants up to 2023. Ireland submitted its NRRP in July 2021, and it was reviewed by the European Commission shortly afterwards.

C. Brexit: The End of the Beginning

January 2020 marked the UK's formal withdrawal from the EU. The UK then entered a transition period in which it remained part of the single market and customs union for the duration of 2020 while the EU and UK negotiated an agreement as to their future trading relationship. Negotiations commenced in March 2020, but the growing COVID-19 crisis meant that the early rounds of negotiations in March were postponed. Negotiations recommenced in late April by videoconference, and ran through a proposed October deadline into November and December 2020. The negotiations were characterised by high drama and friction. The UK, in particular, raised the stakes in September 2020 by publishing the Internal Market Bill, which in relevant provisions intended to unilaterally modify the Withdrawal Agreement and the Northern Irish Protocol.[18] In total, 10 negotiating rounds occurred before a cliff-edge agreement in principle was reached on 24 December 2020. The EU–UK Trade and Cooperation Agreement was ratified by the UK on 30 December 2020,[19] and provided more or less[20] for free trade in goods, but with a large increase in 'red tape' requirements,[21] while allowing limited access in services, but importantly excluding provision for financial services. There was significant industry uncertainty at the end of 2020 as to the viability of the land bridge as a means of transporting goods to and from Ireland to the Continent due to the increase in technical barriers to trade and, in consequence, to the viability of supply chains. New and expanded direct routes to the Continent through the Rosslare Europort were launched in January 2021 in an attempt to offset these difficulties.[22] The consequence of Brexit not only hastened the

[17] The report was rather anodyne, but did note ongoing issues in this area in particular. See European Commission, '2020 Rule of Law Report – Country Chapter Ireland' (30 September 2020) 2–7, https://ec.europa.eu/info/sites/default/files/2021_rolr_country_chapter_ireland_en.pdf.

[18] In its clauses 42, 43 and 45, which were later removed.

[19] In UK domestic law, it is implemented by the European Union (Future Relationship) Act 2020. It was ratified by the European Parliament on 28 April 2021. See European Parliament, 'Parliament Formally Approves EU–UK Trade and Cooperation Agreement', Press Release (28 April 2021) www.europarl.europa.eu/news/en/press-room/20210423IPR02772/parliament-formally-approves-EU-UK-trade-and-cooperation-agreement.

[20] But VAT would apply, and so would sanitary and phytosanitary requirements. Also, these rules are subject to rules of origin requirements.

[21] ie a large increase in technical barriers to trade, including customs formalities and documentation requirements.

[22] See R Lough and P Halpin, 'After Brexit, Ireland and France Cut out the Middleman – Britain' (22 January 2021) www.reuters.com/article/uk-britain-eu-maritime-trade-idUSKBN29R1ME.

need for pragmatic solutions for new barriers to trade, but reawakened older quarrels. Conflicting claims about the extent of territorial waters re-emerged in 2020, with Ireland's and the UK's long-dormant dispute over Rockall and Lough Foyle coming back onto the political agenda.[23]

D. Taxation, State Aids and the Irish Model

Judgment was given in the 'Apple Tax case' by the European General Court (EGC) in 2020.[24] It will be recalled that the Ireland and the EU 2019 Report mentioned its significance against the background of wider criticisms of Ireland's over-reliance on corporation tax.[25] The background to the EGC's decision was a European Commission decision to impose a recovery order for the sum of circa €13 billion because it decided that Ireland's corporate tax law and regulation constituted an illegal state aid.[26] The EGC ruled against the Commission primarily because it did not demonstrate that the Irish taxation regime constituted an advantage, owing to errors in the Commission's assessment of the activities of the Apple Group.[27] However, the EGC did not accept Ireland's wider argument that the Commission's state aid decision infringed Ireland's tax sovereignty in the division of competences between the EU and its Member States. The Commission has since appealed the EGC's decision to the CJEU. In a broader sense, while the case is very significant for the Irish economic model, it has been somewhat outpaced in significance by OECD co-operation in 2021 towards introducing a global corporate tax rate of 15 per cent, which challenges Ireland's competitive advantage in regulatory competition over taxation.[28] Ireland belatedly, in 2021, joined the Base Erosion and Profit Shifting Agreement, but its future impact on Irish finances remains uncertain.[29]

II. PRELIMINARY RULINGS IN 2020

A. Asylum

The preliminary reference in *MS v the Minister for Justice* arose against the background of Ireland's unique[30] and complex international protection legislative

---

[23] For a detailed discussion, see R Derrig, 'Irish State Practice on the Law of the Sea 2020' in this volume.

[24] Joined Cases T-778/16 and T-892/16 *Ireland v Commission* ECLI:EU:T:2020:338.

[25] R Condon, 'Ireland in the European Union 2019' (2021) 14 *Irish Yearbook of International Law* 137.

[26] See European Commission, 'State Aid: Ireland Gave Illegal Tax Benefits to Apple Worth up to €13 Billion' (30 August 2016) https://ec.europa.eu/commission/presscorner/detail/en/IP_16_2923.

[27] *Ireland v Commission* (n 24) para 312; see also paras 249 and 310.

[28] See OECD, '130 Countries and Jurisdictions Join Bold New Framework for International Tax Reform' (1 July 2021) www.oecd.org/newsroom/130-countries-and-jurisdictions-join-bold-new-framework-for-international-tax-reform.htm.

[29] On receipt of some clarifications and reassurances, eg that the headline rate of 15% for multinational corporations is a maximum rate and not a minimum rate, which had been previously indicated. For an overview, see www.oecd.org/tax/beps/.

[30] Unique in the sense that of the EU27, Ireland is the only country in which, as will be shown, the regime straddles two legislative frameworks.

framework.[31] The governing domestic legislative enactment, the International Protection Act 2015, provides that in circumstances in which refugee status or subsidiary protection has been granted in another Member State, an asylum application will be declared inadmissible.[32] This legislative provision is consistent with Directive 2013/32/EU (the 2013 Directive), which Ireland did *not* adopt.[33] The 2013 Directive is a procedures directive associated with Dublin Regulation III,[34] which Ireland adopted, and it provides specifically that a Member State may declare an application inadmissible where the applicant has been granted subsidiary protection in another Member State.[35] Dublin Regulation III provides an alternative 'take back and take charge' transfer procedure for international protection applicants.[36] However, given that Ireland did not adopt the 2013 Directive, the procedures governing the grant of international protection in EU law are regulated by Directive 2005/85/EC (the 2005 Directive),[37] which is associated with Dublin Regulation II.[38] The earlier 2005 Directive did not explicitly identify inadmissibility as an option for situations in which subsidiary protection, as distinct from refugee status, had been granted in another Member State. In effect, Ireland has a foot in two distinct legislative frameworks, namely the 2005 Directive, which supplements Dublin Regulation II, and the Dublin III Regulation.[39] Therefore, the underlying interpretative question in *MS* is: given that the 2005 Directive did not on its face provide for inadmissibility where subsidiary protection had been granted, is the 2015 Act incompatible with EU law?

The claimants in *MS* were three asylum seekers who had previously been granted subsidiary protection in Italy, and of whom two had failed to inform the Irish authorities of this fact. Both the International Protection Office and the International Protection Appeals Tribunal decided that, pursuant to section 21(4)(a) of the 2015 Act, their claims were inadmissible. On appeal to the High Court, Humphreys J referred three questions to the CJEU concerning the interpretation of the 2005 Directive, effectively querying whether a ground of inadmissibility where

---

[31] Case C-616/19 *Minister for Justice and Equality (Demande de protection internationale en Irlande)* ECLI:EU:C:2020:1010.

[32] International Protection Act, 2015, s 21(2)(a).

[33] Directive 2013/32/EU of the European Parliament and of the Council of 26 June 2013 on Common Procedures for Granting and Withdrawing International Protection [2013] OJ L180/60.

[34] Regulation (EU) No 604/2013 of the European Parliament and of the Council of 26 June 2013 establishing the Criteria and Mechanisms for Determining the Member State Responsible for Examining an Application for International Protection Lodged in one of the Member States by a Third-Country National or a Stateless Person, [2013] OJ L180/31.

[35] 2013 Directive, Art 33(2)(a). As confirmed by the CJEU in Joined Cases C-297/17, C-318/17, C-318/17 and C-438/17 *Ibrahim v Bundesrepublik Deutschland and Bundesrepublik Deutschland v Magamodov* ECLI:EU:C:2019:219, para 71.

[36] See Dublin Regulation III, chs V and VI.

[37] Council Directive 2005/85/EC of 1 December 2005 on Minimum Standards on Procedures in Member States for Granting and Withdrawing Refugee Status [2005] OJ L326/13.

[38] Regulation (EC) No 343/2003 of 18 February 2003 Establishing the Criteria and Mechanisms for Determining the Member State Responsible for Examining an Asylum Application Lodged in one of the Member States by a Third-country National [2003] OJ L50/1.

[39] AG Saugmandsgaard Øe referred to Ireland's 'very specific context', which distinguished Ireland for all other Member States. See the Opinion of Saugmandsgaard Øe in Case C-616/19 *MS v Minister for Justice* ECLI:EU:C:2020:648, para 3.

subsidiary protection had been granted in another Member State could be read into the directive. More precisely, section 25 of the 2005 Directive provides a number of grounds of inadmissibility including the prior grant of refugee status in another Member State.[40] Section 25(2)(d) provides that where 'a status equivalent to the rights and benefits of the refugee status' has been granted by the 'member state concerned', an application can be declared inadmissible. Humphreys J asked whether the reference to the 'member state concerned' in section 25(2)(d) and (e) of the 2005 Directive referred to the second Member State (Ireland) or the first Member State (Italy). The thrust of this question is whether the 2015 Act is compatible with EU law, because if the reference is to the second Member State, Ireland could not validly declare the applications inadmissible. The second question concerned whether, in circumstances in which a claimant has applied for subsidiary protection in a first Member State and subsequently applies for international protection in a second Member State, such conduct constitutes an abuse of rights. The third question concerned, in essence, whether, assuming the 2005 Directive did not contemplate inadmissibility for subsidiary protection, Ireland was free to legislate for inadmissibility in these circumstances.

The CJEU's decision largely and explicitly followed AG's Saugmandsgaard Øe's analysis.[41] In *Ibrahim*, the CJEU had decided that the proper interpretation of Article 25 of the 2005 Directive precluded a Member State from declaring a claim inadmissible where subsidiary protection had been granted in another Member State.[42] Outside the procedure in Article 25, Article 16 of Dublin Regulation II provided a mandatory 'take charge and take back' procedure by the Member State responsible. The CJEU found in *Ahmed* that in circumstances in which subsidiary protection had been granted in another Member State, Dublin Regulation III precluded a Member State from using the 'take back and take charge' procedure.[43] It followed that since Ireland adopted Dublin Regulation III, it appeared that Ireland was precluded from declaring applications inadmissible where subsidiary protection had been granted in another Member State pursuant to the 2005 Directive, and from transferring applicants pursuant to Dublin Regulation III. In effect, where 'secondary movements' had occurred and subsidiary protection had been granted in another Member State, Ireland would be obliged to hear all these applications. The CJEU, however, distinguished *MS* from *Ibrahim*. While *Ibrahim* meant that the 2005 Directive read in the light of Dublin Regulation II precluded inadmissibility as a ground for refusing an application for subsidiary protection where it had been previously granted in another Member State, Ireland's legislative framework came 'partially' within the Dublin Regulation III regime.[44] In these unique circumstances, the CJEU ruled that where the 2005 Directive referred to the Dublin Regulation II, these references should be construed as referring to the Dublin Regulation III,

---

[40] See s 25(2)(a).
[41] See *MS* (n 31), explicitly at paras 35, 38 and 50.
[42] *Ibrahim* (n 35) para 71.
[43] Confirmed in Case C-36/17 *Ahmed v Bundesrepublik Deutschland* ECLI:EU:C:2017:273, para 41.
[44] Saugmandsgaard Øe (n 39) para 59.

which explicitly repeals Dublin Regulation II.[45] Construing the 2005 Directive in the light of Dublin Regulation III, the CJEU read inadmissibility into the 2005 Directive, because a more restrictive interpretation of the 2005 Directive would conflict with the overall legislative objectives of the Common European Asylum System. The 'objectives pursued by Directive 2005/85 and by the Dublin III Regulation'[46] were consistent, as both the Dublin Regulation II and III regimes contemplated that where an applicant obtained 'refugee status or otherwise sufficient protection' in another Member State, a second Member State should not be obliged to entertain their application for international protection.[47] Any contrary interpretation would risk encouraging secondary movements between Member States, which is precisely what both the 2005 Directive and Dublin Regulation III are designed to avoid.[48] Because the CJEU adopted this purposive interpretation, there was no requirement to separately answer Ireland's third question and, additionally, the CJEU did not deem it relevant to answer the second question either.[49]

The CJEU's decision in *MS*, first, rescued Ireland from a difficult and self-imposed legal quandary. Ireland adopted most of the 'phase 1' Common European Asylum System directives in the area of freedom, security and justice, but it did not adopt any of the 'phase 2' directives, which supplement Dublin Regulation III. While this approach is perfectly legitimate and has a clear legal basis, *MS* highlights the costs associated with straddling two legislative frameworks. Had the CJEU taken a more literal approach and decided that inadmissibility could not have been read into the 2005 Directive, Ireland would be in the invidious position of being unable to declare inadmissible claims from individuals who had previously received subsidiary protection in another Member State and would not have been able to transfer those individuals to another Member State. In effect, Ireland would have to evaluate all claims de novo and a real risk of 'asylum shopping' would have arisen, which is precisely what the Dublin regime aims to counteract. Secondly, looking at the judgment in its broader context, *MS* highlights Ireland's ongoing difficulties with formulating a coherent and effective legislative approach to international protection.[50] The reason why Ireland did not adopt the 2013 Directive, it seems, stems from practical concerns about the strict time limit requirements set out in the Directive for

---

[45] *MS* (n 31) para 43. The CJEU pointed to direct textual support for this interpretation, namely Art 48 of Dublin Regulation III, which explicitly repeals the Dublin Regulation II.

[46] ibid para 46.

[47] ibid para 47.

[48] ibid para 52.

[49] Saugmandsgaard Øe (n 39) para 94 stated that a subsequent application for international protection is not an abuse of rights per se.

[50] This is not the first time that Ireland's approach has been criticised. The McMahon Report recommended that the Dublin III regime should be adopted *in toto*. See Department of Justice, 'Working Group to Report to Government on Improvements to the Protection Process, including Direct Provision and Supports to Asylum Seekers' (June 2015) www.justice.ie/en/JELR/Report%20to%20 Government%20on%20Improvements%20to%20the%20Protection%20Process,%20including%20 Direct%20Provision%20and%20Supports%20to%20Asylum%20Seekers.pdf/Files/Report%20to% 20Government%20on%20Improvements%20to%20the%20Protection%20Process,%20including%20 Direct%20Provision%20and%20Supports%20to%20Asylum%20Seekers.pdf.

the processing of asylum applications.[51] In the circumstances, the legislator took a pragmatic approach and, while adopting Dublin Regulation III, it de facto adopted the relevant criteria of assessment in the 2013 Directive through section 21(2)(a) of the 2015 Act, but did not formally adopt the 2013 Directive. The result is a 'unique' approach to international protection among the EU27 Member States that effectively adopts some of the elements of Dublin III regime, but domestic acts must be interpreted in the light of directives related to Dublin II. This approach is complex, and defeats clarity and coherence in law.

B. Environmental Law

The important preliminary ruling in *Friends of the Irish Environment v An Bord Pleanála*[52] concludes a long-standing legal dispute, which has its origins in *Commission v Ireland*.[53] In that dispute, the ECJ held in 2007 in infringement proceedings that Ireland had not properly transposed Articles 6(3)–(4) of the Habitats Directive[54] because it had assimilated the conducting of an environmental impact assessment pursuant to the Environmental Impact Assessment Directive (EIA Directive)[55] with an 'appropriate assessment' pursuant to the Habitats Directive into a single evaluation.[56] The CJEU ruled, in particular, that Article 6(3) of the Habitats Directive mandates a two-stage test involving, first, a screening test and, secondly, a precautionary principle-based risk assessment. Three months later, An Bord Pleanála (ABP) granted planning permission under the expedited section 146B procedure of the Planning and Development Act 2006 for a gas terminal in the Shannon Estuary near two Natura 2000 protected sites.[57] The section 146B procedure is a special statutory procedure governing strategic infrastructure development, which allows a developer to make an application directly to ABP.[58] As part of the decision-making process, ABP conducted a mandatory EIA for the gas terminal,[59] but did not consider the Habitats Directive-relevant impact of the development

---

[51] ibid para 3.175, ie Art 31 of the 2013 Directive, which lays down a general rule that a first instance decision must be made within six months.

[52] Case C-254/19 *Friends of the Irish Environment Ltd v An Bord Pleanála* ECLI:EU:C:2020:680 (*FIE 2020*).

[53] Case C-418/04 *Commission v Ireland* ECLI:EU:C:2007:780.

[54] Directive 92/43/EEC of 21 May 1992 on the Conservation of Natural Habitats and of Wild Fauna and Flora [1992] OJ L206/7.

[55] Directive 2001/42/EC of the European Parliament and of the Council of 27 June 2001 on the Assessment of the Effects of Certain Plans and Programmes on the Environment [2001] OJ L197/30.

[56] See Directive 92/43/EEC; *Commission v Ireland* (n 52) paras 231–33. See also EC (Natural Habitats) Regulations 1997 (SI No 94/1997), reg 27(1)–(2).

[57] Natura 2000 sites are protected sites pursuant to the Birds Directive (formerly Directive 79/409/EEC, now replaced by Directive 2009/147/EC) and the Habitats Directive, which are designated as protected for the conservation of endangered birds' species as well as the protection of flora and fauna.

[58] See *Friends of the Irish Environment v An Bord Pleanála* [2019] IEHC 80 (Simons J), para 14 (*FIE 2019*).

[59] Planning and Development Act 2006, s 146B requires public participation where the changes are 'material', which is a threshold question. Ultimately, after public consultation, ABP concluded that the alternations were not material. See ibid (Simons J) para 30.

or mention the Natura 2000-protected sites, although it did undertake an ad hoc screening exercise.[60] Section 146B does not, on its face, require an 'appropriate assessment' required by Article 6(3) of the Habitats Directive. The planning permission contained a 10-year commencement of construction clause. No works took place during the 10-year period, and in 2018 ABP granted a further five-year extension to the planning permission, again pursuant to section 146B. On this occasion, ABP did not conduct an 'appropriate assessment' in accordance with Article 6(3) the Habitats Directive.[61] In the interim between ABP's 2008 decision and its 2018 extension decision, the geographical range of the protected sites had been significantly increased such that the proposed gas terminal was now directly adjacent to the protected sites.[62] It is the latter 2018 decision that was challenged by way of judicial review in *Friends of the Irish Environment*.[63]

In his judgment, Simons J concluded that section 146B could never be an appropriate legal basis for the grant of an extension of a development consent; instead, section 42 of the Planning and Development Act (PDA) 2000 'represent[ed] a form of lex specialis' for planning extension requests.[64] This was an important finding because whereas section 146B was silent as to the requirement of an appropriate assessment, section 42 PDA 2000 mandated an 'appropriate assessment' be conducted where a development has not commenced.[65] However, Simons J considered that since the parties had not pleaded this issue, he was not permitted as a matter of Irish procedural law to quash the decision as ultra vires.[66] He did, though, reason that if there was an EU law-based 'own motion' imperative, this path was open.[67] Domestic case law did not favour the claimants, because Barrett J in *Merriman v Fingal Co* held that section 42 PDA 2000 does not alter a planning permission, and in those circumstances there is no obligation to conduct an 'appropriate assessment' of a development's impact on a protected site pursuant to Article 6(3) of the Habitats Directive.[68] This was good law even where the original planning permission breached the procedural requirements laid down in the EIA Directive or the Habitats Directive.[69] The *Merriman* judgment was consistent with existing CJEU jurisprudence that held that in circumstances in which no physical changes were proposed to a protected site, no Article 6(3) 'appropriate assessment' was required.[70] However,

---

[60] An 'ad hoc' inquiry was conducted in 2008 by ABP in which Habitats Directive-relevant considerations were taken into account and the relevant planning permission reflected some of these concerns, but no formal two-stage procedure as required by s 6(3) of the Habitats Directive was followed. See *FIE* 2019 (n 58) para 4. In 2018, a more limited ad hoc screening exercise was conducted, but it related only 'to the effects of the alteration requested rather than the effects of the underlying permitted development' (para 53).

[61] Although, again at this point, it did conduct an ad hoc screening exercise.

[62] *FIE* 2019 (n 58) para 38.

[63] ibid.

[64] ibid para 84.

[65] See s 42(1)(a) (ii)(IV).

[66] See *FIE* 2019 (n 58) para 191. The relevant procedural law is s 50A(5) of the PDA 2000.

[67] There was also some domestic Supreme Court support for this reasoning, see *Callaghan v An Bord Pleanála (No 1)* [2017] IESC 60, para 4.5.

[68] [2017] IEHC 695, paras 236, and 240.

[69] ibid.

[70] Case C-275/09 *Brussels Hoofdstedelijk Gewest & Others* EU:C:2011:154, para 24; Case C-121/11 *Pro-Braine & Others* EU:C:2012:225, paras 31–32.

AG Kokott, in her opinion in *Inter-Environnement Wallonie ASBL*,[71] stated that, in principle, the extension of a development consent is subject to an 'appropriate assessment' per Article 6(3) of the Habitats Directive.[72] This meant that the matter could not be deemed to be *acte clair*. Thus, Simons J's first and central question was whether the Habitats Directive required an 'appropriate assessment' where a planning permission had been extended. When answering this question, Simons J asked whether the lack of an appropriate assessment in relation to the first grant of development consent should be a relevant consideration, whether it was relevant that the first development consent had expired prior to the grant of the second development consent and whether it was relevant that no development works had commenced at all. Secondly, if it were the case that the second development consent triggered the requirement of an appropriate assessment in Article 6(3) of the Habitats Directive, Simons J asked what considerations a competent authority should take into account when conducting the 'stage-1' screening exercise. Of the other questions referred, perhaps the most important question related to the power of a court to raise of its own motion issues not pleaded by the parties.

The CJEU in *Friends of the Irish Environment*[73] focused primarily on whether the 2018 planning extension constituted an 'agreement to a project' such that Article 6(3) of the Habitats Directive applied. The first task was to clarify the meaning of project and, secondly, to clarify the meaning of agreement for the purposes of the Habitats Directive. Regarding the term 'project', the Court stated that it may 'take into account' the definition of project for the purposes of the EIA Directive.[74] The EIA Directive's definition of project is more limited than that of the Habitats Directive and, as such, if the extension were to come within the definition of project within the EIA Directive, it follows that it would also come within the definition of project for the purposes of the Habitats Directive.[75] The CJEU stated that project in Article 1(2)(a) of the EIA Directive refers to 'the execution of construction works or of other installations or schemes' and 'to other interventions in the natural surroundings and landscape including those involving the extraction of mineral resources'.[76] The case law of the Court further clarifies that project refers to 'work or interventions involving alterations to the physical aspect of the site'.[77] The Court stated that the present facts came within this definition and, as such, came within the definition of project for the purposes of the Habitats Directive.[78] The Court then distinguished between recurrent activities, which constitute a single operation and a single project, and circumstances in which the original consent had lapsed. In the latter circumstances, the Court concluded that because the original consent had lapsed, by definition the consent related to a distinct project for the purposes of section 6(3)

---

[71] Opinion of AG Kokott in Case C-411/17 *Inter-Environnement Wallonie ASBL v Conseil des Ministres* ECLI:EU:C:2018:972.
[72] ibid para 170.
[73] *FIE* 2020 (n 52).
[74] ibid para 28.
[75] ibid para 29.
[76] ibid para 31.
[77] ibid para 32.
[78] ibid paras 33–34.

of the Habitats Directive.[79] This was the case 'irrespective' of whether the original consent complied with section 6(3) of the Habitats Directive.[80]

The Court then considered whether it was an 'agreement' to a project. The Court, since the Habitats Directive does not define the term 'agree',[81] considered the definition of development consent in the EIA Directive, which in section 1(2)(c) defines development consent as 'the decision of the competent authority or authorities which entitles the developer to proceed with the project'.[82] Citing its decision in *Wells*,[83] the Court rejected that in circumstances such as the present case such (development) consent required a change to the project.[84] In circumstances in which a consent had lapsed such that 'a new consent was necessary in order to resume the operation of the activity ... [it] replaced not only the terms but also the very substance of the original consent' and that decision 'constituted a new consent'.[85] Therefore, the extension of planning permission in 2018 constituted a new consent under the EIA Directive and, perforce, Article 6(3) of the Habitats Directive, and required an appropriate assessment per the Habitats Directive.[86]

The Court then restated that an 'appropriate assessment' for the purposes of Article 6(3) of the Habitats Directive involves a two-stage test.[87] The first stage involves an assessment of 'the implications of a plan or project for a protected site where there is a likelihood that the plan or project will have a significant effect on the site'.[88] This requires, following the precautionary principle that account be taken of 'the best scientific knowledge in the field', evaluating whether 'the plan or project might affect the conservation objectives of the site'.[89] If there is a risk of a significant effect on the protected site, then, at a second stage, an appropriate assessment is required, and a project can only be authorised where it is determined it will 'not adversely affect the integrity of [the] site'.[90] This 'appropriate assessment' must also rely on the 'best scientific knowledge in the field' and must evaluate 'all the aspects of the plan or project which can, either individually or in combination with other plans or projects, affect the conservation objectives of [the] site'.[91] Where the assessment contains 'gaps, and lacks complete, precise and definitive findings and conclusions capable of removing all reasonable scientific doubt as to the effects of the proposed works on the protected site', it cannot be regarded as appropriate.[92] The Court clarified that 'earlier assessments carried out for earlier consents' may be

---

[79] ibid paras 38–39.
[80] ibid para 39.
[81] ibid para 42.
[82] ibid para 43.
[83] ibid para 44; Case C-201/02 *Wells* EU:C:2004:12.
[84] *FIE* 2020 (n 52).
[85] ibid.
[86] ibid para 47.
[87] ibid para 50.
[88] ibid para 50.
[89] ibid para 51.
[90] ibid para 52.
[91] ibid. This also follows precautionary reasoning as there must be 'no reasonable doubt' as to the deleterious effects of the plan or project on the site.
[92] ibid para 53.

taken into account, but they are not determinative for new consent applications.[93] It is, as a matter of general guidance, for the competent authority to determine what weight should be given to earlier assessments and, in particular, they might preclude the requirement of conducting an appropriate assessment.[94] This competent authority will decide on whether the assessment must apply to the project as a whole or to parts of it, and should take account of 'previous assessments that may have been conducted and changes in the relevant environmental and scientific data as well as changes to the project and the existence of other plans or projects'.[95] However, in the instant case, because the previous consent did not constitute 'complete, precise and definitive conclusions capable of removing all reasonable scientific doubt as to the effects of the proposed works on those sites',[96] and since the project may have a significant effect on two protected sites, nothing short of a 'full assessment of the implications of the entire project for those sites' was required.[97] The Court did not consider it had enough material before it to answer the *ex officio* question referred, but did note that where the claimant raised Article 6(3) of the Habitats Directive directly, the issue of the *ex officio* application of EU law did not arise.[98] Finally, it was irrelevant for the purposes of determining whether the second development consent engaged Article 6(3) of the Habitats Directive that the original consent was not in compliance with the Habitats Directive.[99]

In sum, in *Friends of the Irish Environment*, the CJEU gave a straightforward and affirmative answer to Simons J's central question, namely whether a new development consent came within the scope Article 6(3) of the Habitats Directive. Where a new planning application has been made, even if it is in substance an extension to a previous grant of planning permission, once it has a potential impact on a protected site, in circumstances in which a previous assessment was defective, a fresh and full Article 6(3) appropriate assessment inquiry is required. In other circumstances, in which the previous assessment is not defective, the new planning application can take account of the previous assessment, but it must be 'updated' in the light of new environmental and scientific knowledge, and changes to the project and the existence of other plans and projects. Taking a broader view of the dispute, the original impetus behind the reference was AG Kokott's invitation in *Inter-Environnement Wallonie ASBL* to revise CJEU jurisprudence on project extensions, which the Court subsequently accepted.[100] The driver behind this revised interpretation was the requirement of rendering EU law compliant with the Aarhus Convention (the United Nations Economic Commission for Europe Convention on Access to Information, Public Participation in Decision-Making and Access to Justice in Environmental Matters) and, as such, of giving the term 'project' in the EIA Directive a wider interpretation

---

[93] ibid paras 54–55.
[94] ibid paras 54 and 56.
[95] ibid para 56.
[96] ibid para 57.
[97] ibid para 58.
[98] ibid para 69.
[99] ibid para 73.
[100] Case C-411/17 *Inter-Environnement Wallonie ASBL v Conseil des Ministres* ECLI:EU:C:2019:622, para 145.

than it had previously received; a fortiori, the term project in the Habitats Directive. In other words, whatever else project may imply within the meaning of the Habitats Directive, it must at a minimum be interpreted in a way that is compatible with the Aarhus Convention. This demonstrates how the interpretation of EU law, and indeed national law, occurs against a background of international law obligations. Of course, the threshold of project as something likely to have a significant effect on the environment is broader than the threshold for project in the EIA, but reference to the EIA and, by extension, the Aarhus Convention is considered an important yardstick to ensure that the EU's international legal obligations are fulfilled.

C. Intellectual Property Law

The preliminary reference in *Recorded Artists Actors Performers Ltd* at its simplest arose as a preliminary matter in a contractual dispute between the eponymous RAAP and Phonographic Performance (Ireland) Ltd (PPI) about the distribution of payments from the use of sound recordings in public.[101] RAAP, a collective management organisation for performers, and PPI, a licensing body for copyright owners, contracted to regulate how licence fees collected by PPI ought to be distributed between producers and performers.[102] The contract defined several terms by reference to the Copyright and Related Rights Act, 2000 (the CRR Act). Determining the proper interpretation of the contract required the Court to determine the restrictions placed on any such interpretation by statute. PPI maintained that the licensing fee should be paid to producers alone, while RAAP argued that the sums collected should also be distributed to performers. According to the CRR Act, a performer is entitled to 'equitable remuneration' if he or she is an Irish citizen or domiciled or resident in Ireland, or if he or she is domiciled or resident in an EEA country.[103] Non-EEA performers, therefore, are not entitled, in domestic law, to a share of moneys gained through licensing payments. This distinguished performers from producers, since producers, pursuant to the CRR Act, are entitled to 'equitable remuneration' regardless of their residency status. However, the CRR Act appeared at first sight to be inconsistent with the WIPO Performances and Phonograms Treaty (WPPT),[104] which in Article 4(1) accords to nationals of states parties a right to equal treatment and equitable remuneration, which is further specified in Article 15. The WPPT also cross-refers to the Rome Convention 1961, which contains a general non-derogation principle,[105] buttressed by a more specific reference in Article 3(2) to the requirement

---

[101] *Recorded Artists Actors Performers Ltd v Phonographic Performance (Ireland) Limited* [2019] IEHC 2 (Simons J) (*RAAP* 2019).

[102] Collected through the use of sound recordings by the playing of sound recordings in public, eg nightclubs, bars and broadcasters.

[103] Relevant sections of the CRR Act include ss 38, 184 and 287.

[104] *RAAP* 2019 (n 101) para 14.

[105] The WIPO Convention was ratified by both Ireland and the EU in 2009, and its Art 1(1) contains a non-derogation clause in relation to 'existing obligations' under the Rome Convention.

to comply with the criteria for national treatment contained in Articles 4 and 5 of the Rome Convention.

Article 4 of the Rome Convention defines the criteria for which performers and producers shall be entitled to national treatment. Article 5 qualifies producers to national treatment in certain circumstances; however, by dint of Article 4(2), performers are extended the same qualifying criteria as those specifically addressed to producers in Article 5. Article 5(2) of the Rome Convention, in particular, includes a rule by which it affords national treatment to publications made in a non-contracting state as if it were published in a contracting state within 30 days of first publication. This was relevant because the USA was not a signatory to the Rome Convention. The USA was, however, a signatory to the WPPT and, as such, it was argued that its performers should benefit from the wider Rome Convention protection via the gateway of Articles 1(1) and 3(2). In this rather roundabout and esoteric way, it appeared that the rule in the CRR Act that conferred national treatment on non-EEA producers was only inconsistent with the WPPT because it excluded performers from the same treatment contrary to Article 4(2) of the Rome Convention.[106] However, it is well established in Irish law that international treaties are not directly applicable in disputes before domestic courts.[107] In the premises, the EU had also ratified the WPPT,[108] although it did not sign the Rome Convention, and Directive 2006/115/EC (the Directive) was enacted to give effect to the EU's WPPT international law obligations and, as a mixed agreement in a field of shared competence, was binding on the Member States of the Union.[109] Therefore, the dispute in RAAP concerned the interpretation of the Directive as a 'gateway' for international law obligations into domestic law. Article 8 of the Directive closely resembled Article 15 WPPT, concerned with equitable remuneration to be shared between producers and performers. A key question for resolution was whether the principle of national treatment had been incorporated into the Directive or Ireland had the discretion to define the term 'relevant performers' in Article 8(2) of the Directive to whom equitable remuneration was due. The legal dispute was further complicated by the fact that the USA had entered a reservation to Article 15(1) WPPT in respect of the right of performers and producers to equitable remuneration.[110] The WPPT[111] and general principles of international law as codified in the Vienna Convention on the Law of Treaties declared that reciprocal limitations could in these circumstances be placed on the nationals of the reserving state party.[112] Did Ireland have the discretion to do so in a field of shared competence? And could Ireland differentiate between producers

---

[106] *RAAP* 2019 (n 101) para 30. It was aptly described in argument as the performer 'piggyback[ing]' on the fact that the producer has qualified under Art 5 of the Rome Convention.

[107] Bunreacht na h-Éireann, Art 29.6. See also *In Re Ó Laighléis* [1960] IR 93; more recently, see *McD v PL* [2009] IESC 81.

[108] Ratification of Ireland and the EU was contemporaneous done on 14 March 2010.

[109] See Directive 2006/115/EC of the European Parliament and of the Council of 12 December 2006 on Rental Right and Lending Right and on Certain Rights Related to Copyright in the Field of Intellectual Property [2006] OJ L376/28.

[110] This was provided for in Art 15(3) WPPT.

[111] See Art 4(2) WPPT.

[112] See Vienna Convention on the Law of Treaties of 23 May 1969 (United Nations Treaty Series, vol 1155, 331), Art 21(b).

and performers, or did the principle of reciprocity require that producers also be excluded from protection?

Thus, the first and most relevant legal question referred concerned the proper interpretation of Article 8(2) of the Directive, and in particular whether it should be read in the light of the WPPT and the Rome Convention.[113] For Simons J, the issue of the extent of the obligation to interpret the Directive in the light of the WPPT and the Rome Convention could not be said to be *acte clair*.[114] While it was clear that there was an obligation to interpret the Directive in the light of 'equivalent concepts' in the WPPT in order to give effect to the EU's international obligations,[115] the existing case law pertained to situations in which the relevant term in the Directive had a 'direct equivalent'[116] term in the WPPT.[117] There was no direct equivalent to Articles 4 and 5 of the Rome Convention, and its concept of national treatment, in the Directive. If Article 8(2), however, were interpreted in the light of the Rome Convention[118] and Article 15 WPPT, it could be argued that although it contained no explicit reference to national treatment, non-discrimination against performers was required to give effect to the objectives of the WPPT and the Rome Convention.[119] In the circumstances, Article 8(2) of the Directive closely resembled Article 15(2) WPPT, but did not explicitly mention the term 'national treatment'. Thus, the first question referred concerned whether, where there was no equivalent concept in the Directive to the concept of national treatment in the WPPT, a national court was obliged to interpret the Directive in the light of the WPPT. A second and subsidiary question related to whether Member States nevertheless retained the discretion to define 'relevant performers' by limiting its definition to performers who are domiciled in the EEA or resident nationals, or where the performance takes place within an EEA country.

The third question referred concerned whether, in circumstances in which a state party had entered a reservation pursuant to Article 15(3) WPPT, any, and if so what, legal consequences followed. Given that it was a field of shared competence, did Member States retain the discretion to take counter-measures? If they did, should any restrictions be mirroring or reciprocal restrictions, or could a Member State treat producers and performers differently? Fourthly, the Court asked whether it was permissible to confine the right to equitable remuneration to producers only. Finally, the High Court seemed to query, although it did not formally ask the question,[120]

[113] The questions are set out in full in the annex to the judgment.

[114] *RAAP* 2019 (n 101) para 83.

[115] This is evident from the *SCF* decision. See Case C-135/10 *Società Consortile Fonografici v Marco Del Corso* ECLI:EU:C:2012:140 (*SCF*). WPPT, Art 2(g) defines 'communications to the public', and this expression is also present in the recitals of the Directive and Art 8 thereof.

[116] *RAAP* 2019 (n 101) para 83, eg 'communication to the public' or 'equitable remuneration', referring to *SCF* in this respect.

[117] *SCF* (n 115).

[118] Through the gateway of national treatment in Art 4 WPPT, which refers to Art 3(2) WPPT, which in turn refers to the 'criteria for eligibility' in the Rome Convention.

[119] Rather, Art 8(2) of the 2006 Directive refers to the requirement that 'equitable remuneration' is shared between producers and performers, but states that in the absence of agreement between performers and producers, it is for Member States to 'lay down the conditions as to the sharing of this remuneration between them'.

[120] See *RAAP* 2019 (n 101) paras 108–14.

whether, given the dispute concerned two private parties in circumstances in which national law might be incompatible with a Directive and where a conforming interpretation could not be given, the parties could in any event rely directly on Article 8(2) of the Directive.[121]

The CJEU's ruling in *RAAF* focused, first and foremost, on whether the Directive should be interpreted in the light of the WPPT and the Rome Convention.[122] The Court recalled that where the terms of a provision make no express reference to the law of Member States, it must be given an autonomous and uniform interpretation in EU law, and that such interpretation must take account of 'the wording of that provision, its context and the objectives pursued by the rules'.[123] It followed that the term 'relevant performers' in Article 8(2) should bear an autonomous and uniform meaning.[124] The term 'relevant performers' is silent as to whether it refers to performers who are nationals of states to which the Directive applies or to performers who are nationals of another state, but in the case of doubt, this provision must be interpreted in the 'context and the objectives of' the Directive.[125] The Court then noted recitals 5–7 of the Directive, which set out the objectives of the Directive, including securing an adequate income, which state that these objectives are to be achieved 'in such a way as not to conflict with the international conventions on which the copyright and related rights laws of many Member States are based'.[126] Therefore, there is a requirement to interpret concepts in the Directive in the light of 'equivalent concepts' in international conventions such as the WPPT.[127] The WPPT defines 'performer',[128] and Article 8(2) of the Directive confers on those persons a right to compensation for the public communication of their work, and it is a right to equitable remuneration that is shared with producers.[129] The Directive does not distinguish between EEA nationals and non-EEA nationals, and, pursuant to the primacy that international obligations have to secondary legislation, the Directive must be interpreted, as far as possible, in a manner consistent with the international obligation.[130] In other words, Article 8(2) of the Directive must be interpreted in the light of Articles 3(2), 4 and 15 WPPT. Articles 3(2) and 4, in particular, carry into the WPPT the national treatment provisions of the Rome Convention.[131] The effect of these provisions in the Rome Convention and WPPT is to embody a non-discrimination principle for all nationals of contracting states. Since Article 8(2) of the Directive applies Article 15 WPPT, then it is not within the discretion of Member States to limit protection to nationals from EEA states only.[132] Therefore, limiting

---

[121] See para 110.
[122] Case C-265/19 *Recorded Artists Actors Performers Ltd v Phonographic Performance (Ireland) Ltd* ECLI:EU:C:2020:677 (*RAAP* 2020).
[123] ibid para 46.
[124] ibid para 48.
[125] ibid paras 49–50.
[126] ibid.
[127] ibid paras 51 and 52.
[128] In Art 2(a) WPPT, and Art 2(b) explicitly defines phonograms as including sound recordings.
[129] ibid paras 54–55.
[130] ibid paras 61–62.
[131] ibid para 66.
[132] ibid para 68.

protection to performers from these states is incompatible with the Directive.[133] The Court did not address the 'no horizontal direct effect' argument head on. The fact that the dispute arose in the context of a dispute between private parties did not fetter a private party's right to raise Article 8(2) of the Directive, or the requirement to interpret the Directive in the light of the WPPT, where Ireland was also a defendant.[134] However, it is submitted that this finding did not resolve the issue as to whether the incompatibility of the CRR Act and the Directive meant that the Directive could be relied on directly as against a private party to disapply national law.[135]

The second main limb of the CJEU's decision concerned the effect of reservations entered into by states parties other than EEA Member States. General principles of international law as codified in Article 21 of the Vienna Convention meant that where another state party to a treaty enters a reservation, this modifies the provision to same extent for the other party in its relations with the reserving state.[136] As several states, including the USA, had derogated in whole or part from the requirement of providing equitable remuneration in Article 15(1), could Ireland also limit the right to equitable remuneration in respect of performers or was the matter solely within the competence of the EU legislator? The CJEU first noted that Article 4(2) WPPT and the Vienna Convention included a principle of reciprocity that modifies the provision to the same extent for other states parties.[137] However, this modification was interpreted by the Court as a power which the relevant state party could, but was not obliged to, exercise.[138] The fact that another state party had entered a reservation under Article 15(3) WPPT did not, of itself, modify the property rights of third country nationals.[139] This was the case notwithstanding that the unequal treatment of EEA nationals vis-à-vis US nationals raised public interest and public policy issues.[140] However, a clear legal basis for such limitations of the single equitable right to remuneration was required because this right was 'an integral part of the protection of intellectual property enshrined in Article 17(2) of the Charter of Fundamental Rights',[141] and any such limitation must comply with the principle of proportionality.[142] Importantly, the CJEU added that since Article 8(2) 'is a

---

[133] ibid para 69.

[134] ibid para 74.

[135] If the defendant were Ireland alone, then there would be an obligation to do so. But where the dispute relates to a contractual dispute between RAAP and PPI in which the CRR forms part of the contract, it seems doubtful that the presumptively clear words of the CRR can be disapplied. The obligation in these circumstances is rather one of 'indirect effect' or conforming interpretation reaching its limits at a *contra legem* interpretation, and the latter is precisely what Simons J considered would be required. See, more recently, Case C-441/14 *Dansk Industri (DI) acting on behalf of Ajos v Estate of Rasmussen* ECLI:EU:C:2016:278, paras 30–34.

[136] See Vienna Convention, Art 21(b).

[137] *RAAP* 2020 (n 122) para 79.

[138] ibid para 80.

[139] ibid para 87.

[140] ibid paras 82–84.

[141] ibid paras 85 and 86.

[142] This is implied by reference to the Charter, Art 52(1), para 86. Art 52(1) specifically mentions the proportionality principle.

harmonised rule, it is for the EU legislature alone and not the national legislatures' to determine the legitimate limits on the right to equitable remuneration.[143] In other words, the partial limits placed on the right by Ireland in the CRR Act were incompatible with EU law.[144]

The legal consequence of the CJEU's decision in *RAAF* is that it clarifies that Ireland has failed to properly transpose the Directive. However, as Simons J rightly clarifies in *Recorded Artists Actors Performers Ltd v Phonographic Performance (Ireland) Limited*, the significance of this finding of non-transposition has yet to be determined in the context of the underlying contractual dispute.[145] Directives do not ordinarily have horizontal direct effect, but in the context of a horizontal dispute they require Member States' courts only to give a conforming interpretation of national law where it is possible to do so. The Member State court is not obliged to stretch this principle so far as to give a *contra legem* interpretation. In his 2019 judgment, however, Simons J underlined that since the CRR Act was clear and unambiguous in its differential treatment of producers and performers, such a conforming interpretation was precluded.[146] It is debatable whether this is a correct interpretation as required by the principle of conforming interpretation; it may well be so, but it does seem, respectfully, that Simons J settled on a certain meaning of the CCR Act, based on a literal reading, before considering the Directive rather than using the Directive to interpret the statute.[147] It might have been more appropriate to construe the CCR Act as far as possible in the light of the Directive before reaching a conclusion as to its meaning.[148] This conforming interpretation requirement is, one would imagine, stronger when set against the fundamental right to property in the Charter of Fundamental Rights of the EU (the Charter)[149] which the Court has recognised has an indirect horizontal effect in private legal disputes.[150] Assuming, however, that Simons J is correct and national law does not admit of a conforming interpretation, the CJEU ruling offers little succour to the claimants, and it appears that the only way to bring Irish law into conformity with EU law is through amending the CCR Act.

---

[143] *RAAP* 2020 (n 122) para 88.

[144] In ibid paras 92–96, the CJEU answered the High Court's fourth question as to whether Ireland could voluntarily extend protection to producers only separately, but it seems to be surplusage since the answer to the reservation question determined the answer to the final question.

[145] *Recorded Artists Actors Performers Ltd v Phonographic Performance (Ireland) Limited* [2021] IEHC 22, paras 18–20.

[146] *RAAP* 2019 (n 101) para 6.

[147] Of course, in this respect, Simons J was guided by the pleadings of the parties, who both accepted that the CRR Act had a clear meaning.

[148] See S Prechal, *Directives in EC Law*, 2nd edn (Oxford, Oxford University Press, 2006) 209, criticising similar UK methods of interpretation: 'There is an important difference between, on the one hand, looking to see whether national law is ambiguous and only in the case of an affirmative answer turning to the directive, and, on the other hand, giving proper consideration to the directive first and then seeking to interpret national law accordingly.' In the instance case, the long title of the CRR Act makes it clear that, inter alia, it is enacted to give effect to Directive 92/100/EEC, the predecessor of the Directive, which contains an article identical to Art 8(2).

[149] Art 17(2).

[150] For a discussion, see T Rendas, 'Fundamental Rights in EU Copyright Law: An Overview' in E Rosati (ed), *The Routledge Handbook of EU Copyright Law* (Abingdon, Routledge, 2021) 18–38.

Focusing more broadly on the effect of the CJEU's ruling on the domestic legal order, it appears to be yet another illustration of how international law through the backdoor of section 3 of the European Communities Act 1973 Act enters the domestic legal order and qualifies a rigid understanding of Article 29.6 of the Irish Constitution (Bunreacht na h-Éireann).[151] This has recently been quite clearly illustrated in case law stemming from the Aarhus Convention, another treaty in a field of shared competence, and such backdoor reception of international law will likely be an increasing feature of legal disputes in the future.[152] There is, moreover, a more subtle influence on Irish copyright law that is based on the CJEU's decision to characterise the status of performers as a fundamental right, namely that Irish copyright law gradually becomes unmoored from its common law roots.[153]

The decision also clarifies that the requirements of EU law in the field of copyright extend beyond simply an EU27 non-discrimination principle and, given the fundamental nature of the right to property, which has a charter footing, it also extends protection to non-EEA performers.[154] Of course, this protection may be restricted, in the public interest, by the EU legislature, but any such restriction must be proportionate. Because the Directive harmonised the concept of equitable remuneration, it now falls within the exclusive competence of the EU legislator to determine its requirements notwithstanding it is a directive in a field of shared competence. This also extends to the appropriate response to reservations made by third countries. Additionally, it impacts on the interpretation of agreements, such as the Rome Convention, to which the EU is not a signatory, but which impacts on agreements such as the WPPT, to which the EU is a signatory.[155]

D. Data Protection

Data Protection Commissioner v Facebook Ireland Ltd and Maximillian Schrems (*Schrems II*) related to the transfer of personal data from the EU to the USA and, in particular, the lawfulness of data transfers in the context of the USA's mass surveillance

---

[151] 'No international agreement shall be part of the domestic law of the State save as may be determined by the Oireachtas.' The seminal case is *In Re Ó Laighléis* (n 108). See D Fennelly, *International Law in the Irish Legal System*, 1st edn (Dublin, Round Hall, 2014) para 2.03: 'As more international agreements take effect in Ireland through the EU legal order, the effect of Art.29.6 of the Constitution is increasingly being influenced, and indeed *qualified*, by the position in EU law' (emphasis added).

[152] eg similar to the treatment of Art 9(3) of the Aarhus Convention, in *Conway v Ireland* [2017] IESC 13.

[153] See M Borghi, 'The Universal Nature of Performers' Rights under EU Law (a Note on Case-265/19, Recorded Artists Actors Perfomers v Phonographic Performance Ireland)' (2021) CIPPM/Jean Monet Working Papers No 01-2021, 2–3, 12–15 focusing on the personality-based, continental approach to performers' rights in contrast to the common law 'functional' (or economic) approach.

[154] AG Tanchev in *RAAP* 2020 (n 122) para 53 was even more emphatic than the Court: 'Fundamental rights are universal in nature and what is at issue here is the right to property.'

[155] Additionally, per Borghi (n 153): 'The harmonisation of the law absorbs the competences of the Member States in relation to equivalent provisions laid down in treaties to which only the Member States are parties, such as the Rome Convention' (10).

programmes.[156] In *Schrems I*, Mr Schrems had filed a complaint with the Office of the Data Protection Commissioner (the Commissioner) requesting it to make an order to prohibit the transfer of personal data from Facebook Ireland, an Irish subsidiary, to its parent company, Facebook Inc, which is based in the USA.[157] The claimant's basic argument was that the transfer of personal data, and its legal basis, the Commission's Safe Harbour Decision, was invalid.[158] When the Commissioner rejected his complaint, he appealed its decision to the High Court and, in turn, the High Court made a preliminary reference to the CJEU.[159] The CJEU, in essence, decided that the US legislative framework failed to offer adequate protection of personal data, and that the Safe Harbour Decision was invalid.[160] It also held that the Commissioner should be able to engage in legal proceedings where it formed the view that a complaint was well founded.[161] This resulted in the Commissioner's decision being annulled, and the matter returned before the Commissioner for decision. Before the Commissioner, it emerged that the legal basis of the continuing transfer of personal data to the USA was the Standard Contractual Clauses (SCC) Decision.[162] There are three legislative pathways through which personal data may be transferred to a third country: first, pursuant to a Commission adequacy decision; secondly, pursuant to SCCs, which are meant to provide adequate safeguards in the absence of an adequacy decision; and, thirdly, in circumstances in which the data subject consents to the transfer of their data.[163] In other words, SCCs enable the transfer of personal data to third countries by compensating for the absence of an EU Commission adequacy decision. SCCs are, essentially, boilerplate provisions binding data exporters and importers, which contain procedural and remedial safeguards against the improper sharing of personal data. The Commissioner doubted the validity of the SCC Decision, particularly because SCCs did not bind US authorities and because of the US legal framework which appeared to impugn them, and brought an action to the High Court for decision. The High Court decided to refer no fewer than 11 questions to the CJEU for preliminary ruling. The most important questions

---

[156] Case C-311/18 *Data Protection Commissioner v Facebook Ireland Ltd and Maximillian Schrems* ECLI:EU:C:2020:559 (*Schrems II*). Mass surveillance programmes include spying and intelligence-gathering programmes, which are authorised by the US Foreign Intelligence & Surveillance Act 2008, s 702.

[157] Case C-362/14 *Maximillian Schrems v Data Protection Commissioner* ECLI:EU:C:2015:650 (*Schrems I*).

[158] Commission Decision 2000/520/EC pursuant to Directive 95/46/EC.

[159] *Data Protection Commissioner v Facebook Ireland & Maximillian Schrems* [2017] IEHC 545 (Costello J).

[160] *Schrems I* (n 157) para 98.

[161] The Commissioner could not overturn a Commission Decision, such as the Safe Harbour Decision, because the validity of EU law could only be pronounced upon by the CJEU. The Court clarified in *Schrems I* that where no validity decision had been taken, the Commissioner was bound by the relevant decision, but nonetheless she could initiate proceedings before the national court where it had doubts as to its validity, which in turn could refer a question to the CJEU for determination of validity.

[162] Their legal basis was Commission Decision 2010/87, and Art 26(4) of the pre-GDPR Directive, Directive 95/46/EC, declared that they provided sufficient safeguards of data privacy. The actual boilerplate contractual clauses were contained in the Annex of the 2010 decision.

[163] Directive 95/46/EC, Arts 25 and 26; GDPR, Arts 45, 46 and 49 respectively. See Regulation (EU) 2016/679 of the European Parliament and of the Council of 27 April 2016 on the Protection of Natural persons with Regard to the Processing of Personal Data and on the Free Movement of such Data, and Repealing Directive 95/46/EC (General Data Protection Regulation) [2016] OJ L119/1.

concerned, first, whether the Charter applied to the transfer of personal data to third countries where that information would be processed in that country for purposes of national security; secondly, the compatibility of the SCC Decision with Articles 7 and 8 of the Charter;[164] thirdly, the adequacy of protection afforded to non-US citizens in the light of Article 47 of the Charter;[165] fourthly, whether the Data Privacy Shield reaches the threshold of adequate protection; and fifthly, what obligations are incumbent on national data protection authorities and, in particular, whether they should prohibit transfers under the SCCs. In the interim, and in response to *Schrems I*, the Commission adopted the Privacy Shield Decision.[166] Additionally, the General Data Protection Regulation (GDPR) entered into force.

The CJEU, in *Schrems II*, first decided that the transfer of personal data between two legal persons for commercial purposes comes within the scope of 'processing of personal data' under the GDPR. The Court rejected, in particular, the relevance of Article 4(2) of the Treaty of the European Union (TEU). Article 4(2) TEU, among other things, obliged the EU to 'respect' the national security of Member States, as well as recognising it as the 'sole responsibility' of Member States.[167] However, the Court interpreted this provision as applying to the relationship between the EU and Member States, and, in consequence, as being not relevant to the relationship between the EU and third countries.[168] Therefore, it could not be read in conjunction with the exceptions to the scope of application of Articles 2(2)(a), (b) and (d) GDPR.[169] These exceptions refer to processing of personal data by state authorities and, in the circumstances, a strict interpretation excluded the transfer of personal data between two private companies from their purview.[170] This conclusion was reinforced by the fact that Article 45(2)(a) GDPR contemplated that the Commission, when investigating whether a third country provides adequate protection to personal data, should, among other things, take account of that third country's national security law.[171]

The second matter concerned the level of protection of personal data required by Articles 46(1) and 46(2)(c) GDPR in relation to SCCs. These Articles belong to Chapter V of the GDPR, which is concerned with the transfer of personal data to third countries. Article 45 provides the mechanism of an adequacy decision, which is conducted by the Commission, and this decision must ensure third country compliance with the rule of law, human rights, the right to an effective remedy and

---

[164] The SCC governed the contractual relations between Facebook Ireland and its users, but imposed no obligations on US authorities.

[165] While US citizens benefit from US Constitution 4th Amendment rights, non-US citizens do not. This deprives EU citizens of *locus standi*. Additionally, the Privacy Shield Decision created an ombudsperson for complaints from non-US citizens for violations of their privacy; however, it was suggested that it was not a tribunal within the meaning of Art 47 of the Charter.

[166] Commission Implementing Decision (EU) 2016/1250 of 12 July 2016 pursuant to Directive 95/46/EC of the European Parliament and of the Council on the Adequacy of the Protection provided by the EU–US Privacy Shield [2016] OJ L207/1, primarily by the creation of an ombudsperson.

[167] TEU, Art 4(2).

[168] *Schrems II* (n 156) para 81.

[169] ibid para 85.

[170] ibid para 86.

[171] ibid para 86.

international law requirements.[172] It requires, in other words, that the Commission ensures that third countries give 'essentially equivalent' protection to personal data in line with the standards guaranteed within the EU.[173] However, if this adequacy decision does not occur, Article 46 applies. Article 46 states that a transfer of personal data can only occur in these circumstances where the 'controller or processor' of personal data has provided 'adequate safeguards, and on condition that enforceable data subject rights and effective legal remedies for data subjects are available'.[174] Article 46(2)(c) states, however, that the appropriate safeguards may be provided for without the requirement of supervisory authority authorisation by SCCs, which are approved by the Commission. The relevant legal question concerned whether the level of protection contained in Article 45 differed from the level of protection required by Article 46. The CJEU found that it did not. Drawing on recitals 107 and 108 GDPR and the compensatory function of Article 46, the Court decided that where data is transferred pursuant to SCCs, the level of protection provided should be 'essentially equivalent' to the level of protection guaranteed within the EU, thereby equating the level of protection required under Articles 45 and 46.[175] While Article 46 did not specify what constituted 'appropriate safeguards', the CJEU read Article 46 in the light of Article 44, which contained the general principles of transfer and applied to all Chapter V provisions.[176] With regard to Article 46(2)(c), in particular concerning the factors that should be taken into account by a national court when determining whether SCCs comply with the requirement of adequate protection, the CJEU specified that the competent authority must examine the contract between the data controller or processor and the third country data recipient against the background of the third country legislative framework for public authority access to personal data. The criteria should, in particular, correspond to the 'non-exhaustive' criteria in Article 45(2), which include rule of law and human rights compliance.[177] The CJEU added that the level of protection in Article 46 should be read in the light of the Charter, and not in the light of national law.[178]

Article 58 GDPR confers a range of investigative and corrective powers on supervisory authorities, and Articles 58(2)(f) and (j) include the power to order the temporary and permanent suspension of data processing and the suspension of data flows to third countries. Thirdly, the CJEU, in this respect, considered whether the competent supervisory authority is obliged to suspend or prohibit a transfer of personal data to a third country if, pursuant to the SCCs' adequacy decision adopted by the Commission, the Supervisory Authority is of the view that the SCC Decision fails to comply with Articles 45 and 46 GDPR and the Charter. The Court, recalling *Schrems I*, first clarified that the relevant supervisory authority has the responsibility to monitor compliance with the GDPR, and this responsibility included, and is

---

[172] Art 45(2) is quite extensive, but these are the main headline requirements.
[173] ibid para 94.
[174] Art 46(1).
[175] ibid para 96.
[176] ibid para 92.
[177] ibid para 104.
[178] ibid para 101.

of particular importance when, personal data is transferred to third countries.[179] This responsibility is meant to ensure the right of each person to an effective judicial remedy, which is also a right according to the Charter, since each person may lodge a complaint with the supervisory authority per Article 58, and the supervisory authority must exercise due diligence in order to vindicate this right.[180] This may include a requirement to suspend or prohibit the transfer of data where a third country does not comply with the requirement of essentially equivalent data protection.[181] This is the general rule if no adequacy decision has been adopted by the Commission. However, where the Commission has adopted an SCC pursuant to Article 46(2)(c), the supervisory authority's responsibility is not *ipso facto* discharged.[182] Instead, the supervisory authority has a continuing obligation to evaluate compliance. The adoption of an SCC means, however, that the supervisory authority cannot declare the agreement invalid, but rather must comply with the Commission's decision.[183] Instead, where a complaint is lodged, and in circumstances where the supervisory authority doubts the compliance of the Commission's SCC decision with the GDPR, they must bring an action to the national courts.[184] The national courts, where appropriate, should refer its validity for a preliminary ruling.[185]

The CJEU, fourthly, evaluated whether the relevant SCC decision in issue complied with Articles 7, 8 and 47 of the Charter in respect of the right to adequate protection. Articles 46(1) and 46(2)(c) essentially reproduced provisions of the SCC Decision.[186] A particularly relevant feature of the SCCs was that they did not bind third country public authorities, but only controllers and recipients of data who were in contractual privity.[187] The CJEU concluded from this fact that whether an SCC ensures adequate protection of personal data will, in essence, depend on a case-by-case analysis. In certain circumstances, the presence of an SCC between the EU27 data controller and the non-EU recipient may be sufficient to guarantee adequate protection, but in other circumstances the law and practice, including public authority surveillance practices, may render the SCC nugatory.[188] The Court went on to emphasise that merely because the SCC decision does not bind public authorities, it does not render the SCC Decision invalid. SCCs are essentially boilerplates, which of themselves do not ensure that appropriate safeguards are in situ. Indeed, unlike an adequacy decision pursuant to Article 45(1) GDPR, they do not require an extensive review of third country law and practices before they are adopted.[189] Where no such Article 45(1) adequacy protection decision has been adopted, it falls to the data processor or controller to provide the appropriate safeguards.[190] In other words,

---

[179] ibid paras 107–08.
[180] ibid paras 110–12.
[181] ibid paras 112–13.
[182] ibid para 115.
[183] ibid paras 116–18.
[184] ibid paras 119–20.
[185] ibid.
[186] ibid para 124.
[187] ibid paras 123 and 125.
[188] ibid para 126.
[189] ibid para 130.
[190] ibid para 131.

the data controller or processor must supplement the relevant SCC with additional protections in order to ensure compliance with Charter rights.[191] If the controller or processor is unable to plug any gap, as it were, between third country legislation and practices and the requirements of EU law, then they must suspend or prohibit personal data transfers.[192] Thus, while the validity of the SCC Decision is not impugned by this interpretation, it places a significant burden on 'private' parties to ensure compliance with EU law requirements.

The CJEU, fifthly, considered whether supervisory authorities are bound by the Commission's Privacy Shield Decision, which stated that the USA provides an adequate level of protection of personal data. The Privacy Shield Decision was adopted subsequent to the Data Commissioner's hearing, but it was necessary to determine its validity in order to give guidance as to EU law because the Data Commissioner had yet to make a decision in relation to the underlying complaint. A particular feature of the Privacy Shield Decision was the establishment of an office of Ombudsperson in the USA as a way to safeguard the rights in Article 47 of the Charter. The question of whether it was binding on the Data Commissioner or not required the CJEU to review its validity per the GDPR read in the light of the relevant provisions of the Charter.[193] In effect, the CJEU was required to review the declaration of adequate protection made by the EU Commission pursuant to Article 45(3) GDPR.[194] The CJEU turned first to Articles 7 and 8 of the Charter. Article 7 provides that 'everyone has the right to respect for his or her private and family life, home and communications', whereas Article 8 expressly confers a right to personal data protection. The Court recognised that the processing of personal data fell squarely within the scope of protection of these rights, and these rights are interfered with where personal data is transferred to public authorities.[195] However, while fundamental rights, these rights are not absolute and 'must be considered in relation to their function in society'.[196] Any interference, however, must be subjected to a proportionality test.[197] This formed the analytical framework through which the US legal framework was analysed. Section 702 of the US Foreign Intelligence Security Act 2008 (FISA) was a measure that empowered the Foreign Intelligence Surveillance Court to authorise a series of mass surveillance programmes and to verify whether those programmes related to the objective of acquiring foreign intelligence information, but did not verify whether individuals were 'properly targeted to acquire foreign intelligence information'.[198] Because it was, in this way, undiscriminating, the FISA failed to meet the standard of essentially equivalent protection required by the Charter and failed the proportionality test.[199] While there were in-built legal safeguards, they

---

[191] ibid para 134.
[192] ibid para 135, 'or failing that, the competent supervisory authority ...'
[193] Charter, Arts 7, 8 and 47. The Privacy Shield Decision declared in Art 1(1) that it provided adequate protection pursuant to Art 45(1) GDPR.
[194] ibid para 162.
[195] ibid paras 170–71.
[196] ibid para 172.
[197] ibid para 174.
[198] ibid para 179.
[199] ibid para 180.

did not grant data subjects actionable rights before US courts.[200] The CJEU then examined the US office of Ombudsperson in the light of Article 47 of the Charter. Article 47, as is well known, confers on 'everyone' the right to an effective remedy before an independent and impartial tribunal. In this respect, it was clear that the Ombudsperson was not independent of the US State Department because it reported directly to the Secretary of State.[201] Moreover, although there was a 'commitment' on behalf of the US government that the intelligence services would correct violations of rules detected by the Privacy Shield Ombudsperson, the latter lacked enforcement powers to compel compliance.[202] In these circumstances, the CJEU decided that the Ombudsperson mechanism violated the rights protected by Article 47 and, as such, the Privacy Shield Decision was invalid.[203]

Schrems II is a very significant case. As Costello J stated in the High Court, its outcome affects the personal data of millions of people within the EU and beyond, and its implications for EU–US trade can be counted in the billions.[204] It might be viewed politically as a continuing rebuke to the post-9/11 state of exception through which intelligence gathering in the USA, particularly in relation to non-US citizens, was largely exceptionalised from traditional rule of law concerns. However, as Costello J in the High Court was apt to remark, the decision has a firm legal basis in EU law. One might speak, therefore, in terms of a clash of cultures of privacy across the Atlantic as much as one might speak of a Brussels effect. The consequences of *Schrems II* is that the Commission must rethink its approach to data sharing once again.

III. CONCLUSION

There was a steady number of preliminary rulings given in 2020. More significant than the number of rulings given, however, were their complexity and wider importance for the EU27 and beyond. *Schrems II* was, of course, the most significant and highly anticipated CJEU decision because of its broad economic and political impact. The CJEU seized the occasion to clarify the requirements of data controllers and supervisory authorities, and, once again, rebuked the European Commission–US data sharing practices. The *Friends of the Irish Environment* and *RAAF* decisions are perhaps of more interesting and lasting impact for Irish law and legal culture because they confirm the fact that the process of Europeanisation is also a process of internationalisation, which blurs the lines between domestic law and international law obligations. While Ireland is a dualist state, this is a simplification of the legal reality, and a more nuanced understanding of Ireland's obligations is developing. Apart from their theoretical significance, they are important decisions in terms of

---

[200] ibid paras 181 and 182.
[201] ibid para 195.
[202] ibid para 196.
[203] ibid paras 197 and 201.
[204] *Schrems* (n 159) para 5.

the substantive decisions reached in each case. In *Friends of the Irish Environment*, the CJEU confirmed that the obligation to conduct appropriate and precautionary assessments of the environmental impact of developments is an ongoing obligation, which recurs so long as a development has not been commenced or at the expiry of its operating licence, and must reflect the current state of knowledge and not the state of knowledge when planning permission was initially granted. In *RAAF*, the CJEU clarified that EU law obliges a more even sharing of revenues between performers and producers, and enshrines this within the framework of fundamental rights. *MS* highlights the difficulties that derive from straddling two legal regimes or, in other words, of taking an à la carte approach to harmonisation, where bits and pieces of different regulatory frameworks are adopted. Overall, 2020 was a year of very significant and engaged judicial dialogue between Irish courts and the CJEU against the background of a significant public and economic health crisis, with the latter even eclipsing Brexit on the popular and political agenda.

Human Rights in Northern Ireland 2020

ESTHER McGUINNESS*

JANUARY 2020 GAVE people of Northern Ireland (NI) cause for hope. The devolved institutions had finally been restored based on the New Decade, New Approach (NDNA) agreement,[1] which was underpinned by a range of detailed commitments, including the establishment of an Ad Hoc Committee on a Bill of Rights[2] and progressing long-unfulfilled commitments in relation to Irish language legislation[3] and an anti-poverty strategy.[4] There was also the eagerly anticipated introduction of legislation to implement the legacy aspects of the Stormont House Agreement within the first 100 days.[5] Then COVID-19 struck.[6]

As a result, the rest of the year has been dominated by the Northern Ireland Executive dealing with an unprecedented public health challenge, leading to difficult decisions being made in real-time with limited contemporary experience to draw on.[7]

Human rights do not take a back seat during public emergencies. For civil and political rights, including, for example, freedom of thought, conscience and religion and freedom of assembly and movement, a set of principles has been developed on the parameters within which such limitations can be applied. The Siracusa Principles on the Limitations and Derogation Provisions[8] in the United Nations International Covenant on Civil and Political Rights[9] were published by the American Association of the International Commission of Jurists in 1984.[10]

The Principles provide that any restrictions on rights must be prescribed in law, with adequate safeguards and effective remedies, and must not be arbitrary or unreasonable. Such measures taken, and their severity and scope, should be no more than strictly necessary to deal with the emergency and be proportionate to the threat

---

* Ulster University School of Law.

[1] NI Office, 'New Decade, New Approach' (NIO 2020) chrome-extension://efaidnbmnnnibpcajpcgl-clefindmkaj/https://assets.publishing.service.gov.uk/government/uploads/system/uploads/attachment_data/file/856998/2020-01-08_a_new_decade__a_new_approach.pdf.

[2] ibid para 28.

[3] ibid para 5.21.3.

[4] ibid 9.

[5] ibid para 16.

[6] www.bbc.co.uk/news/uk-northern-ireland-51665704.

[7] See https://nihrc.org/publication/detail/annual-statement-2020, 6.

[8] UN Commission on Human Rights, *The Siracusa Principles on the Limitation and Derogation Provisions in the International Covenant on Civil and Political Rights* (28 September 1984) E/CN.4/1985/4, www.icj.org/wp-content/uploads/1984/07/Siracusa-principles-ICCPR-legal-submission-1985-eng.pdf.

[9] UN General Assembly, *International Covenant on Civil and Political Rights*, United Nations, Treaty Series, vol 999 (16 December 1966) 171, www.refworld.org/docid/3ae6b3aa0.html.

[10] www.idealist.org/en/nonprofit/de6ff061867f43a8aad6760e98dea0ec-the-american-association-for-the-international-commission-of-jurists-new-york.

posed.[11] Any restriction should last for no longer than required and, in the case of a public health emergency, should give due regard to the international regulations of the World Health Organization (WHO).[12] Moreover, certain rights can never be derogated from even in an emergency, including the rights to life, freedom from torture, cruel and inhuman treatment, freedom from slavery and freedom of thought, conscience and religion.[13] The principles are not binding in domestic law, although they remain an excellent yardstick to judge any diminution of rights.

In response to the COVID-19 pandemic, a number of temporary legal reforms were introduced with a view to tackling the virus and preventing its spread.[14] The Northern Ireland Human Rights Commission (NIHRC) commented that 'governments in London, Belfast and Dublin have taken unparalleled powers and sweeping measures, unheard of in peace times and long cherished freedoms have been curtailed'.[15] Consequently, the following section provides an overview of the temporary legislative reforms that were applicable to NI during the pandemic and outlines how those reforms impacted the human rights framework, before moving on to address outstanding issues within the human rights and equality landscape in NI.

I. COVID-19 AND ITS IMPACT ON HUMAN RIGHTS IN NORTHERN IRELAND

In terms of legally enforceable rights under the European Convention on Human Rights (ECHR) and the UK Human Rights Act 1998, some rights must be strictly adhered to. These include the right to life (Article 2 ECHR) and the right to freedom from torture, inhuman or degrading treatment or punishment (Article 3 ECHR). Other rights can be limited under a range of circumstances. These include the rights to liberty (Article 5), education (Protocol No 1, Article 2 ECHR), respect for private and family life (Article 8 ECHR) and peaceful assembly (Article 11 ECHR).[16] However, in March 2020, when the WHO confirmed that global measures to prevent the spread of COVID-19 and preserve the life and health of those affected or under threat of infection, particularly the most vulnerable, were legitimate aims, the international community responded with emergency legislation. The Coronavirus Act 2020 was subsequently enacted in the UK on 25 March.[17]

While organisations such as the Committee on the Administration of Justice in NI argued that the pandemic raised 'the spectre of the securitisation of health and the

---

[11] *The Siracusa Principles* (n 8) 6–7.

[12] ibid 8, para 28.

[13] ibid 12, para 58.

[14] See 'The Territorial Impact of COVID-19: Managing the Crisis across Levels of Government' www.oecd.org/coronavirus/policy-responses/the-territorial-impact-of-covid-19-managing-the-crisis-across-levels-of-government-d3e314e1/.

[15] NIHRC Annual Statement 2020, 6.

[16] It depends on the individual right and circumstances as to when such a right can be limited and to what extent, but generally any limitation must be provided for in law, be necessary and proportionate, and pursue a legitimate aim.

[17] www.legislation.gov.uk/ukpga/2020/7/contents.

dangers of COVID-19 restrictions becoming a pretext for fortified surveillance and policing infrastructures and thus exacerbating existing inequalities in the treatment of marginalised groups'.[18] The Coronavirus Act introduced new emergency powers to help contain and cope with COVID-19. These powers have a time limit of two years and can only be used where necessary to deal with the COVID-19 public health crisis.[19] I In terms of holding the UK government to account in its use of these powers, the Coronavirus Act was reviewed by the UK Parliament after six months, after which the Secretary of State is obliged to provide a report on the powers that are used every two months until all restrictions are lifted.[20]

The initial versions of the legislation were introduced for the purposes of restricting movement, services and social interaction within NI, in a bid to curb the spread of COVID-19. From 15 May 2020, the NI Executive had been gradually taking steps, including enacting amended versions of the original legislation, to ease the restrictions in place since 28 March 2020. In September 2020, the NI Executive started implementing some localised restrictions for set periods, guided by medical advice. In October 2020, increased restrictions were expanded across the whole of NI for set periods. The tightening and loosening of restrictions were subject to constant review by the NI Executive, guided by the Department of Health and medical advice. This approach continued into 2021.

A. Domestic Abuse: Inhuman and Degrading Treatment

In June 2020, the Police Service NI reported that it received on average 570 domestic violence calls per week between February 2019 and March 2020.[21] However, between 8 April 2020 and 30 June 2020, the average number of calls per week was consistently above 600, with a spike of 721 calls in mid-April 2020 and one of 727 at the start of June 2020.[22] These increases were consistent with reports in England and

---

[18] https://caj.org.uk/2020/12/11/caj-annual-report-2020/, 4.

[19] It is possible that some of the powers set out in the Act may never be applied.

[20] These include: Health Protection (Coronavirus Restrictions) Regulations 2020 and subsequent versions; Temporary Modification of Education Duties Notice (NI) 2020 and subsequent versions; Children's Social Care (Coronavirus) (Temporary Modification of Children's Social Care) Regulations (NI) 2020 and subsequent versions; Planning (Development Management) (Temporary Modifications) (Coronavirus) Regulations (NI) 2020; Statutory Paternity Pay, Statutory Adoption Pay and Statutory Shared Parental Pay (Normal Weekly Earnings etc) (Coronavirus) (Amendment) Regulations (NI) 2020; Maternity Allowance and Statutory Maternity Pay (Normal Weekly Earnings etc) (Coronavirus) (Amendment) Regulations (NI) 2020; Working Time (Coronavirus) (Amendment) Regulations (NI) 2020; Discretionary Support (Amendment No 2) (COVID-19) Regulations (NI) 2020; Statutory Sick Pay (General Coronavirus Amendment No 3) Regulations (NI) 2020; and Private Tenancies (Coronavirus) Modifications Act 2020.

[21] 'Domestic Abuse Calls Received by Police in Northern Ireland: Weekly Management Information on Domestic Abuse Calls Received by PSNI since Covid-19 Lockdown Measures Were Introduced on 23 March 2020', 2, www.psni.police.uk/globalassets/inside-the-psni/our-statistics/domestic-abuse-statistics/covid-19/domestic-abuse-calls-to-26.05.20.pdf.

[22] ibid.

Wales during the same period.[23] Nexus, the NI Rape Crisis Centre, also confirmed that the number of visits to its domestic and sexual abuse website had doubled in the same period.[24] In June 2020, the Department of Health provided Women's Aid with an additional £60,000 to provide an initial care package for families who have experienced, or been a victim of, domestic abuse.[25] Notably, other governments within the UK had provided significantly more additional funding to domestic violence organisations during the COVID-19 crisis. The Scottish government provided £1.35 million to Scottish Women's Aid and the UK government committed an additional £28 million package for domestic violence victims and £3.8 million for community-based domestic abuse and modern slavery services in England and Wales.[26]

B. Health and Social Care: Right to Private and Family Life

The statistical updates provided by the Department of Health indicated around half of COVID-19 related deaths involved care home residents, either in the care home or in hospitals. High numbers of deaths within care homes may have been linked to the slow introduction of testing within such settings, discharging patients to care homes without those individuals being tested for COVID-19, the late arrival of personal protective equipment, the delay in including care home deaths in COVID-19 statistics to enable an understanding of the issue, and the relative underfunding and general neglect of the care home sector.[27] In May 2020, these concerns were highlighted in a joint statement by the Commission and Commissioner for Older People NI.[28] Subsequently, in September 2020, it was reported that the Health and Social Care Trusts in NI had discharged patients to care homes without those individuals being tested for COVID-19. Follow-up investigations found that almost 70 patients confirmed as having or suffering potential symptoms of the virus were discharged from hospitals to care homes in one health trust.[29] Overall, it has been found that

---

[23] www.ons.gov.uk/peoplepopulationandcommunity/crimeandjustice/articles/domesticabuseduring thecoronaviruscovid19pandemicenglandandwales/november2020.

[24] ibid.

[25] Department of Health, 'Press Release: Cross Government Response to Tackling Domestic and Sexual Abuse during COVID-19' (26 June 2020) www.health-ni.gov.uk/news/cross-government-response-tackling-domestic-and-sexual-abuse-during-covid-19-0.

[26] Home Office, 'COVID-19: Home Office Extraordinary Funding for Domestic Abuse Support Services (reopened)' https://assets.publishing.service.gov.uk/government/uploads/system/uploads/attachment_data/file/897709/COVID-19_Home_Office_Extraordinary_Funding_for_Domestic_Abuse_Support_Services_Bid_Prospectus_Reopened.pdf.

[27] NI Human Rights Commission, 'Women and Equalities Committee's Inquiry into the Unequal Impact of COVID-19: Disability and Access to Services' (NIHRC, 2020) https://nihrc.org/publication/detail/women-and-equalities-committees-inquiry-into-the-unequal-impact-of-covid19-disability-and-access-to-services.

[28] 'Joint Statement: Relentless Focus on Protecting Older People's Rights Needed as We Deal with the Next Phase of the Pandemic', www.copni.org/news/2020/november/joint-statement-relentless-focus-on-protecting-older-people-s-rights-needed-as-we-deal-with-the-next-phase-of-the-pandemic.

[29] T Fowles, 'NI Health Trust Discharged 70 Covid Patients into Care Homes' *Belfast Telegraph* (Belfast, 9 September 2020) www.belfasttelegraph.co.uk/news/health/vulnerable-dungannon-care-home-resident-petrified-after-staff-called-police-in-toast-row-39502213.html.

between 1 March and 15 April 2020, 318 patients were discharged to care homes, of whom only 52 were tested for COVID-19 prior to discharge.[30]

In response to COVID-19, the visiting rights of residents in care homes within NI were significantly curtailed. On 17 March 2020, initial guidance on COVID-19 restrictions for residential care homes was issued and this was followed with an updated version on 26 April 2020.[31] While acknowledging that there would be situations where individual care homes would have to amend their approach depending on the risk to their residents, in principle, it was decided that care homes should facilitate one face-to-face visit by one person per week, per resident. According to published guidance at the time, every effort should have been made to enable other forms of visiting to ensure residents and patients maintain important social connections, such as using technology. Additional consideration was to be given to residents at the end of life. Care homes were also encouraged to introduce the concept of care partners, to help support residents' physical, mental and emotional well-being. However, it has been reported that only a small number of care homes in NI implemented the care partners scheme.[32]

C. Right to Work and to Just and Favourable Conditions of Work

In March 2020, to stop the spread of COVID-19, schools and childcare facilities were closed, which, due to the lack of alternative childcare available, impacted on parents/guardians' ability to work. The potential loss of wages and limited paid parental leave available risked increasing household poverty. This applied particularly to parents of disabled children, as childcare for children with disabilities is extremely limited even in ordinary circumstances. Some schools remained open for the purpose of providing childcare and education for the children of key workers. However, there was a lack of childcare provision for pre-school ages. NI's situation can be contrasted to that of Wales, where free childcare was rolled out for children of key workers aged under five years old.[33] Childcare for key workers employed outside school hours was also difficult to source.

In October 2020, Carers UK reported that there were up to 310,000 unpaid carers in NI. Of the 826 carers surveyed in NI, 702 (85 per cent) reported they were providing more care. For 305 surveyed unpaid carers in NI (37 per cent), this was due to the needs of the person they care for having increased, whereas for 371 (45 per cent) it was because local services were reduced or closed.[34] In terms of the impact on unpaid carers, 479 (58 per cent) of those surveyed in NI reported feeling

[30] ibid.

[31] Department of Health, 'COVID-19: Guidance for Nursing and Residential Care Homes in NI' (DoH, 2020) www.health-ni.gov.uk/covid-19-guidance.

[32] 'COVID-19 Visiting Scheme in Place at "Small Number" of Care Homes' (BBC News, 23 November 2020) www.bbc.co.uk/news/uk-northern-ireland-55042413.

[33] Welsh Government, 'Coronavirus: Childcare for Under Five Year Olds Parents Guidance' (Welsh Government, 2020) https://gov.wales/childcare-coronavirus.

[34] Carers UK, 'Caring behind Closed Doors Six Months on: The Continued Impact of the Coronavirus (COVID-19) Pandemic on Unpaid Carers' (Carers UK, 2020) 30, www.carersuk.org/images/News_and_campaigns/Caring_Behind_Closed_Doors_Oct20.pdf.

more stressed and 437 (53 per cent) said it had an impact on their health and well-being.[35] This included 503 (61 per cent) of those surveyed in NI not being able to take any break from their caring role during the COVID-19 pandemic, 140 (17 per cent) unable to take as many breaks as they felt they needed and 223 (27 per cent) worried about being able to care safely, due to a lack of knowledge, information or equipment.[36] Additionally, 594 (72 per cent) of unpaid carers surveyed in NI were worried about how they would cope if further lockdowns or local restrictions were introduced, 602 (73 per cent) reported feeling exhausted and worn out as a result of caring during the COVID-19 pandemic and 363 (44 per cent) of carers felt lonely and cut off from people.[37] Financial strain was also a concern for a number of unpaid carers surveyed in NI, with 231 (28 per cent) struggling to make ends meet, 74 (9 per cent) experiencing debt as a result of caring, 74 (9 per cent) having reduced working hours to manage their caring responsibilities and 33 (4 per cent) having given up work to care since the COVID-19 pandemic.[38] The Carer's Allowance in NI has not changed to address increasing needs due to COVID-19,[39] unlike in Scotland, where an extra Carers Allowance Supplement was paid in response to the pandemic.[40]

D. Right to Adequate Standard of Living and to Social Security

In March 2020, the Minister for Communities, Carál Ní Chuilín MLA, and the Minister of Education, Peter Weir MLA, announced plans to provide direct payments to families in receipt of Free School Meals during term-time school closures due to COVID-19.[41] Some 97,000 children have benefited from this scheme. In June 2020, the Minister of Finance, Conor Murphy MLA, allocated funds for a summer food scheme, which extended free school meals to during the school holidays.[42] The Minister of Education had not committed to continue Free School Meals during school holidays as standard, stating that children going hungry during school holiday periods, 'while it may be exacerbated this year by COVID-19, … is something that causes concern during every holiday period' and that it requires 'a cross-departmental effort to address this issue including consideration of the continuation

---

[35] ibid.
[36] ibid.
[37] ibid.
[38] ibid.
[39] R Russell, 'Research and Information Service Briefing Paper: Background Information and Statistics on Carers in NI' (NI Assembly, 2017), 7, https://niopa.qub.ac.uk/bitstream/NIOPA/4518/1/2517.pdf.
[40] Scottish Government, 'Coronavirus Carer's Allowance Supplement', www.mygov.scot/carers-allowance-supplement/coronavirus-carers-allowance-supplement/.
[41] Department of Education, 'Press Release: Ministers Take Action in Relation to Free School Meals Payment' (26 March 2020) www.education-ni.gov.uk/news/ministers-take-action-relation-free-school-meals-payment-0.
[42] Department of Finance, 'Press Release: Murphy Allocates Funds for Health, Childcare & Free School Meals' (30 June 2020) www.finance-ni.gov.uk/news/murphy-allocates-funds-health-childcare-free-school-meals.

of the scheme'.[43] However, in November 2020, the NI Executive agreed to extend the free school meal scheme over the school holidays until Easter 2022.[44]

In late March 2020, the Department for Communities agreed with the NI Housing Executive and Housing Associations that any social housing tenant facing difficulties paying rent during COVID-19 would not be evicted.[45] In May 2020, the Private Tenancies (Coronavirus Modifications) Act 2020 came into force. The Act protects private tenants from eviction during the period of the health crisis by extending the notice to quit period from four weeks to 12. The Act was originally due to apply for only six months. However, in August 2020, the Minister for Communities stated that 'given the need to prepare for a possible second wave of the virus, and as the various additional economic supports such as the furlough scheme wind down in the autumn, I have decided it is necessary to extend the emergency period'.[46] On 29 September 2020, the Private Tenancies (Coronavirus Modifications) Regulations (NI) 2020 came into operation, which extended the application of the 2020 Act to 31 March 2021.

A sector-led, multi-agency group was set up with the assistance of funding from the Department for Communities to co-ordinate the response to homelessness and COVID-19, which helped ensure no one slept rough during the strictest period of lockdown.[47]

E. Right to Health

The Coronavirus Act 2020 enabled temporary modifications to the commenced aspects of the Mental Capacity Act (NI) 2016, primarily deprivation of liberty safeguards. The temporary provisions relaxed some of the statutory requirements of those safeguards during the COVID-19 pandemic, to ensure that persons could be deprived of liberty during the pandemic crisis when staff availability may have been significantly reduced.[48] The details are set out in the Mental Capacity Act (NI) 2016 Emergency Code of Practice Coronavirus Act 2020, which confirms that 'the provisions in the Coronavirus Act are permissive and do not remove the normal

---

[43] NI Assembly Hansard, 'Response to Written Questions: Free School Meals – Peter Weir MLA – AQW 7681/17–22' (8 October 2020) http://aims.niassembly.gov.uk/questions/writtensearchresults.aspx?&qf=0&qfv=1&ref=AQW%2021068/17-22.

[44] R Meredith, 'Free School Meals: Meals to Be Funded during Holidays until 2022' (BBC News, 20 November 2020) www.bbc.co.uk/news/uk-northern-ireland-55009536.

[45] Department for Communities, 'Press Release: Housing Support Crucial in This Crisis – Hargey' (27 March 2020) www.communities-ni.gov.uk/news/housing-support-crucial-crisis-hargey.

[46] Department for Communities, 'Press Release: Minister Ní Chuilín Announces Extension of Legislation to Protect Renters' (19 August 2020) www.communities-ni.gov.uk/news/minister-ni-chuilin-announces-extension-legislation-protect-renters.

[47] N McCrudden, 'No Going Back: Tackling NI's Homelessness under COVID-19' (Campbell Tickell, 30 July 2020) www.campbelltickell.com/2020/07/30/no-going-back-tackling-northern-irelands-homelessness-under-covid-19/.

[48] Department of Health, 'Press Release: Coronavirus and Temporary Regulations' (1 April 2020) www.health-ni.gov.uk/publications/coronavirus-act-2020-and-temporary-regulations.

procedures. Rather they provide an alternative when the normal procedures cannot be followed'.[49] The Health and Social Care Trusts are required to monitor the use of the modified provisions and must provide a report to the Department of Health within three months of the emergency ending.[50]

Terminations have been legal in NI since 31 March 2020.[51] To date, the Department of Health has not commissioned the required healthcare services to implement these regulations. The Department of Health also failed to provide guidance to cover these services during the pandemic. Unfortunately, this lack of action made it incredibly difficult for women, girls and transgender men that required or who sought access to terminations in NI, particularly during the initial stages of the first lockdown when significant travel restrictions were in place and many airlines were not operating flights. Consequently, in April 2020, the Health and Social Care Trusts in NI, guided by the new regulations, gradually started providing certain termination services within their existing resources and without formal support from the Department of Health. At the time, the NIHRC stated that this approach was neither 'appropriate nor sustainable'.[52] In October 2020, due to the continued strain on the Trusts' existing resources and a lack of commissioning by the Department of Health, these services started to experience significant roll-back. The Northern Health and Social Care Trust ceased all termination services, which the remaining four trust areas did not have the resources to fill, creating a disparity in service provision across NI. Additionally, while some trusts initially offered termination services beyond 10 weeks, this service as a whole has now ceased across NI.

F. Right to Education

The disruption to education caused by COVID-19 prompted a number of calls for academic selection to be suspended in 2020. In May 2020, this led to the NI Commissioner for Children and Young People writing to the Board of Governors and principals of selective post-primary schools urging them to not use academic selection for admitting pupils to the 2021 school year.[53] In June 2020, the Catholic Principals' Association called for transfer tests to be scrapped until 2021.[54] Transfer tests were subsequently postponed to January and February 2021.

---

[49] Department of Health, 'Mental Capacity Act (NI) 2016 Emergency Code of Practice Coronavirus Act 2020' (DoH, 2020) 1, www.health-ni.gov.uk/mca.

[50] ibid para 28.

[51] Abortion (NI) Regulations 2020; Abortion (NI) (No 2) Regulations 2020, www.legislation.gov.uk/uksi/2020/503/made.

[52] NIHRC Annual Statement 2020 (n 15) 22.

[53] G Connolly, 'Schools Urged to Avoid Transfer Tests after Lockdown' (Q Radio, 27 May 2020) www.goqradio.com/belfast/news/q-radio-local-news/listen-schools-urged-to-avoid-transfer-tests-after-lockdown/.

[54] J Toner, 'Coronavirus: Catholic Heads Call for Suspension of Selection Tests in NI' *Belfast Telegraph* (Belfast, 15 June 2020) www.belfasttelegraph.co.uk/news/health/coronavirus/coronavirus-catholic-heads-call-for-suspension-of-selection-tests-in-northern-ireland-39285056.html.

The Temporary Modification of Education Duties Notice (NI) 2020[55] and its subsequent iterations temporarily modified legal duties covering special educational needs, including assessment and the provision of statements. This modification only applied where an inability to comply with a legal duty was attributable to the temporary closure of schools and the reallocation of Education Authority NI and health and social care resources to meet other essential services. These changes applied for 28 days at a time. All schools in NI reopened the week commencing 31 August 2020.[56] Since then, some schools took individual decisions, guided by the Public Health Agency, to partially or fully close for a set period when there were COVID-19 positive cases within the school community. In October 2020, the NI Executive decided on the basis of medical advice to close all schools in NI for a further period of two weeks.

II. THE WITHDRAWAL AGREEMENT AND THE IRELAND/NI PROTOCOL

In January 2020, the UK signed the UK–EU Withdrawal Agreement and Ireland/NI Protocol.[57] On 31 January 2020, the UK left the EU in accordance with the Withdrawal Agreement.[58] Much of the Withdrawal Agreement is dedicated to setting out the terms of the transition period, and Part Two sets out the commitments in relation to citizens' rights after the UK leaves the EU. Under Article 2 of the Protocol, the UK commits to

> ensur[ing] that no diminution of rights, safeguards or equality of opportunity, as set out in that part of the 1998 Agreement entitled Rights, Safeguards and Equality of Opportunity[,] results from its withdrawal from the Union, including in the area of protection against discrimination, as enshrined in the provisions of Union law listed in Annex 1 to this Protocol.[59]

Annex 1 contains six equality directives, related to access and supply of goods and services, employment, self-employment, racial or ethnic origin and social security, which will continue to set the standards in NI as EU law evolves.[60] This list does

---

[55] www.education-ni.gov.uk/publications/notice-coronavirus-act-2020-temporary-modification-education-duties-no10-notice-northern-ireland.

[56] ibid.

[57] Agreement on the Withdrawal of the UK of Great Britain and NI from the EU and the European Atomic Energy Community 2020, www.legislation.gov.uk/eut/withdrawal-agreement/contents/adopted.

[58] ibid.

[59] Protocol on Ireland/NI to the Agreement on the Withdrawal of the UK of Great Britain and NI from the EU and the European Atomic Energy Community 2020, https://assets.publishing.service.gov.uk/government/uploads/system/uploads/attachment_data/file/840230/Revised_Protocol_to_the_Withdrawal_Agreement.pdf.

[60] Directive 2004/114/EC 2004, 'EU Council Directive on the Principle of Equal Treatment between Men and Women in Access to and Supply of Goods and Services', 23 December 2004; Directive 2006/54/EC, 'EU Council Directive on the Principle of Equal Opportunities and Equal Treatment of Men and Women in Matters of Employment and Occupation', 5 July 2006; Directive 2000/43/EC, 'EU Council Directive on the Principle of Equal Treatment between Persons Irrespective of Racial and Ethnic Origin' 29 June 2000; Directive 2000/78/EC, 'EU Council Directive of a General Framework for Equal Treatment in Employment and Occupation', 27 November 2000; Directive 2010/41/EU, 'EU Parliament and EU Council Directive on the Principle of Equal Treatment between Men and Women Engaged in Self-employment', 7 July 2010; Directive 79/7/EEC, 'Directive of the Council of European Communities on the Principle of Equal Treatment for Men and Women in Social Security', 19 December 1978.

not include directives concerning parental leave, pregnant workers or the rights of victims, but the UK government has confirmed that

> provided that the rights in question are relevant to the aforementioned chapter of the Agreement, they are in scope of the UK Government's commitment that there will be no diminution of rights as a result of the UK leaving the EU.[61]

The additional scope of the Ireland/NI Protocol remains to be seen and it is unclear to what extent the EU Charter of Fundamental Rights can be implied into the commitments in the Protocol. In September 2020, the NIHRC and the Equality Commission NI provided oral evidence to the NI Assembly Committee for the Executive Office on Article 2(1) of the Ireland/NI Protocol, reiterating the requirement to ensure that there is no diminution of rights due to Brexit and to set out the role of the Commissions as the appointed dedicated mechanism.[62]

In February 2020, the UK government set out its approach to negotiations of the future relationship to the EU:

> [I]t is a vision of a relationship based on friendly cooperation between sovereign equals, with both parties respecting one another's legal autonomy and right to manage their own resources as they see fit. Whatever happens, the [UK] Government will not negotiate any arrangement in which the UK does not have control of its own laws and political life. That means that we will not agree to any obligations for our laws to be aligned with the EU's, or for the EU's institutions, including the Court of Justice, to have any jurisdiction in the UK.[63]

In September 2020, the UK government's chief negotiator, David Frost, made it clear that 'a number of challenging areas remain and the divergences on some are still significant', but that the UK is 'committed to working hard to reach agreement by the middle of October'.[64] In response, the EU's chief negotiator, Michel Barnier, noted that 'the EU has shown flexibility to work around the UK's red lines and find solutions ... in particular with regard to the role of the European Court of Justice, the future legislative autonomy of the UK, and fisheries'.[65] However, the EU was 'missing important guarantees on non-regression from social, environmental, labour and climate standards' and on 'essential safeguards for judicial cooperation and law

---

[61] NI Office, 'UK Government Commitment to "No Diminution of Rights, Safeguards and Equality of Opportunity" in NI: What Does It Mean and How Will It be Implemented?' (NIO, 2020) https://assets. publishing.service.gov.uk/government/uploads/system/uploads/attachment_data/file/907682/Explainer__ UK_Government_commitment_to_no_diminution_of_rights__safeguards_and_equality_of_opportu-nity_in_Northern_Ireland.pdf.

[62] NI Assembly Committee for the Executive Office, 'Oral Evidence: Article 2(1) of the Protocol on Ireland/NI – Equality Commission for NI and NI Human Rights Commission' (16 September 2020) www.equalityni.org/Footer-Links/News/Delivering-Equality/Joint-statement-on-Brexit-evidence-to-NI-Assembly.

[63] HM Government, 'The Future Relationship with the EU: The UK's Approach to Negotiations' (HM Government, 2020) para 5, https://assets.publishing.service.gov.uk/government/uploads/system/uploads/ attachment_data/file/868874/The_Future_Relationship_with_the_EU.pdf.

[64] D Frost, 'Statement after Round 8 of the Negotiations' (10 September 2020) https://no10media. blog.gov.uk/2020/09/10/lord-frost-statement-after-round-8-of-the-negotiations/.

[65] EU Commission, 'Press Statement by Michel Barnier following Round 8 of the Negotiations for a New Partnership between the EU and the UK' (10 September 2020) https://ec.europa.eu/commission/ presscorner/detail/en/STATEMENT_20_1612.

enforcement'.[66] In October 2020, the Vice President of the European Commission, Maros Sefcovic, stated 'deal or no deal that the Withdrawal Agreement must be respected' and that the UK and European Commission had 'managed to strike a constructive approach'.[67]

In October 2020, the UK government introduced draft regulations to extend the power to depart from retained EU case law to additional courts, including the Court of Appeal NI. The draft regulations preserve the normal operation of precedent between decisions of UK courts by making it clear that the identified courts (including the Court of Appeal NI) will be bound by the decision of another court which would normally bind them on the question of whether or not to depart from retained EU case law. As at July 2021, the matter remained under review.[68]

The Immigration and Social Security Co-ordination (EU Withdrawal) Bill 2019–21, which became an Act in July 2021, aims to end European Economic Area nationals' right to free movement. It enhances Common Travel Area rights by allowing free movement of British citizens into Ireland and Irish citizens into the UK, regardless of whether the journey originated outside of the Common Travel Area. It does not reciprocate legislation in Ireland, which rules out deportation of UK citizens.[69]

In 2020, the Joint Committee of the NIHRC and the Irish Human Rights and Equality Commission published a legal analysis and proposals for reform to uphold the birth right provision in the Belfast (Good Friday) Agreement within UK immigration law[70] and research on continuing EU citizenship rights in NI after the UK leaves the EU.[71] The New Decade, New Approach agreement, which committed the UK government to reviewing its rules on migration, noting that 'taking into account the letter and spirit of the Belfast Agreement and recognising that the policy should not create incentives for renunciation of British citizenship by those citizens who may wish to retain it',[72] endorsed the birth right provision and bound the UK government to change the rules.[73]

By May 2020, the Home Office had released a Statement of Changes in Immigration Rules, which provides for a 'relevant person of NI' to access EU free movement law protections.[74] On 24 August 2020, these changes came into force and remained in

---

[66] ibid.
[67] European Commission, 'Press Statement: Speech by Vice-President Sefcovic on Behalf of President von der Leyen at the European Parliament Plenary on the Conclusions of the European Council Meeting of 15 and 16 October 2020' (21 October 2020) https://ec.europa.eu/commission/presscorner/detail/en/SPEECH_20_1961.
[68] See NIHRC Annual Report 2020, 62.
[69] Aliens (Exemption) Order 1999, www.irishstatutebook.ie/eli/1999/si/97/made/en/print.
[70] A Harvey, 'A Legal Analysis of Incorporating into UK Law the Birthright Commitment under the Belfast (Good Friday) Agreement 1998' (NIHRC and IHREC, 2020) www.ihrec.ie/documents/legal-analysis-of-incorporating-into-uk-law-the-birthright-commitment-under-the-belfast-good-friday-agreement-1998/.
[71] S de Mars, C Murray, A O'Donoghue and B Warwick, 'Continuing EU Citizenship "Rights, Opportunities and Benefits" in NI after Brexit' (NIHRC and IHREC, 2020) https://nihrc.org/uploads/publications/Rights_Opportunities.pdf.
[72] NI Office, 'New Decade, New Approach' (n 1) 48.
[73] Statement of Changes in Immigration Rules (14 May 2020) CP 232.
[74] Home Office, 'Statement of Changes in Immigration Rules CP232 (HO, 2020) 10.

place until the EU Settlement Scheme closed to new applications in June 2021.[75] A relevant person of NI is now defined as someone who is a British citizen, an Irish citizen, or both British and Irish and was born in NI to a parent who was British, Irish or both, or otherwise entitled to reside in NI without any restriction on their period of residence. The right of NI-born Irish citizens to avail themselves of EU free movement rights in relation to family members from non-EU states had been legally challenged by Jake Parker De Souza.[76] The challenge had reached the Court of Appeal in NI, but was withdrawn following changes to the EU Settlement Scheme to include family members of people of NI.

The House of Commons Committee on the Future Relationship with the EU published a report on implementing the Withdrawal Agreement and citizens' rights in October 2020. The cross-party report urges the UK and EU to ensure that citizens' rights protections in the Withdrawal Agreement are fully implemented for UK nationals living across the EU and EU citizens in the UK, including their right to live and work in the country where they reside.[77]

The Citizens' Rights (Frontier Workers) EU Exit Regulations were published in October 2020, creating a permit scheme for frontier workers. The regulations are likely to apply to a number of EU citizens travelling between Ireland and NI for work. Anyone applying must do so before 1 July 2021. The lack of consultation and an impact assessment in advance of producing the regulations was raised by a number of civil society organisations, including the Committee for the Administration of Justice, the Centre for Cross Border Studies and the Irish Congress of Trade Unions.

III. DEALING WITH THE PAST

A. Legacy Inquests and Conflict-Related Deaths

Funding for legacy inquests had been delayed for a number of years. In 2019, following a legal challenge,[78] the Department of Justice NI established a new Legacy Inquest Unit within the Coroner's Service under the remit of the Lord Chief Justice. The Legacy Inquest Unit is to complete its work within five years, starting in 2019/2020. There is a legacy caseload of 52 cases relating to 93 deaths. These are made up of one inquest in which findings have been given and a final legal ruling is awaited, five inquests (the Ballymurphy series) in which findings are awaited, two in which hearings have commenced and are adjourned, and 44 which are pending.[79] The first full

---

[75] NI Human Rights Commission, 'EU Settlement Scheme Extended to the People of NI: What Does It Mean for Me?' (NIHRC, 2020) https://nihrc.org/publication/detail/eu-settlement-scheme-extended-to-the-people-of-ni-what-does-it-mean-for-me.

[76] *Secretary of State for the Home Department v Jake Parker De Souza* [2019] UKUT 355.

[77] House of Commons Committee on the Future Relationship with the EU, 'Implementing the Withdrawal Agreement: Citizens' Rights' (HC, 2020) https://publications.parliament.uk/pa/cm5801/cmselect/cmexeu/1095/109502.htm.

[78] *In the Matter of an Application by Brigid Hughes for Judicial Review [2018] NIQB 30*, at para 12.

[79] 'CoE Committee of Ministers Communication from the Authorities in the *McKerr Group of Cases v UK* (Application No 28883/95)' (28 October 2020) DH-DD(2020)931, 4, https://rm.coe.int/09000016809e90b0.

hearings were to start in April 2020. However, due to COVID-19, all non-urgent court business, including legacy inquests, were adjourned on 20 March 2020 and a new schedule is subject to ongoing review.[80] The UK government has stated that the delay due to COVID-19 'will have an impact on the timeline for the Five Year Plan, however, because the full impact of the pandemic on legacy inquests is not yet known, the overall impact on the timeline cannot yet be assessed'.[81]

However, on 18 March 2020, the Secretary of State for NI, Brandon Lewis MP, issued a written ministerial statement outlining the UK government's new approach to addressing the legacy of the past in NI. This statement indicates a significant roll-back on the commitments made in New Decade, New Approach and the Stormont House Agreement. In the Secretary of State for NI's view, 'it is clear that, while the principles underpinning the draft Bill as consulted on in 2018 remain, significant changes will be needed to obtain a broad consensus for the implementation of any legislation'.[82] His statement continued:

> [T]he [UK] Government will ensure that the investigations, which are necessary are effective and thorough, but quick, so we are able to move beyond the cycle of investigations that has, to date, undermined attempts to come to terms with the past. Only cases in which there is a realistic prospect of a prosecution as a result of new compelling evidence would proceed to a full police investigation and if necessary, prosecution. Cases which do not reach this threshold, or subsequently are not referred for prosecution, would be closed and no further investigations or prosecutions would be possible – though family reports would still be provided to the victims' loved ones. Such an approach would give all participants the confidence and certainty to fully engage with the information recovery process.[83]

In April 2020, the NIHRC wrote to the Secretary of State for NI expressing concerns that this new approach by the UK government is not human rights compliant, particularly regarding Article 2 ECHR.[84] In October 2020, the NI Affairs Committee published an interim report to its inquiry, finding that the UK government's proposals were a

> unilateral and unhelpful departure from the Stormont House Agreement rather than a positive and progressive evolution' and that the proposed 'permanent closure of a case in which a serious crime has been committed raises profound legal, ethical and human rights issues.[85]

Additionally, the NI Affairs Committee stated that it was 'dismayed' by the lack of engagement and consultation by the UK government with stakeholders, NI parties

---

[80] Judiciary NI, 'Press Release: Statement from the Presiding Coroner Mrs Justice Keegan – Legacy Inquests' (4 May 2020) www.judiciaryni.uk/legacy-inquests-general.

[81] 'CoE Committee of Ministers Communication' (n 79) 4.

[82] NI Office, 'Press Release: UK Government Sets Out Way Forward on the Legacy of the Past in NI' (18 March 2020) www.gov.uk/government/news/addressing-northern-ireland-legacy-issues.

[83] ibid.

[84] Letter from NI Human Rights Commission to Secretary of State for NI, Brandon Lewis MP, 1 April 2020, 68, https://nihrc.org/publication/detail/annual-statement-2020.

[85] House of Commons NI Affairs Committee, 'Addressing the Legacy of NI's Past: The Government's New Proposals (Interim Report)' (NIAC, 2020) paras 15 and 38, https://committees.parliament.uk/publications/3186/documents/29458/default/.

and the Government of Ireland both before and after publication of the ministerial statement.[86] The NI Affairs Committee stated that the UK government 'must, as soon as possible, introduce legislation that is consistent with the six principles of the Stormont House Agreement'.[87] At the time of writing, these matters remain outstanding.

B. The Stormont House Agreement

On 23 December 2014, the Stormont House Agreement was reached.[88] The Agreement sets out a structure for the effective investigation of conflict-related deaths, including the Oral History Archive;[89] Victims and Survivors' Services (including a Mental Trauma Service, pension for severely physically injured victims and advocate-counsellor assistance);[90] the Historical Inquiries Unit;[91] the Independent Commission on Information Retrieval;[92] and the Implementation and Reconciliation Group.[93] The UK government has committed within the financial annex of the Stormont House Agreement to provide up to £150 million over five years to help fund the bodies to deal with the past.[94]

In 2020, following the re-establishment of the NI Assembly, the New Decade, New Approach document stated that:

[I]n moving to a better, more prosperous and shared future the parties recognise the need to address the legacy of the past. To that end, the parties are committed to working together and to doing everything possible to heal wounds and eliminate the issues that divide us.[95]

The UK government committed to:

[W]ithin 100 days, publish and introduce legislation in the UK Parliament to implement the Stormont House Agreement, to address NI legacy issues. The [UK] Government will now start an intensive process with the NI parties, and the Irish Government as appropriate, to maintain a broad-based consensus on these issues, recognising that any such UK Parliament legislation should have the consent of the NI Assembly.[96]

At the time of writing, there have been limited concrete government actions to address the outstanding issues.

---

[86] ibid 24.
[87] ibid 15.
[88] Stormont House Agreement, 23 December 2014, www.gov.uk/government/publications/the-stormont-house-agreement.
[89] ibid para 22.
[90] ibid paras 26–29.
[91] ibid para 30.
[92] ibid para 41.
[93] ibid para 51.
[94] NI Office, 'Stormont House Agreement: Financial Annex' (NIO, 2014) 1. The Stormont House Agreement includes a further broad financial commitment to all sections covered within the Agreement. It is stated within the Financial Annex that: 'the total value of the Government's package is additional spending power of almost £2 billion'.
[95] NI Office, 'New Decade, New Approach' (n 1) 14.
[96] ibid 48.

C. Statute of Limitations

In April 2017, the House of Commons Defence Committee issued a report on an investigation into fatalities in NI involving British military personnel. Since then, there have been numerous calls for the introduction of a statute of limitations to protect from prosecution members of the Armed Forces who served in NI.[97] The most recent of these came from Prime Minister Boris Johnson.[98] The Queen's Speech in December 2019 also referenced bringing 'forward proposals to tackle vexatious claims that undermine our Armed Forces'.[99] The matter remains under review.

D. The Case of Pat Finucane

In February 2020, the UK government stated that it would provide a formal response to the UK Supreme Court's decision in the Pat Finucane case,[100] 'within a matter of weeks'.[101] The formal response was not provided. In October 2020, a representative of the Secretary of State for NI committed to the UK government providing a decision on whether it would undertake an inquiry into Pat Finucane's death by the end of November 2020.[102] Subsequently, on 30 November 2020, the Secretary of State for NI confirmed that the UK government does not intend to hold a public inquiry into Pat Finucane's death at this point in time, stating that 'I am not taking the possibility of a public inquiry off the table at this stage, but it is important we allow ongoing Police Service NI and Police Ombudsman NI processes to move forward'.[103] The Police Service NI later issued a statement confirming there are currently no new lines of inquiry and it will decide if a further review is necessary. If so, it is highly likely that any review will need to be conducted independently of the Police Service NI due to the 'accepted position of State involvement in this matter'.[104] Highlighting the

---

[97] HC Deb 9 July 2018, vol 644, col 686; HC Deb 21 May 2019, vol 663, col 85WS.

[98] Conservative Party, 'Press Release: Conservatives in General Election Manifesto Pledge to End "Unfair Trials" for NI Veterans' (13 November 2019) www.niconservatives.com/news/conservatives-pledge-protect-our-veterans.

[99] Gov.UK, 'Press Release: Queen's Speech December 2019' (19 December 2019) www.gov.uk/government/publications/queens-speech-december-2019-background-briefing-notes.

[100] *In the Matter of an Application by Geraldine Finucane for Judicial Review (NI)* [2019] UKSC 7.

[101] C McCurry, 'Government to Respond to Supreme Court Ruling over Pat Finucane Death "in Weeks"' *Belfast Telegraph* (Belfast, 21 February 2020) www.belfasttelegraph.co.uk/news/northern-ireland/government-to-respond-to-supreme-court-ruling-over-pat-finucane-death-in-weeks-38978993.html.

[102] A Erwin, 'Pat Finucane Public Inquiry Decision by End of November, Pledges Brandon Lewis' *Belfast Telegraph* (Belfast, 12 October 2020) www.belfasttelegraph.co.uk/news/northern-ireland/pat-finucane-public-inquiry-decision-by-end-of-november-pledges-brandon-lewis-39613129.html.

[103] 'Pat Finucane: No Public Inquiry into Belfast Lawyer's Murder' (BBC News, 30 November 2020) www.bbc.com/news/uk-northern-ireland-55138030.

[104] Police Service NI, 'Press Release: Statement from Chief Constable Simon Byrne following the Announcement from the Secretary of State on the Murder of Pat Finucane' (30 November 2020) www.psni.police.uk/news/Latest-News/301120-statement-from-chief-constable-simon-byrne-following-the-announcement-from-the-secretary-of-state-on-the-murder-of-pat-finucane/.

UK Supreme Court judgment, the Finucane family has stated that it will continue to campaign for a full public inquiry.[105]

E. Bloody Sunday

In September 2020, the Public Prosecution Service NI confirmed that, following an internal review, it was upholding its decision to not prosecute 15 soldiers that were allegedly connected with the deaths of 10 individuals killed and 10 individuals injured during Bloody Sunday, on the grounds that the evidential test for prosecution had not been met.[106] The families are considering further legal action following the outcome of that review.[107]

IV. RIGHT TO LIFE

In September 2020, the Council of Europe (CoE) Committee of Ministers 'strongly urged' the UK government to 'act, within the shortest possible time frame, on their obligation to put an end to the type of violation identified by the [ECtHR] in the present cases and to secure compliance with the requirements of Article 2 of the [ECHR]'.[108] The Committee of Ministers requested that the UK provided a detailed time frame by 22 October 2020, or it would consider issuing an interim resolution against the UK.[109]

Security statistics released by the Police Service NI for the period between 1 October 2019 to 30 September 2020 shows that there were two security-related deaths during this reporting period, compared to three during the previous 12 months. There were also 15 casualties of paramilitary style shootings, compared to 17 during the previous 12 months. All 15 casualties were aged 18 years or older. The number of paramilitary style shootings increased in Belfast (from five to eight), but substantially decreased in Derry City and Strabane (from 11 to two), compared to the previous 12 months. Overall, there were 44 casualties of paramilitary style assaults, compared to 66 in the previous 12 months. Of the 44 casualties, one was under 18 years old. The greatest number of paramilitary style assaults occurred in Belfast and Mid and East Antrim (10 in each district). Although Belfast experienced 10 such assaults, this was approximately half the number that occurred in the district during the previous 12 months (21 assaults). There were 18 bombing incidents

---

[105] 'Pat Finucane: No Public Inquiry into Belfast Lawyer's Murder' (BBC News, 30 November 2020) www.bbc.com/news/uk-northern-ireland-55138030.

[106] Public Prosecution Service NI, 'Press Release: PPS Upholds Decision Not to Prosecute 15 Soldiers in Connection with Bloody Sunday' (29 September 2020) www.ppsni.gov.uk/news-centre/pps-upholds-decision-not-prosecute-15-soldiers-connection-bloody-sunday.

[107] Statement from Madden & Finucane Solicitors, https://madden-finucane.com/2020/09/29/bloody-sunday-30-january-1972/.

[108] 'CoE Committee of Ministers Decision: *McKerr Group v UK* (Application No 28883/95)' (3 September 2020) CM/Notes/1377bis/H46-44, para 6, https://rm.coe.int/0900001680a1b20e.

[109] ibid.

and 42 shooting incidents, compared to 15 and 39, respectively, in the previous year. The report also shows that there were 79 persons arrested under section 41 of the Terrorism Act 2000, compared to 178 during the previous 12 months. The number of persons subsequently charged decreased from 22 to 14 over the same period.[110]

V. FREEDOM FROM TORTURE, INHUMAN AND DEGRADING TREATMENT

A. Allegations of Torture and Cruel, Inhuman or Degrading Treatment or Punishment Overseas

On 18 March 2020, the Overseas Operations (Service Personnel and Veterans) Bill 2019–21 was introduced to the UK Parliament. The Bill aims to create protections for members of the armed forces and the UK government relating to the legal consequences of events that occur in the course of military operations overseas, by derogation from the ECHR. It seeks to impose a six-year statutory limitation on taking cases against UK service personnel and veterans involved in overseas operations. The Bill excludes alleged crimes by UK military personnel within NI, but raises concerns as to the UK government's commitment to adhering to human rights standards in the broader context, including conflict-related investigations concerning NI. By the start of November 2020, the Bill was progressing through Parliament at pace, reaching the Second Reading stage of the House of Lords. In the Secretary of State for NI's ministerial statement on the UK government's revised approach to proposals for dealing with the legacy of the past in NI, this Bill was referred to as a way 'to provide greater certainty for service personnel and veterans who serve in armed conflicts overseas'.[111] However, at the time of writing, the Northern Ireland Office has published an EQIA on the UK government's proposals for legislation to address the legacy of the Troubles.

B. Historical Abuse of Children and Adults

On 31 March 2020, the Historical Institutional Abuse Redress Board was established, in line with the Historical Institutional Abuse (NI) Act 2019. On 3 April 2020, the application process for eligible candidates opened and will run for five years. The NI Criminal Injuries Compensation Scheme 2009 was amended in June 2020 so that anyone previously denied compensation under the same household rule, or put off from coming forward because of it, will be able to make a fresh application. The time limit for applications to be received is two years from 9 June 2020. However,

---

[110] Police Recorded Security Situation Statistics 1 October 2019 to 30 September 2020, www.psni.police.uk/globalassets/inside-the-psni/our-statistics/security-situation-statistics/2020/september/security-situation-statistics-to-september-2020.pdf.

[111] NI Office, 'Press Release: UK Government Sets Out Way Forward on the Legacy of the Past in NI' (18 March 2020) www.gov.uk/government/news/addressing-northern-ireland-legacy-issues.

the time limit may be waived if the Department of Justice considers there is a good reason for the delay and it is in the interests of justice to do so.[112]

In October 2020, Fiona Ryan was appointed as Commissioner for Victims and Survivors of Historical Institutional Childhood Abuse.

C. Domestic and Sexual Violence and Abuse

The Domestic Abuse and Family Proceedings Bill was introduced to the NI Assembly on 31 March 2020. The Bill provided for a new domestic abuse offence capturing patterns of psychological abuse, violence and/or coercion of a partner, ex-partner or family member. It also includes a statutory aggravation of domestic abuse, which may attract enhanced sentencing for other offences. In contrast to the Domestic Abuse Bill, currently before the UK Parliament, this Bill does not include provision for Domestic Violence Protection Notices and Domestic Violence Protection Orders or a Domestic Abuse Commissioner. The Department of Justice intends the Bill to be enacted in early 2021.

D. Spit and Bite Guards

In March 2020, spit and bite guards were introduced by the Police Service NI to protect officers working in specialist functions, such as the COVID-19 Response Teams, custody suites, cell vans and armed response, during the COVID-19 pandemic.[113] There have been a number of incidents reported where police officers were spat at by individuals claiming to have COVID-19.[114] Despite a commitment from the Police Service NI that the use of spit and bite guards would cease by December 2020,[115] a letter from the Police Service NI to the NIHRC has stated that, from 18 December 2020, spit and bite guards will be issued to a wider range of police officers, including all local policing teams, all neighbourhood policing teams, tactical support groups, the Roads Policing Unit, district support teams and C4 Special Operations.[116] The Chief Constable of the Police Service NI, Simon Byrne, has stated that he 'believes that an enhanced roll out to all operational officers fulfils his obligations under health and safety legislation which require ... [the provision of] safe systems of work for all employees'.[117]

---

[112] Department of Justice, 'Press Release: Justice Minister announces changes to the Criminal Injuries Compensation Scheme' (9 June 2020) www.justice-ni.gov.uk/news/justice-minister-announces-changes-criminal-injuries-compensation-scheme.

[113] Report on the Thematic Review of the Policing Response to COVID-19, 67.

[114] A Quinn, 'Man on NI Bus Says He Has COVID-19, Spits at Police Service NI Officers and Is Arrested for Drugs Offences' (*NewsLetter*, 29 May 2020); 'Newtownabbey Man Spat Blood in Policeman's Face before Claiming He Had COVID-19, Court Told' *Belfast Telegraph* (Belfast, 17 June 2020).

[115] Report on the Thematic Review of the Policing Response to COVID-19 (n 113) 12.

[116] Letter from Police Service NI to NI Human Rights Commission, 23 November 2020. See NIHRC Annual Report 2020 (n 68) 37.

[117] ibid 38.

VI. FREEDOM FROM SLAVERY

In May 2020, the NI Local Government Association published guidance on tackling modern slavery for local councils in NI.[118] The Anti-Slavery Commissioner, Dame Sara Thornton, published her annual report in September 2020. Unlike the rest of the UK, Trafficking and Exploitation Risk Orders are not included within legislation in NI. The Anti-Slavery Commissioner had urged the Minister of Justice, Naomi Long MLA, to 'reconsider their value as evidence of effective use in England and Wales and Scotland emerges'.[119] Subsequently, the Department of Justice launched a public consultation on a draft Modern Slavery Strategy for NI 2021/2022. The strategy aims to equip NI to eradicate modern slavery through a collaborative partnership between law enforcement agencies, frontline professionals and the general public to raise awareness of human trafficking and slavery-like offences, support victims and bring offenders to justice.[120]

VII. RIGHT TO LIBERTY AND SECURITY OF PERSON

A. Remand of Children

In 2019/2020, the total number of admissions to the Juvenile Justice Centre was 298, which was 11.6 per cent lower than the 337 admissions in 2018/2019.[121] Of these, 197 (66.1 per cent) were related to the Police and Criminal Evidence Act 1984, 95 (31.9 per cent) concerned remand and six (two per cent) were sentencing admissions.[122] The proportion of admissions attributed to remand decreased from 35.9 per cent in 2015/2016 to 31.9 per cent in 2019/2020.[123]

In 2019/2020, there were 416 movements within the Juvenile Justice Centre, which included 190 (45.7 per cent) to remand.[124] This included new admissions and internal change of status. The number of remand movements decreased by 5.9 per cent from 2018/2019.[125] In 2019/2020, the total average daily population in the Juvenile Justice Centre was 17 children.[126] Of these, 11 (66.7 per cent) were on remand.[127] In 2019/2020, there was a total number of 6177 custody days provided

---

[118] NI Local Government Association, 'Tackling Modern Slavery: Guidance for Councils' (NILGA, 2020) www.nilga.org/news/2020/may/tackling-modern-slavery.

[119] Independent Anti-Slavery Commissioner, 'Independent Anti-Slavery Commissioner Annual Report 2019–2020' (IASC, 2020) para 2.3.3, www.antislaverycommissioner.co.uk/media/1461/ccs207_ccs0520602790-001_iasc_annual-report-2019–2020_e-laying.pdf.

[120] Draft Modern Slavery Strategy 2021/22, https://consultations.nidirect.gov.uk/doj/draft-modern-slavery-strategy-2021-22/.

[121] Analytical Services Group, 'NI Youth Justice Agency Annual Workload Statistics 2019/20' (DoJ, 2020) 12, www.justice-ni.gov.uk/news/northern-ireland-youth-justice-agency-annual-workload-statistics-201920-published-today.

[122] ibid.

[123] ibid.

[124] ibid 18.

[125] ibid.

[126] ibid.

[127] ibid.

by the Juvenile Justice Centre.[128] Of these 4122 custody days (66.7 per cent) were attributed to children on remand, a decrease of 16.6 per cent from 2015/2016.[129]

In November 2020, the Minister of Justice, Naomi Long MLA, confirmed that the Justice (Miscellaneous Provisions) Bill, which is due to be introduced to the NI Assembly in early 2021, would include proposals that

> aim to strengthen the right to bail for children, and introduce specific conditions which must be met before a child can be remanded in custody, with a view to ensuring that custody is used as a last resort, in line with our international obligations.[130]

The Bill is yet to be enacted.

B. Child Sexual Exploitation

In June 2020, the Criminal Justice Inspection NI published its inspection report on child sexual exploitation, which considers the frontline response and investigation of child sexual exploitation.[131] This report noted concern 'that little was known about the perpetrators of child sexual exploitation and the criminal justice system was urged to develop its response in this respect'.[132] It also found that:

> [A] review of a sample of files held by the Public Prosecution Service NI showed that where the Police Service NI had passed files to prosecutors, evidence of case building and identification of factors pertinent to child sexual exploitation was at times good. However, the Public Prosecution Service NI needed to better support prosecutors to reflect how factors related to exploitation and grooming had been weighted in decisions. Myths and stereotypes including about children having 'demonstrated affection' required to be addressed in the planning of cases. Public Prosecution Service NI staff instructions specific to child sexual abuse and exploitation were needed.[133]

It also found that 'where cases did progress to court, support for children was required'.[134] It noted positive steps, such as the National Society for the Prevention of Cruelty to Children Young Witness Service and Victim Support NI's pilot Children's Independent Sexual Violence Advocate Service, but highlighted that consideration should be given to the Gillen Review recommendations.[135] It also noted that:

> [W]ithin the Public Prosecution Service NI and the NI Courts and Tribunals Service, a tailored child safeguarding procedure to enhance internal governance and direction on this, including the considerations that the Equal Treatment Bench Book outlined, would be of benefit.[136]

---

[128] ibid 39.

[129] ibid.

[130] NI Assembly Hansard, 'Written Question – Custody of Children – Naomi Long MLA – AQO 992/17–22', 2 November 2020.

[131] Criminal Justice Inspection NI, 'Child Sexual Exploitation in NI: An Inspection of the Criminal Justice System's Response' (CJINI, 2020) www.cjini.org/getattachment/31173a89-f283-4e24-ac04-4aab3cbd0d04/Child-Sexual-Exploitation-in-Northern-Ireland.aspx.

[132] ibid 80.

[133] ibid 8.

[134] ibid.

[135] ibid.

[136] ibid.

In October 2020, following a consultation on proposals aimed at implementing the Independent Inquiry into Child Sexual Exploitation in NI's recommendations, the Minister of Justice committed to legislative amends. These focus on introducing provisions that remove terms such as 'child prostitution' from current legislation, legislate against adults masquerading as children online and include live streaming in relevant sexual offences. These changes are to be included within the Miscellaneous Provisions Bill, and scheduled to come into force in 2022.[137]

VIII. RIGHT TO A FAIR TRIAL

In 2020, the Department of Justice consulted on the use of live link technology in a review of detention by a superintendent from 24 to 36 hours and a magistrate for up to 96 hours, under Articles 43 and 44 of the Police and Criminal Evidence (NI) Order.[138] The Department of Justice published a summary of the consultation responses in October 2020, which largely welcomed the proposed amends 'while stressing that the rights, voice and participation of the detainee must be maintained at all times'.[139] The Department of Justice intends to include the proposed amends to the use of live links within the Miscellaneous Provisions Bill that is currently being prepared for introduction to the NI Assembly in 2021.[140]

In February 2020, the Minister of Justice established an Implementation Team to co-ordinate phased actions aimed at addressing the Gillen report on the handling of serious sexual offences cases, as agreed by the Criminal Justice Board.[141] In June 2020, the Department of Justice published the Implementation Team's plan.[142] By 2021, the implementation plan had changed to include a commitment to introduce separate legal advice/representation for complainants pre-trial, Case Progression Officers, an Achieving Best Evidence interview, improved disclosure and a bespoke Indictable Cases Process that takes into account the unique nature of sexual offences cases.[143] The plan also committed to remove, by 2022, the use of oral evidence as part of the committal process, and to introduce new arrangements whereby relevant cases can bypass the committal process entirely, thus ensuring that those cases are transferred to the Crown Court at an earlier stage. This is subject to

---

[137] Department of Justice, 'Press Release: Measures to Strengthen Laws Protecting Children from Sexual Exploitation to Be Taken Forward' (20 October 2020) www.justice-ni.gov.uk/news/measures-strengthen-laws-protecting-children-sexual-exploitation-be-taken-forward.

[138] Department of Justice, 'Consultation on Proposals on the Use of Live Links for Police Detention/Interviews' (DoJ, 2020) www.lawsoc-ni.org/DatabaseDocs/new_7500809__consultation_document_live_links_april_2020_final.pdf.

[139] Department of Justice, 'The Use of Live Links for Policy Detention/Interviews – A Consultation: Summary of Responses' (DoJ, 2020) para 3.2, www.lawsoc-ni.org/DatabaseDocs/new_7500809__consultation_document_live_links_april_2020_final.pdf.

[140] ibid paras 3.3 and 3.4.

[141] Department of Justice, 'Press Release: We Must Work Together to Deliver Real Change for Victims of Serious Sexual Assault: Long' (3 February 2020).

[142] Department of Justice, 'Implementation Plan: The Gillen Review into the Law and Procedures in Serious Sexual Offences in NI' (DoJ, 2020) www.justice-ni.gov.uk/publications/gillen-review-implementation-plan.

[143] ibid 6–7.

the passage of the Criminal Justice (Committal Reform) Bill, which was introduced to the NI Assembly in November 2020.

IX. RIGHT TO PRIVATE LIFE

A. Access to Financial Support for Unmarried Couples

In August 2018, the UK Supreme Court ruled that the requirement that couples are married in order to access the Widowed Parent's Allowance was in violation of the right to private and family life under Article 8 ECHR and was also discriminatory, contrary to Article 14 ECHR.[144] Despite the UK Supreme Court's ruling, substantive proposals to change the law have yet to be introduced in the UK Parliament. In October 2019, the Work and Pensions Committee published a report, noting the continued delay in remedying the position and meeting its stated aim of 'making bereavement benefits more accessible as quickly as possible'.[145]

In July 2020, the Parliamentary Under-Secretary of State for Employment, Mims Davies MP, announced the UK government's intention to lay a Remedial Order to remove the human rights incompatibilities by extending entitlement to the Widowed Parent's Allowance and the Bereavement Support Allowance to cohabitees with children.[146] At the time of writing, this has not been progressed by the UK government and further proceedings are pending.

B. Anonymity and Children in Pre-trial Proceedings

Section 44 of the Youth Justice and Criminal Evidence Act 1999 prevents anyone under 18 allegedly involved in an offence from being named in the media.[147] However, unlike in England and Wales, NI has not enacted this provision. Article 22 of the Criminal Justice (Children) (NI) Order 1998 places reporting restrictions for minors in post-charge and court scenarios, but not for minors who are pre-charge.

In 2020, a challenge was brought on behalf of a child hacker who was named in the press. In 2015, the applicant, who was then 15 years old, was arrested and interviewed by the Police Service NI as a suspect in an alleged cybercrime involving the hacking of customer details retained by the company Talk-Talk. Shortly after his arrest, details of the applicant's identity, including his name, age, place of residence and photograph, were published by various media outlets. The applicant sought a declaration that the Department of Justice's failure to enact section 44 of the Youth and Justice Criminal Evidence Act was unlawful and to not extend the protection of

---

[144] *In the Matter of an Application by Siobhan McLaughlin for Judicial Review (NI)* [2018] UKSC 48.

[145] House of Commons Work and Pensions Committee, 'Bereavement Support Payment – First Report of Session 2019–20' (WPC, 2019) para 75, https://publications.parliament.uk/pa/cm201919/cmselect/cmworpen/85/8506.htm.

[146] HC Hansard 27 July 2020, 'Response to Written Question: Bereavement Benefits – Mims Davies MP – 76930', https://questions-statements.parliament.uk/written-questions/detail/2020-07-20/76930.

[147] This provision applies in England, Wales and NI.

Article 22 of the Criminal Justice (Children) (NI) Order 1998 to pre-charge minors was unfair. The applicant also sought to obtain an order requiring the Department of Justice to immediately enact legislation to provide for reporting restrictions in pre-charge situations. The High Court NI found that the applicant, who was in a pre-charge situation, was 'not in a relevantly analogous situation to children who actually appear before a court' and that there was 'nothing unfair or irrational in the State's approach'.[148]

C. Biometric Data

In 2015, the UK Supreme Court ruled that the indefinite retention of a person's DNA profile was not a disproportionate interference with Article 8 ECHR. The claimant, Mr Gaughran, had pleaded guilty to a recordable offence, namely, a drink driving offence, for which he was fined and banned from driving for 12 months.[149] Mr Gaughran subsequently brought his case to the European Court of Human Rights (ECtHR). In February 2020, the ECtHR found that the policy of indefinite retention was a disproportionate interference with the applicant's right under Article 8 ECHR, stating that:

> the indiscriminate nature of the powers of retention of the DNA profile, fingerprints and photograph of the applicant as person convicted of an offence, even if spent, without reference to the seriousness of the offence or the need for indefinite retention and in the absence of any real possibility of review, failed to strike a fair balance between the competing public and private interests ... Accordingly, the respondent State has overstepped the acceptable margin of appreciation.[150]

In 2020, with a view to addressing the ECtHR's ruling, the Department of Justice consulted on proposals to amend the legislation governing the retention of DNA and fingerprints in NI.[151] The Department of Justice proposes amending the Criminal Justice Act (NI) 2013 to end indefinite retention, instead using the 75, 50 and 25 year model for retaining DNA and fingerprints of convicted individuals. It is also proposed that this new approach would include a review system that would be put in regulations that have yet to be published.

D. Stop and Search

In February 2020, the Court of Appeal NI considered whether the Police Service NI's Code of Practice for Monitoring Community Background imposes insufficient

---

[148] *In the Matter of an Application by JKL (A Minor) to Apply for Judicial Review and the In the Matter of a Decision of the Department of Justice* [2020] NIQB 29, paras 70 and 72.
[149] *Gaughran v Chief Constable of the Police Service of NI* [2015] UKSC 29.
[150] *Gaughran v UK* [2020] ECHR 144, 96.
[151] Department of Justice, 'Consultation on Proposals to Amend the Legislation Governing the Retention of DNA and Fingerprints in NI' (DoJ, 2020) www.justice-ni.gov.uk/consultations/proposals-amend-legislation-governing-retention-dna-and-fingerprints-ni.

safeguards to ensure that the impugned powers are not exercised arbitrarily. The Court of Appeal noted that:

> [A]lthough there is no specific methodology required under the Code for the monitoring of community background we accept that the monitoring and supervision requirements of the Code establish a duty on the part of the Police Service NI to devise a methodology of enabling such monitoring and supervision ... The evaluation of the pilot by the Police Service NI has tended to suggest that the best option may be assessment by the individual police officers of community background. We understand that such an option has not yet been implemented but we are satisfied that the requirements of the Code are that some proportionate measure is put in place in order to ensure that there can be adequate monitoring and supervision of the community background of those being stopped and searched.[152]

The Court of Appeal agreed with the High Court that, taking into account the scheme as a whole, it was satisfied that there were 'sufficient safeguards to protect the individual against arbitrary interference', but found a breach of Article 8 ECHR on the basis that the Police Service NI did not record the basis for the search.[153]

Following this ruling, the Independent Reviewer of the Justice and Security (NI) Act 2007, David Seymour, reported that:

> [T]he Court of Appeal in Ramsey has now made it clear that the Code establishes a legal duty on the Police Service NI to devise a methodology for monitoring the community background of those who are stopped and searched under the Justice and Security (NI) Act ... if the issue of community monitoring is to be taken forward [there would be benefit in], refining and publishing an analysis of the impact of General Data Protection Regulation on the Police Service NI's ability to record the community background of those who are stopped and searched under the Justice and Security (NI) Act.[154]

X. FREEDOM OF RELIGION AND BELIEF, EXPRESSION, ASSOCIATION AND THE RIGHT TO PARTICIPATE IN PUBLIC AND POLITICAL LIFE

A. Freedom of Expression of Journalists

In April 2020, a journalist working for the *Irish News* was warned by the Police Service NI of a threat against them.[155] In May 2020, further threats were issued against journalists working for the *Sunday Life* and *Sunday World*.[156] An open letter published by #StandUpforJournalism on 20 May 2020 called 'for the immediate

---

[152] *In the Matter of an application by Stephen Ramsey (No 2)* [2020] NICA 14, paras 55–58.

[153] ibid 68.

[154] D Seymour, 'Report of the Independent Reviewer Justice and Security (NI) Act 2007: Twelfth Report – 1 August 2018–31 July 2019' (NIO, 2020) paras 7.30–7.44, https://assets.publishing.service.gov.uk/government/uploads/system/uploads/attachment_data/file/957086/12th_Report_1819.pdf.

[155] G Moriarty, 'Threats against NI Journalists Broadly Condemned' *Irish Times* (Dublin, 20 May 2020) www.irishtimes.com/news/ireland/irish-news/threats-against-ni-journalists-broadly-condemned-1.4257680.

[156] ibid.

withdrawal of all threats against journalists in NI and for the freedom of press to be respected and protected'.[157]

In July 2020, the NI High Court published its judgment on whether the search warrants issued against journalists Barry McCaffrey and Trevor Birney were lawful. The Court confirmed 'that on the basis of the material that has been provided to us we see no overriding requirement in the public interest which could have justified an interference with the protection of journalistic sources in this case'.[158]

B. Parades and Protests

In May and June 2020, there were a series of anti-racism protests in NI in response to the global 'Black Lives Matter' movement. At that time, the existing iteration of the Health Protection (Coronavirus, Restrictions) (NI) Regulations, which were aimed at preventing the spread of COVID-19, prohibited gatherings in public spaces of more than two people with limited exceptions. The Regulations also provided the Police Service NI with the powers to restrict freedom of movement and protests for this purpose. The Police Service NI issued a number of fines to Black Lives Matter protestors under the Regulations.[159] However, subsequent protests by the NI Cenotaph Protection Group reportedly took place without fines being issued.[160] The Police Ombudsman NI investigated the use of police powers in relation to large public gatherings during this period. The findings of that investigation, which were published in late 2020, found that 'PSNI acted in an unfair and discriminatory manner', paid mere 'lip service' to human rights, and found its use of the Serious Crime Act against peaceful protestors to be 'entirely disproportionate'.[161]

In addition, in November 2020, the Policing Board NI, in its review of the Police Service NI's response to COVID-19 gatherings overall, acknowledged that there was an 'apparent inconsistency in approach to the enforcement of all large gatherings of people during April, May and June 2020'.[162] The Policing Board NI recommended that the Police Service NI should report to the Board on any lessons learnt; hold

---

[157] 'Stand Up for Journalism: Initiative Condemning Threats against NI Reporters Receives Widespread Support' *Belfast Telegraph* (Belfast, 20 May 2020) www.belfasttelegraph.co.uk/news/northern-ireland/stand-up-for-journalism-initiative-condemning-threats-against-ni-reporters-receives-widespread-support-39218960.html.

[158] *In the Matter of an Application by Fine Point Films and Trevor Birney for Judicial Review and the in the Matter of an Application by Barry McCaffrey and the in the Matter of an Application by Police Service NI and Durham Constabulary for Search Warrants* [2020] NIQB 55, para 55.

[159] 'Coronavirus: Anti-racism Rallies in Belfast and Londonderry' (BBC News, 6 June 2020) www.bbc.com/news/uk-northern-ireland-52934110.

[160] J Bell, 'Police Ombudsman to Probe Difference in Police Service NI Approach to Black Lives Matter Rallies and Belfast Cenotaph Protest' *Belfast Telegraph* (Belfast, 17 June 2020) www.belfasttelegraph.co.uk/news/northern-ireland/police-ombudsman-to-probe-difference-in-psni-approach-to-black-lives-matter-rallies-and-belfast-cenotaph-protest-39293099.html.

[161] Police Ombudsman NI, 'Press Release: Police Ombudsman to Look at How Police Have Enforced Regulations on Large Public Gatherings' (17 June 2020) www.policeombudsman.org/Media-Releases/2020/Police-Ombudsman-to-look-at-how-police-have-enforce.

[162] Policing Board NI, 'Report on the Thematic Review of the Policing Response to COVID-19' (PBNI, 2020) 56.

discussions with organisers 'to ensure peaceful protests are facilitated and that both sides understand the positive obligations of the police and the key role of the organisers'; create an Independent Advisory Group on protests; and hold a seminar with key stakeholders, to assist 'with ensuring a consistent approach to all protests'.[163]

C. Participation and Language Rights

The New Decade, New Approach agreement committed the First Minister and Deputy First Minister to 'sponsor and oversee a new framework both recognising and celebrating NI's diversity of identities and culture, and accommodating cultural difference'.[164] The agreement committed that this framework would consist of the establishment of an Office of Identity and Cultural Expression, a commissioner to recognise, support, protect and enhance the development of the Irish language in NI and another commissioner to enhance and develop the language, arts and literature associated with the Ulster Scots/Ulster British tradition.[165] The framework was also to include recognition of the status of the Irish language and the Ulster Scots language in NI.[166] The three Bills that were intended to provide for this legislative framework were published with the agreement – NI Act 1998 (Amendment No 1) Bill, NI Act 1998 (Amendment No 2) Bill, and NI Act (Amendment No 3) Bill. These Bills were to be presented to the NI Assembly by April 2020,[167] they remain outstanding.

In July 2020, the Committee of Experts of the European Charter for Regional or Minority Languages published its monitoring report on the UK. The Committee of Experts noted the 'ongoing political resistance' by the NI Executive and considered that 'such legislation should be passed at central governmental level and comprehensively regulate the use and promotion of Irish'.[168] On Ulster Scots, the Committee of Experts stated that 'due to the lack of information in the State periodical report on the situation of Ulster Scots ... [it] was unfortunately not able to conclude on numerous undertakings'.[169] Of the information that was provided, the Committee of Experts noted that 'Ulster Scots continues to have a weak presence in public life' and recommended the adoption of 'a strategy to promote Ulster Scots in education and other areas of public life'.[170]

On the basis of the Committee of Experts' report, the CoE Committee of Ministers published its recommendations regarding application of the European Charter for Regional or Minority Languages by the UK. The recommendations identified

---

[163] ibid 55–57.
[164] NI Office, 'New Decade, New Approach' (n 1) 15.
[165] ibid 16.
[166] ibid.
[167] ibid 36.
[168] 'Fifth Report of the Committee of Experts on the European Charter for Regional or Minority Languages in respect of the UK' (1 July 2020) CM(2019)84-final, para 1.2.
[169] ibid para 22.
[170] ibid paras 1.2 and 2.4.2(I)(a).

three matters of priority across the UK, including that the UK government and NI Executive 'adopt a comprehensive law and strategy on the promotion of Irish in NI'.[171]

XI. RIGHT TO HEALTH

A. Mental Health

In 2018, the NI Commissioner for Children and Young People published its rights-based review into mental health services provided for children and young people in NI.[172] In February 2020, the NI Commissioner for Children and Young People published its first monitoring report analysing the NI Executive's response to the recommendations set out in the review.[173] Regarding progress to date, the NI Commissioner for Children and Young People expressed particular concern in relation to funding for effectively implementing the recommendations and a continued lack of progress on effective data collection and addressing delays related to Child and Adolescent Mental Health Services.[174]

The New Decade, New Approach agreement committed to publishing a Mental Health Strategy by December 2020.[175] To date, this target has not been met due to the increased demands on the Department of Health posed by COVID-19 and the subsequent impact which the pandemic has had on waiting lists.[176] The Department of Health has committed to publish a Mental Health Strategy that is 'co-produced with multi-disciplinary and multi-sectoral participation in its development, be evidence based, take a whole life approach, focus on population need, be trauma informed and place the need and experiences of the persons using the system at its centre'.[177] The strategy remains under review.

In June 2020, Siobhán O'Neill was appointed interim Mental Health Champion for NI. This role includes being a public advocate for mental health, a consensus builder to integrate mental health and well-being across government, an adviser to senior stakeholders and a challenger of decisions and policies related to mental health.[178]

---

[171] 'Recommendation of the CoE Committee of Ministers to Member States on the Application of the European Charter for Regional or Minority Languages by the UK' (1 July 2020) M/RecCHL(2020) 1.

[172] NI Commissioner for Children and Young People, 'Still Waiting: A Rights Based Review of Mental Health Services and Support for Children and Young People' (NICCY, 2018) www.niccy.org/about-us/our-current-work/mental-health-review-still-waiting/still-waiting-a-rights-based-review-of-mental-health-services-and-support-for-children-and-young-people-in-northern-ireland/.

[173] NI Commissioner for Children and Young People, 'Still Waiting: Monitoring Report' (NICCY, 2020) www.niccy.org/about-us/our-current-work/mental-health-review-still-waiting/.

[174] ibid 12.

[175] NI Office, 'New Decade, New Approach' (n 1) 27.

[176] Department of Health, 'Mental Health Action Plan' (DoH, 2020).

[177] ibid 8.

[178] University of Ulster, 'Press Release: Professor Siobhán O'Neill Appointed Interim Mental Health Champion for NI' (24 June 2020).

In October 2020, the NIHRC made an amicus curiae intervention in a mental health case being considered by the NI High Court.[179] The High Court was considering the lawfulness, particularly in relation to Article 5 ECHR (right to liberty), of releasing an individual who had been convicted and detained within a mental health hospital who now appeared to have mental capacity. The Belfast Health and Social Care Trust sought conditions upon the individual's discharge; however, drawing from recent UK Supreme Court jurisprudence,[180] the Review Tribunal did not consider that it had the power to authorise a conditional discharge as it amounted to a deprivation of liberty. In November 2020, Justice Keegan highlighted that if mental capacity legislation can be utilised in NI in relation to an individual without capacity seeking conditional discharge but cannot be utilised in the same way by a person with capacity in the same situation, then the individual with capacity is left at a disadvantage. Mindful of the human rights considerations, Justice Keegan indicated that she was considering using the Court's inherent jurisdiction to address this. Justice Keegan adjourned the case on the basis that further evidence and consideration of the legal issues is required.

B. Legislative Reform on Termination of Pregnancy

On 31 March 2020, in line with the NI (Executive Formation etc) Act 2019, the Abortion (NI) Regulations 2020 came into force. This was in addition to the decriminalisation of termination of pregnancy in October 2019.[181]

On 14 May 2020, the original regulations were revoked and replaced by the Abortion (NI) (No 2) Regulations 2020. This was for administrative reasons, with no substantive changes to the circumstances in which terminations can be performed in NI and the procedural requirements attached to this. Consequently, since 31 March 2020, terminations have been legalised in NI under any circumstances up to 12 weeks and where there is a risk to physical or mental health up to 24 weeks. Terminations with no gestational limit are also now legal in NI where there is an immediate necessity, a risk to life or grave permanent injury to the physical or mental health of a pregnant woman or in cases of severe foetal impairment or fatal foetal abnormality. However, the Department of Health has not yet commissioned the required healthcare services to implement these regulations. The Department of Health has also not provided guidance on the provision of services in general or to cover services during the pandemic, particularly given the travel restrictions imposed by COVID-19. Between mid-April and the start of June 2020, health and social care trusts in NI, guided by the regulations, started providing certain services within their existing resources and without financial support from the Department of Health. This approach is not sustainable in the longer term, which was confirmed in October 2020, when certain services provided by health and social care trusts experienced roll-back.

---

[179] *Belfast Health and Social Care Trust v O and R* [2020].
[180] *Secretary of State for Justice v MM* [2018] UKSC 60.
[181] NI (Executive Formations etc) Act 2019, s 9(2).

On 2 June 2020, the NI Assembly debated a motion put forward by the DUP 'that this Assembly welcomes the important intervention of disability campaigner Heidi Crowter and rejects the imposition of abortion legislation to all non-fatal disabilities, including Down's syndrome'. An amendment was added by Sinn Fein 'that this Assembly welcomes the important intervention of disability campaigner Heidi Crowter and the specific legislative provision in the abortion legislation that goes beyond fatal foetal abnormalities to include non-fatal disabilities, including Down's syndrome'.

The DUP's motion was carried (46:40) and Sinn Fein's amendment was rejected (32:52). This outcome did not impact the 2020 Regulations; however, the motion and amendments continue to be incompatible with the UN Committee on the Elimination of Discrimination against Women (CEDAW)'s inquiry recommendation regarding severe foetal impairment.[182]

Consequently, the UK government has committed to

establish[ing] a mechanism to advance women's rights, including through monitoring authorities' compliance with international standards concerning access to sexual and reproductive health, including access to safe abortions, and ensure enhanced coordination between the mechanism with the Department of Health, Social Services and Public Safety and the NI Human Rights Commission.[183]

XII. THE RIGHT TO EDUCATION

In June 2020, almost 300 children in NI with a statement of Special Educational Needs were still without a school place for September 2020.[184] In September 2020, the NI Audit Office issued a follow-up report on special educational needs in NI from an earlier inquiry in 2017.[185] The earlier report found that neither the Department of Education nor the Education Authority NI could demonstrate value for money in the provision of special education needs support in mainstream schools.[186] The follow-up report found that, of 10 recommendations made in 2017, none had yet been fully addressed.[187] Further, it noted that it had been 13 years since the Department of Education had begun a review of special educational needs in NI and that review had still to be completed.[188]

Elsewhere, the Education Authority NI is working on implementing 10 recommendations identified by the internal audit and the Committee for Education, who

---

[182] 'UN CEDAW Committee Inquiry Concerning the UK of Great Britain and NI under Article 8 of the Optional Protocol to the UN CEDAW Report of the Committee' (6 March 2018) CEDAW/C/OP.8/GBR/1, para 85(b)(iii).

[183] ibid para 85(e).

[184] R Meredith, 'Hundreds of Special Needs Children Have no September Place' (BBC News, 24 June 2020) www.bbc.com/news/uk-northern-ireland-53152284.

[185] NI Audit Office, 'Impact Review of Special Educational Needs' (NIAO, 2020) www.niauditoffice. gov.uk/publications/impact-review-special-educational-needs.

[186] NI Audit Office,' Special Educational Needs' (NIAO, 2017) www.niauditoffice.gov.uk/publications/special-educational-needs.

[187] NI Audit Office, 'Impact Review of Special Educational Needs' (n 185).

[188] ibid.

will monitor how the implementation is progressing.[189] This includes drafting a report on lessons learned from the Special Educational Needs admissions process and the use of Interim Specialist Resource Provisions, which is to inform discussions with the Department of Education on the way forward.[190] The Department of Education established a Special Educational Needs Governance Group, chaired by the Department of Education's Permanent Secretary and including the Education Authority NI, to provide strategic oversight to the programme of Special Educational Needs improvements.[191]

XIII. EQUALITY AND NON-DISCRIMINATION

A. Sexual Orientation Strategy

The New Decade, New Approach agreement committed to publishing a sexual orientation strategy.[192] In October 2020, the Department for Communities published an indicative timetable for the development and publication of the sexual orientation strategy. Development of this strategy adopts a co-design approach, which includes appointing an Expert Advisory Panel and undertaking ongoing engagement with a Co-Design Group and cross-departmental working group made up of key stakeholders. The Expert Advisory Panel has been tasked with gathering evidence to inform the strategy and is due to provide a report to the Department for Communities by mid-2021.[193]

B. The Lee Case

In 2018, the UK Supreme Court found that the refusal of a bakery to make a cake with a slogan supporting the extension of civil marriage to same-sex couples was not discriminatory.[194] In 2019, Mr Lee made an application to the ECtHR on the grounds that the UK Supreme Court failed to give appropriate weight to his ECHR rights.[195] In March 2020, the ECtHR requested that the parties provide their views on how Mr Lee exhausted domestic remedies, whether there has been an interference

---

[189] NI Assembly Hansard, 'Committee for Education: Special Educational Needs Assessment and Statementing Audit – Education Authority NI', 4 March 2020.

[190] NI Assembly Hansard, 'Response to Written Question – Special Educational Needs – Peter Weir MLA – AQW 7523/17–22', 1 October 2020.

[191] ibid.

[192] NI Office, 'New Decade, New Approach' (n 1) https://assets.publishing.service.gov.uk/government/uploads/system/uploads/attachment_data/file/856998/2020-01-08_a_new_decade__a_new_approach.pdf.

[193] Department for Communities, 'Social Inclusion Strategies' www.communities-ni.gov.uk/articles/social-inclusion-strategies.

[194] *Colin McArthur, Karen McArthur and Ashers Baking Company Ltd v Gareth Lee* [2018] UKSC 49.

[195] 'Ashers "Gay Cake" Row Referred to European Court' (BBC News, 15 August 2019) www.bbc.co.uk/news/uk-northern-ireland-49350891#:~:text=A%20case%20involving%20a%20Christian,of%20Human%20Rights%20(ECHR).

with Articles 8, 9 and 10 ECHR and if this can be justified, and the appropriate test to be applied in a dispute of a 'purely private nature'.[196] To date, there is no record of the UK government having responded.

C. Equal Marriage and Civil Partnerships

Section 8 of the NI (Executive Formation etc) Act 2019 required that regulations be introduced on or before 13 January 2020 by the Secretary of State for NI that provide for the extension of civil marriage to same sex couples and civil partnerships to couples not of the same sex in NI. On 13 January 2020, the Marriage (Same-sex Couples) and Civil Partnership (Opposite-sex Couples) (NI) Regulations 2019 came into force, which permitted same-sex civil marriage and opposite-sex civil partnerships in NI. However, these regulations did not include religious same-sex marriages, or the ability to convert a civil partnership into a marriage or vice versa.

On 20 January 2020, the NI Office launched two consultations, seeking views on permitting same-sex religious marriage in NI (alongside the appropriate protections)[197] and whether to allow same-sex and opposite-sex couples to convert their civil partnerships to marriage, and vice versa.[198]

On 1 September 2020, the Marriage and Civil Partnership (NI) Regulations 2020 came into force. These regulations remove the prohibition of same-sex religious marriages and enable religious bodies to nominate their officiants to solemnise same-sex marriage. They also set out the protections for those religious bodies and officiants who do not wish to marry or perform civil partnership ceremonies for same-sex couples. This includes an 'opt in' system for same-sex religious marriage, allowing individual officiants to be appointed to solemnise same-sex religious marriage where the governing authority of the religious body they belong to gives its written consent to same-sex marriage to the Registrar General. It also includes protections and exemptions so that these changes do not amount to unlawful discrimination for a religious body, or an officiant, to refuse to marry a couple because they are of the same sex.

In October 2020, the UK government laid the Marriage and Civil Partnership (NI) (No 2) Regulations 2020 before the UK Parliament, and these came into force on 7 December 2020. These regulations provide a three-year window in which same-sex couples can convert an existing civil partnership formed in NI into a marriage and opposite-sex couples can convert an existing marriage formed in NI into a civil partnership. These conversions will be backdated, meaning that the resulting relationship will be treated as having existed from the date the original relationship was formed.

---

[196] P Johnson, '"Gay Cake" Case Communicated by ECtHR' (*ECHR Sexual Orientation Blog*, 30 March 2020) http://echrso.blogspot.com/2020/03/gay-cake-case-communicated-by-european.html.

[197] NI Office, 'Same-sex Religious Marriage in NI – Government Consultation' (NIHRC, 2020) https://assets.publishing.service.gov.uk/government/uploads/system/uploads/attachment_data/file/901458/FINAL_Government_response_to_the_same_sex_marriage_consultation._16_July_2020.pdf.

[198] NI Office, 'Marriage and Civil Partnership – Conversion Entitlements in NI – Government Consultation' (NIHRC, 2020) https://assets.publishing.service.gov.uk/government/uploads/system/uploads/attachment_data/file/928771/GOVERNMENT_RESPONSE_-_Marriage_and_Civil_partnership_-_Conversion_entitlements_in_Northern_Ireland.pdf.

D. Gender Equality Strategy

The New Decade, New Approach agreement committed to publishing a Gender Strategy.[199] In October 2020, the Department for Communities published an indicative timetable for the development and publication of the gender strategy. Development of this strategy adopts a co-design approach, which includes appointing an Expert Advisory Panel and undertaking an ongoing engagement with a Co-Design Group and a cross-departmental working group made up of key stakeholders. The Expert Panel has been tasked with gathering evidence to inform the strategy and is due to provide a report to the Department for Communities by the end of December 2020. The Co-Design Group and the cross-departmental working group are due to meet regularly from November 2020 until at least the finalisation of themes and the action plan in June 2021. The strategy is due to be subject to public consultation in August 2021, followed by its publication in December 2021.

E. Gender Recognition

In 2019, the Department of Health asked the Health and Social Care Board to undertake a review of the Regional Gender Identity Service pathway. A multi-agency Gender Identity Service Pathway Review Group was established to take this forward. In 2020, despite some delays due to COVID-19, the group developed a draft set of objectives to help inform the future direction of the service in the region. Once agreed, the development of a set of objectives will provide the baseline from which a number of options will be developed and assessed to identify how to deliver a gender identity service that addresses existing need and is capable of meeting demand.[200] Civil society organisations have welcomed the creation of the multi-agency group, but have raised concerns that a number of persistent issues need immediate action, including significant delays in receiving support and treatment from Brackenburn Clinic and the need to support those self-medicating as a result.[201]

F. Hate Crimes

In early 2020, the Independent Hate Crime Review Team undertook a public consultation on reviewing hate crime legislation in NI. In addition to encouraging written submissions, the team, led by Judge Desmond Marrinan, hosted several meetings and events with key stakeholders. The Commission submitted a response to the consultation, providing human rights advice on the various issues raised within the scope of

---

[199] NI Office, 'New Decade, New Approach' (n 1), at 27.
[200] Health and Social Care Board, 'Gender Identity Service Review of the Pathway' www.hscboard.hscni.net/gender-identity-service/.
[201] Email correspondence with Transgender NI and NI Human Rights Commission, 21 October 2020. Taken from NIHRC Annual Report 2020 (n 68) 28.

the consultation.[202] On 1 December 2020, following a delay due to COVID-19, the findings and recommendations of the Review Team were published.[203] The Minister of Justice, Naomi Long MLA, is taking time to consider the 'complex and wide-ranging' recommendations.[204]

G. Persons with Disabilities

The New Decade, New Approach agreement committed to publishing a Disability Strategy.[205] In October 2020, the Department for Communities published an indicative timetable for the development and publication of the disability strategy. Development of this strategy adopts a co-design approach, which includes appointing an Expert Advisory Panel and undertaking ongoing engagement with a Co-Design Group and cross-departmental working group made up of key stakeholders. The Expert Panel has been tasked with gathering evidence to inform the strategy and is due to provide a report to the Department for Communities by the end of December 2020. The Co-Design Group and cross-departmental working group are due to meet regularly from November 2020 until at least finalisation of themes and the action plan in June 2021. The strategy is due to be subject to public consultation in August 2021, followed by its publication in December 2021.

H. Independent Living Fund

The UK-wide Independent Living Fund was closed on 30 June 2015 and future responsibilities were transferred to the individual jurisdictions.[206] This fund seeks to support persons with disabilities in the UK, including NI, to achieve positive independent living outcomes, and to have greater choice and control over their lives. In NI and Scotland, the Independent Living Fund for existing applicants has been retained and is administered by the Independent Living Fund Scotland.[207] As these new arrangements restricted continued eligibility of the fund to existing users, they will lead to the fund's eventual closure. In early 2020, Independent Living Fund Scotland, with the support of the Department of Health, publicly consulted on whether the fund should continue and be reopened for new applicants. This is following ongoing work with the Independent Living Fund Working Group established by the Department of Health.

---

[202] NI Human Rights Commission, 'Submission to the Hate Crime Review Consultation' (NIHRC, 2020) https://nihrc.org/uploads/publications/NIHRC-Hate_Crime_Review-FINAL_(002).pdf.

[203] Department of Justice, 'Hate Crime Legislation in NI: Independent Review' (DoJ, 2020).

[204] Department of Justice, 'Press Release: Long Welcomes Completion of Review into Hate Crime Legislation' (30 November 2020) www.justice-ni.gov.uk/news/long-welcomes-completion-review-hate-crime-legislation.

[205] NI Office, 'New Decade, New Approach' (n 1).

[206] Independent Living Fund, 'Press Release: Decision on the Future of the ILF' (6 March 2014) www.gov.uk/government/news/future-of-the-independent-living-fund.

[207] S Preece, 'NI Independent Living Fund to be Administered in Scotland' (*Welfare Weekly*, 28 January 2018) https://welfareweekly.com/northern-ireland-independent-living-fund-to-be-administered-in-scotland/.

In September 2020, after two years of consultation with the disability sector, the terms of reference of the UN Convention on the Rights of Persons with Disabilities (CRPD) Independent Mechanism in NI's Disability Forum were finalised.[208] Reflecting Article 33(3) of the UN CRPD and the UN CRPD Committee's General Comment No 7,[209] this forum was established to provide a dedicated space to ensure disabled people and their representative organisations are at the core of the Independent Mechanism's work in promoting, protecting and monitoring the implementation of the UN CRPD in NI. It builds on the previous engagement and involvement of disabled people and their representative organisations in the Independent Mechanism's UN CRPD related work. At the time of writing, the Forum have held their first meeting.

In 2020, the NI Union of Supported Employment expressed concern about the absence of any clear plan to ensure continuous funding for European Social Fund projects after March 2022, when such funding will no longer be available due to the UK leaving the EU.[210]

XIV. SOCIAL RIGHTS

A. Child Poverty Strategy

In March 2019, the existing Child Poverty Strategy expired.[211] The New Decade, New Approach agreement committed to publishing a new Child Poverty Strategy.[212] A timeline for producing this strategy was due to be published by April 2020; however, this is yet to be provided. In September 2020, the Minister for Communities, Carál Ní Chuilín MLA, announced that the existing child poverty strategy had been extended to May 2022. This is on the basis that the Minister for Communities considers there may be scope to take child poverty forward within the wider anti-poverty strategy that has also been committed within the New Decade, New Approach agreement.[213] The Department of Communities has established an Expert Panel,

---

[208] UN CRPD Independent Mechanism of NI, 'IMNI Disability Forum: Maximising the Involvement of People with Disabilities in the Realisation of the UN CRPD in NI' (NIHRC and ECNI, 2020) www.equalityni.org/ECNI/media/ECNI/Publications/Delivering%20Equality/IMNI-DisForum-OverviewAndContext.pdf.

[209] CRPD/C/GC/7, 'UN CRPD Committee General Comment No 7: Participation of Persons with Disabilities, Including Children with Disabilities, Through their Representative Organisations, in the Implementation and Monitoring of the Convention' (9 November 2018) www.ohchr.org/en/hrbodies/crpd/pages/gc.aspx.

[210] NI Union of Supported Employment, 'Briefing Paper: June 2020' (NIUSE, 2020) https://northernireland.mencap.org.uk/sites/default/files/2020-10/NIUSE%20Briefing%20Paper%20June%20 2020%20pdf.pdf.

[211] NI Executive, 'The Executive's Child Poverty Strategy' (NI Executive, 2016); Department for Communities, 'Press Release: Minister Announces Extension to Child Poverty Strategy' (11 September 2020).

[212] NI Office, 'New Decade, New Approach' (n 1) 27.

[213] Department for Communities, 'Minister Announces Extension to Child Poverty Strategy' (n 211).

Co-Design Working Group and cross-departmental working group for the purposes of drafting the anti-poverty strategy, which was published in December 2021.[214]

B. Social Security

In March and June 2020, the Department for Communities extended the social security reform mitigation package through agreement with the Department of Finance under the Budget Act (NI) 2020 and Budget (No 2) Act 2020. The arrangements were in place until December 2020 and were being kept under review in the absence of amendments to the Welfare Reform (NI) Order 2015.[215] In September 2020, the Minister for Communities confirmed that she intends to introduce primary legislation to amend as a matter of urgency the Welfare Reform (NI) Order 2015 to provide for an extension of social security mitigation payments for people affected by the bedroom tax.[216] It is also the Minister's intention to address the two-child tax credit and bedroom cap in future legislation and regulations.[217]

In October 2020, the UK Supreme Court heard the Child Poverty Action Group's appeal concerning the lawfulness of the two-child tax credit limit, after failing with its challenge in part on human rights grounds in the Court of Appeal.[218] Unfortunately the case was subsequently dismissed by the Supreme Court in 2021.

XV. CONCLUSION

A lot has changed since the last Human Rights in NI Report for the *Yearbook*. A global pandemic gripped the planet for more than two years, leading to over 68 million cases of COVID-19 infection and over one and a half million deaths caused by the virus; and the eruption of the Black Lives Matter movement, sparked by killings of black people by police in the USA, has given a new impetus to a global anti-racist struggle. Closer to home, the British government's introduction of the Internal Market Bill, which breaches the NI Protocol, international law and the Good Friday Agreement, once again throws the spotlight onto this region in the context of the still incomplete (at the time of writing) negotiations between the UK and the EU. 2020 also witnessed the re-establishment of the institutions at Stormont based on the New Decade, New Approach document, which contains many progressive commitments, and while the Executive has stumbled at times to act in a unified manner in relation to the pandemic, it remains clear that devolution hangs by a thread and the threat of direct rule is never far away.

---

[214] Department for Communities, 'Social Inclusion Strategies' www.communities-ni.gov.uk/articles/social-inclusion-strategies.

[215] NI Assembly Hansard, 'Oral Questions: Welfare Mitigations Schemes Primary Legislation – Cara Hunter MLA – AQO 594/17–22', 8 September 2020; email from Cliff Edge Coalition to NI Human Rights Commission, 29 September 2020.

[216] AQO 594/17–22 (n 215).

[217] ibid.

[218] *R (on the application of SC, CB and 8 children) (Appellants) v Secretary of State for Work and Pensions and others (Respondents)* [2019] UKSC 135.

Book Reviews

Lori Allen, *A History of False Hope: Investigative Commissions in Palestine* (Redwood City, CA, Stanford University Press, 2020) 432pp ISBN: 9781503606722 (hardback) Price: $30.00

In the field of international law and legal history, reflections on the tensions between law and politics, between adjudication and advocacy and between positivism and realism in international relations tend to be the order of the day: there is a long-established tradition of legal, historical and philosophical enquiry. This is less so in the field of the history of emotions and almost non-existent in the history of hope, a particular emotion which, claims the author, has fuelled scholarly and popular engagements with international law in Israel/Palestine. The book explores Palestinians' emotional engagements with international law through the lenses of the international commissions of enquiry sent from the Mandate Period to the present day to examine the question of sovereignty in Palestine. Allen claims that the role of investigative commissions, composed of diplomats, lawyers, academics, military generals and legal experts, and thus largely favoured by governments,[1] has been to determine the 'nature of authorised conversations' and to 'promote a form of liberal rationality' that has narrowed political vision and action.[2] This has happened through the creation of new sites of hope and faith in international law, institutions and values that were regularly unattended and frustrated on the ground.

The book enriches our understanding of how international law operates in practice by looking at lived experiences well beyond the canonical sources of the law and the affective engagements it produces. It dwells extensively on elites' and ordinary citizens' 'structure of feelings', generated by the liberal international legal order and its tools, to reveal how the hegemonic force of the law came to be ingrained into Palestinians' minds and modes of thinking. While exposing liberalists' contradictions and false claims to neutrality and objectivity, it pushes the reader to critically reflect on and to question core values of truth and justice. If these commissions gathered so many facts, yet with no political results even remotely getting closer to a 'just peace', then, the author asks, 'what still motivates Palestinians to turn to international law?' How and why, after so many failures and disappointments, do they keep investing faith and hope in the idea of a just peace? The reply to these questions relies on the capacity of liberalism and its promoters, ie legal scholars and practitioners, to offer new opportunities and venues promising an 'empathetic listening' and a sense of being cared about, which, the author argues, substantiate much of the power of international law as an ideology. However, these hopes are 'false' because, she claims, international law produces often undeliverable expectations, thus 'acquiring the capacity to divert attention and energy from the collective work required for political change, and thus, actively preventing and limiting the range of Palestinians' political imagination'.[3]

---

[1] L Allen, *A History of False Hope: Investigative Commissions in Palestine* (Redwood City, CA, Stanford University Press, 2020) 3.
[2] ibid 27–28.
[3] ibid 29.

Allen focuses on six of the 22 investigative commissions sent to Israel/Palestine since the collapse of the Ottoman Empire, which are listed at the beginning of the book. She starts with the King–Crane Commission sent in March 1919 to gather facts and provide instructions to the peace conference in Paris designed to assign the mandates. The first chapter provides a detailed account of the care taken by Palestinians in welcoming and assisting the work of the commission during their visit to the most active and industrious towns of Greater Syria: while visiting Damascus, Beirut, Homs, Safed, Nablus, Haifa, Bethlehem and Jerusalem, the commission was struck by the amount of information gathered through personal accounts, reports from the press and cultural associations, petitions and other written and oral material sent to them between April and August 1919. Indeed, Arab-Palestinians, full believers in the guiding principle that settlements would be guided by the interests of the population concerned, imagined establishing their own state according to the logic of the newly found liberal order: religious tolerance, democratic procedure of self-governance, progress towards equality and refusal of sectarianism were conceived as the constitutional pillars of the new state. Allen argues that the postcolonial framework of Third World nationalism did not confront Palestinians in this era. The Arabs engaged in the competition to have their civilisational status recognised through mastering the rational methods of good governance and through mobilising the common terms of references established by the prototypical liberal regime of the League of Nations: scientific commissions of enquiry, minorities treaties and the petition processes were the channels substantiating their faith in and requests for rights and public accountability.

From the very first chapter, Allen describes the vicious circle of the 'false hope' of liberalism: the feeling of being heard, consulted, recognised and cared about by an international, albeit 'nebulous', community that promised to deliver but failed to do so; the vicious circle of reports and recommendations regularly disregarded or dropped, which fuelled the need and substantiated the further hope of putting the record straight. The King–Crane Commission fulfilled Arab demands and its report recommended a limit to Jewish immigration, the creation of a single Syrian state under Faysal and the USA as a mandatory power. However, its recommendations were not circulated, and the report became irrelevant. Nevertheless, Allen argues, it did convince the Arabs they had a shared common ground with Western societies, fuelling their engagements with international law.

The second chapter focuses on the Royal Peel Commission, sent to Palestine in 1936 amid the Arab Revolt, which lasted until 1939. The author argues that the uniqueness of this commission came from its rejection by the Arabs, who, for the first time, had grown frustrated with the tools of liberal governance and disappointed with the British. The prolonged Arab boycott of the Peel Commission, she contends, must be understood in the context of the contested geopolitical space of the 1930s. That was the age of the rising 'pans' – pan-Africanism, pan-Islamism, pan-Arabism and black internationalism – in which Palestine and the Arab Revolt became symbols of the struggle for liberation against foreign colonisation as well as the site of the battle for national legitimacy to foster self-governance and broader transnational solidarity networks. According to Allen, the boycott marked a moment of 'disillusionment' and 'refusal of the colonisation of consciousness'[4] for Palestinians, solidly anchored in humanist values: 'we are humans and have the rights of humans, and the natural right to govern ourselves', said 'Abd al-Hadi.[5] The liberal humanist grammar was evident in the claims to the universal notions of justice and dignity, humanitarianism and human rights. Yet Arab public opinion, as shown by, for example, the Arab Women's Committee of Jerusalem, condemned the British liberal hypocrisy of promoting justice 'for some' only, which had been proved once again by the recent secret accords between the UK and France to give Ethiopia, the first non-Western nation of the 'family of nations', to Italy.[6] Despite the Palestinian women's movement's engagement with the petition systems since the dawn of the mandate in an attempt to bring the daily injustices of the political and economic inequalities of the mandate system to international attention, colonial violence once again resurfaced during the state of emergency imposed by the British to quell the revolt. As home demolitions, collective punishments, executions and killings became the order of the day, the leaders of the rebellion, such as Akram Zu'aytir, vowed that they would not be sucked into another investigative commission[7] and pushed for the Arab Higher Committee in exile in the Seychelles not to engage with the Royal Peel Commission, but to support the popular boycott. However, popular resistance was far away from the interests and class markers uniting the foreign and national elites. Pressured by Arab kings and princes and deceived by the 'royal' sponsorship of the Peel Commission, the Arab Higher Committee finally engaged with it.

Considering that the reasons for Palestinians' engagements with international law are part of the central question asked by the author, it is a pity that she glosses over how it happened, simply restating yet again the vicious circles at the core of the book. Elsewhere, historians of the League of Nations, such as Pedersen, Dubnov and Robson, have identified the uniqueness of the Peel Commission in its proposal on partition, and explicit recognition of the unworkability of the two contradictory – Balfour and McMahon – promises;[8] here, Allen argues instead that the novelty of the Peel Commission should be seen in the Arab boycott, as the emblem of their right to represent themselves 'in ways not exhausted by liberalism', and as a glimpse of a 'possible alternative order of politics based in a shared anticolonial sentiment'.[9]

---

[4] ibid 85.

[5] ibid 101.

[6] N Arekat, *Justice for Some: Law and the Question of Palestine* (Redwood City, CA, Stanford University Press, 2019).

[7] Allen (n 1) 95.

[8] A Dubnov and L Robson, *Partitions: A Transnational History of Twentieth-Century Territorial Separatism* (Redwood City, CA, Stanford University Press, 2019); S Pedersen, *The Guardians: The League of Nations and the Crisis of Empire* (Oxford, Oxford University Press, 2015).

[9] Allen (n 1) 99–101.

Following Scott's suggestion on the goal of colonial histories, that the 'question should not be how the colonised accommodate or resisted their conditions but rather how colonial power altered conditions on the ground to make viable routes of accommodation or resistance possible',[10] chapter three looks at the post-WW2 world. It argues that the destruction of European Jewry produced a shift in the criteria necessary for the 'good liberal' to claim and be recognised as worthy of nationhood and self-determination, and how the call to humanism and justice came to be articulated in humanitarian terms: sympathy for Jewish suffering, the author argues, became part of the international 'habitus', a system of values and rules of conduct to guide international behaviours and practice.[11] Despite the reasonable (though not enough for the commissioners) argument made by Fayez Sayegh that 'to alleviate sufferings of the Jews by causing equal suffering to other people is not only an unreasonable attempt ... nor only an imprudent attempt, but also and primarily an unjust attempt',[12] Allen argues a new policing of affect became the subsequent feature of the next commission of enquiry sent to Palestine. The 'Report of the Anglo-American Committee of Enquiry Regarding the Problems of European Jewry and Palestine' was published by the Anglo-American Committee of Inquiry (AACI), which met in Washington in January 1946. However, the legitimacy and authority of the AACI was disputed by both Arabs and Zionists. Nevertheless, while insisting on their natural right to self-governance, the Arabs cooperated with the commission and presented their case for an independent constitutional government and representative democracy as the solution to the problem of Palestine (albeit with some contradictions: in the words of Jamal Al-Husayni, 'Palestine Arabs cannot bind themselves finally by the Committee's decisions, even if they are prepared to put their case before it'[13]). Further protagonists in this chapter are Fayez and Charles Issawi Sayigh, Cecil and Albert Hourani and Ahmed Al Shuqayri, all self-professed liberals who would continue to work at the United Nations in various capacities, and who continued, in accordance with the liberal etiquette, to adhere to the principles of tolerance, democracy and equality.[14] However, Allen argues, their attachment to these values was considered too 'heated' and a sign of 'obstructive intransigence' by the commissioners.[15] The tone, as well as the substance, she claims, was not sympathetic enough to the pains and suffering of the European Jewry and failed to reach those standards of humanitarian feeling and morality that had raised the barometer of liberalism.[16] Protestant humanitarianism in the Middle East during this period was marked by the 'identification with Jews as symbols of historical injustice and violence in the world ... requiring the fulfilment of history's atonement to them'.[17]

---

[10] ibid 74.
[11] ibid 104.
[12] ibid 141.
[13] ibid 109.
[14] ibid 110.
[15] ibid 111.
[16] ibid 126–27.
[17] ibid 116.

According to Allen, despite the vast literature today focusing on the representation of suffering as a feature of human rights politics that can justify political interventions, what has remained understudied is 'the humanitarian structure of feeling',[18] a cluster of moral principles at the core of ethical claims and political strategies. It is this 'structure of feelings' which, albeit not further explored in the book, is understudied in the context of the Israel/Palestine question.[19] Building on the work of Lauren Berlant, an Afro-American scholar and theorist who magisterially asserted how the core practice of democracy should be seen, not as abstract-oriented deliberations, but rather as a platform 'for the orchestration of public feelings of politics and as a scene of emotional contestation',[20] the uniqueness of the AACI should be found, Allen argues, in the assertion of universal humanitarian sympathy for the suffering of the Jews. This became a political moral value, a standard not met by the Arabs, which 'could have not been both politically reasonable and humanly sympathetic as this would have upset the hierarchy of the suffering of the Jews as a universal value'.[21] The Commission's recommendations unleashed the wrath of the Arabs: the revocation of the White Papers limiting the immigration and sale of land once again engendered frustration and disillusionment in the Arabs, who rejected the outcome of the inquiry while the Palestine question shifted to the United Nations.

Chapter four focuses on the 1960s and 1970s as the 'hothouse of hope' for Palestinians. Allen argues that the nature of the commissions changed after the creation of the State of Israel, their aims moving from 'gathering facts to recommend policies' to 'gathering facts to ascertain violations of international law'.[22] The chapter focuses on the less well-known UN Special Committee to Investigate Israeli Practices Affecting the Human Rights of the Population of the Occupied Territories, established by the UN General Assembly in 1969 to investigate the violations and analyse the nature of the military occupation of the West Bank, Gaza, East Jerusalem, the Golan Heights and Sinai after the 1967 Six-Day War. After the basic resolutions passed during the 1960s and 1970s,[23] a surge of optimism again entered Palestinians' engagements with the international legal system, revolving around the centrality of Palestine to forging a Third World solidarity network and agenda. It is this solidarity, at times 'mythical, romanticised, and depoliticised',[24] at times powerful, attractive, and impactful, which remains understudied by anthropologists, and is beyond the realpolitik of international relations scholars or the micropolitics which have been the focus of historical and legal disciplinary approaches to the

---

[18] ibid 106.

[19] The concept is borrowed from P Redfield and E Bornstein, 'An Introduction to the Anthropology of Humanitarianism' in P Redfield and E Bornstein (eds), *Forces of Compassion: Humanitarianism between Ethics and Politics* (Santa Fe, NM, School for Advanced Research Press, 2010) 3–30.

[20] Allen (n 1) 142.

[21] ibid 132–35.

[22] ibid 143.

[23] GA Resolution 181 confirming the partitioning; GA Resolution 194 affirming the right of return for Palestinian refugees; SC Resolution 242 reasserting the inadmissibility of the acquisition of territory by force after the 1960 UN Declaration of Granting Independence to Colonial Countries.

[24] Allen (n 1) 157.

Bandung years.[25] To fill this academic void, Allen recentres the role of emotional assessments in forging anticolonial dynamics and narrating its history. Emotions, she argues, become part of the performance of personal and collective national identity and morality.[26] In fact, both the emotional assessment of state delegates and witnesses to human rights violations came under investigation by the commissioners (from Ceylon, Yugoslavia and Somalia) called to record the truth of the abuses and grant rectification for their violation.

Notwithstanding the impossibility of interpreting emotions in the archives, what the author analyses is the creation of the UN as an 'echo chamber of the right to have rights under international law',[27] with the double effect of reinforcing its authority as a tool of governmentality while at the same time preventing change on the ground due to its structural impotence in enforcing systemic change.[28] Here, the main argument of the book is restated in observing through anthropological lenses the working of a machine as 'in perpetual motion but that remains in one place'.[29] However, it is not clear what is included in this mechanistic view (international law, the international legal system or the UN). The vicious circles are again reproposed: any legal innovations fuelled Palestinians' 'hope'. These could be a resolution or a new catalogue of Israeli abuses vested with the authority of an international legal commission of enquiry. Yet, they are falsely posited on an international law which has always failed to deliver for the better and which requires further correction, clinging to the redemptive power of knowledge and witnessing.

The focus of chapter five is the Mitchell Committee, an international fact-finding group aimed at developing recommendations to furthering the peace negotiations and agreements on the issues that Oslo had left unsettled: water, refugees, settlements and border security. These were the hot topics in which young legal professionals excelled in faith and performance at the Negotiation Support Unit (NSU) to aid the Negotiating Affairs Departments headed by Abu Mazen in 1998. From here on, the book's tone changes as the methods of the historical inquiry change. The author now relies on her PhD fieldwork, notes and first-hand encounters in Palestine before and during the Oslo years and the Second Intifada.[30] The Mitchell commissioners, from Britain, Norway, the Netherlands and Sweden, as well as funders of European NGOs operating in Palestine, were headed by US senator George Mitchell, appointed for his diplomatic success in negotiating the Good Friday Agreement in Northern Ireland. The chapter argues that the specialty of this investigative commission was represented by its open endorsement of a

---

[25] The Bandung conference was a meeting of 29 African and Asian States which took place on 18–24 April 1955 in Bandung, West Indonesia, to grapple with the legacies of imperialism, colonialism and racism for non-Western states and to build new alliances of sovereign states in the postcolonial world order. I refer here to the 'Bandung years' to signal the contested meanings and the different conceptualisation of both Bandung's origin and scopes. L Eslava, M Fakhri and V Nesiah, *Bandung, Global History and International Law: Critical Pasts and Pending Futures* (Cambridge, Cambridge University Press, 2017).

[26] Allen (n 1) 163.
[27] ibid 175.
[28] ibid 152.
[29] ibid 175.
[30] ibid 182.

liberal communicative framework and the superiority of liberal communicative ideals over the assertion of juridical principles.[31] Openness, equality of communicative opportunity, ability to communicate freely without coercion and balance were the new guiding principles of the commission performing a 'democratic listening'.[32] It even managed to engage a very sceptical Israel Ministry of Defence in the investigation which, at the time, was fearing an international intervention because of Sharon's militarised incursion in Haram al-Sharif, the site of the Dome of the Rock and the third holiest place in Islam, which had triggered the Second Intifada. Yet again, Allen argues, we are confronted with an intensification of violence leading to an investigative commission 'ostensibly to support a just solution but that often simply leads to the establishment of the status quo'.[33] The NSU, surrounded by the violence of the Second Intifada, shifted its work from providing recommendations to further the Oslo process to developing recommendations for ending the violence and translating the anger and frustration of the Palestinians, mostly directed at a 'national Vichy-style government', the Palestinian Authority, acting under the aegis of the Israelis.

The language of international law then becomes the 'Rosetta stone that translates conditions of injustice into a language anyone could hear'.[34] What characterises this commission, she claims, is its performance as a 'democratic listener', its ability to compassionately and equanimously listen to both sides. It focused on the mission of making both 'parties feel heard as a crucial point of being free'. However, Allen asserts, 'being heard is not the quandary of political change but rather its liberalism's ideological obfuscation that makes it appear as such'.[35] These factfinders were indeed hardly guided by neutrality, and they were impacted more by the tour of the occupation than by the legal argument painstakingly put together by the NSU: disdain, pity and revulsion opened the committee members to understanding the pain of the occupation. Yet the recommendations scolded each side for not understanding the other's perspective and focused on a balance of concern and understanding which, argues the author, had the effect of erasing the settler colonial takeover of Palestine and the history of imbalance which characterised the conflict:[36] the lack of a mechanism to implement its recommendations and the disconnection between the two US leaderships doomed the commission's report to failure.

Lastly, chapter six focuses on the aftermath of Operation Cast Lead, an Israeli military offensive which took place between December 2008 and January 2009, and on the Goldstone Investigative Commission sent by the Human Rights Council to investigate Israel's violations of international humanitarian and human rights law. Yet again, Allen argues, the commission worked to reinforce convictions and hopes not only in relation to international legal rule (on the protection of human rights and on the principle of distinction and proportionality), but also in relation

---

[31] ibid 177.
[32] ibid 179.
[33] ibid 181.
[34] ibid 198.
[35] ibid 197.
[36] ibid 209.

to the ethical principles that human suffering matters, and that Palestinians' suffering mattered too. The Goldstone Commission was sent to Israel/Palestine to investigate the crimes committed in Gaza, where the bombing, full blockade and use of banned weapons constituted flagrant violations of humanitarian law. The uniqueness of this commission resides, according to Allen, in the shift from 'democratic' – balanced, equal to the Mitchell experience – to an 'ethical' practice of listening. The commissioners, among whom were international legal scholar Christine Chinkin, Hina Jilani of the Supreme Court of Pakistan and Desmond Trevers, former member of the Irish Defence Force, were led by Richard Goldstone, a Jewish and Zionist supporter, a former South African constitutional judge and former Chief Prosecutor at the UN International Criminal Tribunals for Yugoslavia and Rwanda. Israel refused to engage with the commission and barred them from entering Gaza from Israel, forcing them to travel via Egypt. 'Ethical loneliness' is a term coined by the philosopher Stauffer to indicate the experience of being abandoned by humanity and by those who have the power to help.[37] Allen uses this concept to further argue that what commissioners performed in front of the 'ethical loneliness' of the people of Gaza could be recognised as an 'ethical listening', ie an accentuated and emphasised communicative manner of bearing witness to Palestinians' isolation.[38] Their actions were admittedly aimed at readdressing the tendency of the law to silence people's voices, therefore altering the relationship of the law to neutrality and objectivity. Borrowing from Peter Redfield the notion of a 'motivated truth',[39] she argues that an assemblage of fact and witnessing, and of reason and sentiment, guided the commissioners during their investigations and interviews.[40] Internationally, the commission was considered pivotal in stressing in its recommendations the need for accountability and the end of impunity for the State of Israel. Worldwide, the commission again inspired hope, knotted with grief and outrage. Despite its critiques, mostly from the Israeli side, accusing Goldstone of being a self-hating Jew and holocaust denier, the Goldstone Report represents an unprecedented document of condemnation. However, yet again recommendations went unimplemented and, as scholars Perugini and Gordon explained,[41] eventually its most important effect was to unleash a wave of repression of human rights and human rights campaigners in Israel.[42]

The book poses central questions for a wide readership in history, law and politics. Despite the field of inquiries and investigative commissions being relatively new in international legal scholarship,[43] the book points out two distinctive features

---

[37] J Stauffer, *Ethical Loneliness: The Injustice of Not Being Heard* (New York, Columbia University Press, 2018).

[38] Allen (n 1) 225–26.

[39] P Redfield, 'A Less Modest Witness' (2006) 33 *American Ethnologist* 1, 3–26.

[40] Allen (n 1) 222.

[41] N Perugini and N Gordon, *The Human Right to Dominate* (Oxford, Oxford University Press, 2015).

[42] Allen (n 1) 236.

[43] P Parisi, 'Fact-finding in Situations of Atrocities: in Search of Legitimacy' (2021) 1 *Journal of International Humanitarian Legal Studies* 14.

characterising the debate around fact-finding commissions in international law: the flexibility of both the common and substantive procedural features that character-ise these mechanisms, and the problem of legitimacy and authority they carry with them. The sharp ability of the author to turn profound juridical dilemmas into a cri-tique of the liberal order must be commended. So must the historiographical weight of the book, which will surely be of help to students, academics and readers inter-ested in a critical and situated account of Palestinian history and thought. Subaltern histories of interventions, engagements, solidarity, cooperation and negotiations within the international legal order before the 1960s are still much too scarce in the history of international law and, where they do exist, are often too Eurocentric and mainstream. It is surely another merit of the book to have brought them to light again, locating Allen's contribution to transnational legal histories of empire, as well as histories of subaltern knowledge production.

The book offers compelling and thought-provoking reflections, and has undeni-able merits. It presents a historical account, chronicling Palestinians' engagements in the international legal system and its production of alleged undeliverable expec-tations. Its broader contribution to the emerging field of legal anthropology or anthropological and critical approaches to international law lies in its sophisticated analysis of the emotional workings of law. From a historiographic point of view, the author admirably performs the insurmountable task of reading emotions resurfac-ing through archival documents and artefacts with sensitivity and soundness, and accomplishes the difficult chore of recovering Palestinians' agency and voice and of writing international law from 'below'. Theoretically, some of the book's critical ele-ments of the Israel/Palestine quandary are extremely urgent: what is the legal truth, and what are the effects of the juridification of facts in the political sphere? What is the legitimacy of commissions of enquiry? What is the future of transitional justice in the region? If the reader possesses a bare minimum background in both interna-tional law and/or politics, and in the history of the Arab/Israeli conflict, they will find in the book a cogent narrative and insightful answers, with depth, awareness and understanding.

However, while human rights fact-finding commissions can be conducted at different levels and by different actors, the absence of an attempt by the author to distinguish between the witnesses and leaders involved, and types of fact-finding activities and reference to their function or internal features, sometimes creates challenges for readers looking for a compass with which to orient them-selves. Similarly, those who are not so well versed with the history of the Israeli/ Palestinian conflict may encounter some difficulties in navigating the complexities of the legal and circumstantial changes that characterise not only the history of international enquiries, but also the history of the creation, interpretation and application of international norms in Palestine. Furthermore, some key issues remain indeterminate, such as a statement as to the scope of the book and the main terms used; for example, 'liberalism' as a potentially endless, unbounded political category should not be identified with international law, nor 'fairness and equity' with liberalism.

Moreover, there is no easy answer to the set of metaphysical questions the book raises on the meaning of truth and justice. For example, Allen writes: 'UN delegates and Palestinians insisted on this *undefined* but inextricable connection between the act of recording the truth of abuses and their rectification' (emphasis added)[44] and asks, throughout the book, why do Palestinians and legal scholars continue to invoke (international) law? Why do they commit and dedicate themselves to truth and justice? Why do people seek accountability for unjust behaviours? Why, even when facing repeated failure, frustration, neglect and disappointments, do they still believe, act and hope? Most likely realising the author's desired effect, these distressing questions have left me uncomfortably puzzled and bewildered. Are these hopes, invested in the morality of the laws of humanity which, unenforceable by human will or authority, claim to propose a future of justice for all, merely false hopes? It may be worth bearing in mind the ancient meaning of the words *juris prudentia*: in medieval Latin, *prudentia* did not mean 'caution', but rather the ability to foresee and foretell. *Juris prudentes* were those who, able to know the *jure*, the laws, were able to foresee the direction of the future. By making, interpreting and applying the laws, jurists hope, and direct others to hope, for a better and more just future. The question is, do they have any other choice?

In conclusion, *A History of False Hope: Investigative Commissions in Palestine* is an interdisciplinary and challenging publication for students and academics in anthropology, history and international law. It achieves its stated aim, to give anthropologists a perspective to look at people's affective engagements with the international, global and transnational dimensions of the conflict and to unsettle international legal practitioners and academics, challenging their deep certainties on how truth and justice are felt and acted upon in Palestine. Finally, it establishes the foundations for further academic research identifying the emotional dimensions of the investigative commissions and connecting them to critical and decolonial approaches to international law.

Paola Zichi,
Postdoctoral Research Assistant, School of History,
Queen Mary University of London

---

[44] Allen (n 1) 164.

Ntina Tzouvala, *Capitalism as Civilisation: A History of International Law* (Cambridge, Cambridge University Press, 2020) 268 pp ISBN: 9781108684415 (online), 9781108497183 (print) Price: £85.00 (hardback)

On occasion, a theory is so digestible in its basic formulation – yet has so many applications – it lodges in your mind and becomes apparent in many diverse situations. Speaking personally, Antonio Gramsci's notion of hegemony and David Kennedy's centre–periphery framework are two such examples.[1] The thesis Ntina Tzouvala sets out in *Capitalism as Civilisation* is a third.[2] As Tzouvala helpfully reminds her reader at every turn in the development of her argument, the notion of the standard of civilisation, as it is used in the context of international law, can be understood 'as an argumentative pattern that oscillates between disciplining the state along the lines of capitalist modernity and confining some communities to a lower legal status due to their purportedly inherent inferiority'.[3] To put it another way, there is a notable contradiction in how civilisation has been employed throughout the modern history of international law. On the one hand, 'civilised' Western states have used the term to denote how 'uncivilised' non-Western states must change to shake their lower status – what Tzouvala terms the 'logic of improvement'.[4] Simultaneously, non-Western states are unable to shake the 'uncivilised' label due to racial and gendered hierarchies enforced by the civilised states. This is the other pole of the argumentative pattern, that of the 'logic of biology'.[5] In essence, non-Western states were constantly presented with a standard that they must meet in order to be heard in the realm of international law. However, this goal remained unattainable so long as the uncivilised states were constructed as non-white and non-male.

Tzouvala's analysis does not rest on an assumed Western/non-Western binary, nor is that what *Capitalism as Civilisation* is attempting to unveil. Rather, Tzouvala maintains that we must appreciate how the standard of civilisation, understood as an argumentative pattern, has aided the global expansion of capital. As Tzouvala takes us through how the standard of civilisation has been employed in the historical debates surrounding extraterritoriality,[6] the League of Nations Mandate System,[7] the South West Africa saga[8] and the post-9/11 War on Terror,[9] it is the interests of

---

[1] A Gramsci, *Selections from the Prison Notebooks of Antonio Gramsci* (Q Hoare and G Nowell-Smith eds, New York, International Publishers, 1971) 181; DW Kennedy, 'Law and the Political Economy of the World' (2013) 26 *Leiden Journal of International Law* 7.
[2] N Tzouvala, *Capitalism as Civilisation: A History of International Law* (Cambridge, Cambridge University Press 2020).
[3] ibid 167.
[4] ibid 2.
[5] ibid.
[6] ibid 73–84.
[7] ibid 88–128.
[8] ibid 129–66.
[9] ibid 167–211.

capital that continually come out on top. In one sense, the logic of improvement ensures the ideals of capitalism expand into new terrains through demanding that uncivilised states adopt market-friendly measures, such as an emphasis on juridifying legal rights. However, it was the logic of biology that granted civilised states the authority to make such demands in the first place. As Tzouvala puts it,

> non-Western political communities were both morally inferior and politically and economically backwards and … it was only through the stewardship and guidance of the West in general, and of Western international lawyers in particular, that they would achieve the necessary transformation in order to be considered civilised.[10]

However, to describe the two poles of the standard of civilisation as a contradiction or as an inherent tension would undermine how both sides of the argument coexist and were simultaneously deployed. The logic of improvement constructed market-friendly structures as morally superior, meaning non-capitalist systems could be described as morally substandard, reinforcing the gendered and racial hierarchies that supported the logic of biology.

Capitalism as Civilisation's heavy use of examples is not intended to merely add purchase to the overall argument; rather, Tzouvala's engagement with legal text adheres to a 'theory of reading'.[11] To put it another way, Tzouvala asks her readers to remind themselves what they are really doing when they read law and advocates for 'a productive rather than revelatory understanding of reading of/for international law'.[12] For Tzouvala, every reading of a text is influenced by a 'problematic' that might cause the reader to emphasise something the author originally felt was benign, or to unearth a hidden bias in a seemingly neutral argument. Why such a practice should be encouraged is that, first of all, it lets the reader shed the internal logic of law as a discipline and, secondly, removes international legal texts from a pedestal. As such, engaging with classic texts and debates of international law that have already been well trodden will unveil fresh insights. As Tzouvala puts it, 'my own "symptomatic reading" aims to recover not only what is said, but also what remains unsaid, not because of an oversight but as a logical consequence of the problematic of the text'. In other words, dismissing a new interpretation on the basis that a text was 'the product of its time' closes off all the ways that classic texts can contribute to the understanding of a certain 'problematic'.

As Tzouvala's thesis has the aforementioned mental sticking power, it is also easily condensed and repeated. This is a blessing in the sense that the reader familiarises themselves with *Capitalism as Civilisation*'s central argument with ease and then brings that perspective with them, long after finishing the book. The theory's succinctness may also prove to be a curse in that it could be easily removed from its Marxist roots. This would be a mistake and a great shame. As Tzouvala explains, the internal tension in the standard of civilisation is only legible 'in the context of imperialism as a specifically capitalist phenomenon'.[13] The expansion of capitalism

---

[10] ibid 68.
[11] ibid 8.
[12] ibid 10.
[13] ibid 2.

as a mode of production has been a historically violent, uneven and messy process that 'does not bring about the homogenisation of life-worlds, economic development or legal systems'.[14] As such, international law and the actors that shape it are in a sense playing catch-up as they make efforts to explain the flawed logic of capitalist development. Part of what makes the logic of imperialism and capitalist development so flawed is the exploitation that inevitably comes in their wake. Tzouvala recites Marx's analysis of the surplus value that a labourer creates for the capitalist, whereby the labourer works beyond what is needed to create value for themselves. The significance of this for international law is how the capitalist mode of production required a replenishing supply of 'masses in possession of nothing else but their ability to work'.[15] The role of the state here is crucial, as the reproduction and discovery of new labourers is not a natural phenomenon. Rather, the laws of the state play 'a crucial role in organising the subjugation of this very special commodity, labour-power'.[16] As capitalism expanded into new lands, the pre-existing social relations had to be dismantled so that native labourers could use their work to produce value for the capitalist, not just themselves. Once again, the law was indispensable in ensuring the continued subjection of these colonised people and their land. Additionally, this narrative contains invocations of racial and gender hierarchies, which are not only reproduced through capitalist development, but simultaneously relied upon to justify these development processes. As Tzouvala puts it, 'these ideological and material categories have entered the international legal argument and have been constantly conditioning our collective imagination of what is possible and plausible and what is not'.[17]

The standard of civilisation first entered the conversation when international law lost its religious footing in the nineteenth century and needed further bases for its universalising mission. Or, in other words, 'international lawyers turned away from universal moral truths to factual assessments' based on ethnographic or anthropological assumptions to preserve momentum.[18] The running thread through *Capitalism as Civilisation* is how important this argumentative approach was for capitalist expansion. Tzouvala takes the words of Pasquale Fiore as an example: 'civilised countries in order to find new outlets for their ever increasing activity, need to extend their present possessions and to occupy these parts of the earth which are not of any use to uncivilised peoples'.[19] In a few words, Fiore unwittingly ties together the standard of civilisation argument and the Marxist primitive accumulation theory. However, uncivilised nations required an incentive to enact political reform that would satisfy the interests of capital, which is where the logic of improvement becomes relevant again as it became a conduit for 'systematising and legitimising a wide range of juridical practices' such as individual property rights and a state apparatus made

---

[14] ibid 4.
[15] ibid 23.
[16] ibid 25.
[17] ibid 33.
[18] ibid 48.
[19] ibid 42; P Fiore, *International Law Codified and Its Legal Sanction* (translated from the 5th Italian edn by EM Borchard, New York, Baker, Voorhis & Co, 1918) 46.

independent from the economy.[20] The inadequacy of the legal systems of uncivilised states also fuelled the narrative that colonisation was an inevitability due to the aforementioned moral superiority of Western political systems and, in this context, 'non-Western polities were given the option to either assimilate or perish'.[21]

Thus, we see how the standard of civilisation must be appreciated beyond its conception 'as a legal term to be interpreted'. In order to fully understand the standard of civilisation in the history of international law, the effects it produced in practice must also be scrutinised.[22] As well as justifying imperialist policies, the standard of civilisation as employed in the nineteenth century also shaped interstate legal relationships, specifically in the area of extraterritoriality. Extraterritoriality refers to the ability of a state to construct and apply law outside its own jurisdiction, and, as Tzouvala writes, its use in the nineteenth century focused on ensuring Western nationals were exempt from the laws of 'semi-civilised' states such as Japan or the Ottoman Empire.[23] The standard of civilisation shone a light on the supposed incomplete legal systems of these countries; to subject Westerners to such lacklustre rules and courts would leave them unfairly exposed. However, when lawyers from semi-civilised nations tried to use the logic of improvement to argue for their place within the circle of civilised decision-makers, this served to further validate the argumentative pattern itself, 'elevating capitalist modernity' in the process.[24]

Tzouvala goes on to describe how the standard of civilisation survived the significant intellectual shifts that ran alongside the rise of the welfare state and the period of decolonisation after World War II. As the likes of Wolfgang Streeck have remarked, capitalism and democracy have irreconcilable demands and the modern state, through measures such as welfare programmes, has sought to moderate this tension.[25] A similar pattern unveils itself in the interwar period and the League of Nations Mandate System, where international law reformed to account for the worst excesses of capitalist development, albeit incrementally and insignificantly. In order to exit the Mandate System, Iraq, for example, was required to adhere to 'a minimum standard of state intervention in health, education and labour'.[26] However, the turn to welfarism has a sinister undertone when subject to Marxist analysis, which says that uncontrolled worker exploitation benefits the individual capitalist but diminishes the labour force in the long term.[27] The advent of minimal social standards coincided with a departure from explicit invocations of civilisation, with Western lawyers instead preferring the seemingly neutral language of technocracy.[28] Despite the best efforts of the West to cloak its intentions, the logic behind the Mandate System rested on the same argumentative pattern of the

---

[20] Tzouvala (n 2) 59.
[21] ibid 69.
[22] ibid 83.
[23] ibid 75.
[24] ibid 83.
[25] W Streeck, 'The Crisis of Democratic Capitalism' (2011) 71 *New Left Review*.
[26] Tzouvala (n 2) 114.
[27] ibid 116.
[28] ibid 109.

standard of civilisation. Article 22 of the League Covenant enshrined the Mandate System and the logic of improvement is evident in its temporal nature – ie states aspiring towards independence required a period of supervision so that improvements could be externally approved. At the same time, as Tzouvala exemplifies, the Mandate System included policies concerning alcohol as non-Western states 'were physically and culturally unable to consume alcohol without descending into moral decay', echoing the logic of biology.[29]

Following the Second World War and the collapse of the League, the standard of civilisation came to the fore once again as the Third World's participation in international law accompanied decolonisation. Tzouvala uses the South West Africa saga to illustrate how Third World lawyers grappled with the argumentative pattern in a period of new hope and confidence, with the final International Court of Justice (ICJ) opinion issued just before the New International Economic Order gained momentum.[30] According to the South African government of the time, its annexation of South West Africa was legal as the region was not covered by the trusteeship regime, which, under the UN Charter, replaced the Mandate System.[31] Ethiopia and Liberia challenged South Africa's administrative record over South West Africa through 'a tactical deployment of' the argumentative pattern of the standard of civilisation.[32] In essence, the applicants argued that South Africa had instituted a system of continued economic exploitation based on racial segregation, whereby, for example, workers were subject to criminal charges in the event of a breach of employment contract and barred from joining a union.[33] These measures, the applicants argued, were incompatible with South Africa's responsibility under its 'civilising mission'.[34] However, this attempt to use the standard of civilisation argument against its previous advocates could not equate to Namibian liberation as it still served the narrative that only the civilised could enjoy independence. In other words, South Africa was depriving South West Africa of its chance to prove itself under the auspices of the logic of improvement. Regardless, the ICJ did not assess the merits of the arguments and instead ruled that Ethiopia and Liberia did not have the standing to obtain a decision.[35]

The standard of civilisation still has a place in contemporary centre–periphery relations, as exemplified by Tzouvala's use of the example of the 2003 invasion of Iraq.[36] As the inner workings of capitalism have changed to ensure its continued hegemony, so too have the contours of the standard of civilisation. As Iraq

---

[29] ibid 97.

[30] *Legal Consequences for States of the Continued Presence of South Africa in Namibia (South West Africa) notwithstanding Security Council Resolution 276* (Advisory Opinion) [1971] ICJ Rep 16.

[31] Tzouvala (n 2) 136; 'Statement by Dr Steyn (South Africa)', *International Status of South West Africa* [1950] ICJ Pleadings 273, 290.

[32] Tzouvala (n 2) 150.

[33] ibid 151; 'Memorial Submitted by the Government of Ethiopia', *South West Africa (Ethiopia v South Africa, Liberia v South Africa)* [1966] 1 ICJ Pleadings 32, 126–30.

[34] Tzouvala (n 2) 150.

[35] *South West Africa (Ethiopia v South Africa, Liberia v South Africa)* (Second Phase) [1966] ICJ Rep 6.

[36] Tzouvala (n 2) 172.

was coerced into enacting measures to conform with a post-Cold War neoliberal model,[37] the justification was based on gaining the acceptance of the international community. In a macro sense, neoliberalism can be understood as the use of both deregulation and 'regulation-in-denial' to ensure the market wins out in the battle between capitalism and democracy.[38] As such, the role of the state is far more significant that the term 'neoliberalism' suggests. In a micro sense, and specifically in the case of Iraq, the occupying authorities created business for the defence industry, private security and pharmaceuticals, thereby transferring vast amounts of wealth into the private sector.[39] According to Tzouvala, the Iraqi experience of British and American occupation 'can be understood as efforts to remake states in the Global South in accordance with the imperatives of a historically singular convergence between neoliberalism and militarisation'.[40] As the logic of improvement was used to advance the interests of Western capital, the logic of biology ensured the rules of the game were never out of Western control. For instance, high-ranking members of the Ba'ath party were prohibited from occupying public positions.[41] One might question the explanatory potential of examples such as this, and point out that changes to how certain states contribute to the international legal order may instead be based on, say, upholding human rights norms. However, I believe Tzouvala's structuralist analysis makes room for such developments. As she states from the outset, 'this book attempts to integrate historical movement and change with the deciphering of persistent argumentative structures'.[42] In other words, whilst political pressure demands that a certain human rights-friendly register is used when employing the standard of civilisation, the end result remains the same.

Capitalism as Civilisation is a rewarding read but a real pain to review – no sooner has one critique come to mind than Tzouvala has already answered it. One of the strongest examples of this is found in the Tzouvala's discussion of the 'unwilling or unable' doctrine.[43] Tzouvala argues that the logic of biology is invoked in this context to only grant 'victim state' status for 'those who can persuasively position themselves as being reasonable, potent and restrained'.[44] However, before the reader can proclaim that Turkey – a state that has historically not dictated the shape of international law – has relied upon the unwilling or unable doctrine in response to Kurdish separatists, Tzouvala already has an answer.[45] People and states are racialised and

---

[37] For an account of the relationship between law and neoliberalism, see DS Grewal and J Purdy, 'Introduction: Law and Neoliberalism' (2014) 77 *Law and Contemporary Problems* 1.

[38] J Peck, *Constructions of Neoliberal Reason* (Oxford, Oxford University Press, 2010) 2; Streeck (n 25) 12.

[39] Tzouvala (n 2) 176.

[40] ibid.

[41] ibid 179.

[42] ibid 6.

[43] The doctrine refers to the supposed entitlement of a 'victim state' to use force in another jurisdiction, or the 'territorial state', if the victim state is under an attack from non-state actors based in the territorial state that is unwilling or unable to prevent the attacks; Tzouvala (n 2) 190. For an account of the alleged legal basis for the doctrine, see A Deeks, '"Unwilling or Unable": Toward a Normative Framework for Extra-territorial Self-Defense' (2012) 52 *Virginia Journal of International Law* 483.

[44] Tzouvala (n 2) 202.

[45] ibid.

gendered according to a reference point and historical contingencies. As such, when previously excluded states rely on the standard of civilisation argumentative pattern, it does not undermine their existence. Rather, 'we ought to understand these processes of feminisation or racialisation as the complex articulations of material relations of oppression and exploitation'.[46] Tzouvala's explanation is also crucial for the book's main takeaway because, as new invocations of the standard of civilisation emerge in the future, analysts should not look to the actors involved (or some set of inherent characteristics) for the first sign of the argument's reappearance. Instead, as economic power, race and gender are relational, examples of the standard of civilisation position will be found where capital requires the power dynamics and malleability of international legal argument.

As outlined at the start of this review, the argument set forth in *Capitalism as Civilisation* is brilliant in its simplicity and impressive in its application. Tzouvala is meticulous in her engagement with the standard of civilisation and shows, at every instance of its invocation, how its use cannot be separated from the interests of capital. Whilst the book does not attempt to ask existential questions of international law as a discipline, Tzouvala's work does call into question the motives of the so-called 'liberal international legal order'.[47] From the West's engagement with its trading partners through extraterritoriality, through to its justification for wrestling control of the Iraqi economy, the pretence has always been that no one is in a better position to guide the world to a better place. *Capitalism as Civilisation* shows that the real winner all along has been capital and the mask may be slipping for many others around the world, as confidence in the liberal international legal order is giving way to rising extremism. However, rather than read this as a departure from a form of civilised liberalism, Tzouvala demonstrates that coercion and exploitation have always been synonymous with Western international lawyers.

Niall O'Shaughnessy,
PhD Researcher, Department of Law,
European University Institute

---

[46] ibid 203.
[47] ibid 210.

James Upcher, *Neutrality in Contemporary International Law* (Oxford, Oxford University Press, 2020) 336pp ISBN: 9780198739760 Price: £80

The law of neutrality had its heyday – often described as its 'golden age' – in the nineteenth century. Amidst the habitual violence between European colonial powers, neutral states sought to consolidate legal privileges which allowed them to continue to engage in commerce and trade uninhibited. As international law at the time was largely orientated around the absolute right of states to wage war, the recognition of a legal status of neutrality and the associated freedoms afforded to neutral merchant ships provided neutral states with an unprecedented freedom to remain at peace while continuing to fully engage politically and commercially on the world stage. In fact, early developments in the twentieth century suggested that the law of neutrality would retain its importance, if not stand to increase its profile. In particular, the introduction of neutral rights in the 1907 Hague Conventions V and XIII, where previously there were largely only duties, put neutral states in a stronger legal position than ever before.

Yet this sense of momentum was ultimately short-lived. The creation of the League of Nations, the successive World Wars, the introduction of the UN Charter and the *jus ad bellum*, the evolution of naval affairs and the law of the sea, and a prevailing sense through a notable portion of the twentieth century that neutrality was a relic of the past culminated in the law of neutrality becoming of increasingly marginal interest. That said, despite being understudied and overlooked, neutral states, including 'permanently neutral' states, continue to assert themselves to be bound, and privileged, by the law of neutrality during both international armed conflicts and peacetime, and orientate their foreign policies, at least ostensibly, around the form and substance of the Hague Conventions. Ireland can be counted amongst such states, defining itself somewhat ambiguously as 'militarily neutral'. It is for this reason that James Upcher's posthumous effort on the topic is to be welcomed as an insightful and rigorous interrogation of the law's contemporary content.

At the outset, Upcher, borrowing a line from Lauterpacht, identifies neutrality as being at the 'vanishing point' of international law.[1] It is no coincidence, therefore, that so much time is spent justifying the subject matter of his inquiry. Chapter one – on neutrality, the supposed indeterminate status of 'non-belligerency' and the prohibition on the use of force – and chapter two – on the application of the law of neutrality and its termination – concern themselves, above all else, with carving out the position of neutrality alongside more contemporary international legal principles. For example, in chapter two, Upcher tackles the distinction between the now outdated and subjective concept of 'war', upon which the Hague Conventions – and thus their codifications of the law of neutrality – are

---

[1] J Upcher, *Neutrality in Contemporary International Law* (Oxford, Oxford University Press, 2020) 1.

based, and the contemporary, objective notion of 'armed conflict', which governs modern international humanitarian law. Being an exercise essentially rooted in customary international law, the approach taken is to survey state practice and *opinio juris*, and to weigh contrasting positions, including the notion that neutrality is solely applicable when war is formally declared,[2] when an international armed conflict reaches the nebulous threshold of constituting an 'extended' armed conflict[3] and the view that neutrality is applicable in all international armed conflicts, as was famously asserted by the International Court of Justice in its *Threat or Use of Nuclear Weapons* Advisory Opinion.[4] While Upcher ultimately, and compellingly, concurs with the latter Advisory Opinion, it is the clarity and precision with which he undertakes this analysis and outlines each position that is most striking at this early stage of the book – a methodological vigour which is present throughout the volume.

Reading further through chapter three – on the duties and rights of neutral states – and chapter four – on neutrality in the context of the UN Charter – the wide doctrinal scope of Upcher's inquiry becomes increasingly clear. This is a direct consequence of the subject matter. Although concerned with war, or international armed conflict, the law of neutrality in effect peers into hostilities from the outside. As Upcher puts it, neutrality in truth belongs to the laws of peace, not the laws of war, governing the peaceful relations of third states with belligerents which are, coincidentally, engaged in hostilities with each other.[5] Therefore, existing in tandem with international humanitarian law, it is at once wedded to this area of law and yet entirely separate from it. A comprehensive work on neutrality, such as Upcher's, must consider not only international humanitarian law, but also such diverse issues as the use of inter-state force, the law of international organisations, principles of state responsibility and the law of the sea. Further, the law of neutrality, presented alongside these areas of contemporary international law, reveals the extent to which the now century-old principles of the law of neutrality, codified in 1907, are akin to a fish out of water. Whereas such contemporary areas pride themselves on their (relative) precision, the law of neutrality is markedly antiquated – as a case in point, the Hague Conventions pre-date the widespread use of the aeroplane in warfare, which rendered them arguably outdated upon the outbreak of World War I.

This presents certain challenges which are apparent throughout the book. First, Upcher is confronted routinely with ambiguities in the intersections of these areas of law. On one end of the spectrum, the lack of explicit and codified provision for the status of neutral airspace is unproblematic due to growing recognition of the extension of principles of neutrality to aerial warfare.[6] On the other end, however, it becomes clear that with the scarce state practice available it is virtually impossible to be certain as to the law's content on the duties and rights of neutral states, tackled in chapter three, and the rights of belligerents, broached in chapter five. A significant question mark is left over, for example, the duties of neutral states with regard to the

---

[2] ibid 47–48.
[3] ibid 48–50.
[4] ibid 50–54.
[5] ibid 177.
[6] ibid 107–10.

arms trade in the context of the neutral prohibition on the supply of war material, an area over which Upcher notes that 'the law is in a considerable state of disarray'.[7] Further questions are left concerning the interaction between neutrality and the law of the sea.[8] The notion of belligerent rights is similarly unclear. However, Upcher posits that in the specific context of the visit, search and potential seizure of neutral shipping and contraband, the law of neutrality may be supplemented and clarified through the assistance of modern principles of the *jus ad bellum* and self-defence under the UN Charter.[9] Perhaps surprisingly, this is not the case in chapter four, which specifically explores the Charter, and more specifically its Chapter VII. Here, Upcher deftly tackles what many writers, particularly in the last century, considered to be neutrality's death knell and provides a convincing, and ostensibly practicable, vision as to how the law of neutrality may function in the wake of a Chapter VII resolution from the UN Security Council.

The strength of Upcher's analysis, however, is in the recognition of these shortcomings in the law. Rather than speaking to a weakness of scholarship, the indeterminacy of chapters three and five are better read as a sincere recognition of the neglect of the law of neutrality in international legal scholarship over the past century. The strength of the book lies in its potential to renew interest in the law of neutrality, and to serve as a basis for further reflection and interrogation of the inconsistencies and ambiguities it identifies. That said, this is obscured somewhat by the book's framing around contemporaneity. Despite Upcher's own recognition that 'The law of neutrality must be grasped historically',[10] the editorial decision was made to relegate much of his material on neutrality's legal history prior to 1907 to an Annex,[11] albeit a very carefully and thoughtfully written one. Upcher's book then feels somewhat conflicted; it is at once a call to arms to re-engage with the law of neutrality directed towards legal scholars and an attempt to provide a practicable overview of the law for legal practitioners and diplomats. Ultimately, due to the inherent limitations in the subject matter, discussed above, and state attitudes towards the law of neutrality since the introduction of the UN Charter, the volume's real contribution will likely be in the former.

Finally, it is worth noting a number of curious decisions made in the text. First, for a book concerned with neutrality and contemporary international law, it is notable that the question of cyberwarfare is not meaningfully addressed. Some mention is made of the renewed attention to the traditional prohibition on the belligerent erection of communications devices in neutral territory, with Upcher stressing that 'there is a clear need to update the rules regarding the use of communication facilities that are based in neutral territory'.[12] However, this is limited to only two paragraphs. Given that the book aims to focus on the contemporary application of the law of neutrality, this omission is all the more striking when one reads the sections on questions which are today of largely academic interest, such as the distinction between absolute and conditional contraband, or the doctrinal bases for naval blockades.

---

[7] ibid 86.
[8] See, inter alia, ibid 121.
[9] ibid 169–70.
[10] ibid 3.
[11] ibid xi.
[12] ibid 104.

Second, throughout the book, Upcher displays a curious methodological disposition in favour of British primary sources above all others. While ample reference to national military manuals is understandable when one is seeking to interrogate customary international law relevant to armed conflict and the use of force, it is nonetheless notable that Upcher's primary point of call is, in the vast majority of instances, the UK manual,[13] whether he agrees with its content or not.[14] Upcher does make reference to state practice outside of the west – for example, he repeatedly returns in particular to Iran, Iraq and Kuwait during the 1980–88 Iran–Iraq War – however, a more diverse set of case studies, if available, would have been appreciated. Nonetheless, despite the centrality of the British perspective throughout the volume, Upcher's analysis and argumentation are based on a sound doctrinal footing and are routinely subjected to rigorous internal scrutiny.

The law of neutrality is unlikely to enjoy a second 'golden age'. It is also, put frankly, unlikely to re-emerge as a focus of mainstream international legal scholarship. Yet there is considerable work that can be done on this topic, and its application in the modern day. As noted above, some of this work orbits around the emerging frontier of cyberwarfare; other facets of this work gravitate around outer space, peacekeeping, permanent or 'peacetime' neutrality, the question of non-international armed conflicts and neutrality in the context of peacekeeping and peace enforcement operations. More traditional approaches to this question have taken place in the arena of legal history. On a separate note, neutrality continues to be debated in fields such as political science, international relations and history, in a manner increasingly divorced from its basis in international law. In the specific context of Ireland, neutrality has taken on a somewhat confused political currency of its own, one without any sound doctrinal understanding as to what the term means. This was on particular display during the national debate on Ireland's engagement with the EU's 'Permanent Structured Cooperation' (PESCO) initiative, which largely overlooked the legal dimensions of an Irish claim to 'military neutrality'.

Works capable of bridging the diffuse modern concepts and principles which intersect with the law of neutrality are accordingly sorely needed, and further work will surely be done on this question. Unfortunately, this work will not be done by James Upcher himself. As noted above, *Neutrality in Contemporary International Law* was published posthumously, following the author's tragic death in an accident in 2017; the book itself opens with a preface – essentially a professional eulogy – from Upcher's friend, Ioannis Konstantinidis. Even so, without having the opportunity to refine its content through subsequent works, Upcher's volume on the law of neutrality will undoubtedly feature prominently in ongoing and future debates concerning the law of neutrality.

Pearce Clancy
Irish Centre for Human Rights
National University of Ireland, Galway

---

[13] UK Ministry of Defence, *The Manual of the Law of Armed Conflict* (Oxford, Oxford University Press, 2014).
[14] For an example of the latter, see Upcher 70–71.

Morten Bergsmo, Wolfgang Kaleck and Kyaw Yin Hlaing (eds), *Colonial Wrongs and Access to International Law* (Torkel Opsahl Academic EPublisher, 2020) 622pp ISBN: 9788283481334 Price: £30

I. INTRODUCTION

The impunity surrounding colonial wrongs rarely evokes a robust and viable response. Global politico-legal discourse largely converges on locating and imputing culpable actors for contemporary violations, disavowing colonial-era wrongdoings. *Colonial Wrongs and Access to International Law* makes a vital contribution towards bolstering the groundwork that can support and advance the active acknowledgement and redressal of colonial grievances. This book examines how international law – which has itself served as a tool for enabling and legitimising colonial subjugation, may be used to address colonial grievances and establish legal accountability for colonial crimes. Central to this book is the argument that international law must enable the redressal of colonial grievances in order to secure its legitimacy and universality in the contemporary world.

The ethnic violence against Rohingyas in present-day Myanmar serves as a key point of reference for the book and has been used to demonstrate the need to address the colonial-era policies which set the stage for such violence to occur. The 18 chapters within this anthology also traverse a range of colonial sites, including China, Africa and Cambodia, and shed light on the violence against indigenous communities in Canada and Norway. These accounts demonstrate the complicity of colonial laws and policies in sustaining the oppression and marginalisation of colonised subjects. These 'case studies' within the book offer a distinct advantage by allowing an increased understanding of the complexities of each region and enabling the formulation of strategies for redressal. The chapters in this anthology have been written by a diverse range of authors, including international lawyers and academics whose work does not necessarily focus on postcolonial or Third World approaches to international law (TWAIL) scholarship. This serves as an important step towards broadening the space for critical engagement with international law and moving beyond the historicisation of this topic or its confinement to TWAIL. The book offers multiple points of entry into a holistic and effective discussion over the issue of colonial wrongs and its acknowledgement through international law. It further advances critical engagements with the structures and processes of international law, and indicates the increasing need to grapple with its deficiency in addressing colonial injustices.

II. CONFRONTING COLONIAL HISTORIES

Several chapters in this book offer a historical background to highlight the harmful and lasting repercussions of colonial policies that remain unaddressed by international law. Jacques P Leider's chapter on 'The Chittagonians in Colonial Arakan: Seasonal and Settlement Migrations' provides a historical account of the migration

from Lower Bengal (Chittagong) to Rakhine (Arakan). It underscores the resulting demographic shift, which was actively fuelled by the colonial administration
to further its own politico-economic interests in the region. This account is further supplemented by Ryan Mitchell's chapter on 'Myanmar and the Hegemonic
Discourse of International Criminal Law'. This chapter outlines the role played
by colonial policies in spreading communal disharmony between the Arakanese
and the settling Bengali immigrants through preventing mutual communication and
providing opportunist incentives to minorities. In this backdrop, Mitchell notes
how the International Criminal Court (ICC) was able to 'find' its jurisdiction when
the Pre-Trial Chamber authorised an investigation into the situation in Bangladesh/
Myanmar and yet is unable to account for the colonial wrongs committed by and
through the population transfer of Rohingyas into Arakan.

This duality of standards is effectively captured in Morten Bergsmo's chapter on
'Myanmar, Colonial Aftermath, and Access to International Law', where his analysis
foregrounds the 'double standards' pervading international law. Bergsmo notes how
the massive transfer of civilians into colonial Burma – which engendered today's
communal confrontation – may constitute grave violations of international law and
yet the law is only being applied selectively to punish Burmese actors for the violence
in Rakhine. His chapter underscores how the situation in Myanmar presents an
occasion to account for these colonial wrongs and make an attempt to rescue international criminal law from the threat these 'double standards' pose to its legitimacy.
Contrarily, Derek Tonkin, in his chapter titled 'Migration from Bengal to Arakan
During British Rule 1826–1948', suggests that there is no demonstrable evidence to
show that the British government actively arranged the transfer of Bengali migrants
to Burma. Tonkin argues that this migration happened quite organically owing to
the socio-political and economic circumstances at the time. The inclusion of these
divergent accounts in the book is remarkable.

It foregrounds the need to engage with multiple historical realities and also examine ways in which colonial policies may have tacitly led to the creation of an overall
coercive environment in the area in which such migration occurred.

III. THE ROAD TO REDRESSAL

A distinguishing feature of this anthology is the authors' attempt to throw light
on actionable means of redressal for colonial wrongs across several regions. For
instance, in the case of Myanmar, Ryan Mitchell recommends ways through which
the historical context of colonial wrongs in Rakhine can be made part of the ongoing proceedings in the International Court of Justice. This can be done by adding
to these proceedings a claim by Myanmar against the UK for its colonial policies
that may have violated customary international law. Matthias Neuner's chapter on
'The Notion of Continuous or Continuing Crimes in International Criminal Law'
is also of key importance in this regard. This chapter indicates how the crime committed by an occupying power via transferring its own civilian population into the
territory occupied, as prohibited by the Rome Statute, can be used to account for

the demographic turmoil and the physical and proprietorial harm caused by such transfer over a period of time. Neuner suggests that the existence of settlements in an occupied territory can evince the earlier act of transferring one's own population into such territory. Neuner also employs the example of other crimes, such as enforced disappearance, sexual slavery and forced conscription of children, to uncover the space for punishing continuous offences in international criminal law.

Christophe Marachand, Crépine Uwashema and Christophe Deprez analyse the statutory impediments to prosecuting international crimes in their chapter on 'Possible Limitations to Justice for Colonial Crimes: A Belgian Perspective'. They highlight the indeterminacy attached to the application of temporal limitations and retroactivity for international crimes, and recommend enacting appropriate legislative regulations at the domestic level to overcome such challenges. Mutoy Mubiala, in his chapter on 'Addressing Colonial Wrongs in the Great Lakes Region of Africa', suggests the establishment of a joint claims tribunal to address colonial wrongdoings which have already been identified as precursors to mass atrocities in the region. Hugo van der Merwe and Annah Moyo, in their chapter on 'Transitional Justice for Colonial Era Abuses and Legacies: African versus European Policy Priorities', signify the shifting paradigms of transitional justice mechanisms that acknowledge colonial legacies and the underlying socio-economic injustice. They suggest that these transformations have made transitional justice an important legal tool for addressing colonial-era violations. Similarly, Wolfgang Kaleck, in 'On Double Standards and Emerging European Custom on Accountability for Colonial Crimes', reposes faith in transitional justice mechanisms but also broadly in advancing criminal litigation and recognition of colonial crimes under international criminal law.

Looking beyond the traditional legal framework, Brigid Inder OBE emphasises truth-telling as a means for achieving a greater sense of justice or vindication for colonial grievances. A similar assertion is made by Shannon Fyfe in the chapter titled 'The Transfer of Civilians as a Collective Harm (and Wrong)'. Fyfe unpacks the notion of individual and collective harm to underline the wide range of setbacks and infringements caused by the act of transferring civilians into a territory. It is then argued that the extent of harm to the individual and collective preferences or interests through such an act cannot be fully captured within the law and demands means through which collective accountability can be established within the community.

Other authors explore the means for accountability for the colonial subjugation of indigenous peoples. Joshua Castellino, in 'Colonial Crime, Environmental Destruction and Indigenous Peoples: A Roadmap to Accountability and Protection', describes the role played by international law in legitimising environmental exploitation and destroying indigenous lands. Castellino argues that the preservation of biodiversity through maintaining 'protected areas' leads to the dispossession of indigenous communities and the exclusion of traditional knowledge that is vital for sustainable environmental conservation.

Such systematic violence against indigenous communities has also been outlined in Gunnar M Ekelove-Slydal's chapter, titled 'Past Wrongdoing Against Romani and Sámi in Norway and the Prism of Modern International Criminal Law and Human Rights'. Ekelove-Slydal argues that the Norwegian assimilation policies against the indigenous communities, including territorial intrusion, forced sterilisation, separation of children from families and the eradication of native language and religion, infringed the core values protected by international human rights and international criminal law norms. The determination of these past wrongs as violation of international human rights law and international criminal law can point towards the state as the violator and facilitate redressal. Ekelove-Slydal states that such redressal is also significant in order to address the duplicity in Norway's support towards establishing accountability for current human rights violations elsewhere, while committing these violations at home. Similarly, Asad G Kiyani, in the chapter titled 'Avoidance Techniques: Accounting for Canada's Colonial Crimes', notes the double standards in Canada's approach to limiting its own domestic legal liability for perpetrating cultural genocide against indigenous peoples while continuing to advocate for its prosecution in other parts of the world.

The inclusion of such accounts in this book is notable. These chapters portray the various means and mechanisms through which colonialism and imperialism, as an ideological practice, manifest in nations that are themselves colonised by other powers. This provides a critical space to engage with the colonial practices of postcolonial nations and affords a holistic view of how colonialism is materialised and reinforced through laws and policies of the contemporary postcolonial nation-state.

Disparate colonial sites can also present distinct challenges, given the necessity to engage with multiple socio-political and cultural dimensions. Thus, recognising colonial wrongdoings also necessitates acknowledging the complicity of national and local actors in pronouncing ethnic and religious divisions, thus exacerbating harm. For instance, Kyaw Yin Hlaing's chapter on 'The Importance of Hearing Colonial Wrongs in Myanmar' highlights the role played by influential national leaders of Myanmar in justifying discrimination and racial hatred in the name of righting colonial wrongs. In this light, it is important to ensure that the discourse on the acknowledgment of colonial wrongs does not 'evacuate the agency of postcolonial states'[1] over their role in preserving and perpetuating harmful narratives and structures. The investigation of colonial wrongdoings, then, must not militate against rightful attribution of guilt and the recognition of the role played by postcolonial nations in forging their own futures. As highlighted in this book, disallowing any interruption of the ongoing processes for international justice assumes importance in this regard.

Besides outlining particular sites of unremedied colonial violence, this book also brings forth larger questions pertaining to the colonial underpinnings of international law. An overarching quest within the book is to identify ways through which international law mechanisms can be used to account for colonial crimes. Yet accessing international law for the vindication of colonial grievances may also be characterised as an act reinforcing its 'civilising mission'. The historical origins and contemporary structures of international criminal law are embroiled with the notion

---

[1] R Rao, 'A Tale of Two Atonements' in D Otto (ed), *Queering International Law* (London, Routledge, 2019) 21–22.

of exclusion and civilisation. Antony Anghie has demonstrated how the narrative of international law constructed the non-European 'uncivilised other' who needed to be brought into the universal and 'civilised' fold of international law.[2] This dynamic also pervades international criminal law, where individual accountability for international crimes becomes the universal and civilised response to atrocity.[3]

In this book, Kevin Crow indicates this notion in the chapter titled 'Winds of Justice: Post-Colonial Opportunism and the Rise of the Khmer Rouge'. Crow notes how establishing the Extraordinary Chambers in the Courts of Cambodia and the conviction of former leaders of the Khmer Rouge for crimes against humanity represents an idealised vision of temporally bound 'international justice' which is inconsonant with local conceptions of justice that are unbound by narrow notions of time and causation. Thus, an appeal to international law for remedying colonial wrongdoings can be said to reinstall the agenda of its 'civilising mission' and imperil a holistic and impactful response to colonial atrocities. This book does the crucial task of creating a space where such arguments can be asserted and contested. It also poses larger questions about the postcolonial implications of approaching colonial wrongs through the architecture of international law.

Further fortifying the relevance of its topic, the book indicates how colonialism continues to signify contemporary operations of international law. Ling Yang's chapter, titled 'On the Relevancy of Chinese Colonial Grievances to International Law', describes how the resulting impunity surrounding past colonial crimes translates into resistance or reluctance by nation-states in engaging with international law. Furthermore, Ambassador Narinder Singh's foreword explains how the lack of experience and resources hinders the capacity of postcolonial nations in shaping and influencing the formation of international law. Ambassador Singh points out that until decolonialisation, these nations were far removed from having a role in the formation of international law and still continue to face challenges in consistently engaging with the myriad of ongoing negotiations. This exclusion and incapacity continue to inform present-day perceptions over international legal obligations and question the truly 'universal' character of international law.

IV. CONCLUSION

In February 2021, the ICC found Dominic Ongwen, a military commander, guilty of crimes against humanity and war crimes committed in Northern Uganda between 2002 and 2005.[4] Among other crimes, the court found Ongwen guilty of conscripting child soldiers and using them to participate actively in hostilities. Notably, Ongwen himself was a child soldier, having been abducted at the age of nine and

[2] A Anghie, 'The Evolution of International Law: Colonial and Postcolonial Realities' (2006) 27 *Third World Quarterly* 739, 742.

[3] C Nielsen, 'From Nuremberg to The Hague: The Civilizing Mission of International Criminal Law' (2008) 14 *Auckland University Law Review* 81, 108.

[4] 'Dominic Ongwen Declared Guilty of War Crimes and Crimes against Humanity Committed in Uganda' (International Criminal Court, 4 February 2021) www.icc-cpi.int/Pages/item.aspx?name=pr1564.

inducted into the Lord's Resistance Army (LRA) – a Ugandan armed group involved in massive atrocities against civilian populations.[5] In Uganda, colonial policies led to the deepening of ethnic divisions and the destabilisation of political structures, ultimately enabling radical groups such as the LRA to flourish.[6] Yet, while international law can hold Ongwen's conduct to account, it is unable to hold colonial actors responsible for sustaining endemic violence and unrest in the nation. The socio-political and cultural dimensions that underpin the violence thus remain unattended by the law.

Several contemporary violations of international law can be traced back to colonial policies and conducts. Yet such actions are often characterised merely as historical events, rather than culpable and actionable wrongs. This book does the crucial task of visualising what attempts to such redressal may entail. It provides further impetus to the increasing relevance of a postcolonial enquiry into the form and substance of international law.

However, this book does not constitute an exhaustive exploration of colonial grievances and the scope for their redressal within international law. Issues raised and recommendations offered throughout the chapters raise critical questions that require detailed exploration. For instance, truth and reconciliation mechanisms, consultation processes with victims and impacted communities, joint claims tribunals and other relevant remedies for colonial grievances need to be outlined and examined. Relevant standards for the nature of reparations and restitutions need to be developed. Practical challenges in investigating colonial crimes and getting responsible actors to participate in reparative processes also need to be confronted.

Yet the text makes crucial inroads into what is a complex and multidimensional theme. As contemplated in the foreword by the editors, a second, expanded edition of the book will certainly be welcome. This anthology can function as an excellent resource for international legal researchers and practitioners looking to analyse and address the issue of colonial wrongs through international law. The text is both lucid and eclectic in style, making it useful and accessible for scholars from a range of disciplinary backgrounds. The forewords by Ambassador Singh and Brigid Inder OBE provide excellent and valuable conceptual direction. The book is replete with detailed historical accounts, philosophical approaches, theoretical analysis and political insight pertaining to the issue at hand. Parts IV and V of the book especially provide a crucial glimpse into how colonialism manifests in different regions and contexts, prompting such critical engagements for other regions and communities around the world.

Harshit Rai,
School of Law, University of Warwick

[5] RLA Pangalangan, 'Dominic Ongwen and the Rotten Social Background Defense: The Criminal Culpability of Child Soldiers Turned War Criminals' (2018) 33 *American University International Law Review* 605, 606.

[6] F Van Acker, 'Uganda and the Lord's Resistance Army: The New Order No One Ordered' (2004) 103 *African Affairs* 335, 341–42.